VLADISLAV ZUBOK

The World of the Cold War: 1945–1991

A PELICAN BOOK

PELICAN
an imprint of
PENGUIN BOOKS

PELICAN BOOKS

UK | USA | Canada | Ireland | Australia
India | New Zealand | South Africa

Penguin Classics is part of the Penguin Random House group of companies whose addresses can be found at global.penguinrandomhouse.com

Penguin Random House UK,
One Embassy Gardens, 8 Viaduct Gardens, London SW11 7BW

penguin.co.uk

First published 2025
001

Text copyright © Vladislav Zubok, 2025

The moral right of the author has been asserted

Penguin Random House values and supports copyright.
Copyright fuels creativity, encourages diverse voices, promotes freedom of expression and supports a vibrant culture. Thank you for purchasing an authorized edition of this book and for respecting intellectual property laws by not reproducing, scanning or distributing any part of it by any means without permission. You are supporting authors and enabling Penguin Random House to continue to publish books for everyone.
No part of this book may be used or reproduced in any manner for the purpose of training artificial intelligence technologies or systems. In accordance with Article 4(3) of the DSM Directive 2019/790, Penguin Random House expressly reserves this work from the text and data mining exception.

Book design by Matthew Young
Set in 11/16.13pt FreightText Pro
Typeset by Jouve (UK), Milton Keynes
Printed and bound in Great Britain by Clays Ltd, Elcograf S.p.A.

The authorised representative in the EEA is Penguin Random House Ireland, Morrison Chambers, 32 Nassau Street, Dublin D02 YH68

A CIP catalogue record for this book is available from the British Library

ISBN: 978-0-241-69614-9

Penguin Random House is committed to a sustainable future for our business, our readers and our planet. This book is made from Forest Stewardship Council® certified paper.

Contents

LIST OF ILLUSTRATIONS ... ix

LIST OF MAPS ... xiii

Introduction: An Unlearned History ... 3

PART ONE: THE TIME OF MARS, 1945–1952

CHAPTER 1
The Fate of Europe ... 23

CHAPTER 2
The Conflict Takes Shape ... 53

CHAPTER 3
The Asian Front ... 83

CHAPTER 4
Domestic Frontlines ... 103

PART TWO: THE TIME OF VULCAN, 1953–1962

CHAPTER 5
After Stalin ... 127

CHAPTER 6
The Wind from the East
165

CHAPTER 7
Russian Roulette
199

PART THREE: THE TIME OF JANUS, 1963–1980

CHAPTER 8
Vietnam and the Origins of Détente
233

CHAPTER 9
Brezhnev's Peace Project
259

CHAPTER 10
A Partnership of Rivals
281

CHAPTER 11
The Destruction of Détente
311

PART FOUR: THE TIME OF MINERVA, 1981–1991

CHAPTER 12
Another Round
353

CHAPTER 13
The Advent of Gorbachev
381

CHAPTER 14
The End of Confrontation
411

CHAPTER 15
Other Endings
435

Conclusion: The Time of Mercury – After the Cold War 455

FURTHER READING	479
NOTES	487
INDEX	503

List of Illustrations

Part One

1.1 A Soviet woman traffic controller in Berlin after the Red Army took the Reich's capital, 1945. Copyright © Serge Plantureux / Corbis via Getty Images. — 27

1.2 Truman and his advisers: Robert Lovett, George Kennan and Charles Bohlen, 1947. Copyright © Bettmann via Getty Images. — 66

1.3 The communist coup in Czechoslovakia, February 1948. Copyright © Hulton-Deutsch Collection / CORBIS / Corbis via Getty Images. — 72

1.4 Marshall Plan delivered to Greece, around 1948. Copyright © Bettmann via Getty Images. — 81

1.5 China's communists carry Stalin's portrait during the anniversary of their victory, October 1951. Copyright © Library of Congress / Corbis / VCG via Getty Images. — 101

1.6 An American housewife watches Joseph McCarthy on TV, early 1950s. Copyright © Bettmann via Getty Images. — 105

Part Two

2.1 A memorial event in Beijing after Stalin's death, March 1953. Copyright © Imaginechina Limited / Alamy Stock Photo. — 135

LIST OF ILLUSTRATIONS

2.2	Nikita Khrushchev and other Soviet leaders celebrate the 4th of July with the American diplomatic community in Moscow, 1955. Copyright © Bettmann via Getty Images.	145
2.3	Dwight Eisenhower and Gamal Nasser. Egypt's nationalization of the Suez Canal in 1956 brought US power to the Middle East. Copyright © Walter Kelleher/NY Daily News Archive via Getty Images.	156
2.4	Khrushchev and Vice President Richard Nixon vie for superiority at the model of the American kitchen, American exhibition in Moscow, July 1959. Copyright © Associated Press/Alamy Stock Photo.	185
2.5	Patrice Lumumba, First prime minister of independent Congo, became the first high-profile casualty of the Cold War in Africa, 1960. Copyright © Everett Collection Inc./Alamy Stock Photo.	194
2.6	Soviet scientists and the military inspect the 100-megaton Tsar Bomba, tested in October 1961. Copyright © Album/Alamy Stock Photo.	210
2.7	Stanley Kubrick's *Dr Strangelove* became the best black comedy about the Cold War, 1964. Copyright © Atlaspix/Alamy Stock Photo.	217
2.8	Castro visits the USSR after the Cuban Missile Crisis, 1963. Copyright © Keystone-France/Gamma-Keystone via Getty Images.	220
2.9	Détente possible? Dean Rusk, Khrushchev, US Ambassador in Moscow Lewellyn Thompson, Andrei Gromyko and Soviet Ambassador in Washington Anatoly Dobrynin and US Ambassador in Moscow Lewellyn Thompson, in Pitsunda, the Soviet Black Sea resort, with their wives. Courtesy of the National Security Archive, George Washington University, and reproduced by permission of the family of Lewellyn Thompson.	224

Part Three

3.1 Actress Jane Fonda's controversial visit to North Vietnam during the war, 1972. Copyright © STF/AFP FILES/AFP via Getty Images. — 237

3.2 Breezy *Ostpolitik*. Leonid Brezhnev, Willy Brandt, and Egon Bahr tour Crimea, 1971. Copyright © Associated Press/Alamy Stock Photo. — 260

3.3 Brezhnev is greeted by Kissinger and Nixon in San Clemente, 1973. Copyright © Associated Press/Alamy Stock Photo. — 274

3.4 Pipes, not missiles ... The Soviet gas pipelines from Siberia to central Europe became détente's lasting product. Copyright © Keystone-France/Gamma-Keystone via Getty Images. — 278

3.5 The US campaign for the emigration of Soviet Jews led to a clash between human rights and détente, 1973. Copyright © Michel Laurent/Gamma-Rapho via Getty Images. — 291

3.6 Fear of 'another Cuba' in Latin America. Police in Chile before the coup against Allende, 1973. Copyright © Romano Cagnoni/Getty Images. — 312

3.7 Angola's independence brought the Cold War back to Africa, 1975. Copyright © Keystone Press/Alamy Stock Photo. — 320

3.8 Iranian revolution: women in an anti-US protest, 1979. Copyright © Associated Press/Alamy Stock Photo. — 329

3.9 Carter's kiss to Brezhnev turned out to be a goodbye to détente, 1979. Copyright © World History Archive/Alamy Stock Photo. — 336

LIST OF ILLUSTRATIONS

Part Four

4.1 The three who won the Cold War? Reagan, Secretary of State George Shultz, and Vice President George H. W. Bush. Copyright © Pool via CNP/Getty Images.   356

4.2 Nuclear scientist Andrei Sakharov and Gorbachev both imagined an exit from the Cold War. Copyright © Sergei Guneyev/Getty Images.   385

4.3 New thinking at work. (From right to left) Margaret Thatcher, Soviet Foreign Minister Eduard Shevardnadze, Gorbachev and his wife Raisa, 1987. Copyright © Bryn Colton/Getty Images.   390

4.4 Chinese students in Tiananmen Square wait for Gorbachev, May 1989. Copyright © Associated Press/Alamy Stock Photo.   413

4.5 Violence in Romania capped the series of peaceful anti-communist revolutions in eastern Europe, December 1989. Copyright © Simon Grosset/Alamy Stock Photo.   426

4.6 Russians turn against the communist state, Moscow, February 1991. Copyright © Alain Nogues/Sygma/Sygma via Getty Images.   445

4.7 Bush arrives at the last summit with Gorbachev in Moscow, July 1991. Three weeks later, the coup of hardliners ruins the Soviet Union. Copyright © SHONE via Getty Images.   450

Conclusion

5.1 Statue of Mercury in front of the World Trade Center, Moscow, 2004. Copyright © komskaya/Alamy Stock Photo.   461

List of Maps

Map 1: Post-war territorial changes and division of Europe	19
Map 2: The Cold War Comes to Asia	20–21
Map 3: NATO and the Warsaw Pact: Consolidation of the Cold War	120–21
Map 4: The Cuban Missile Crisis, October 1962	124–25
Map 5: Détente and Global Cold War in the 1970s	230–31
Map 6: Retraction of Soviet Power in 1989–91	350–51

The World of the Cold War

Introduction:
An Unlearned History

'The Cold War was like the Wagnerian cycle *The Ring*: it was massive and seemed to never end.' I heard those words in London in 1998, from Jeremy Isaacs, director of the Royal Opera House, Covent Garden. Sir Jeremy was about to produce a milestone twenty-four-part documentary film, *Cold War*, sponsored by CNN founder Ted Turner. I was a scholar from the former Soviet Union and one of the series' consultants, alongside historians John Lewis Gaddis and Lawrence Freedman. Everyone grappled with the magnitude of the task, but I was in a league of my own. While growing up and studying in the Soviet Union in the 1970s, I heard the term 'Cold War' only rarely and only in quotation marks, used in sentences like 'The United States unleashed the so-called "Cold War" against the Soviet Union . . .' In Moscow libraries, it was impossible to find a solid book on the subject. Those that existed were published in the West and were available only with special permissions. Much of what I learned about the great conflict, therefore, had been written by my Western colleagues.

Once the Soviet archives became accessible after 1991, I devoted my time to studying and interpreting them. Much of the narrative from the Eastern perspective in this book is based on the new evidence that I and a few fellow historians discovered in those archives. But how to interpret this wealth of evidence? Communist ideology and censorship had collapsed, but among Russians there was no agreement on what had happened since the end of the Second World War. A few liberals believed that the entire confrontation with the West was caused by the aggressive communist regime. Many more believed that the Soviet Union was defeated and destroyed, perhaps by internal treason. There were even those who thought that the Cold War had never truly ended: the West was still out to destroy Russia.

A four-decade long conflict is not easy to synthesize; indeed, *The Cambridge History of the Cold War* was published in three thick volumes. In this short book, I draw from my dual perspective of three decades in the USSR followed by three decades in the West, to interrogate the key issues and developments of the war.

We all live and write in space and time. As T.S. Eliot wrote: 'What is actual is actual only for one time and only for one place.' Had this book been written ten years ago, it would have appeared as a record of dangerous, but ancient times. Not so now. The world has become perilous again: the COVID-19 pandemic, the climate catastrophe, and the return of large-scale conflicts – the Russia–Ukraine war, and the growing sense that we are living through a 'new cold war' between the United States and China. Stability and peace are no longer the natural state of things. Diplomacy ceases to work, treaties are broken. International institutions, courts, and norms cannot prevent conflicts. Technology and internet communication do not automatically promote reason and compromise, but often breed hate, nationalism, and violence.

Should we be surprised? There is something unchanging about human nature and conflicts. Exiled general and self-made historian Thucydides famously wrote in the 5th century BC that the war among the Greeks was the result of 'the rise of Athens, and fear that this produced in Sparta'. Fear, honour, and interest – for Thucydides those qualities were natural, and naturally contributed to the tensions between the Greeks. Twenty-five centuries after Thucydides, French novelist Marcel Proust observed the naivety of those who expect wars to only erupt when countries are not satisfied with their borders and territories. War has countless causes. Seeing the 'other' as an enemy, a need for moral superiority, ideological delusions – all of these contribute to conflicts between countries. Insecurity is an irrational feeling that tends to become paranoia. And conflict almost inevitably breeds the conviction that the only way to settle a dispute is through the force of arms, pre-emptive offensives, and persevering at any cost.

People, of course, are not a pre-programmed species with unchanging emotions and invariable reactions. They are products of their life experience. We read about wars of the past not as neutral observers but from the vantage point of our life and education – now largely shaped by the 21st century. In a similar way, the policymakers in 1945–47, when the Cold War was starting, looked back to the past and saw thirty years of catastrophes – predominantly two world wars, the Great Depression, and a pandemic. Those calamities shattered many illusions about security, liberal values, and capitalist economy. Incidentally, the period between the outbreak of the First World War and the outbreak of the Cold War is roughly equal to that which has elapsed since the fall of the Berlin Wall.

The Cold War, most people argue, was an existential battle – between capitalist democracy and totalitarian communism. There were other 'isms' at stake: liberalism, imperialism, racism, colonialism. Those key phenomena had shaped the history of Europe and North America for about a century until 1914. Then came the First World War, the collapse of great empires, and the rise of new ideologies such as communism, fascism, and Nazism. After 1945, the United States became a global superpower. It waged the Cold War against the Soviet Union; its weapons of choice were containment by nuclear weapons and construction of an international capitalist liberal order, called 'the West'. Yet racism, imperialism and colonialism continued to define that 'West', and made Soviet communism look to many like an attractive alternative and a viable rival. Communist doctrine preached that capitalism was the foundation of other pernicious 'isms' and that it would perish from its own contradictions, yet before doing so, it might unleash another world war. Thus, it was necessary to contain the Western imperialists by force and help those around the world who were struggling against them.

The conflict was bound to last until one of the sides gave up. Many believe that the US-led West simply outspent and thus defeated the Soviet Union. The picture is different when one looks beyond the East–West rivalry. The Cold War was an almost uninterrupted string of proxy wars in Africa, Latin America, and Asia, and the people of those parts of the world paid the ultimate price for it. The Cold War for them was primarily about a contest between models and ideas of how to achieve de-colonization, development, modernization, and greater justice. Did the superpowers' stand-off help or delay this process? The debate about it continues to this day and is rather heated.

How did the Cold War affect the transformation of liberal capitalism? As a young man growing up in the Soviet Union, I heard from Western radio broadcasters that reached Moscow, such as the BBC and Voice of America, that capitalism had become humane, socially conscious, and was even 'people's capitalism'. This message certainly helped to erode the image of the enemy created by communist propaganda. Ironically, in the 1980s, capitalism began to swing back to its classical form: with global financial markets bringing an abrupt end to social programmes, with stagnant and declining incomes among the middle classes, and with skyrocketing income inequality. This trend continued after the Cold War ended. Liberal capitalist globalization continues to create its contradictions and discontents.

All of this was on my mind while writing this book. Why did this conflict erupt so soon after the Second World War and escalate so rapidly? What were the primary drivers of the confrontation, aside from ideology? How could the Soviet Union, a country so depleted by war and with limited finances, compete with the United States, sometimes successfully, for several decades? Did nuclear weapons prevent the conflict from intensifying or were there other constraints?

The standard narrative outline in most American histories of the Cold War is that the United States, thanks to its overwhelming superiority, entrepreneurial and democratic values, thriving economy, and cooperation with strong allies, successfully contained the Soviet Union and ultimately triumphed in Europe and elsewhere. There is much truth to this, but this narrative is too deterministic and reflects a winner's vantage point. Curious readers may wonder why capitalism did not prevail in the 1950s or 1970s. This book restores the drama and uncertainty to the story of the Cold War, one of the longest global conflicts in contemporary history. Soviet and non-Western actors are just as prominent in this book as Western voices – perhaps even more so, to compensate for their silencing in previous narratives. I also seek to demonstrate how intelligent strategies produced unintended consequences; how words and images could be more potent than arsenals of nuclear weapons; and how capitalist wealth provoked Soviet resilience, and only much later led to an accommodation and Western triumph.

Much of the recent writings about the Cold War seeks to 'decentre' the conflict, to bring in lesser-known developments and figures, primarily in Africa, the Middle East, Asia, and Latin America. And yet, the main proponent of the 'global Cold War', historian O.A. Westad, posits that the key ideas that fuelled the confrontation came from Europe – Enlightenment values, nationalism, imperialism, liberalism, communism – and that the conflict started and ended in Europe. Nor can the best-known aspects of the story, such as the Truman Doctrine and the Marshall Plan, the Berlin Crisis, or the Euromissile crisis, be 'decentred': they are too important, and it is necessary to put them in context.

This book consists of four parts, each focused on a distinct period of the long confrontation. With a nod to Thucydides and Proust as well as to ancient Rome, I have chosen to name each period after Roman divinities. Their names serve as metaphors for the specific zeitgeist of each era. The first part, entitled 'The Time of Mars', is on the origins of the Cold War. The US–Soviet hostilities grew directly from the two world wars, and earlier failures to prevent those conflicts. Only the alliance between the leading capitalist democracies and Stalin's Soviet Union could ensure the defeat of Germany, but this alliance was bound to lead to the occupation and split of Europe, prostrate and powerless, into two zones of influence. Washington, Moscow, and London trod cautiously, yet the urgency to build an order in Europe, above all in Germany, made them take steps, such as the Marshall Plan, that split the continent and led to confrontation. Many on both sides of the divide believed that a new great war was likely and imagined it ending, in Manichaean terms, either in victory or in unconditional surrender. At the same time, fear of a major war in Europe contained both sides, on that continent and also in Asia. It was only the outbreak of the Korean War, an outcome of the communist victory in China and of mutual miscalculations, that fully mobilized the West and the East for a global conflict. It was at the end of this period when the statesmen on both sides began to realize that the conflict had to be limited to a Cold War, and not escalated into World War III.

The second part is 'The Time of Vulcan', Vulcan being the maker of weapons in the Roman pantheon. This period marked the peak of the conflict. Stalin died in 1953, and there was hope that the confrontation might ease, both in Europe and in Asia, into a truce between the great powers. The main driver of this vision was the threat of thermonuclear 'revolution' that made an extinction of humanity possible. Ultimately, both sides focused not on negotiations, but on the arms race and shoring up their respective blocs. The Soviet leaders did this by launching Sputnik and sending tanks into Hungary in November 1956. NATO had its own crisis in the same month over Suez, yet American economic contributions and markets were too important for western Europeans to lose. Western Europe also began to discover the economic and political benefits of a common market, under the US nuclear umbrella. The thermonuclear revolution, instead of nudging the opposite sides towards a compromise, pushed them to build massive nuclear arsenals to deter each other. The United States reached the peak of its nuclear predominance, but, unsurprisingly, felt extremely vulnerable. The Americans even feared losing the 'race' to the Soviets. This emboldened Khrushchev to try to deter Americans in turn, and he ultimately overreached in Berlin and Cuba. The Cuban Missile Crisis made both superpowers, but especially the Soviets, step back from the brink.

Decolonization shaped this period tremendously. The rise of new sovereign countries in Asia and the crumbling of European colonial empires in Africa gave a unique opening to the messages of communism. And the Soviet breakthrough in space created an illusion that Moscow might replace Western capitalism as the main vehicle of modernization. The American reaction to this threat was neuralgic and exaggerated: the main consequence of it was the doctrine of 'falling dominoes' and the US expansion in Indochina. Both Moscow and Washington couched their policies in the universalist language of global development and scientific-technical progress – an epic struggle for the hearts and minds of all humanity. The realities on the ground were more sordid and messier, particularly the Wall in Berlin and the war in Vietnam.

The third part of the book is 'The Time of Janus', named for the Roman two-faced god who opened doors alternately to war and peace. Stark confrontation gave way to reversals and about-faces, elusive promises, and ambiguous policies. Both superpowers suffered from internal crises of faith. In the Soviet Union, communist ideology became ossified after the denunciation of Stalin and the suppression of the 'Prague Spring' in Czechoslovakia. American society was split over the Vietnam War and shocked by the Watergate scandal. Many believed that the US was losing the Cold War. Yet ultimately the protean and vibrant nature of American democracy proved to be much more robust than Soviet communist autocracy. In Europe, there was an urge for negotiations, trade, and treaties (what became known as 'détente'), generational change, and common fatigue from violence and nuclear fears. Europeans, especially the French and the Germans, became the main architects of rapprochement, alongside Soviet leadership under Leonid Brezhnev. Many hoped that détente would pave the road to the end of the Cold War. The Helsinki conference of 1975 and the resulting Helsinki Final Act seemed to point in this direction. The Iron Curtain remained, yet there were promising attempts to regulate the arms race. This moment could not be sustained. Most importantly, influential forces in the United States viewed peaceful process in Europe with suspicion and rejected an accommodation with the authoritarian Soviet Union as immoral and unreliable.

In the 1960s and 1970s, the world, having finally overcome the wounds of the Second World War, went through rapid decolonization, and suffered the first shocks of new globalization. The Cold War had never been bipolar: the UK, France, Poland, China, India, Algeria, Egypt, Iran, Cuba, Chile, and others had played distinct, sometimes crucial roles at various junctures. And during the 1970s, the US–Soviet bipolarity was challenged from all directions. China exited the Cold War and then became an ally – albeit a provisional one – of the United States. Iran exploded in the Islamic revolution against both liberal and communist poles. Various figures and forces in the Middle East, Africa, and Latin America continued to align with the East or the West, according to their own interests. In Latin America especially, military dictatorships turned to Washington for support against social democratic movements. The Third World was the main source of friction and mistrust between Moscow and Washington.

The increasing Soviet adventurism in Angola, Mozambique, and Ethiopia convinced the US media and policymakers that détente was merely a cover for Soviet expansionism. And the ideology of human rights helped the US to reinvent Cold War liberalism, overcome the trauma of Vietnam, and restore American leadership in the West. The Soviet leadership, meanwhile, entered a period of collective sclerosis. Brezhnev, who began as an energetic peacemaker, became a hostage to his failing health, parochial interests, and vanity. His personal demise, like Nixon's before, doomed the US–Soviet partnership.

The final part of the book is called 'The Time of Minerva', she being the goddess associated with the wisdom of hindsight. In the last decade of the Cold War, capitalism became truly global; financial capital became deregulated and reinvigorated the Western economies, above all the US economy;

the West took advantage of new technologies of computerization and robotization. This part also deals with the Cold War policies of the Reagan administration, the Euro-missile crisis, and the return of nuclear fears. The international developments of the 1980s had their roots in the previous decade but were also rich in unexpected reversals. The main achievements of the East during détente – such as the construction of oil and gas pipelines from Siberia to Europe, and access to Western credit, technologies, and consumer goods – turned into the main source of vulnerability for the Soviet bloc. Another major reversal happened when Ronald Reagan, formerly the main enemy of détente, showed he was ready to talk about nuclear disarmament and found his partner in Mikhail Gorbachev.

Much of this part is dedicated to how the Cold War ended. The main developments took place in the Soviet Union and eastern Europe. Mikhail Gorbachev's course of *perestroika* and *glasnost* reflected the yearning for change yet failed to find a viable reformist course. Gorbachev's economic policies and lifting of repressions put the Soviet Union, and eastern Europe, on the fast track towards the uncontrollable collapse of the communist system. For many Europeans, the end of the confrontation became linked to the spectacular fall of the Berlin Wall and communist regimes in eastern Europe. For Gorbachev, the end came down to the renunciation of ideological dogmas and an offer of partnership to the United States. For the Americans, the nature and timing of the end were disputed: from 1989, to the reunification of Germany in 1990, and all the way to the Soviet Union's disappearance in 1991. American reluctance to believe that the game was over was understandable. Gorbachev's rush to end the conflict, however, remains much less understood. Gorbachev could have bowed out of the Cold War like China. Instead, he offered a radically idealistic joint project: a nuclear-free world and a 'common European home' based on the convergence of democratic capitalism and democratic socialism. Gorbachev brought back genuine socialist idealism, but the rapid dissolution of Soviet power, triggered by unsuccessful reforms, buried the last sparks of this idealism.

The Soviet collapse distorted the way many would look at the end of the Cold War. While the end of the Soviet system and state might have been determined by domestic factors, its rapid meltdown made the end of the Cold War appear as an absolute Western victory – with far-reaching consequences. Gorbachev, a visionary peacemaker and socialist reformer, ended up as a supplicant of Western financial assistance. The United States, with its Western allies, suddenly became the only pole in a new global order. In the West, pessimism and the exaggeration of Soviet power gave way to triumphalism and hubris. As often before, the unintended outcomes of history set the stage for the illusions and mistakes of the following period, even beyond the Cold War.

As for the conclusion, the only appropriate title is 'The Time of Mercury', invoking the god of money and commerce, who also became a symbol of unbridled economic liberalism. The unipolar world seemed to open unlimited opportunities for a liberal global capitalism, with the United States in the dominant role, and with alliances, institutions, and rules from the Cold War. NATO and the European Union were successfully extended to eager entrants in eastern Europe.

And in Asia, China seemed to be on a track of rapid integration into global capitalist markets. The triumphalist mood was punctured by the terrorist attacks of 9/11, yet this tragedy did not shatter the enthusiasm about the global liberal order. On the contrary, the United States attempted to convert even the Middle East to 'democracy'.

Twenty years later, the triumphal mood is over. The rise of aggressive, neoimperialist Russia, and above all the growth of powerful China, which has replaced the Soviet Union as the second pole in the international system, have presented severe challenges to the liberal global order. Many observers have begun to speak about the idea, mentioned above, of a 'new cold war' and warn that the previous decades have been 'a holiday from history'. The remarkable way the West rallied after Putin's invasion of Ukraine gave some respite from pessimism, but not enough to dispel worries about the future. Will Western institutions and practices inherited from the Cold War be sufficient to grapple with new challenges? China is a much more formidable rival than the Soviet Union ever was, economically and technologically. Will the nations of the developing world, rapidly catching up with the developed countries, opt to support or to challenge the Cold War winner? Will the countries of the global south remain neutral towards the West and China, trying to benefit from their tensions? And if a new great power conflict erupts, where will its main fronts be, and what will be its preferred weapons? Whatever happens, this primer to the 'first' Cold War will help us better predict what the future may have in store.

PART ONE
The Time of Mars, 1945–1952

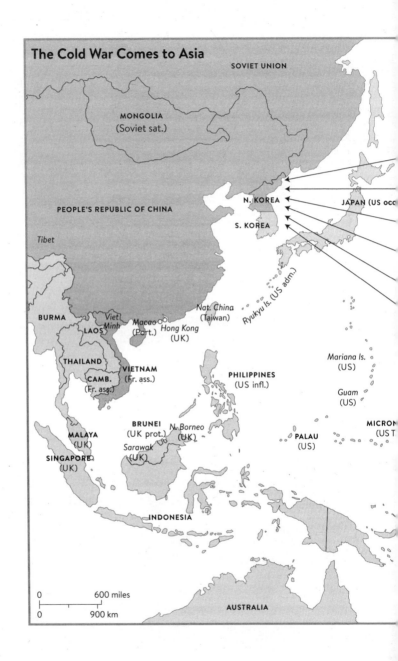

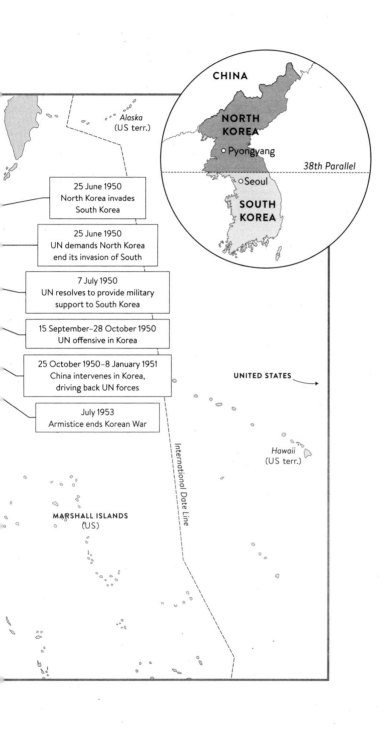

CHAPTER 1
The Fate of Europe

Origins

Why did the United States and the Soviet Union, who had allied against Hitler and Japan from 1941 to 1945, collide so soon after? Why did this conflict, within just a few months, come to be regarded by both sides as irresolvable, existential, and even more dangerous than the war against Nazism that had just ended? What made these two giants, separated by half a globe and never before in conflict, suddenly insecure and hostile?

Some would immediately answer: the struggle between freedom and totalitarianism. Others would say: the struggle between capitalism and communism. My preferred approach is less abstract: it was the struggle for the fate of Europe. Mars, the Roman god of war, had haunted Europe for hundreds of years before Marx and Engels famously wrote the same about 'the spectre of communism'.[1] For at least three centuries, Europe remained the world's powerhouse – financially, militarily, and culturally. Europeans colonized Latin America, then Asia and Africa. Europe was also the main battlefield for wars between the great powers. The quarrelsome family of European monarchies and empires clashed, made peace, and sometimes even organized 'concerts' of great powers that temporarily established international order. The most famous of these resulted from the Congress of Vienna of 1815, at which the victors over Napoleon – including the Russian tsar, the Austrian emperor, and the king of Prussia – shared a ballroom parlour with British politicians and even with the statesmen of the defeated France. The Concert of Europe maintained the balance between the great powers, all of them European at the time, for the rest of the 19th century, preventing another Napoleon, or any sole power, from dominating the continent.

In 1914 this world abruptly fell victim to the furies of the First World War. During the next few years, social upheaval and revolutionary violence consumed the Russian empire of the Romanovs, the *Kaiserreich* of Germany, and the Austro-Hungarian empire. The most spectacular change occurred in Russia: its imperial realm was resurrected as the Union of Soviet Socialist Republics, headed by the Bolshevik (communist) party. Vladimir Lenin, Leon Trotsky, and other Bolsheviks preached a world communist revolution and declared themselves enemies of the capitalist order and the system of European colonial domination over the rest of the world. Great Britain and France, the victors of the First World War, attempted to build a *cordon sanitaire* against the Soviet Union, consisting of Poland and other eastern European countries. They also tried to tame the revolutionaries by extending recognition and offering lucrative trade. They did not succeed. The spectre of Soviet communism continued to haunt the rest of Europe. Crucially, the restoration of a concert of great powers in Europe became impossible: the Bolsheviks would have been more out of place in such an order than a bull in a china shop.

The First World War also demonstrated the dangerous power of Germany. On the continent, this dynamic, populous, and industrialized country had no match. The United Kingdom and France had colonies over half of the world yet could not have defeated Germany without the peasant armies of Russia, and, after Russia collapsed in 1917, required support from the United States, a distant overseas democracy that had never previously involved itself in European wars. US president Woodrow Wilson was the most powerful figure at the peace conference convened in Paris in 1919. He offered a new system of collective security, the League of Nations, to replace the discredited concert of great powers. Yet Wilson failed to bring his own country along. The United States refused to join the League and instead practised isolationism, which meant it had its self-declared zone of influence in the Western hemisphere and no binding commitments to the rest of the world.

Stability and peace in Europe were, de facto, left to Great Britain and its weaker partner France to manage. This proved to be disastrous, especially in a financial and economic sense. There were too many discontents of the postwar settlement, above all in Germany and Italy. London and Paris were busy with their colonial empires in Africa, the Middle East, and Asia, and they did not have the armies nor the money to reintegrate Europe into any kind of concert. When the international economy crashed with the Great Depression from 1929 onwards, the British and the French preferred to retreat into the safety of their colonial trade blocs, leaving the struggling Germans and eastern Europeans to their own devices.[2]

Adolf Hitler took advantage of this. The leader of German

National Socialism promised the humiliated and impoverished Germans 'a thousand-year Reich', domination of Europe, and colonies in the East. British appeasement and French weakness helped Hitler to take over Austria and swallow Austria and Czechoslovakia in 1938. After striking a tactical pact with the Soviet dictator Joseph Stalin in August 1939, Germany attacked Poland, and the country was divided between Germany and the Soviet Union. London and France declared war on Germany, but not on the Soviet Union. Some British diplomats and military officials thought that communism was much worse than Nazism and hoped that Hitler would strike against the Soviet Union. Instead, the Wehrmacht took over Denmark and Norway, then, in a lightning campaign, crushed France and brought the United Kingdom to the brink of defeat.

Only when British prime minister Winston Churchill refused to sign a peace treaty with Hitler, and the German–British war became one of attrition, did the Führer finally take his greatest gamble (and make his biggest mistake): in June 1941 he invaded the Soviet Union. And in December 1941, with German troops at the gates of Moscow, he declared war on the United States. With those decisions, the German dictator accomplished what no other architect of international relations could have done: in a few years the Russian armies and the colossal power of the US would come to occupy the heart of Europe. Unwittingly, the Führer created the unique setting for a future Cold War.

In 1945, the Red Army converged on the Third Reich from the east across Prussia and Poland; the American troops, with the support of the British and French armies, did the

Figure 1.1
A Soviet woman traffic controller in Berlin after the Red Army took the Reich's capital, 1945.

same across France, Belgium, and Italy. On 2 May 1945, Soviet soldiers, in a staged performance of victory, hoisted the hammer-and-sickle red flag over the Reichstag, the charred edifice of crushed German might.

In February 1945, the three leaders of the anti-Hitler coalition – Stalin, Churchill, and US president Franklin D. Roosevelt – had met in Yalta, on the southern coast of Crimea. Photographers pictured them as an amiable trio, as if they were old gentlemen taking a break from their poker game. The new concert had slim chance of lasting. The Grand Alliance was Hitler's inadvertent creation and could last only as long as he lived. Much of Europe lay prostrate, unable to manage its economy and finances, at the mercy of the liberators. The European vacuum and the devastation left by Nazism invited more discord than collaboration between the

Allies. And because Europe was the hub of imperial and colonial domination in the Eastern hemisphere, its fate had global implications.

Had there only been British and Americans soldiers in Europe in 1945, they would have hastened to go back home as soon as possible. Yet the presence of the Red Army made Churchill plan for the worst: what if Stalin decided to move his troops all the way to the English Channel? Who would stop them? Would the Americans fight? This was wild supposition, yet recent history had proven that nightmares could quickly become real. Stalin was not hair-trigger Hitler, yet he was the opposite of the well-intentioned Russian emperor Alexander of 1815. Back then, the victorious Russian troops had occupied Paris, but had then returned home. In 1945, Stalin's armies took Berlin, Vienna, Prague, Warsaw, and Budapest, and had no intention of retreat.

Stalin was the recognized leader of global communism. But how much did this matter? In 1943, after the victory at Stalingrad, Stalin had ordered the disbandment of the Communist International (Comintern), the Moscow-based headquarters of the global movement that preached revolution, the overthrow of capitalist order, and decolonization. In his correspondence with his Western partners, he presented himself as a traditional leader of 'Russia', caretaker of its security and national interests, as well as a member of the great powers' club, only interested in his legitimate sphere of influence. Roosevelt and Churchill seemed to agree that the Soviet Union *was* Russia, warts and all, no longer bent on world revolution. The only problem was the limit of Russian ambition, and how to manage that ambition. Until 1946, Western expectations and actions regarding the Soviet Union stemmed from these assumptions. Most Europeans wanted the Russian bear to slink back into its Eastern lair. Yet the enormity of the double collapse, of both prewar Europe and Hitler's 'New Order', made radical changes inevitable. There would be no return to the world of British dominance, arrogant aristocracy, ostentatiously rich bourgeoisie, angry proletarians, and poor peasants. European nations such as Germany and France that once believed themselves to be at the top had miserably failed and would have to adopt or import new ways of life. Their future was now contested and caught between two powerful projects: American liberal capitalism and Soviet planned socialism. In Parisian cafés, in the factories and trattorias of Milan, and even in the pubs of London, intellectuals and many in the working classes opted for communism, while the middle classes were keen to embrace the 'American way'.

It would be wrong, however, to assume that ideas were the primary reason for a confrontation. The experience of the past was an even more powerful factor in shaping domestic and international politics. In Washington, Moscow, London, Paris, and Rome, policies and decisions were guided primarily by the experience of recent catastrophes, rather than by ideology. The spectre of Mars, not Marx, led to the division of Europe into east and west. The expectation of another battle for Europe and further carnage among the great powers remained the predominant fear in the minds of many leaders and elites in the years after 1945. Alcide De Gasperi, the Christian Democratic leader of Italy, was one of many who thought that the presence of the United States in Europe and the Mediterranean would be 'a guarantee against a new war'.³ This presence, however, came with a price: a divided Europe and four decades of the Cold War.

Protagonists

The Second World War sent more than 16 million Americans across the Atlantic and the Pacific to fight. The most powerful American trauma from the war was not Hitler's aggression but the attack by the Japanese empire on the US Pacific Fleet in Pearl Harbor, Hawaii. On 6 and 9 August 1945 the US had its revenge: two atomic bombs destroyed Hiroshima and Nagasaki. Japan surrendered, its government was dissolved, and the former empire was occupied by American troops.

While the war in the Pacific attracted national attention, Roosevelt and the American business elites were more concerned about the Atlantic and the fate of Europe. Both Pearl Harbor and Hiroshima pointed to one clear conclusion: American security and prosperity could no longer be protected by the two oceans and the US Navy. It was too dangerous to leave Germany, as well as Japan, unattended, free to make their own choices. While Japan was firmly under full American control, Germany was divided into Soviet, American, French, and British zones. The economic and political future of Europe, with all its trade routes, interdependencies, and colonies, now became an American problem too.

In the Soviet Union, Stalin and the Soviet people looked at the Second World War through a very different lens. The war against Hitler came to be known as the Great Patriotic War. Thirty-four million Russians, Ukrainians, Belorussians, Kazakhs, Tatars, Georgians, Armenians, and many others were mobilized for the Soviet army – one in every six citizens. Over 10 million of them did not return home. The Eastern front and the territories there occupied by Hitler and his allies became the 'bloodlands' of Europe.[4] The total human loss of the Soviet Union was 27 million out of a population of 195 million. This naturally meant millions of widows and orphaned children, while among the returning soldiers there were many amputees and those left maimed and shell-shocked. Adding to the trauma was the fact that many Russians, Ukrainians, Balts, and fighters of other ethnicities had sided with Hitler and fought against the Stalin regime.

The scale of death and suffering made the survivors feel entitled to exact revenge and to establish security arrangements that would create a lasting peace on Soviet terms. Stalin was the dictator and he made the decisions, but he also embodied the expectations of tens of millions. The victory transformed the Soviet Union from an outlier of Europe into a great power. Stalin performed impressively at the Yalta conference in February 1945 and seemed to confirm his partnership with Roosevelt. The Red Army had its troops and tanks in eastern Europe and Soviet generals and secret policemen ruled in Poland and Romania. Stalin was eager to extend Soviet power to the Far East as well. With Roosevelt's blessing, he pressed the Chinese Nationalist (Guomindang) government in Chongqing to sign a treaty that gave the Soviet Union a zone of influence in Manchuria – the area that for decades had been a contested territory between Russia and Japan. Shortly after Hiroshima, the Red Army invaded and occupied this region. The volte-face of history was so amazing that members of the Soviet elites and military felt hubristic. One of them wrote in his diary: 'We Russians can do anything!

Now, the whole world knows it. And this is the best guarantee of our security in the future.'[5] This mood was shared by the master of the Kremlin: no global issue from now on could or should be decided without the Soviet Union. One historian believed that this alone was a recipe for a future clash: the new Soviet 'great power' identity that resulted mainly from its victory in the Second World War 'clashed with America's vision of itself as Europe's liberator and protector'.[6]

Then things began to change abruptly. Roosevelt died of a stroke in April 1945, and Harry S. Truman, a conservative Democrat picked for the vice presidency, stepped into the Oval Office in time to finish negotiations on the postwar order. Truman was as ignorant of world affairs as he was brusque and decisive. In May, he abrogated US assistance to the Soviet Union without alerting the Kremlin. Then he reconsidered and mended fences. In July he went to a peace conference in Berlin to get Stalin's consent for the Red Army to join the war against the Japanese. While there, he was emboldened by the news that the United States had successfully tested an atomic bomb. Truman was not good at negotiations, preferring to tell the Soviets what *should* be done, in the Far East or in eastern Europe. From the Kremlin's perspective, American power suddenly seemed to be everywhere, disrupting Stalin's expansionist designs and recognizing no spheres of influence but their own. Truman's secretary of state James Byrnes boasted he was going to peace talks with the Russians 'with an atomic bomb on his hip'. Stalin did not take this boast lightly.

However, these two great powers, each with its own hegemonic designs and expansive security needs, were in dramatically opposite conditions. The United States, one historian writes, was 'the greatest military and economic power the world had ever known'.[7] That colossus financed, waged, and won what were effectively two enormous wars overseas, one in Europe, the other in the Pacific, while successfully building and financing a pioneering atomic project. The American economy had come roaring back from the Great Depression: it had produced more arms than the Axis powers and the Soviet Union combined and had supplied Soviet and British war machinery on land, at sea and in the air. Half of the world's manufactured goods were 'made in the USA'. It was a financial superpower that held two-thirds of the world's gold reserves and three-quarters of all invested capital. Its navy commanded the Atlantic and the Pacific, and one half of the world's shipping vessels carried the US flag. Much of this had resulted from the war-induced shrivelling of other powers, such as the United Kingdom, yet the global predominance of America was astounding.

And, on top of that, America was a democracy. The 'American century' was not just for millionaires, but for most American people (though, at the time, only the white ones). Europeans tasted American products and watched well-fed GIs with admiration and envy. Hollywood showed millions a polished version of the American world. American consumerism and mass culture defined modernity – and did it more attractively than the discredited Nazi newsreels, not to mention clumsy Soviet propaganda. All this meant the US had a unique appeal for famished and dispirited Europeans. Americans did not seek any conquests in Europe, they did not even want to stay there. Rather, many Europeans, in the apt expression of one scholar, were eager to invite them over; they wanted to become part of an 'American empire' of productivity, prosperity, and consumerism.[8]

The Soviet Union, for all its spectacular victories and hubris, was a country of survivors, exhausted and emaciated. Its impressive concentration of power had been created by the iron will and fist of Stalin, with the help of a unique political and economic system of ubiquitous mobilization and repression. The Soviet Union had almost lost the war to the Wehrmacht in 1941–42 and had marshalled all of its resources to stop and then defeat the German troops. Only then could Stalin redirect its armies against Japan in Manchuria. The Soviet economy could not have sustained the war effort without the US Lend-Lease system: through this scheme, billions of dollars' worth of assistance were given, covering a myriad of Soviet shortages and urgent needs, among them alloys for tank steel, petrol for aircraft, railway engines and trucks to carry troops, communication stations and cables, and canned meat to feed the army.

Soviet victory was Pyrrhic: a term derived from Roman history, referring to irreversible losses that negate the fruits of victory. The Soviet regime concealed the scale of those losses for thirty years, because they were, in part, the result of woeful inefficiency, a criminal waste of human lives, and reflective of the backward nature of the Soviet state, economy, and society. In those decades the Russian peasantry, the main supplier of manpower during the war, never recovered demographically or psychologically. For years to come the people who had stopped Hitler at Stalingrad, and who had taken Berlin, continued to live in abject misery, among ruins, and in hunger. After 1945, the survivors faced the monumental tasks of healing, reconstruction, and modernization. Stalin, however, had his own urgent priorities: in 1945–46 he launched gigantic state-funded projects to match American atomic power and to build missiles and jet aircraft.

History and ideology made the contrast between the would-be antagonists even starker. American elites emerged from the war convinced that the second half of the 20th century would be a culmination of two centuries of amazing US expansion of territory, trade, financial power and prosperity. The collapse of Europe resolved the old American debate between the isolationists, who wanted to stay away from 'the corrupt old world', and the successors to Woodrow Wilson, who wanted to 'save the world for democracy'. Both sides, the former isolationists and the Wilson followers, saw the immense power of America as a product and tool of divine predestination, as well as a natural outcome of the virtues and efforts of Anglo-Saxons and other European immigrants. Myths of Anglo-Saxon superiority in a white democracy built by immigrants of European stock built a democratic, but also racist foundation for American foreign policy. Suppression of American Indigenous people, anti-Semitism, segregation and racial discrimination against Black people, Latinos, and Asians were as integral to American life in the 1940s as were grassroots egalitarianism, rejection of intrusive state bureaucracy, and Christian proselytizing.[9] In 1945, it was the mission of the 'new world', seen as the product of European immigrants and superior values, to give the 'old world' of Europe a new lease of life, transforming it with American ideas, goods, and money.

The Search for a New World Order

In spite of all this, American triumph was darkened by uncertainty and fear. The Great Depression and the two world wars created a deep-seated anxiety about the future. Could more cataclysms come and sap the American capacity for prosperity? The tension between triumph and insecurity could be best resolved by a new mission: with America leading the world towards a better international order under the aegis of the United Nations, teaching humanity to prosper from free trade and business. After Roosevelt's sudden death this enormous task fell on the shoulders of Truman, whose only real prior exposure to the world beyond the US was on the battlefields of France during the First World War, where he served as a captain in the field artillery. He was determined, however, to create 'a federation of the world' with Americans leading from the front.

In the Soviet Union, Stalin and his communist regime told people that their country was the glorious successor to a millennium of Russian history, and at the same time a model of social justice and a paragon of 'all progressive humanity'. The problem lay in the stark gap between these aspirations for greatness and the reality of the country's postwar misery. The mainstays of the regime, some Western observers in Moscow thought at the time, were closer to the autocratic Russia of the 19th century than to a paradise of workers and peasants. The Stalinist state saw the world not as a potential arena for revolutions, but as a source of grave threats. Police surveillance was ubiquitous, while spontaneous social life was driven underground. Official ideology was full of citations from Lenin and Marx, yet reality consisted of omnipotent bureaucracy, oppressed people, and militarism. Stalin and his handpicked elites did what imperial powers had done several centuries earlier: took over land and looted economic resources from their neighbours. The Soviet Union annexed the Baltic states and western Poland, imposed heavy indemnities on Finland, crushed the resistance of the Balts and western Ukrainians under Soviet rule, and deported 'disloyal peoples' from the imperial peripheries to Siberia and the Kazakh steppes.

Many Russians, victims of the regime, found consolation in the superiority complex that the same regime propagated. In contrast to the American sense of superiority, based on growing material and technological abundance, the Soviet sense of superiority was a child of imperial legacy, ideology, and military victory. Marxist-Leninist ideology was no longer in conflict with the Russian imperial past; the two blended into one.[10] 'The USSR must become so powerful,' a former Soviet ambassador to Great Britain wrote to Stalin in January 1944, 'that it would not fear any aggression in Europe or in Asia; more than that – that no one power or combination of powers in Europe or Asia would ever think up an intention like that'.[11] A few educated war veterans thought differently. In their imagination, the victory over fascism was a great opportunity for the Russians to lift themselves out of the historic vicious circle of autocracy and militarism. Those veterans would play an extraordinary role in Soviet history after Stalin's death and would be influential in the last years of the Cold War under Mikhail Gorbachev.

Soviet imperialism was not a global phenomenon. It was

severely constrained by its capacities. 'It is necessary to stay within certain limits,' recalled Soviet foreign minister Vyacheslav Molotov. '[If you swallow too much] you could choke . . . We knew our limits.'[12] The general public and most of the elites dreaded another war. The common expectation was that the Soviet Union would remain in alliance with the United States and Great Britain for a considerable time. War veterans and those who had lost loved ones fervently hoped they would have some respite from misery and suffering. At the same time, history and culture made them look up to a strong state and leadership, who would steer the country into its uncertain future and prevent another war. There was only one leader available: the master of the Kremlin.

Biographies of the great dictator are no longer pieces of guesswork. They benefit from a mountain of archival evidence obtained from Moscow, and Stalin's personal collection of papers has long been open to the public. Stalin comes out as a product of the great revolution, of revolutionary terror, and of geopolitical cataclysms, but also a potentate from Dante's *Inferno*, a tyrant who combines cynicism and calculation.[13] A self-styled disciple of Lenin, Stalin was not an ideological fanatic. For all his ambition, he was prudent and cautious. He walked a thin line between cynical opportunism, cunning prudence, and a revolutionary worldview. The Kremlin ruler was a long-time student of realpolitik; he had learned from such great power masters of the 19th century as Napoleon and Bismarck, as well as from the history of the imperial Russian conquests. Yet he was capable of phenomenal miscalculations and even follies.

In the 1930s, Stalin prepared the Soviet Union for an

inevitable clash with European powers. He refused, however, to believe that Germany would be his main threat, or that the United Kingdom would be an ally. He correctly suspected that many in the West would not mind Hitler marching eastward and destroying the Soviet Union. Still, he expected that 'two groups of imperialists' – Hitler and Western democracies – would have 'a good, hard fight' and weaken each other instead. He was surprised when Hitler quickly defeated France, conquered Europe, and then turned against him. The dictator and his realm survived by the skin of their teeth. In 1945 Stalin was prepared to act in concert with Great Britain and the United States – a country that had never been Russia's rival. Yet the dictator was determined not to get duped and ambushed again.

The United Kingdom, more commonly referred to as simply Great Britain at the time, played an important part in the new great-power game. The British empire still ruled over much of Africa, India, and what were then Burma and Malaya, and its commonwealth sprawled from Canada to Australia and New Zealand. The two world wars dealt mortal wounds to British imperial dominance. Four hundred and fifty thousand British citizens perished between 1940 and 1945. The economic losses were huge: the war cost the empire two-thirds of its exports, a quarter of its merchant marine, half of its overseas investments, and a quarter of its financial reserves. The greatest blows were the humiliating defeats against Japan in Southeast Asia. In the colonies, the foundations of British superiority and right to rule were shattered. The British ruling class had great experience in international affairs, world trade and finances. Yet this could not offset the empty coffers, the costs of the navy and the army, and the imperial overreach.

The British prime minister Winston Churchill had been an early enemy of communist Russia, but he was also a realist. In June 1941, he immediately offered Stalin an alliance against Hitler: he knew the Germans could not be defeated without Russian troops. In the 'Big Three', as the trio of Allied leaders came to be known, Churchill was a secondary partner to Roosevelt and Stalin, and tried to cultivate each behind the other's back. Churchill's principal goal was to preserve the British empire and keep the Russians away from the Balkans and the Mediterranean. As the war brought the Red Army into eastern and central Europe, the British grew worried; they imagined Stalin carrying out the old programme of Russian imperialist expansion and feared the Soviet threat to Crete and the Suez Canal, resulting in an end to British control over the routes to India and Hong Kong. Stalin did little to dispel those fears. Churchill even thought of rearming defeated German troops to prevent the Soviet forces from becoming a dominant power in Europe.

In February 1945, Roosevelt and Churchill flew to Crimea, at high personal risk, to meet with Stalin and talk about the future of Europe after Hitler. The Western leaders' daughters joined them, which was seen as a gesture of familiarity, to make the atmosphere more humane and congenial. Roosevelt believed that the Soviet Union could be made one of the stakeholders of the future world order. He regarded the British empire as the main obstacle to the American global vision. Earlier, in Bretton Woods, a mountain resort in New Hampshire, the Americans had offered the Soviet Union a founding membership in the planned global financial institutions that could stabilize commerce and trade. Stalin was the only leader who did not bring his daughter to Yalta. He played a charming host, yet his purpose was hard bargaining. In exchange for his promise to support Roosevelt's idea of the United Nations and other international institutions, he obtained concessions in eastern Europe, Germany, and the Far East.[14]

Later critics would claim that Roosevelt's inclusive strategy towards Stalin was naive. But it was based in reality. Roosevelt and his advisers expected that, after the war, the Soviet government would not be able to ignore people's demands for a better life and, like everyone else, would turn to the United States for credit and assistance. Stalin knew this. He said in his close circles that Churchill 'would slip a penny out of your pocket'; Roosevelt, he said, 'is not like that. He dips his hand in only for bigger coins.' Later Molotov elaborated: 'Roosevelt believed that Russians would come and bow down to America and beg, since Russia is a poor country, without industry, without bread.'[15] Those crude remarks aside, Stalin and his successors valued the 'Yalta order' enormously and considered it the bedrock achievement that made the Soviet Union a recognized world power. For the rest of the Cold War, every successive Kremlin leader would strive to reach this benchmark again and again, each time coming up against their main detractor, the United States.

Without Roosevelt the inclusive Yalta order stood no chance. His successor Truman had a soft spot for 'Uncle Joe', as he called Stalin, but adopted a low-tolerance policy towards Soviet imperialism. The British leaders were glad to support this new course. In July 1945, Churchill lost out in the general election, to the Labour candidate Clement Attlee, but in March 1946, he would arrive in the US as Truman's guest, to give a commencement speech in a local college in Fulton, Missouri. In his now-famous 'Iron Curtain' speech, Churchill proposed a post-war alliance between the United States and the peoples of the British Commonwealth. Aligning the British empire with enormous American power would bolster the former and would check Russian ambitions everywhere.

Stalin regarded the Fulton speech as a collusion of 'the Anglo-Saxon powers' against the Soviet Union. For decades Soviet propaganda would consider this speech the starting point of a new confrontation. The term 'Cold War' was not used. Instead, the Kremlin preferred to call it 'a departure from the Yalta post-war order'. The 'Fulton line' was intended to replace this order with an alliance between the United States and the British empire, aimed against Soviet security interests. This was an unpleasant surprise for Stalin, who took pride in his ability to side with one 'group of imperialists' against the other and obtain concessions from both. Suddenly, there was nobody to side with. In the international power game between February 1945 and March 1946, the United States was like a joker in a card game: it transformed from Stalin's partner to his most formidable antagonist.

A Conflict Imagined

In August 1945 Truman was still full of respect and admiration for Stalin. By the end of that year he said privately, with great irritation, that he 'grew tired of babying the Soviets'. In late February 1946, a chargé d'affaires at the American embassy in Moscow, George F. Kennan, sent a 'long telegram' to Washington, where he wrote that the erstwhile ally would never become a peaceful partner; that the Russian power expands like 'a malignant parasite'; that the Soviet worldview is 'neurotic.' The telegram was an instant success in Washington and across the American diplomatic community. Just as Truman hosted Churchill and accompanied him on a train to Missouri.

Kennan's analysis suffered from weaknesses and contradictions. Kennan, who spent several years in Moscow as a US diplomat, was torn between his affection for the Russian people ('talented, vital, friendly to an outside world') and his loathing of the despotic state, claiming that its 'neurotic view of world affairs' betrayed a 'traditional and instinctive Russian sense of insecurity'. The loathing prevailed in the telegram as Kennan used emotive and powerful images of Russian threat, rather than strategic arguments. He compared the Soviet regime to a pathological virus, a product of Russian history and Marxist ideology. He claimed that Soviet leaders were impervious to reason and alien to Western civilization. And he treated Soviet security claims as limitless, contrary to what we now know to be true. In an oft-quoted sentence, he defined the Soviet threat as 'a political force committed fanatically' to the destruction of the American way of life and US authority. It is not clear to this day what convinced him of this.

One of Kennan's biographers, who studied his private diaries, wrote about the emotions, frustration and resentment that guided him. Kennan, like other American diplomats in

Moscow, was badly exposed to the realities of the tyrannical, xenophobic regime, which prevented contact with the 'wonderful Russian people'. Stalin alone reserved the right to host foreigners, a charming Dr Jekyll who could, in an instant, become a lethal Mr Hyde. One after another, friendly Americans who came to Moscow turned into militants who began to believe that no compromises with Moscow were possible. This wild oscillation between unrealistic expectations and frustrated Russia-bashing would become a hallmark of American attitudes to the Soviet Union throughout the Cold War and beyond.[16]

The classic Western interpretation of the origins of the Cold War focuses on the brutality of Soviet expansionism and Stalin's regime, with its sweeping arrests and deportations, its aggressive xenophobia and militarism, and its ideology preaching the inevitability of another world conflict. In eastern Europe, as the Red Army pushed back the Germans, Stalin's secret police followed up by 'cleansing' actual and potential enemies, including the underground resistance, prewar politicians, clergy, and some intellectuals. Stalin annexed the lands that Hitler had given him as his 'sphere of influence' in 1939, including the Baltic states of Lithuania, Latvia and Estonia, which became 'republics' within the Soviet Union. Two-thirds of Poland, and parts of Slovakia, Hungary, and Romania, were attached to the Soviet republics of Byelorussia and Ukraine, constituent parts of the USSR. Eastern Europeans considered themselves victims of the 'Yalta order' and blamed the British and the Americans for this betrayal of their interests and freedom. Roosevelt's indifference to the fate of this region does seem shocking in retrospect. His defenders answer that it was the price that had to be paid for victory over Hitler: without the Soviet army, many more American lives would have been lost in Europe.

The US and UK did not recognize the legality of the Soviet annexation of the Baltic states but accepted it as a fact. The future of Poland was a much larger bone of contention. Modern Poland was resurrected in 1918, on the rubble of three empires, and viewed itself as a shield and spear protecting Europe from Soviet expansion. The Soviet–German pact and later a 'treaty of friendship' dismembered and destroyed Poland. When Stalin joined Roosevelt and Churchill as a member of the Big Three, the sordid past had to be swept under the rug, at least for as long as the Russians were 'on the good side' of history. Churchill desperately sought to convince Stalin to restore Poland's independence. Stalin and his diplomats responded with an existential argument: Poland had always been a rival of Russia. Also, being too weak, Poland could not prevent the Germans from invading Russian lands. The Soviet leader even argued he wanted to make 'a stronger Poland' by changing Polish geography. He 'compensated' the Poles for their eastern lands and cities Wilno and Lvov with industrial and urban territories annexed from the defeated German Reich. The ethnic cleansing of Germans and 'ethnic exchanges' of Poles and Ukrainians followed. Stalin wanted to make a new Poland, dependent on Soviet protection, rather than on its traditional allies, Britain and France. For additional safety, the Kremlin ruler staffed the post-war Polish government with Polish communists, many of them of Jewish descent, and Soviet advisers. The American and British diplomats powerlessly watched all this.

In Romania and Bulgaria, Stalin did not even bother to do what he had done in Poland. The Soviet leadership viewed those countries, formerly within the German zone of influence, as the keys to Soviet security in the Black Sea. The secret police made members of the pre-war political elites disappear or flee westward. The Soviet ruler was convinced that the United States would not quarrel with him over those countries, in an area far from American trade interests. He was wrong: Washington would scrutinize Soviet encroachments in any part of the world, even the lands which Americans could not properly find on the map. The US diplomats and military began to make plans to respond to Soviet 'aggression' anywhere: from the Black Sea to the Pacific, from the Arctic to Palestine.

In early 1946, the attention of Truman's diplomats and military was redirected from Europe to the lands that had served as traditional flashpoints of past confrontations between Russian and British powers – Iran and Turkey. In the American as well as the British imagination, those countries were 'Oriental' and 'backward'. In both countries, the Europeanized tiny elites, a militarized autocracy in Ankara, and a kleptocratic oligarchy in Tehran, struggled to reinvent the remains of the Ottoman and Persian empires, respectively, into modern nation-states – with limited success. For the British empire-builders, they were purely pawns in the geopolitical chess game. For the Americans, however, they represented aspirants to modernization: wronged by European colonizers, they deserved to see the light of progress brought by the United States.

Stalin's main goals were to gain Soviet control over the Turkish straits, where Europe meets Asia and the Black Sea has a narrow egress into the Mediterranean. In Iran, Stalin wanted oil concessions, like the British had earlier gained. Complicating his games, the Kremlin ruler covered his geopolitical demands with the fig leaf of 'national self-determination'. He pressed the Turks to cede contested territories that Georgians and Armenians had once peopled. In Iran, the Red Army had occupied the northern territories since 1941, per consensus with the British and the United States; Stalin took advantage of this by setting up Azeri and Kurdish 'autonomies' in the zone of occupation, dependent on Soviet support. He pressed the Iranian government to get the deal sealed, but Iranian politicians resisted Russian imperialism and turned to the British and the Americans for support. Stalin assumed that in the age of imperialism he could act like the Russian tsars had done in the past. He did not want to export communism; he wanted to have a territorial buffer of dependent states and statelets along the Soviet borders.

Stalin miscalculated, because his policies aroused US suspicions and clashed with the American idealist vision. The new world order Americans imagined did not have room for Moscow's imperialism. Stalin's pitch backfired when he failed to withdraw his troops from Iran in March 1946. The Truman administration sided with London and took the case to the United Nations Security Council when it opened its first session. Stalin had to announce a gradual withdrawal. The reputational damage, however, was irreparable; many took the Soviet retreat as a result of America's superiority as an atomic power. In his memoirs, Truman even argued, falsely, that an atomic ultimatum made Stalin walk away. At the end of 1946, the Iranian government, which had only recently paid homage to Stalin, crushed the Soviet-instated Kurdish and Azeri autonomies. The Soviet Union did nothing. Stalin, poised against Turkey, was also unable to act against that country. 'It is good that we retreated in time,' Molotov recalled, 'or [the crises in Turkey and Iran] would have led to joint aggression against us.'[17] Moscow tacitly recognized that Iran and Turkey were off limits, but publicly did not stop bullying those countries.

Stalin suspected that his lieutenants were prone to making concessions to the Americans in peacetime. Already in the autumn of 1945, he had begun to crack the whip, bringing them more forcefully into line. Only 'the policy of tenacity and steadfastness', he wrote to them, could make Washington and London respect the Soviet Union as a great power. The Kremlin dictator expected that the Yalta order could be preserved only through hard bargaining and demonstrations of strength, not concessions. This approach, however, only helped to cement the US–British alignment. Time after time, first in the Middle East, then in Europe, Stalin overreached and then had to retreat – without admitting his miscalculation. He retreated because he was not ready for an open confrontation with the Americans and still hoped to delay any such showdown.

Before long, Stalin's spies obtained a copy of Kennan's telegram; Soviet intelligence reported on the change in Washington's attitudes. The US Treasury Department, once very favourable to Soviet inclusion into the global capitalist financial institutions (the World Bank, the International Monetary Fund), was now taken over by different people, who were not eager to meet Moscow's desire for post-war reconstruction loans. Americans no longer wanted to loan Moscow money and technology; they linked their assistance in Soviet recovery to political conditions. Stalin decided to wait and prepare for a long-haul conflict. The Soviet ratification of the Bretton Woods agreements, creating the World Bank and the International Monetary Fund to stabilize the world economy, was put on hold – in the end, it never took place. He took steps to organize, in total secrecy and with great urgency, an atomic project. He estimated the bomb would be ready after three years. This, he hoped, would redress the balance of power with the United States.

Subsequently, a small group of men in Washington decided that a confrontation with the Soviet Union was inevitable and began to prepare for it. The group included, among others, secretary of defense James Forrestal, secretary of state James F. Byrnes, and under-secretaries of state Dean Acheson and William Clayton. George Kennan arrived from Moscow in 1946 as an expert on Russia. The group faced a tall task. The American public did not want an alliance with the British empire and another major conflict abroad; Congress cut down on military expenditure. In November 1946, the Republicans, long known for isolationist policies, took control of both houses of Congress for the first time since 1933. Fortunately, the Truman administration had ample time. The Soviet Union, for all Stalin's bravado, was weakened; the formidable Red Army had shrunk due to demobilization, illness, and sheer exhaustion. There was no military threat from Moscow to western Europe or even the Middle East. In his telegram, Kennan had acknowledged this. He wrote that the Soviet regime, in contrast to Hitler, did not have a fixed timetable for war and conquest: Russian communists believed that capitalism was doomed. In his diaries, Kennan wrote with confidence that 'we can contain Soviet power until Russians tire of this game'.[18]

In the 5th century BC, the Athenian general Thucydides described how the combination of power, arrogance, insecurity, and moral superiority pitted Athens and Sparta, two centres of ancient Greece, against each other in a war that lasted for a quarter of a century. There were no strong reasons for a war, he wrote, but Sparta feared the rapid ascendancy of Athens. In 2017, Harvard political scientist Graham Allison popularized this ancient story by writing about 'Thucydides's Trap'.[19] He wrote that a war could emerge just from fear that a new power could displace the dominant one in a crucial region of the world. The Soviet–American–British triangle produced exactly such a trap in 1945–46. The British were pivotal to this triangle: their waning as a great power made the vacuum palpable, and by aligning with the US, they tipped the balance of fear. In a devastated Europe, hegemony was up for grabs and there were only two contenders: the Americans and the Russians.

Thucydides had another insight that could be applied to the Cold War. He famously wrote that the strong and rich states 'do what they want' and the weak and poor 'do what they must'. There was only one rich and powerful side in the conflict: the United States. In 1946, its leadership convinced itself that the next confrontation, in the style of previous great-power conflicts, would be with the Soviet Union, and began to prepare to contain Soviet power. While the Soviet Union looked formidable, it was insecure, depleted, backward, and poor. The Soviet leaders were aware of their vulnerability and their weaker hand, yet they were ready to do anything to deter another conflict. Stalin's iron will, the exhausted Red Army, and the incessant mobilization of the emaciated population were the only assets they possessed to achieve this tall order.

The Cold War emerged in the way it did largely because the Americans 'did what they wanted' and Stalin refused to 'do what he must'. This is not to say that the Americans launched the confrontation and that the Soviet Union was the passive side. Rather, the Americans had real means and ways to become a dominant power on both sides of the Atlantic. They had the strongest economy, fleets of strategic bombers, a huge navy, and the biggest money pot in the world at their disposal. And they had the atomic bomb. Those Western authors who have claimed that the Americans had to act to save Europe from Stalin have exaggerated the threat. Europe did not fall for communism after the First World War, and was not going that way after the Second World War, despite economic misery, political turmoil, and large communist parties in Italy and France. I side with those who claim that the Cold War was caused by the American decision to build and maintain a global liberal order, not by the Soviet Union's plans to spread communism in Europe. US policymakers did not want to return to the failed international system that had rested on balance between great empires. Instead they decided they were on a mission to build a new international order. In particular, they sought to resurrect the liberal capitalist Europe that had been destroyed by Hitler and fascism, and to contain and weaken the Russians. Their belief in this mission changed the optics as they measured up the Soviet threat. The trials of the Nazi leaders at Nuremberg, which lasted for almost a year until October 1946, reflected this huge change. By the end of the trials, the US and British media publicized Soviet crimes next to Nazi crimes. The top Nazis were hanged, but a historian of this event concluded that the Soviet Union 'lost its victory' at Nuremberg.[20] For the American and British leaders, 'the valiant Russians' had transformed from gallant allies into barbarians at the gates of Western civilization.

CHAPTER 2
The Conflict Takes Shape

The A-Factor

The use of nuclear weapons in Hiroshima and Nagasaki created an atmosphere in which the prospect of another geopolitical struggle was inevitably imagined as an atomic conflict. As the laws of physics were universal and scientific knowledge could not be monopolized, it was just a matter of time until the United States that had created the 'winning weapon' would itself become its target. Truman and the British prime minister Attlee stated the obvious in their declaration in November 1945: 'We recognize that [regarding the atomic weapons] there can be no adequate military defence, and . . . no single nation can in fact have a monopoly.'[1] As if to illustrate the point, the US government published a booklet on the atomic bomb, or A-bomb, which became known as the Smyth Report, that explained the basic principles of how the new weapon worked. Meticulously censored, all scientific and technological secrets excluded, the publication nevertheless provided a valuable blueprint that was translated into many languages. Veterans of the Soviet atomic project later joked it became a 'bible' for them.

Bernard Brodie, an American strategist from Yale University, was the first to comment on the implications of a future atomic war, arguing that, from now on, the main task for the United States would not be to win wars but to deter them. In 1946, he wrote: 'It is clear that the monetary cost is no barrier to any nation worthy of the name. The two billion dollars which the bomb development project cost the United States must be considered small for a weapon of such extraordinary military power.' Another scholar wrote that Soviet–American relations were at a crossroads: 'Either, both sides should recognize that cooperation and some kind of mutually observable rules would be a way to reduce anxiety about the atomic threat to their respective countries and cities. Or fear of the new weapon would strain the relations between the two countries rather than associating them in a common enterprise.'[2] Shelves upon shelves of writing about the nuclear arms race in the years to follow would simply restate these early insights.

In the context of American democracy, with its clash between different, often opposite political views, some people leaned towards the need for a world order that would tame the atomic danger, and others took the opposite view, that the A-bomb would help to secure peace, as long as it was in American hands – but would become a mortal threat if the Soviet Union got hold of it. The former view was shared not only by Roosevelt's followers and left-leaning Americans but initially by several conservative American statesmen, such as Henry Stimson, Dean Acheson, and, at least in part, by Truman himself. In January 1946, the US government initiated the creation of the United Nations Atomic Energy Commission, to explore what to do with the new existential challenge. Truman appointed a special committee to prepare American proposals, headed by Acheson. Robert Oppenheimer, the lead designer of the atomic bomb, a brilliant thinker whose left-leaning views were well known, became the most influential adviser to this committee. His plan, detailed in what came to be called the Acheson–Lilienthal Report, was to create a hugely powerful UN body that would take over the atomic arsenal and all uranium mines around the world. Admitting that the Soviet political regime was not compatible with such a scheme, Oppenheimer insisted that the American position 'should be to make an honourable proposal and thus find out whether they have the will to cooperate'.[3]

Truman read the report, but by that time he had changed his mind decisively on the Soviets. There could not be an honourable proposal to those without a sense of honour. The Canadian intelligence service and the FBI learned from a Russian defector, Igor Gouzenko, about the extent of a Soviet spy ring in North America that was active throughout the entire war and had targeted US atomic secrets. In Washington, the spy scandal shook those who still hoped to cooperate with Stalin, including Acheson. Truman decided to shelve the Acheson–Lilienthal Report. Instead he appointed Bernard Baruch, a New York-based financial donor to the Democratic Party, to lead the talks on international atomic energy. The so-called 'Baruch Plan' did not pass any US atomic facilities to an international authority, and demanded that all countries, including the Soviet Union, first open their territory to foreign inspections. This was not the 'honourable offer' that Oppenheimer had intended.

The spying scandal also made Truman's young councillors

Clark Clifford and George Elsey pen a secret memo. They wrote: 'Our ability to resolve the present conflict between Soviet and American foreign policies may determine whether there is to be a permanent peace or a third World War.' They still proposed 'to demonstrate to the Soviet Union that we have no aggressive intentions, and that peaceable coexistence of Capitalism and Communism is possible'.[4] The last point was quickly dropped in favour of Kennan's uncompromising line: no other way but containment of the Soviet Union. The phrase about 'peaceable coexistence' disappeared from the American diplomatic vocabulary. It would come back repeatedly, but every time the American side would dismiss it as a slogan of Soviet propaganda.

The impact of atomic spying should not be exaggerated. Even aside from the Soviet Union's behaviour across Europe, the conservative and nationalist tide in American society was too strong to ignore. Truman was an *American* internationalist, after all, and was not going to internationalize US nuclear facilities that had cost US taxpayers so dear. The conservative and deeply provincial bulk of the American political class thought the same. The United States ended up promising atomic 'partnership' to the United Kingdom, but in the end did not share all its industrial and scientific secrets even with its British allies. Truman's secretary of state James F. Byrnes meant to use the bomb to cut a deal with Stalin that would be favourable to the United States.

Being forced to accept the US-led 'atomic order' was enough to infuriate Stalin, as it placed the Soviet Union in the position of an excluded third (behind the US and UK), a secondary power. Clumsy, direct diplomacy by Truman and

Byrnes made Western media write about 'atomic diplomacy'. There was a consensus throughout the Kremlin that in this situation the best the Soviets could do would be to pretend to ignore it. The problem was, however, that the bomb was very real, and Stalin knew it. For him it was obvious that in the short term the Soviet Union must behave with even more assertiveness and not yield to American–British pressures anywhere. In practical terms, this translated into Soviet intransigence, which only fanned the early flames of the Cold War. Stalin repeatedly demonstrated to Byrnes and Truman that he did not care for the US atomic monopoly; moreover, he wanted the US to make concessions. The atomic factor did not dissuade the Soviet leader from making his demands on Turkey and Iran, rather it induced him to be more brazen. And in Stalin's view, as two historians of the early Cold War assert, possession of the bomb became 'an absolute necessity for the survival of the Soviet Union' to counterbalance the US atomic monopoly.[5] After Molotov rejected all American proposals on atomic control and inspections on the Soviet territory, the Americans' view was also confirmed: an arms race with the Soviet Union was inevitable.

In July 1946, two Soviet observers were invited to attend a US atomic test on Bikini atoll. The Americans were keen to impress foreign observers. One of the guests used a personal camera to record the test and brought a film to Moscow. Meanwhile, a first crisis occurred in the Black Sea area, where US intelligence detected some suspicious movements of Soviet divisions and interpreted them as a possible attack against Turkey. For the first time, the Joint Chiefs of Staff in Washington made plans for the atomic bombing of

Soviet cities and crucial hubs, such as the oil refineries of Baku. Soviet intelligence duly caught wind of these Western preparations. Stalin took those warnings seriously: whatever Soviet military moves were taking place, he stopped them. Still, he could not admit to the Americans, nor perhaps to himself, that he had made concessions. In his interview with an American journalist in August 1946, which he edited before publication, Stalin inserted the following line: 'Atomic bombs are intended for intimidating weak nerves, but they cannot decide the outcome of war, since atom bombs are by no means sufficient for this purpose.'[6]

Stalin did not have 'weak nerves' but on the importance of the bomb he prevaricated. He kept pushing Lavrenty Beria, the man in charge of the Soviet atomic project and the dreaded head of secret police, to produce a Soviet atomic bomb, a copycat of the American 'Fat Man' that hit Nagasaki, by January 1948.

Stakes in Germany

In this context policymakers in Washington and Moscow decided that a conflict was coming. At the same time neither was ready for it. Several developments in 1947 forced their hands. On the American side, it was domestic politics. The Republicans in Congress wanted to dismantle the 'New Deal' policies of Roosevelt, including his foreign policy. Many of them engaged in anti-communist demagogy, blaming FDR for his concessions at Yalta and excoriating the State Department as a conspiracy of 'appeasers' of Moscow. The Truman administration felt weak and decided to project an image of toughness against the 'communist threat'.

Then came the shocking news from London: the Labour government had confidentially told the Americans that Britain could no longer take 'responsibility' for Greece and the Turkish straits. This meant the end of an era of Britain's role as policeman of the Mediterranean trade routes and the power that could block Russian advances there. The British economy was a shambles. London took an American loan to prop up the weakened pound, yet this came at a high cost and with strings attached. The government of Clement Attlee focused on 'British socialism' and sought to cut colonial costs hard and fast. It set a countdown timer on the independence of India and decisions taken at this time also spelt the beginning of the end for the British mandate in Palestine. In London, the cabinet and the Foreign Office decided that the best option was to lean on 'the American cousins' in order to preserve Britain's great power role. Americans wanted to pry open the British colonies to make them accessible for American goods and money. Now they received a price tag for this: take care of Britain's imperial commitments. This helped to focus the State Department's minds on Greece and Turkey.

There were also significant developments on the ground in Germany. During July–November 1946, the victorious powers had agreed on peace treaties for Germany's wartime allies – Italy, Finland, Hungary, Romania, and Bulgaria. Yet they had failed to work out a settlement on Germany itself. At the Potsdam meeting of the Big Three in the summer of 1945, the occupied Germany had been divided into four zones, administered by the four victorious powers (including France), as a temporary measure before conclusion of a peace treaty and creation of a German state. Stalin had agreed that Berlin would also be temporarily divided into four zones. The occupying powers, however, never managed to create a common German government. In the British, US, and French occupational zones of Germany, the economy went from bad to worse. Inflation, misery, and the black market determined everyday life. The British faced the need to obtain food for the population of the industrial Ruhr, their zone of occupation; with many hungry mouths at home, they refused to do it. The French, to whom the British ceded part of their zone, wanted Germany to remain divided and impotent. The head of the American military administration in Germany was General Lucius Clay: all the problems of the Western zones ended up on his desk. He felt that time was running out. Millions of Germans from eastern German lands flooded the Western zones. They were driven out of their homes by fear, as well as by the Soviets, the Poles and the Czechs. For Clay, the situation amounted to calamity, a recipe for chaos and communism. Those pressures dictated a change of course for America in Germany.

The facts on the ground in Germany and eastern Europe also forced the Soviet hand, in rather unexpected ways. Soviet activities in Germany were the products of Soviet insecurity, uncertainty, and backwardness. Stalin signed over a swathe of East German lands to Poland and augmented his own empire by annexing East Prussia. At first Stalin did not know what a future Germany would look like: the Soviets stripped their zone of occupation of many of its industrial assets and carted them off to the Soviet Union, claiming they were acting in accord with the initial agreement of the Big Three. Soviet authorities destroyed some German plants, including those underground, to deny a future Germany its military potential. The SVAG, the Soviet military administration in Germany, struggled with the same problems as the British and American occupational authorities – above all, how to feed German cities. There was famine in many areas of the Soviet Union, but unlike the British government, Stalin insisted on sending food to the Soviet zone of occupation. The Soviets faced large occupation costs as well and helped themselves by using their printing press (each occupational power had one) to print occupational currency and pay for their expenses. This contributed to runaway inflation.

Because of his paranoia, Stalin missed a chance to accept a promising offer from the United States on the future of Germany. The opportunity came from secretary of state James Byrnes, who wanted to pose as a great diplomat. Byrnes offered Moscow a US–Soviet agreement for twenty to twenty-five years to ensure a demilitarized Germany. Stalin considered this offer and rejected it. He viewed this as an American ruse: an attempt to legitimize the American presence in Europe for a long time. He explained to his underlings that 'the US may hereafter, in league with England, take the future of Europe into their hands'. Stalin's analysis was simple: after the Americans, with their dollars, goods, and troops, became ensconced in post-war Europe, nothing would dislodge them from the continent. He would be proved correct, though at this point the dictator still hoped that the United States would succumb to isolationism.

During 1946, the Soviet authorities in Germany, instructed by the Kremlin, proceeded unilaterally and improvised to build some kind of order in their zone. As one historian aptly put it, they did it in the only way they knew: they began to build a party-state.[7] They invited the survivors of the German Communist Party and social-democratic parties into the new Socialist Unity Party of Germany (SED). Moscow appointed two loyalists, Wilhelm Pieck and Walter Ulbricht, to the command posts of this party. They acted on one guiding principle: everything in the zone should appear democratic, but must be in our hands. This kind of 'order' triggered alarm bells in Washington. In the autumn of 1946, the Truman administration realized that the US had to stop seeking a consensus with the Soviets and instead take over the burden of running the other Western zones, at least in economic and financial terms. In September 1946, the secretary of state James Byrnes, increasingly irked by Soviet shenanigans, went to Stuttgart in the US zone of occupation. He announced that the Americans would not leave Germany, nor, in fact, Europe, as they had after the First World War. Byrnes did not mention the Soviet Union, yet indirectly blamed Soviet and French misconduct for the hardships inflicted on the German people. He offered the 'economic unification' of Germany and financial reforms to ensure its economic revival. Unilaterally, the United States switched from a message focused on punishing Germany to one of hope, even protection – from the Russians. As Byrnes emphasized: 'we do not want Germany to become the satellite of any power or powers or to live under a dictatorship, foreign or domestic.'[8]

For Moscow, the speech served as an official announcement that the Americans would fight them to the bitter end for the minds and resources of Germany. Appropriating the language of the speech, while inverting its message, Soviet propaganda told the Russian people: Americans want Germany to be a satellite and enact revenge on the East again. Blow by blow, the Americans and the Soviets launched the struggle for the soul and resources of Germany – which meant the struggle for Europe. Thucydides's Trap snapped.

Containment

In March 1947, Truman addressed both houses of Congress with a speech that announced the American resolve to assist Turkey and Greece, to the value of $400 million. The pledge, immediately branded as the Truman Doctrine, was the first public statement of the United States' new containment policy, although the Soviet Union was not even mentioned. Truman called on Congress, in which the Republicans now had a majority, to transcend the Monroe Doctrine, which had stood for the last 120 years and which had made the US a self-appointed protector of the Western hemisphere only. Now the entire world fell into two zones: the 'totalitarian' Soviet Union and those nations that it coerced into submission, and 'freedom-loving people' whom Truman pledged to assist and protect. In fact, Stalin had repeatedly refrained from helping communists in Greece and had done nothing against Turkey other than make verbal demands. Yet the Truman administration wanted to project their clarity of purpose and threat. The worst kind of aggression was expected from the Russians, in this case a pincer movement into the Mediterranean, across Yugoslavia and Turkey. Only a pre-emptive show of resolve could forestall a war with Moscow.⁹

The Republicans and conservative southern Democrats

in Congress supported the emerging Cold War policies. The people who had earlier been reluctant to fight Hitler now formed a bipartisan coalition, a marriage of convenience. For those politicians, containing communism also meant rolling back Roosevelt's 'socialism' and preserving racist legislation and traditional gender roles, as well as necessitating lucrative defence contracts. During May–July 1947, Congress set up a new set of institutions, including the National Security Council and the Central Intelligence Agency, to advise the president how to protect and promote US interests around the world. State secrecy, which had found little place in the American republic, became entrenched by such measures as the Atomic Energy Act of 1946. The amount of classified information closed to American democracy began to multiply exponentially. And the power of the FBI to fight foreign espionage in peacetime increased as well.[10] It was the birth of the US national security state and the start of the gradual emergence of a professional group of people who would run US foreign policy and security apparatus – and indeed 'the free world'.

In Washington, in the spring of 1947, the new secretary of state, George Marshall, set up the Policy Planning Staff in the State Department and asked George Kennan to turn the chaos of new developments and American improvisations into a clear strategy. Previously, Roosevelt and other US presidents had drawn up foreign policy highly informally. Wilson had relied on his friend Edward House to do most of the sensitive tasks. Roosevelt had asked his associate Harry Hopkins to do the same. There was no tradition of planning foreign policy. The Council on Foreign Relations on East 68th Street in New York acted as a semi-private discussion club where corporate lawyers, philanthropists, and other internationally minded gentlemen identified problems and discussed the future. For quite a while, those informal ways prevailed in the State Department as well, despite reorganizations. In his office, Kennan single-handedly wrote directives that amounted to a new policy prescription. Republicans in Congress concurred with his arguments and recommendations, as long as they reflected their views of being tough with communists. Quickly, Kennan's texts became self-fulfilling prophecies.

During 1947–48 Kennan came up with the concept of containment of the Soviet Union. He believed it could work if the United States could deny Moscow any control over major centres of industrial power. Among those centres were the Ruhr in Germany and areas of Japan, the UK, and northern France. *Foreign Affairs*, the journal of the Council on Foreign Relations, asked Kennan to write something for the general public. The article appeared in July 1947 under the pseudonym 'X'. This text was even more deterministic than Kennan's 'long telegram' a year and a half before. Kennan portrayed Stalin's regime as a mechanistic force, bent on expansion and responding only to superior force. He presented the Soviet threat as existential for American society, a gross exaggeration of reality. Kennan did not even mention that Soviet society was exhausted by the recent world war and not up to new expansionism. The goal of containment, the piece read, was 'either a break-up or the gradual mellowing of Soviet power'. In his private remarks to American students at the National War College, where he taught a course, Kennan was more nuanced. The Soviet threat to the West, he argued, could be removed by a 'gradual mellowing of Soviet policy

Figure 1.2
Truman and his advisers: Robert Lovett, George Kennan and Charles Bohlen, 1947.

under the influence of firm and calm resistance abroad'. Yet this mellowing, he warned, would be 'slow and never complete'. A more radical option, Kennan said, was 'internal dissension which would temporarily weaken Soviet potential & lead to a situation similar to that of 1919–20', i.e., the Russian civil war. Kennan did not consider such a prospect likely.[11]

Stalin, aged and short of energy, isolated even from his bureaucracy, brooded over how to respond to this American challenge, and found no clear answer. Vibrant discussions among Bolshevik intellectuals on how to ignite a world revolution and divide capitalists were distant history; their participants were dead, in some cases murdered by the secret police. The dictator had only one permanent partner to talk to, his foreign minister Molotov.

When he was alone, Stalin gave full space to his perverse talent to imagine the worst intentions of his foreign adversaries. Yet he was not in a hurry to declare his thoughts aloud. Rather he posed as an oracle, whose utterances were subject to more than one interpretation. This was a deliberately affected manner, to keep his subordinates in constant tension as they struggled to guess what was on the great man's mind. As a result, there is a startling absence of strategic paperwork in Stalin's personal archive for 1946, 1947, and beyond. Historians have pieced together Stalin's revelatory comments during his meetings with foreign leaders and communists, yet have been able to find no 'blueprints' for Europe, even for Germany, comparable to the American memos. Some have even concluded that Stalin was clueless and lived in a bubble of delusions while the Cold War was worsening.

A rare insight into Soviet strategic thinking was the 'Novikov telegram',[12] a kind of Soviet answer to Kennan's long telegram. Molotov commissioned the Soviet ambassador in Washington, Nikolai Novikov, who had no special knack for strategy, to evaluate US motives and actions and cable his thoughts to the Kremlin. In practice, the telegram was heavily edited by Molotov and intended to confirm Stalin's beliefs. It supported Molotov's dogmatic reading of world affairs through a Leninist lens, as a struggle between the US and the British empire. The Roosevelt line of cooperation with Moscow, it said, was being defeated by American reactionary circles. The American goal was 'world domination' and the Soviet Union was 'the chief obstacle' to this objective. Ultimately, the US was in the midst of preparations for a war against the Soviet Union; it had set up military and naval bases around the globe and planned to restore 'German imperialism', as well as Japanese militarism, to fight on their side. The document, just like Kennan's analysis, crudely warped reality and portrayed the other side in a mechanical, deterministic way. The telegram, typically for Soviet internal documents, ended without any recommendations for a Soviet strategic response; making such recommendations was way above the ambassador's pay grade. We do not know how Stalin reacted to this document.

In the summer of 1947, Soviet intelligence and the country's foreign ministry created the Committee of Information. It was vastly different from the institutions at the heart of the US national security state. Stalin brooked no discussion; he wanted full information and trusted only himself to digest it. The Committee simply gathered all information from all spies and condensed it into 'little reports' that were easy for Stalin to read at a glance. The Soviet bureaucracy was short of cadres; very few people knew English and other foreign languages. In Moscow, a new Institute for International Relations was created, to train a crop of young diplomatic and security professionals. It would take years to create new cadres and they would come to prominence only during the 1960s and after, to help shape the course of the second half of the Cold War.

As 1947 progressed, the Soviet reporting from London and Washington, digested by the Committee of Information, received high marks in the Kremlin: not only because the Soviet Union had moles in British and US intelligence, but because US foreign policy objectives increasingly met Stalin's worst expectations. Soviet analysts interpreted Kennan's 'X' article as a call for the preparation for a war against the Soviet

Union, with the goal of destroying the Soviet regime. The intelligence officers who translated Kennan's text into Russian searched for a proper word to translate Kennan's 'containment'. Their bosses pushed them to translate this word as 'strangulation' (*udusheniie*). The correct translation prevailed, but the episode shows how Stalin read US intentions.

Stalin continued to play the oracle: he spoke rarely and little. He kept telling French and Italian communists to hold their fire, cooperate with the Western allies, and avoid provocations that might precipitate a conflict between Moscow and the United States. He also ignored their proposals to restore the Communist International to coordinate their actions. Rather, he preferred to pass his 'advice' in coded messages through secret diplomatic and intelligence channels. Stalin felt, however, that it was increasingly difficult to wear two hats: that of world statesman, the last of the Big Three; and that of potentate of the communist Soviet empire. In April, when US secretary of state George Marshall met with him in Moscow to discuss the German settlement, Stalin continued to be noncommittal and clearly played for time. Perhaps he still expected that the bad streak of 1946 would end, and the capitalist world would experience a recession. Then the Americans would become more accommodating.

The Marshall Plan, announced on 5 June 1947, ended this wait-and-see period. The curt commencement speech by the secretary of state at Harvard University ushered in a far-reaching American strategy: to use billions of US dollars to revive western European economies and synchronize this with financial reform in the combined Western zones in Germany. Once the German economic engine restarted,

European capitalism would be rejuvenated and back on track. The Soviet Union was not explicitly excluded, but Kennan assured US policymakers that Stalin would reject the plan. He knew that the Soviet dictator would be allergic to the idea of an American 'dollar diplomacy' inside the Soviet zone of Germany and Soviet-controlled eastern Europe. Furthermore, Kennan expected that eastern Europe, if deprived of Western markets and US money, would become a cauldron of discontent, and one day would rebel against the Soviet masters. In the State Department, Acheson and Clayton calculated with their eyes on the money: western Europe would do just fine, better than fine, if eastern Europe were to become decoupled from the greater European economy, with its food and raw materials. It was a strategy to 'save' and consolidate economically the most developed part of Europe, while sacrificing its more backward eastern parts.[13]

The Soviet dictator almost ruined these American designs. He agreed with Molotov that the Soviet Union should participate in the discussion of 'the plan of European economic recovery', leading other delegations from 'people's democracies', the moniker for pro-Soviet governments in Poland, Czechoslovakia, Bulgaria, Hungary, and Romania. A big Soviet delegation arrived in Paris for a European conference to discuss American assistance, but at that point Stalin obtained fresh intelligence from his spies in London that corroborated his worst suspicions that the Anglo-Americans were plotting to create a European bloc against the Soviet Union. Stalin's fury was immediate, and it saved Kennan's scheme. The Soviet dictator ordered the governments of Poland and Czechoslovakia, still formally ruled by multi-party coalitions, to pull out of the Paris talks and turn down American money. Finland, eager to obtain a neutral status from Moscow, prudently chose to pull out of the Marshall Plan without expecting a diktat from Stalin.

Stalin decided it was time to stop sitting on the fence. In September 1947 he called the leading European communist leaders to a secret meeting in Poland. Unwilling to travel himself, he sent his trusted lieutenant Andrei Zhdanov to read his instructions to the heads of the French, Italian, Yugoslav, Polish, and Czechoslovak communist parties. The 'Zhdanov Doctrine' responded to American declarations of a 'divided world' with its own version, written in purely Marxist-Leninist language. Stalin edited and corrected Zhdanov's speech and guided his sidekick's every step from the seclusion of his dacha on the Black Sea. Zhdanov said the world had become split into 'two camps': the imperialist one led by the United States, and the 'democratic and peace-loving' one guided by the Soviet Union. Getting ready for the forthcoming struggle, the conference created a Communist Information Bureau (Cominform), a ghost of the Communist International disbanded in 1943. Zhdanov cracked down on the old 'appeasing' line of the French and Italian communists – as if Stalin had not authorized it himself only recently. Now, on Moscow's cue, those communists launched a wave of strikes and demonstrations to derail their countries' participation in the Marshall Plan.

The Marshall Plan forced Stalin's hand. He had to sacrifice his desire to balance his external empire in Europe and his partnership with the United States. It was also clear that the time of Stalin's relatively soft line in eastern Europe was over. In Poland, politicians who were not in the Communist Party prudently fled the country. In Czechoslovakia, the last democracy within the Soviet sphere of influence, the communists staged a coup in Prague in February 1948. The country's democratic foreign minister Jan Masaryk, the son of the founder of Czechoslovakia Tomáš Masaryk, committed suicide or was 'helped' to fall from the window of his office. Stalin's loyalists and helpers from the Soviet secret police could finally act 'in Bolshevik spirit', resorting to terror, imposing one-party control, and eradicating capitalism and the bourgeois classes.

For American strategy, the clear-cut division of Europe into two blocs turned out to be a net benefit. Truman, Acheson, and Marshall gave a sigh of relief as the Russians helped Washington by drawing the lines. The communist bear had

Figure 1.3
The communist coup in Czechoslovakia, February 1948.

showed its claws and temper; the long-needed mobilization of public opinion and resources for the Cold War and containment could now begin in earnest. In March 1948, Congress voted for the largest amount of money in American history to be spent on aid to western Europe in peacetime. In June, Congress reinstated an act permitting the government to draft into the military in peacetime. The British Labour politician Ernest Bevin thought it was a good moment to invite the Americans to maintain their military presence overseas. He and the leaders of France, Belgium, the Netherlands, and Luxembourg signed the Brussels Treaty to form a defensive community; the idea was to turn to the United States for military protection. In a revolutionary break with two centuries of isolationism, both parties in Congress in June 1948 approved the resolution to join the community, which became the North Atlantic Treaty. Its fifth article defined an act of aggression against any European member as an act of aggression against the United States. NATO was born a year later in 1949.

Acheson wrote to Truman years later: 'We used to say that in a tight pinch we could generally rely on some fool play of the Russians to pull us through.'[14] The Marshall Plan and NATO remain to this day the greatest achievements of American foreign policy. Those initiatives also meant a strategic checkmate to Stalin and the Soviet Union.

Splitting Germany

Stalin reacted to the American challenge by consolidating Soviet political and military dominance in eastern Europe. He also intensified a new, hugely expensive arms race, leading with two giant programmes, atomic and missile. Some may see those decisions as a foregone conclusion. In reality, had there been any leader other than Stalin in the Kremlin, it would have been impossible to harness the exhausted, depopulated, and starving country to fulfil such monumental tasks. Half of all Soviet cities, such as Kiev, Minsk, Sevastopol, Stalingrad, and Kharkov, were in ruins. Leningrad (now St Petersburg) was half empty, having lost a million of its population to famine and cold during the German siege.

The Marshall Plan set western Europe on a path towards capitalist revival and even prosperity later, yet eastern Germans and eastern Europeans paid the price. The Stalinist system was imposed on them. Previously, the communist authorities in eastern Europe had avoided fully copying Soviet experience. They had tailored their regimes to the local conditions, albeit with mixed success. The post-1947 regimes, however, had zero tolerance for political pluralism and ideological ambiguity. The idea of specific 'national roads' was discarded, and 'learn from the Russians' became a mantra for all spheres of life. The elites of Poland, Czechoslovakia, and other satellite states could see that they were better educated than 'the teachers' from the east. Yet all ties with the West were cut off and criminalized. Polish intellectual Czesław Miłosz had joined the government, with a view to creating a new Poland, but in 1951 he defected to Paris and described the numbing experience of Stalinization in his pamphlet *The Captive Mind*. Decades later it became an anti-communist manifesto for many eastern European intellectuals.

The Soviet zone in Germany remained the only Soviet-controlled territory to deviate from Stalin's new course. The dictator pursued contradictory goals: he wanted to consolidate communist control in this zone, where the bulk of Soviet military forces were stationed, yet he continued to tempt the people of western Germany with a vision of a united, independent Germany. The Western powers, however, forced his hand again: in March 1948, at a conference in London, they agreed to unite their three zones (the US and British zones had already been merged; the French now added their zone), to introduce a new currency, and to allow German democratic parties to set up a German state. This state would receive Marshall Plan money and US troops in Europe would continue to be stationed there. One Soviet report read: 'The Western powers seek to turn Germany into their stronghold and to include it in their newly formed military-political bloc directed against the Soviet Union and the new democracies.'[15]

Stalin still posed as an advocate of a united future Germany. He could not, however, ignore certain new realities, particularly the danger of a new US-backed German currency. He received eastern German leaders and instructed them to build their own 'democratic' Germany, distinct from any western German state. He ordered his military to gradually limit access routes from Western zones of Germany to West Berlin where American, British, and French troops remained. The explicit aim was to squeeze the Western presence out of the city or at least to make Western powers abrogate their separate currency reform. The head of SVAG, Marshal Vasily Sokolovsky, walked out of the Allied Control Council for Germany, an institution the four powers had set up in 1945. All hopes for a peaceful settlement of the 'German question' were now suspended. The Kremlin leader hoped the Americans would conclude that it was not worth it to fight with the Russians over Berlin, a city deep inside the territory the Red Army controlled. Legally, the Soviet authorities violated nothing, since there were no international agreements on the access routes to Berlin. Still, Stalin proceeded with caution: he did not want to risk a military conflict with the United States. No full-scale blockade of West Berlin was planned; there was no ultimatum. Rather, there was an undeclared campaign of piecemeal restrictions and harassments.[16]

Originally, the Soviet stand on Berlin looked strong. The Western powers clearly violated the 1945 agreements on German unity when they launched a separate West German state. And yet the brutality of the Soviet system, so obviously based on force, lost the battle for the hearts and minds of most Germans. The promise of US dollars, and other Western ways and means, generated popular legitimacy – in contrast to Stalinist crude manipulations. The Soviets responded to the Western currency reform with their own. Two currencies now circulated in Berlin, a highly abnormal situation. The Western Deutsche Mark, backed by the United States, was the natural winner. Sensing this, Stalin responded with the demand that the Deutsche Mark be rescinded in Berlin, and meanwhile imposed a full blockade of trade, people, and goods via air, roads and canal in and out of the city, 'to protect the economy of the eastern zone'.[17]

Western money and resourcefulness organized the resulting airlift to West Berlin. Lucius Clay, who knew his Soviet counterparts well after a few years of running Germany, correctly guessed that the Kremlin would not risk a war and would do nothing to disrupt the air traffic. Over more than eleven months, from June 1948 to May 1949, about three hundred US and British military transportation planes delivered 2.35 million tons of food and fuel to 2 million people in the city. This allowed the Western forces to stay in Berlin and, more importantly, won over the West Berlin population. The Western powers also responded with an economic 'counter-blockade' and threatened to end the supply of coal to East Germans. Once again, Western propaganda was beating Soviet propaganda to the punch. The 'blockade of West Berlin' became the first successful Western story of the Cold War. In some parts of Europe, and of course in the United States, it eclipsed the image of the Red Army as an anti-fascist force. Western sanctions created multiple production breakdowns all over the Soviet bloc. One well-informed historian writes that Stalin 'had no intention whatsoever of starving out the Berlin population with the blockade measures'.[18] Western media, however, presented Soviet activities as blackmail by hunger. Soviet crudeness contrasted with its inability to shut down an 'island of freedom' in West Berlin. The images of American pilots who risked their lives to deliver coal for the Berliners and dropped candy for their children contrasted with the images of the Russian oppressors. The crisis over West Berlin greatly helped the popularity of the German Social Democrats in the city and in the Western zones. Their leader in Berlin, Ernst Reuter, told Clay: 'You worry about the airlift, let me worry about the Berliners.' West Berliners were not ready to surrender to the Russians for a second time. They decided they would stick with the Western Allies and the Deutsche Mark. This choice gave them a new democratic identity they had previously lacked.

After months of stand-off, Stalin gave up. In an interview with a US journalist, he dropped the cornerstone issue of currency. This allowed both sides to untie the knot. Wisely, the Americans used Stalin's gesture to launch secret US–Soviet talks. In March 1949, the Soviet military lifted all restrictions on West Berlin in exchange for an end to the Western counter-blockade. Special agreements were reached that legally assured free access for the three Western occupying powers from their zones to West Berlin. It was a Western victory. Forty British and thirty-one American soldiers lost their lives during the airlift.[19]

After Stalin's death in 1953, Nikita Khrushchev blamed the dictator for triggering the Cold War in Germany, and for making the Soviet position in Berlin worse than it had been before the crisis. He was right. The stand-off over the German future helped to create NATO. The Berlin crisis solidified the American resolve to keep their military in Germany and in West Berlin. And the airlift experience demonstrated that the Soviets were afraid of going to war against the West. All of these events shaped the division of Germany. In October 1949, the Western zones got their constitution (termed Basic Law) and a new state, the Federal Republic of Germany (FRG). Immediately, the Soviets followed suit and proclaimed the creation of the German Democratic Republic (GDR). For all its problems, the FRG got a potent new currency backed by US financial power and economic aid, and West Berlin became an enclave of defiant capitalism in the bosom of the communist empire, a bulwark for Western espionage, propaganda, and, some years later, consumerism.

Deadlock in Europe

Yugoslavia was its own story. Its communist leader, Josip Broz Tito, was the only one in Europe who had seized power in his country without the Red Army's assistance. Initially, Tito and his Yugoslav comrades embraced the Zhdanov Doctrine enthusiastically: the Cominform headquarters were supposed to open in Belgrade. But the Yugoslavs quickly learned that it was not enough to be Stalinists. The new order in eastern Europe required complete subordination to Moscow's wishes and accepting Soviet 'advisers' in every branch of a supposedly sovereign state.

Tito was not ready for such a deal, so Stalin selected him as an apostate, a target for excommunication and elimination. The Kremlin dictator treated foreign communist leaders the same way he treated his minions at home: he designated 'a fifth column' as a pretext for a massive purge and the extermination of potential enemies. Tito defied Stalin's fury and survived, despite Soviet plots to assassinate him. Communist Yugoslavia turned to the United States and the United Kingdom for assistance, and immediately received it – which proved that the Cold War was not as much about fear of the ideology of communism as about fear of the Soviet Union. Other communists in eastern Europe were not so lucky as their Yugoslavian comrades: in the next few years many of them would be put in show trials, tortured and killed, or at best imprisoned, as imagined 'Titoists'. Just like in the Soviet Union during the Great Terror of the 1930s, when Stalin had orchestrated the orgy of denunciations and arrests, loyalty and ideological probity mattered little; it was truly a Russian roulette.

And what about the Russians and other peoples who populated the Soviet Union? The Western architects of containment, such as Kennan and Acheson, would maintain for years that their main goal was to have the Soviet population place pressure on its government, to demand a higher standard of living, dismantle the command economy, and let eastern Europe go. This reasoning, however, was untenable. If there had been a moment when Russians could have pressed their government to relax its grip, it was the post-war period. Russian historians later realized the great extent of the hope of a better life among the Russian people after the war. Stalin had to organize crafty campaigns that divided and atomized the population and crushed all hopes for a better life. There was unending terror. At the same time, many Russians outside the educated elites continued to trust Stalin, and shared the idea that only a strong state was able to protect them from another act of foreign aggression.

The Soviets were also losing the battle for the rest of western Europe's hearts and minds, including in France and Italy, where communist parties were very popular. In Italy, the watershed came in April 1948, when the Italian Communist Party failed to win in the national elections. This outcome was helped by the promise of Marshall Plan money, secret US funds going to the coffers of the anti-communist Italian parties, and the influence of the Vatican on Italian women. Italy remained part of the West. France, despite its strong political left, also remained bourgeois and democratic.

The US strategy of salvaging western Europe worked brilliantly, but the result of this success was a prolonged

Figure 1.4
Marshall Plan Aid delivered to Greece, around 1948.

geostrategic impasse. In 1945–46 the demarcation line between the Anglo-American and Soviet forces was in fact not yet the 'Iron Curtain' that Churchill had claimed: people, goods, and even money continued to travel across the divide. This was no longer possible after the Marshall Plan and the Berlin blockade let the division of Germany, and Europe, harden. The east became a Soviet bloc, with many features of a concentration camp: heavily guarded western frontiers, watchtowers, barbed wire, minefields, and more. Kennan's expectations that eastern Europeans would rebel against this new division came to naught – at least while Stalin remained alive. And the brutal split of Germany and Europe nourished in the public imagination a spectre of probable showdown in the future. Berlin and

Vienna became frontline cities, astride the divisions between East and West, hotbeds of military espionage in both directions. And in Washington, hotheads proposed to 'liberate' the 'captive countries' of eastern Europe by covert operations or even by bold military action.

CHAPTER 3
The Asian Front

The China Shock

The Cold War started in Europe and was caused by huge uncertainty about the fate of the continent. From the start, however, the conflict spread into the Middle and Far East, with Asia looming as a potential second front. Japan, occupied by US troops in September 1945, was another big bone of contention between the Americans and the Russians, second in importance only to Germany. Stalin attempted to get involved in the islands' occupation, Truman bluntly refused, and the dictator took it as a personal offence. The Russian grievances went back to the war of 1904–5, when Russia had suffered a humiliating defeat by Japan. Then had come a long and hard military stand-off during the 1930s, when the Japanese military squeezed the Soviets out of Manchuria and created there a puppet state, Manchukuo, across the border from the sparsely populated and thinly connected Soviet Far East. This had forced Stalin into an urgent military build-up in the Far East, far from Soviet urban and industrial centres. The Kremlin waged a proxy war against the Japanese empire by arming and supporting the Chinese Nationalist (Guomindang) government, led by Generalissimo Chiang Kai-shek.

In 1945, Stalin had word from Roosevelt that the United States would support the restoration of Soviet interests in Manchuria, and Soviet positions vis-à-vis Japan. FDR consented to the Soviets regaining the assets built by imperial Russia and lost to Japan after the war of 1904–5: the naval base Port Arthur, the commercial port Dalian, and the railway from those strongholds to Siberia. In August 1945, Stalin cashed in on American support and pressed the reluctant Chiang to conclude a Sino-Soviet Treaty. Stalin was still in great form as a tough negotiator, a crass imperialist. The Chinese negotiator, a brother-in-law of Chiang Kai-shek, complained to the Americans about 'Russian imperialism', only to be told to comply. Truman still needed the Red Army to help crush Japan in Manchuria. The treaty was Stalin's spectacular achievement in Asia.

The Kremlin, however, feared that Truman would renege on Roosevelt's promises. They especially feared that the United States, after occupying Japan, would turn it into a key anti-Soviet ally. The Red Army moved quickly to occupy Manchuria, and seized the whole range of islands that formed a defensive perimeter around its territory in the Far East. Yet what the Kremlin considered defensive, appeared quite offensive to the American military and planners. The latter already looked at the Soviet threat through the geostrategic lens of the defeated Japanese enemy. What Stalin feared would later come true, although his greatest fears of Japan's remilitarization would never be realized; the United States preferred to keep Japan demilitarized and under its military protection.

As he had initially been in Europe, the Soviet dictator was

highly cautious in the Far East in 1946–47. He did not need to clash with the Americans and valued the Yalta order in Asia based on Roosevelt's promises. Secretly, he advised the leader of the Chinese communists, the young and ambitious Mao Zedong, to form a coalition with the Guomindang to rule a post-war China. Stalin had no reason to believe that Mao would be able to oust the Guomindang; a weak China with the communists inside the government suited him well. Very soon, however, events on the ground radically changed the rules of the game. The most important development was a civil war in China that flared up in 1946. The old enemies, the Guomindang and the communists, hated each other, since bloody clashes in 1927 when Chiang had massacred the communists. This time the Guomindang leader tried to disrupt the fragile truce of 1946 by attacking the communist army, called the People's Liberation Army. Generalissimo Chiang and his coterie of relatives, well connected to politicians in Washington, believed that, no matter what, the Americans would back him in his fight against the communists, at a time when Washington had adopted the strategy of containment in Europe.

Neither the Americans nor Stalin was eager to turn the this giant and poor country in Asia into another huge proxy battlefield. Marshall travelled to China to try to convince Chiang to reform his extremely corrupt and unpopular government, and somehow reach an accommodation with the communists. The Generalissimo continued to act as a wayward dictator, and the Americans concluded that the Guomindang government was hopeless, probably doomed. Stalin assumed the worst from another perspective: he feared that if the Soviet Union sided with the Chinese communists, the

Americans might help Chiang to beat Mao and then perhaps even try to retake Manchuria. The Kremlin leader mistrusted the Chinese communists, who always acted independently from him. In the end, Stalin deliberately distanced himself from Mao, and provided only limited Soviet assistance to the communist troops, doing his best to keep it secret from the United States.

In the end it was not Soviet assistance but Chiang's spectacular failure that determined the outcome of the civil war in China. Chinese peasants and nationalist intellectuals, disgusted by the Guomindang's corrupt regime and lack of reforms, flocked to the communists, who had grandiose plans for China's modernization. One by one, Chiang's generals and competing warlords began to defect to the communist armies. Massive US support to the Guomindang was in vain: American arms ended up in the hands of Mao's armies. The ancient Chinese cycle in which a virtuous warrior seized the 'mandate of heaven' from the corrupt ruler took another turn, except this time the winners carried red flags and preached Marxism-Leninism. The People's Liberation Army rolled across the Yangtze river into China's west and south.

Throughout 1948, Stalin sat on the fence. He treated Mao as a 'peasant leader', not a true communist. In February 1949, however, the communist armies approached the Guomindang's capital Nanjing, and Stalin dispatched his best negotiator, Anastas Mikoyan, on a secret mission to meet Mao at his wartime base of Xibaipo, a mountain village. Mikoyan acted as Stalin's mouthpiece and communicator.[1] The Kremlin leader advised his Chinese comrades to come up with a camouflage of 'peace talks' rather than just proceed towards a complete military victory. This precaution, he explained, would prevent the Americans from making a military intervention similar to the one they had made during the Russian civil war, between 1918 and 1921. Stalin's respect for American power was stronger than Mao's assurances that the United States would not intervene. Stalin also said at the time that the communists should not hurt American business interests in China, but instead direct their attack against the British colony of Hong Kong.

This was to be the second time, after Tito, that a younger revolutionary defied Stalin's advice. Mao was determined to proceed with his revolutionary war. He agreed with Stalin on many counts, yet he insisted on 'clearing the house' of foreigners, above all the Americans. In July 1949, he boldly declared his policy of 'leaning on one side' and aligning with the Soviet Union. By doing this he killed several birds with one stone: he proved his loyalty to Moscow and the world communist movement, captured the rest of China, established himself as a new effective emperor in the eyes of nationalistic Chinese citizens, and chased the defeated remains of the Guomindang off the mainland to Taiwan – without inciting American fury. Instead, the United States 'lost' China without a fight.

How could this happen? In 1947, Truman, Marshall, and Acheson already suspected that the Guomindang would lose their ill-fated war, due to corruption and a lack of popular support. Focused on Europe, the State Department and the US military decided to stay away from the Chinese civil war and to limit the amount of money they poured down the sinkhole of China's corrupt regime. The Americans, just like Stalin, doubted the communists would ever take over all of China. And even if they did, the threat from them to American national interests seemed small. The US focus in Asia was on Japan, the most developed and industrialized country in Asia, which was now an American responsibility. The architects of containment grossly undervalued the huge public impact of the communist victory in China – for Asia and the world. And they disbelieved Mao's 'leaning on one side' move. Backward China, Kennan believed, would become a great drain for Soviet resources. Acheson believed that, down the road, Russian imperialism in Asia would inevitably come to clash with fierce Chinese nationalism.

In January 1950, the new secretary of state, Dean Acheson, gave a speech that reflected the design to decouple China from the Soviet Union. Acheson defined an American 'defence perimeter' in the Pacific with Japan as a bulwark. Taiwan and Korea, sensitive spots for China's nationalism and security, were deliberately excluded from the US zone of responsibility. As for Sino-Soviet relations, Acheson said: 'the Soviet Union is detaching the northern provinces of China' – such as Manchuria, Mongolia, and Xinjiang – 'from China and is attaching them to the Soviet Union.'[2] Many of the American assumptions in Asia after the fall of Nationalist China drew on a flawed reading of history. The Americans, blinded by their own racism, underestimated the virulence of Asian, particularly Chinese, anti-Western nationalism and their wrath at a century of humiliation. Or rather, they assumed it did not concern them.

Mao and his comrades proclaimed the creation of the People's Republic of China (PRC) on 1 October 1949, with its capital in Beijing, with the firm intention to drive Americans and other 'foreign devils' out – except for the Russians. There was no chance for American diplomacy to change this outcome. In addition to Mao's intransigence, American strategy ran into the weeds of US domestic politics. Congress and the media were ablaze with the debate over 'who lost China', and the Republicans pointed their fingers at the arrogant Acheson and his 'treasonous' China experts. The congressional Republicans created a powerful China lobby that demanded the protection of Formosa (Taiwan), where the remains of the Guomindang government and troops had retreated. A host of well-meaning Americans wanted to give Generalissimo Chiang a chance to retake the mainland. A young senator from Wisconsin, Joseph McCarthy, was at the forefront of this movement: in January 1950 he notoriously spoke about 'a list of traitors' in the State Department, who were responsible for China's ignominy. The political witch-hunt would soon ruin the careers and lives of several of Kennan's friends, China experts.

The news of the Soviet atomic bomb compounded the American shock from the China debacle. Soviet scientists supervised by the fearsome secret police chief Lavrenty Beria obtained crucial information on the American bomb from Soviet intelligence, and copied it. They could not create the device in three years, as Stalin demanded, because of the immensity of the technical and industrial tasks involved. They tested the bomb on 29 August 1949, at a remote testing site in the Kazakh steppes, a few years before American intelligence had expected. Stalin wanted to keep the test a secret from the world (he wanted to accumulate an atomic arsenal), yet by pure chance a US reconnaissance plane detected radioactive fallout. On 23 September, just a week before the triumphant declaration of the PRC, Truman made a carefully crafted announcement to the American people. If he wished to lessen the impact, he failed. The uproar about Soviet 'atomic spies' who had given the most precious American secret to the Russians was added to the denunciations of 'traitors' who had lost China to the communists. In November 1949, embattled Acheson was thinking aloud at a government meeting about the potential steps that could be taken to end the Cold War.[3] Naturally, nothing came of this; the genie could not be put back into the bottle.

The summer and autumn of 1949 turned out to be bountiful for Stalin, a welcome respite from the failure of the Berlin blockade, Tito's recalcitrance, and the geostrategic impasse in Europe. In August, he hosted a delegation of senior Chinese Communist Party (CCP) members, whom Mao had sent to Moscow to test the waters. Stalin extolled the victory of the Chinese revolution, and invited the Chinese to attend the Politburo: an honour he did not accord to any other foreign communists. He even boasted about his (still untested) atomic bomb. In December, it was the turn of Mao himself to come to Moscow, to attend the celebration of Stalin's 70th birthday. It was an occasion to gather together representatives of the satellites, members, and tributaries of the Soviet empire and the world communist movement. Mao took a special train across Siberia, his first trip outside China ever, with two goals: to congratulate Stalin, and to legitimize his victory by signing a new Sino-Soviet Treaty, superseding the old one made with the defeated Guomindang. Stalin did not like to be told what to do. At the first meeting with the victorious Chinese leader, Stalin stonewalled him, refusing to change the treaty of 1945. His logic was simple: the abrogation could give the Americans and the British a pretext to question all the Soviet gains granted at Yalta. The talks ended inconclusively. Then Mao surprised his host: after the official festivities, he refused to return to Beijing, under the pretext of touring the Soviet Union. In reality, he remained in Moscow, determined to sit tight as long as necessary for Stalin's change of heart.

There was an awkward pause for a couple of weeks. Then Molotov and Mikoyan convinced the ageing tyrant that sending Mao back to Beijing empty-handed and humiliated was unthinkable. Acheson's speech that meant to drive a wedge between Moscow and Beijing probably helped to change Stalin's mood. The suspicious dictator met with Mao again and told him that there would be a new treaty. When the Chinese leader enquired if the abrogation of the old treaty would invoke inconveniences for the Soviets and endanger the Yalta order, Stalin curtly responded, 'To hell with Yalta.' Chinese foreign minister Chou Enlai was brought over to Moscow to negotiate the specifics. After much haggling, Stalin insisted on temporarily keeping Russian assets in Manchuria, owing to an alleged future threat from Japan.

The new Treaty of Friendship, Alliance, and Mutual Assistance was signed on 14 February 1950. Years later, Mao would speak about how Stalin mistreated him in Moscow and imposed humiliating terms on China like the imperialist powers had done in their 'unequal treaties'. On balance, however, the treaty was a great success for the new communist regime as

Stalin conceded to Mao much more than he had to the Guomindang government five years earlier. True, Stalin refused to give up on the 'independence' of Mongolia, a satellite state under Soviet control, but he recognized China's sovereignty in Manchuria and Xinjiang, and promised to return Soviet bases and railways to the People's Republic of China when Mao deemed it necessary. Mao politely said that he would wait.

Stalin's concessions should be understood in the light of the Cold War. Acheson expected Mao to become the Tito of Asia. Stalin used calculated generosity to prevent this. He told Mao, a great enthusiast of communist revolution, that he should take responsibility for helping Asian communist anti-colonial movements in Indochina and elsewhere. This placed Mao well above Soviet viceroys in eastern Europe – he became Stalin's revolutionary partner in Asia. Mao's desires to conquer Tibet and Taiwan also received Stalin's approval. It was, however, a pretext for Stalin to keep a prudent distance from Mao's adventures. He vaguely promised to give China a fleet and air cover to conquer Taiwan, but it was not to incur the risk of a direct military clash with the United States. The Soviet people, he explained, needed a few years to rest and recover from the previous war.

An Unwanted War

While in Europe Stalin's caution and secret negotiations helped to prevent the worst, it would turn out to be different in Asia. In 1950, Stalin's new partnership with young Mao created an opportunity for an even younger communist conquistador and led to a much more dangerous crisis than that in Berlin. At the end of January 1950, Kim Il-Sung, the 38-year-old North Korean communist leader, wrote to Stalin with a plea to help him unify Korea. The peninsula, like Germany, had been divided by the American and Soviet militaries in August 1945, with a provisional line to avoid skirmishes between US and Soviet troops after the surrender of Japan. The line along the 38th parallel never went away. Inside the US and Soviet zones of occupation, two distinct modes of governments emerged. In North Korea, Korean communists received support from the Soviet army, and soon the young upstart Kim Il-Sung, who had the benefit of military service with the Soviets and was fluent in Russian, moved into the position of leadership for that territory. In 1948, the Korean communists, with Moscow's approval, boycotted elections to form a government representing all of Korea. The government of South Korea was formed by Syngman Rhee, the first Korean to study at Princeton and Harvard, and a fierce anti-communist; Rhee hoped to start a war against the communists and bring back the US forces to defend his regime. By 1949, American and Soviet troops had left the Korean peninsula. This did not help to avoid a confrontation. On the contrary, it helped to make it possible, as both northern and southern Korean rulers itched to bring the fight to its logical conclusion.

One historian has called the Korean War 'an entirely avoidable war', and rightly so.[4] The Kremlin leader wanted to stay out of this fight. In 1948–49, he repeatedly rejected Kim's requests for a military attack on the south. In January 1950, however, Stalin ran out of arguments. The American troops had long left the peninsula. Acheson had excluded Korea from the US defence perimeter. The Truman administration had not intervened in China. And the Soviet Union had its A-bomb. The prospect of Japan becoming the main proxy of American imperialism in Asia continued to bother Stalin. All this helped to bring the Korean peninsula to his attention.

Stalin yielded to young Kim Il-Sung, just as he had earlier to Mao. He agreed to help in this 'serious matter', but delegated the final decision to Mao. If he agreed, then Korea would fall into the Chinese leader's lap. In April 1950, Kim went on a secret trip to Moscow and convinced the Kremlin ruler that it would be a quick operation as South Koreans would embrace 'the liberators' from the north, and Americans would not have time to intervene. Stalin pledged to arm and train the Korean army. Mao in Beijing embraced the enterprise: some Korean divisions had fought against the Japanese as part of the People's Liberation Army, and had then fought against the Nationalists. Now he had to return the favour and help the Korean people. Always cautious, Stalin instructed Kim to stage the operation in June 1950 as a response to a southern military provocation. Kim promised, but then overrode it with a simple and smart pretext. Rhee's armies, he cabled to Moscow, were about to invade North Korea, and he wanted to attack first. The allegation was false, yet for Stalin, who had not been prepared for Hitler's attack in June 1941, it was a winning argument. Mao had demonstrated that there were two big dogs in the communist camp in Asia. Kim now proved that a ferocious puppy could pull the two big dogs into a fight they sought to avoid. Molotov recalled, quite correctly, that the Korean War was 'pressed on us by the Koreans themselves'.[5]

On 25 June 1950, there was a frontal invasion of the

150,000-strong North Korean army, with hundreds of Soviet-made tanks and artillery pieces. Within days, the South Korean forces were smashed and in disarray. Kim was on the verge of military victory, yet in international affairs everything went quickly and terribly wrong for him and his sponsor Stalin. Before the invasion, in Washington, Acheson and the military had argued back and forth as to whether Asia was worth so many American resources. In the domain of strategic thinking, Acheson in the administration believed that the United States should start the mobilization of its military resources, build a huge atomic arsenal and thousands of strategic bombers, and restrain communism in every corner of the world with an awesome military superiority. Another camp, mostly the Pentagon, spoke for moderate containment and a focus on Japan. The outbreak of the Korean War swept this debate aside. Truman immediately decided that this act of communist aggression would not stand and ordered US troops to respond.

The United Nations, under American leadership, passed two resolutions to provide international legitimacy to American military intervention. It entrusted to the United States the formation of a UN force to push back the aggressor. The language surrounding the political goals of the war was deliberately vague: before long, the UN would empower General Douglas MacArthur to 'reunify the peninsula' and liquidate the North Korean communist state. The United Kingdom and Commonwealth countries, including Canada, Australia, and New Zealand (but excluding India), sent their contingents to Korea as well. Stalin's miscalculation and stubbornness helped the Americans: convinced that the war would be brief, he had ordered a boycott of UN proceedings as long as the

Chinese Nationalists, not Mao's communists, sat on its Security Council. This boycott in effect turned the United Nations into an American-controlled organization and provided US troops with the status of a 'peace-restoring mission'.

Nobody talked about the Cold War at that time. Rather, people feared another world war coming. The hostilities took on a momentum of their own and put Moscow and Washington on an extremely perilous collision course. In September–November 1950, events on the battlefields reached their most dramatic point, with each side alternately facing the prospect of a dramatic victory, and then an unexpected crushing defeat. The North Korean forces reached the lowest tip of the Korean peninsula but could not throw the US forces into the sea. Meanwhile, the US Air Force pummelled the North Korean communications with impunity. In September, General MacArthur launched a daring landing operation at Inchon, near Seoul, routed the North Korean forces, then crossed the 38th parallel and dashed into North Korean territory. In early October, Stalin rejected outright the pleas of a desperate Kim to send Soviet troops to Korea. It was again up to Mao's China to decide the fate of Korea: to cede the entirety of Korea to the Americans or to rebuff their forces. Most of the Chinese communist leaders thought that another war, against the United States, would be a folly. Not Mao. After days of hesitation, he decided to send Chinese 'volunteers' to North Korea. This group of soldiers was made up of the battle-seasoned veterans of the People's Liberation Army. At the end of November, 300,000 Chinese soldiers attacked and routed the enemy – this time the US forces under UN flags. It was the gravest defeat of the US Marine Corps in its history.

Stalin and Mao's secret exchanges in early October 1950 represented some of the most dramatic correspondence between communist leaders to date. Up to that moment, the Kremlin dictator had preached caution: the most important thing, according to him, was to avoid American military intervention. After the intervention occurred, however, he changed his tune dramatically. In a secret letter to one of his trusted viceroys in eastern Europe, he argued that the US would get 'entangled' in Korea and 'squander its military prestige and moral authority'. At first, Mao also reversed his stand: he posed as a cautious leader who needed three to five years of peace to consolidate the new China; most of his entourage dreaded a confrontation with the United States. Both understood that a few divisions of 'volunteers' would not be enough to save Kim Il-Sung. Seeing Mao's hesitation, Stalin appealed to his revolutionary ego. The United States would not start a world war over Korea, he wrote, as it would trigger a bigger war with the Soviet Union. A big war may still happen 'for reasons of prestige', Stalin reflected. 'If a war is inevitable,' he continued, 'then let it be waged now, and not in a few years when Japanese militarism will be restored as an ally of the USA and when the USA and Japan will have a ready-made bridgehead on the continent in the form of the entirety of Korea run by Syngman Rhee.'[6]

With a remarkable blend of demagogy and self-interest, Stalin was pushing his junior partner into the firing line. And it worked. Mao convinced himself that another war would allow him to rally all of China and would give him even greater status in the world. He decided to pair his decision to send a big army to Korea with a domestic campaign of revolutionary nation-building under the slogan 'Resist America, assist Korea'. Mao's remarkable audacity, rather than Stalin's cajoling, played the decisive role. And China's intervention had a fateful impact on the history of China, Korea, Japan, and Southeast Asia.

The escalation in Korea transformed the European front of the Cold War. In NATO, the military and intelligence community feared that West Berlin and West Germany could be victims of a Soviet *Blitzkrieg*, in the same manner that South Korea had been attacked. There were urgent plans to create a 'European army' to stop the Russians. Those plans involved the German military, among them officers who had followed Hitler's orders. Macabre scenarios of an imminent world war ballooned; the absence of hard data about Soviet capabilities and intentions fuelled the darkest fears of the American imagination. The two great enemies were not separated by proxies; the US troops faced the Soviet army in Berlin, and in Korea they were just a few miles from the Soviet border in the Far East. At the peak of the tensions, diplomatic and military contacts across the Cold War divide almost ceased. Stalin and Truman had not met and talked for five years. Routine and social contacts with the American diplomats in Moscow and with Soviet diplomats in Washington had become toxic even before the Korean War started. On both sides, diplomacy was at the service of the war mobilization and propaganda machinery. The United Nations, designed to settle disputes and defend international legitimacy and sovereignty, turned into an arena where rhetorical 'gladiator fights' between American and Soviet envoys took place.

As the Korean War escalated, some American public figures,

including Roosevelt's widow, Eleanor, called for negotiations. A group of American Quakers and corporate business leaders offered their services to go to Moscow and talk to Stalin about peace as private citizens. In the State Department, some officials toyed with an idea of backchannel talks to prevent a direct US–Soviet collision, like the discussions that had settled the Berlin blockade. Yet any such ideas ran into a wall of mutual hostility and mistrust. Secretary of state Acheson, under attack for his 'loss' of China, had no credibility to offer any compromises. He also feared that any talks with communists would hurt the preparations for a big war that Washington had embarked upon. By that time, Kennan had been eased out of the government, replaced by a more hawkish successor. He was dismayed to see how the containment he had advocated had turned into a beast that first divided Europe and then engulfed Asia. To the Quakers and corporate leaders who wanted to meet Stalin, he recommended waiting for a thaw in US–Soviet relations. 'For as long as Americans were being shot at by communist forces,' he warned, any act of public diplomacy, any talks with the Russians, would be grossly misrepresented by the American media.[7]

After the initial victory of the Chinese forces in Korea, the Americans pushed back. Truman, however, refused to escalate the war further. He did not declare war on China, an act that would have automatically triggered war against the Soviet Union. And in April 1951, he fired General MacArthur, the main proponent of a war-till-victory against China, as well as the use of atomic weapons. Stalin could be content: he had a major proxy war on his borders, but the danger of escalation into a world war had passed. The United States was bogged down in a protracted and unwinnable war in the Far East, giving the Soviet Union time to consolidate its control over eastern Europe. The Chinese military sacrifices firmed up the Sino-Soviet alliance for years to come. Stalin even sent the Soviet air force to fight with American aircraft in the Korean skies. Hundreds of US and Soviet pilots died in dogfights: the only major case of direct American–Soviet clashes of arms with serious casualties. This did not prevent the American carpet bombing of North Korea, which caused a horrendous loss of civilian lives. Overall, about 3 million Koreans died in this war, and 5 million became refugees. Almost 150,000 thousand Chinese soldiers perished, including Mao's son. Thirty-six thousand US soldiers were killed, over 100,000 were wounded and about 11,000 became prisoners of war and persons missing in action.

After another year of carnage, war fatigue spread in American society. Despite intense propaganda, draftees and their families had little idea why they should go and fight a war of attrition without any tangible results in a small country so far away. The US enjoyed overwhelming technological superiority on the battlefield in 1951–52 but did not send additional troops to Korea. The American military secretly contemplated the use of atomic weapons, yet Truman rejected this option. As for China, its military burnt through its reserves in unsuccessful offensives. Stalin, the main beneficiary of this stalemate, sent only limited assistance to the Chinese, and often demanded payments from his Chinese ally in dollars for Soviet military supplies. An armistice was the logical outcome. In July 1951, military representatives of both sides began preliminary talks in Kaesong, Korea. These talks dragged for the next two years,

Figure 1.5
China's communists carry Stalin's portrait during the anniversary of their victory, October 1951.

chiefly because the Chinese and US did not want to make even symbolic political concessions. The issue of POWs, with many more of them on the Chinese side, was a thorn in the side of Beijing. Americans insisted that most of them did not want to return to China and wanted to go to Taiwan instead, which infuriated Mao and his people.

Aside from Stalin, Japan was the other major beneficiary of the Korean War. The huge US need for military supplies made the Western power place orders in nearby Japan. Japanese *zaibatsu*, corporate groups that specialized in technology and armaments, experienced a revival. The Korean War did for Japan what the Marshall Plan had done for West Germany. In September 1951, six years after the end of the

Second World War, the United States convened a conference in San Francisco to sign a peace treaty with Japan. The Soviet Union was invited, along with fifty other countries, yet Stalin decided to boycott the signing of the treaty. Later historians considered it an error, but the Kremlin dictator had his own reasons. One was the exclusion of the People's Republic of China (the Guomindang government from Taiwan was invited, the PRC was not). Stalin also must have thought about the future of Soviet assets in Manchuria, which he and Mao linked to a revival of the Japanese threat. As a result, the Soviet Union never signed a peace treaty with Japan. And because of the vague language of the treaty, Japan continues to this day to dispute four small islands in Russia's possession.

CHAPTER 4
Domestic Frontlines

American Demons

The Truman administration launched its policy of containment of the Soviet Union as a prudent long-term strategy, but, within four years, US domestic politics, insecurity, and anti-communist fears prevailed over American prudence. China's capture by the CCP, the abrupt end of American atomic monopoly, and the start of the Korean War catapulted the American sense of uncertainty to paranoid heights. Protecting against its political opponents' attacks and seeking to regain the balance, the Truman administration adopted a new doctrine called NSC-68 that reformulated containment in do-or-die terms. Much of the American strategy was now based on the development of much more lethal thermonuclear weapons and the build-up of huge fleets of bombers.

In January 1950, Truman announced that the US would build a super-bomb that would be thousands of times more powerful than the one that had destroyed Hiroshima. After the Korean War began, the Truman Administration almost tripled defense spending. One prominent Quaker, a determined pacifist, recorded in his diary his dismay that 'we must arm to the teeth and be so superior in strength that no one would be able or willing to attack us'. He and many others wondered how the United States had come to this, why was there nothing better.[1] In government circles, the mood was near-apocalyptic. Paul Nitze in the Policy Planning Staff, who replaced the retired Kennan, anticipated an inevitable nuclear collision with the Soviet Union. The secret NSC-68 marked 1954 as 'the year of maximum danger', because by that time the Kremlin would supposedly have accumulated enough atomic bombs to be able to attack the US homeland.

The Cold War did not solely revolve around the dividing lines of Europe and Asia. It affected the societies, cultures, and ideologies of its main protagonists. The inability of the wartime partners to agree on any peace terms shook public faith that an inclusive and stable international order was possible. In the United States, many felt that they, their culture, and their future were being determined by powerful forces outside of their control. The 'New Deal' of the 1930s had promised the working classes a baseline for a decent life, short of European social democracy, but with safety nets for the poorest and the unemployed. This was an American answer to communism and fascism. For the Republicans in Congress, and then the followers of McCarthy, any sign of social democracy was 'un-American'. They believed any such leanings would sap American national spirit, the vital foundation of society.

In the 1930s, many progressive-minded people had collaborated with the Communist Party USA, but by the late 1940s most of them had left its ranks. Those who rooted for Moscow and supplied classified information to Soviet intelligence usually were not communists, but rather anti-fascist intellectuals.

DOMESTIC FRONTLINES

Figure 1.6
An American housewife watches Joseph McCarthy on TV, early 1950s.

The Truman administration, under pressure from Republicans and amid rumours of imminent war, passed legislation with the goal 'to get rid of communists in the government'. The campaign degenerated into witch-hunting. From 1949 until 1954 the nation went through a period of paranoia, with televised sessions of Congress's House Un-American Activities Committee (HUAC), and investigations of Soviet spies and 'fellow travellers'. Among the most prominent casualties were State Department official Alger Hiss, suspected of spying for the Soviets in Yalta, and some Hollywood actors and scriptwriters who were blacklisted as communist sympathizers. The trial and execution of 'atomic spies' Julius and Ethel Rosenberg in 1953 and the denial of security clearance to the 'father' of the US atomic bomb Robert Oppenheimer, capped this macabre period.

The paranoid campaign lost its leader in 1954: McCarthy overreached by attacking Marshall and other top US military. The Senator was censured by Congress. McCarthyism ebbed but left difficult questions and choices. Could America lead the 'free world' while resisting totalitarian trends at home? Would American society be able to sustain its democratic values and habits? Was liberty compatible with the national security state and growing bureaucracy? The traditional institutions of American liberalism – universities, corporate businesses, philanthropic and Protestant religious communities – struggled to find a 'vital center' that would protect them against McCarthy's attacks. The outcome of this soul-searching was a new worldview that would later become known as Cold War liberalism. Those who subscribed to this worldview, such as Arthur Schlesinger, Adlai Stevenson and others, usually from the Ivy League elites, abhorred reactionaries and demagogues in Congress, media, and public life. Cold War liberals had an elitist solution: people with a good education, international experience and professional skills should steer US foreign policy. Thousands of white men and a few women flocked to the State Department, the CIA, and the Pentagon. The Rockefeller, Ford, and Carnegie foundations sponsored 'Soviet studies' at the best universities and funded think-tanks in Washington, New York, and Philadelphia to study the enemy. The growth of these bureaucracies and 'parastatal' structures would mark the evolution of Cold War liberalism for decades to come.[2]

Some historians of American culture and ideology see

the first years of the Cold War as the time when American identity changed. Americans continued to believe in their exceptional destiny and equal opportunities (at least for those of European descent). Yet now this 'American dream' became more conformist, rigid, and expansionist, almost a formal ideology. This rested on three pillars: American greatness, global responsibility to lead the free world, and anti-communism. Only the American way of life was truly modern and a good model for the rest of the world. The last pillar of the trinity, anti-communism, helped to create a consensus among various groups of American society, ranging from ex-socialists in New York City to racial segregationists in the Deep South.[3]

Cold War American anti-communist paranoia was another form of conformism, fed not only by fear of the enemy, but also the fear of losing their post-war achievements: near-full employment, mass consumerism, and increasing prosperity. For two decades, instead of a much-feared economic depression, the United States had seen the rise of a booming middle class that included industrial workers, who began to receive high wages, who bought cars, became home-owners, and could indulge in mass consumption.[4] Former young New Deal socialists abdicated their radical dreams, becoming theorists of liberal economics. Among them was Leon Keyserling, the top economist of the Truman administration during the Korean War, who argued that huge defence expenses would not bankrupt the economy, but would instead drive its permanent growth. This 'pump-priming' economic logic would help to drive American economic prosperity into the late 1960s.

Stalin's Cold War Empire

In the Soviet Union, people's expectations and identities also evolved. Millions of war veterans, returning to a peaceful life, learned to think for themselves and take initiative. They saw European countries where living standards were much higher than in their own towns and villages. Many peasants hoped that the Western allies would apply pressure on Stalin to disband enforced collectivization of land and labour. And Russian educated elites hoped there would be an end to ideological indoctrination and terror, a respite from censorship, and a return of freedom of thought and conscience. Within the Stalinist bureaucratic class, many expected a better life after such a calamitous war. From 1946 to 1950, many of them became frustrated when, contrary to their expectations, there was only more hardship and misery. For a few, there was social mobility, education, and professional careers. For most, the only compensation was alcohol.[5]

Not all Russians trusted Stalin's propaganda claiming that the West was a perfidious enemy. When Stalin, in response to Churchill's 'Iron Curtain' speech, compared the British politician to Hitler, his military doubted his wisdom. The secret police covertly recorded senior officers talking privately. In one of the surviving recordings, two Russian generals, their tongues loosened by alcohol, wondered why Stalin was picking a fight with the Americans while most people in the Soviet Union lived in poverty, and many were hungry. The people, one said, 'are angry about their lives and complain openly, on trains and everywhere. Famine is just unbelievable, but newspapers just lie. Only the [state officials and the secret police] live well, while people are starving.' Another general expressed fear that a war with the Anglo-American bloc would end in Soviet defeat: 'I think before ten years have elapsed, they will whip our ass . . . Nobody will support the Soviet Union.' The critics were later arrested and, after a secret trial, executed as traitors.[6]

In the end, Stalin's terror prevailed over his people's discontent and grievances. The dictator continued to rely on the secret police, numerous secret agents and informers, and the expanded gulag – a giant network of concentration camps. The number of Soviet citizens imprisoned and consigned to slave labour soared after 1945 and reached 5–7 million people (out of a population of 170 million). Terror, however, was not Stalin's only method of rule and policymaking. He used other methods to become a master of people's hearts and minds. If the Americans, in their suburban safety and growing opulence, felt insecure and paranoid, how could the people of the Soviet Union, who had just experienced a genocidal war, not trust Stalin when he warned them about new dangers? Most Russian people had no way of understanding the nuances of international politics. Soviet propaganda repeatedly told them that 'the Anglo-Americans' were taking advantage of their sacrifices and wanted to blackmail them with the atomic bomb, robbing the Soviet Union of its great victory.

Kennan recalled that Soviet propaganda created a 'second reality' where 'real events had to be denied, false ones invented, or true facts distorted beyond recognition'. It was, nevertheless, the story that millions believed: 'The fabricated version having once been created, it at once became the authoritative one, and was then treated with all the respect and seriousness which would have been owing to the actual truth.⁷ Forced by their state into a conformist bubble, many people shut off their minds, adjusted to the official line, and, when anyone raised awkward questions, reacted with denial. Ultimately, most of the Soviet people came to believe that the West had started the Cold War, and the Soviet Union had to defend itself. Such views were shared even by educated elites, professors, and scientists, including the nuclear physicists who designed and tested Soviet atomic weapons. The head of the Soviet atomic program, Igor Kurchatov, and designers of nuclear weapons Yuli Khariton and Andrei Sakharov convinced themselves that without the A-bomb it would be difficult to check American militarism.

Even as early as 1946, Stalin advanced in Soviet propaganda themes and events designed to make Soviet people feel superior to foreigners, both in the East and in the West. The propaganda trumpeted above all the victory over Nazism. The dictator placed Russians at the top of the hierarchy of Soviet ethnic groups, as the 'older brother' of other nationalities, primarily because they were allegedly the most loyal to the regime and had sacrificed more than others. At the same time, while promoting the Russians, Stalin suspected Russian nationalists in the Party and among the elites. From 1949 to 1951, he cracked down on Party leaders from Leningrad, whom he accused of organizing 'a parallel Russian centre' to Moscow. After brutal torture, dozens of them were shot. Other nationalities that populated the Soviet Union, including Ukrainians, Georgians, Armenians, Belorussians, Kazakhs, and Uzbeks, formed 'the family united by the great Russian people'. Down and out of this family were 'punished nationalities' whom Stalin rebuked for their collaboration with the enemy: hundreds of thousands of Lithuanians, Estonians, Latvians, Chechens, Kalmyks, Crimean Tatars, and even ethnic Greeks who lived within the Soviet Union were forcibly deported to the inhospitable lands of Kazakhstan and Siberia. Many perished from the harsh conditions, famine, and cold. A similar fate befell western Ukrainian peasants from the areas annexed from Poland; they had resisted Soviet collectivization and continued to fight Soviet troops into the 1950s. In the end, over 300,000 of them were deported to the gulag camps.[8]

Stalin assigned a special place for Jewish people. After 1917, many of them had benefited from the end of discrimination and had been promoted to the top echelons of Soviet polity, management, culture, science, and propaganda. Many also chose Russification and made a large contribution to Soviet-Russian culture. In the 1940s, however, anti-Semitism came back with a vengeance, apparently with Stalin's full blessing. While in the West many Jewish people sympathized with the Soviet Union (and some of them suffered as a result during the anti-communist campaigns of the early 1950s), Jews in Moscow, Leningrad, and other cities became suspect as 'Zionists in the service of American and British imperialism'. They became the target of Stalin's secret and public campaigns.[9]

From 1946 on, Stalin directed the purge of Soviet state elites, expelling unreliable cadres, above all Jewish people. He also decided to 're-educate' the Soviet intelligentsia and root out 'cosmopolitans' (a new codeword for Jews), and 'genuflection before everything Western'. Cultural-scientific and even personal contact with the West could lead to arrest and a charge of 'espionage'. These campaigns ruined countless careers and lives and were another way to prepare Soviet society for a future war. The establishment of the state of Israel in 1948 was initially approved by Stalin, but soon induced him to even more vicious anti-Semitic policies. As a result, whole groups of Jewish intellectuals were arrested and murdered. In 1952, at the end of his life, Stalin embarked on the last and potentially most lethal of his post-war campaigns: he accused the doctors who had treated him and other top Soviet officials, many of them Jewish, of being involved in a conspiracy with US intelligence and Israel to murder their patients. In January 1953, Moscow broke off diplomatic relations with Israel; a hysterical campaign in the press fomented hatred towards American imperialists and NATO militarists. For many Jews of the Soviet Union, this was a highly dangerous moment; they expected something terrible to begin any day. 'The Kremlin doctors affair' was, however, the last paroxysm of the ageing tyrant. Stalin died on 5 March 1953, left without timely medical assistance.[10]

The empire that Stalin had conquered and consolidated in 1945 persevered and seemed to have withstood all pressures of the confrontation with the US. Moreover, perhaps perversely, the Stalinist regime found an additional reason to exist because of this confrontation. Stalin's objective was to create a military-industrial state that would be impervious to Western ideological influence, with faith in its imperial destiny and superiority, and a mission to expand communism around the globe. For many, even in the West, the Soviet Union recovered from the ruins of the war as if by magic, became a nuclear power, and could draw on seemingly inexhaustible energy and loyalty from its people. This formidable edifice concealed huge cracks: discontent, and open resistance, like in the Baltic states and western Ukraine. Those cracks were only revealed once Cold War tensions abated.

Forging the Enemy

What did people across the dividing lines think of those on the other side? In an age of nationalism and mass propaganda, it takes a remarkably short period of time to dehumanize the adversary and convince oneself that any means possible should be used to defeat them. Because the Cold War followed so closely in the footsteps of the Second World War, it was logical to expect the same thing to happen from 1947 to 1953. The reality, however, was more complicated. On the American side, top Soviet experts, like Kennan, and journalists who worked in Moscow, presented an image of the suffering Russian people and their ruthless oppressive leaders. As one American journalist stationed in Moscow wrote: 'It is essential that the West learn to distinguish between the police state and the Soviet people, for if the former are implacable foes, the latter, unless stupidly antagonized, are potential friends and allies.' Only a few journalists, like Harrison Salisbury, dissented from this simplistic dualism. Most Soviet people, he wrote, followed their leadership. At the same time, he wrote that the Soviet regime actually did not seek war. His colleagues responded that this simply could not be true and was pro-Soviet propaganda.[11] Around the same time, a group of prominent American sociologists was contracted by the US Air Force to conduct an investigation into Soviet society, based on interviews with hundreds of ex-Soviet citizens who had ended up in the West, and essentially came to the same conclusion as Salisbury.[12] Only a few outside the military, however, paid attention to their work.

As the hysteria about a communist conspiracy reared its head in American society, images of Russian communists, who were 'brainwashed' yet insidious, primitive yet cunning, filled the tabloids and Hollywood movies. An assortment of émigrés from eastern Europe, anti-Stalinist intellectuals, and disillusioned ex-members of the Communist Party USA contributed to this picture. Still, this image of Russians as a suffering people under a brutal regime would haunt American popular culture and public imagination into the 1960s. If only the Russians could learn the truth about peace-loving Americans and their prosperity, they would repudiate their regime. Then the Cold War would be won. In 1947, the US government's corporation Voice of America began to broadcast in Russian across the Iron Curtain. In 1953, the CIA set up Radio Liberation and Radio Free Europe to address the Russians, Soviet national minorities, and the nations of eastern Europe that the Soviet Union held 'captive'.[13]

On the other side of the Iron Curtain, Soviet propaganda about the West was not entirely false, but rather a monstrous case of selective exaggeration. With constant nods to Marxist-Leninist theory, it created a caricature of the West, reducing complexity to binary clichés: on one hand, the working people of America and western Europe were suffering under cruel capitalist exploitation; on the other, their ruthless, scheming masters were ready to commit any crime for the sake of capitalist profits. Konstantin Simonov, a hugely popular Soviet poet, wrote a propagandist play about the advent of the Cold War as a conspiracy of Wall Street moguls and journalists who had cheated ordinary Americans. Simonov was on an official tour of the United States in 1946, with a group of Soviet writers. He saw the reality of life in America, which was infinitely more prosperous than in the Soviet Union, yet convinced himself that his play was necessary for the latter to survive in a rivalry against the wealthy and powerful America. Stalin was of the same opinion: he commissioned Simonov's play and even edited it.

In 1947, American novelist John Steinbeck was invited on a similar tour of the Soviet Union, where he met with Simonov in his dacha and ridiculed his play. He noted that the Soviet presentation of American society was in many ways a warped mirror of the Soviet Union's own realities: the cruel taskmasters on top, and the suffering masses below. This did not prevent Simonov from befriending Steinbeck. Many Soviet citizens, despite the Cold War, felt great fondness for their former allies in the struggle against Hitler. They remembered America's and Britain's generous assistance during the Second World War, felt grateful for American food and technical assistance, and admired Western technology and engineering. They also flocked to watch the few American and British films that the Soviets had seized as 'trophies': the Soviet movie theatres were allowed to show licensed copies taken by the Red Army from German and Austrian archives in 1945. Poet Joseph Brodsky, who grew up in Leningrad in the early 1950s, claimed that the American film *Tarzan* was the biggest factor in making him think and act like a free man.

In western Europe, the first decade of the Cold War could

not dislodge earlier memories of the struggles of the 1930s: fascism, Nazism, the war, German occupation, and collaborationism. This experience continued to cause splits and domestic tensions. For many, American governmental policies and especially the Marshall Plan had made a big difference, as had all the things 'made in the US', particularly Hollywood films. Others, especially on the left but also some on the right, resisted Americanization. Intellectual elites in France and Italy, humiliated by the experience of occupation, embraced a new mythology of national resistance to Nazism and fascism. The French and Italian communist parties became the greatest beneficiaries of this narrative. On the left many also continued to idealize Soviet 'socialism' and prided themselves on rejecting American influences. The rise of McCarthyism and the persecution in America of such celebrities as Charlie Chaplin only convinced Soviet sympathizers they were right. The CIA, concerned by this phenomenon, helped to organize and fund the Congress for Cultural Freedom. It became a forum of European Cold War liberals and attracted those, like Miłosz, who had fled from Stalinist oppression in eastern Europe. Émigré Russians also took part in the work of the Congress. One of them was a cousin of the Russian émigré writer Vladimir Nabokov, a lifelong anti-communist.[14]

On 27 July 1953, after three years of carnage and stalemate in Korea, representatives of the US military, the North Korean army, and China's armed units met in Panmunjom, Korea, and signed an armistice. The agreement established a demilitarized zone between the combatants, littered with millions of mines and traps. The world was transformed in many ways during the decade that followed: the decolonization of Asia and Africa, the rise of the Third World's Non-Aligned Movement, the Cuban revolution, the beginning of mass consumerism, the start of the civil rights movement, and the golden age of rock 'n' roll. Yet fears of a global conflict did not die down; rather, they were fuelled by a perpetual state of danger and frequent international crises. Above all this hovered the macabre image of a nuclear mushroom cloud, and the prospect of the extinction of humanity. It affected politics, defined the monstrous arms race, and permeated culture.

The Roman god Vulcan was the master of fire, and much of the decade to follow was haunted by the hellish image of nuclear fire consuming the world.

PART TWO
The Time of Vulcan, 1953–1962

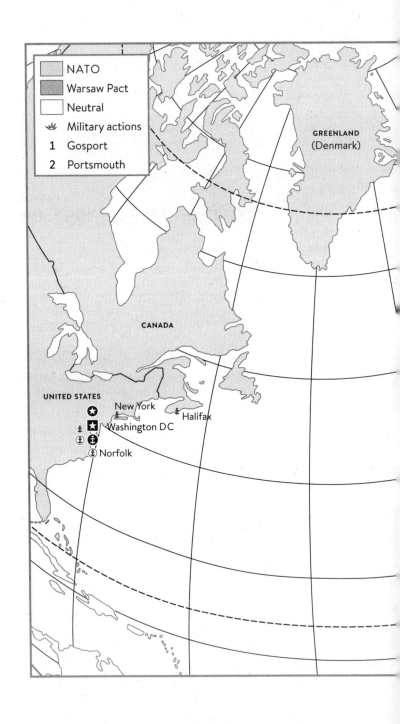

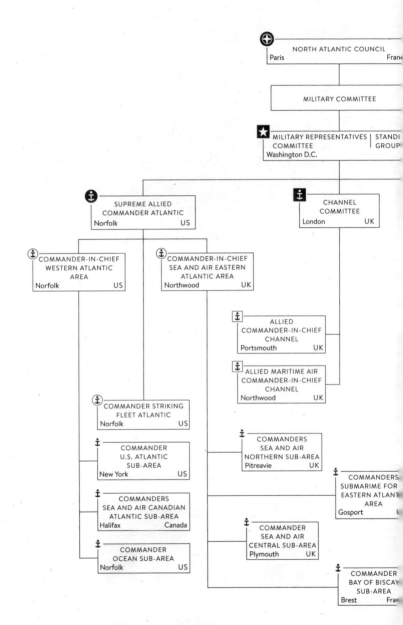

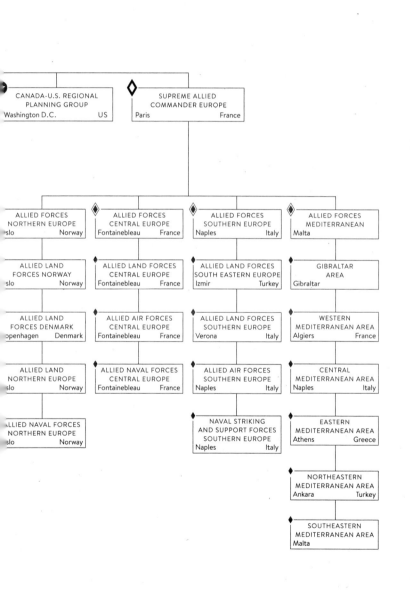

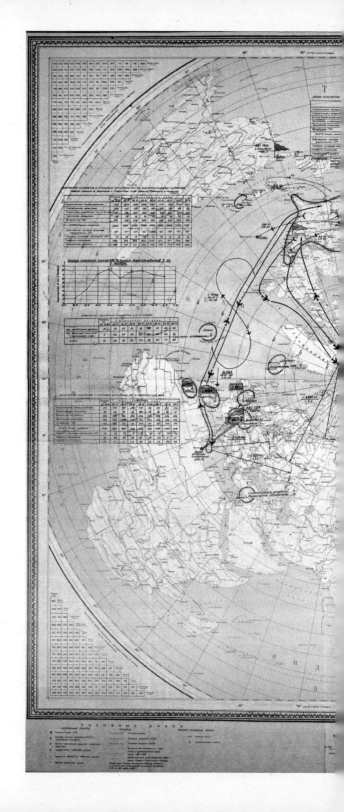

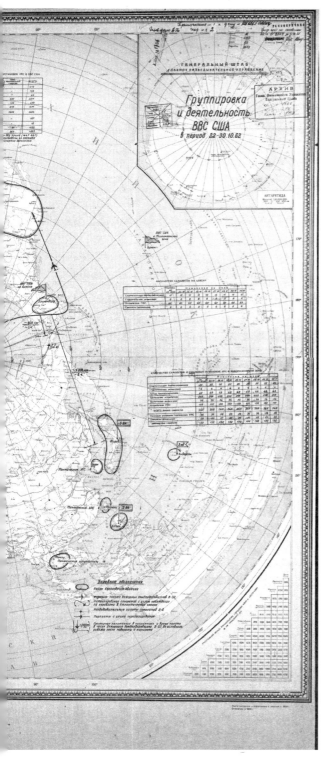

The Cuban Missile Crisis, October 1962

CHAPTER 5
After Stalin

Roll-Back and Nuclear Deterrence

Two deaths were key in the early story of the Cold War. Firstly, Roosevelt's death in 1945 resulted in the abrogation of American attempts to include the Soviet Union in a liberal international system. Secondly, Stalin's death on 5 March 1953 removed the man who wanted to destroy that system. Stalin's funeral resembled mythical ancient rites; millions of mourners across thousands of miles, from Korea to Czechoslovakia, came to bid farewell to the Great Leader. They vowed to continue Stalin's cause. However, after Stalin, the communist empire could no longer be run by terror. Stalin's successors confronted a triple challenge: choose the next supreme leader; convince his subjects that they could govern without Stalin, perhaps even better than him; and avoid a war with the West that Stalin seemed to have been actively preparing for. Nikita Khrushchev, who eventually prevailed in the Kremlin power struggle, recalled that Stalin had repeatedly told his lieutenants: 'Imperialists will smother you like blind kittens!' Facing these challenges, it took a few years for Stalin's successors to learn to stand firmly on their own feet.

The US government did not know how to exploit Stalin's

death. Strangely, for many Americans, Stalin was a symbol of stability, almost reassuring. Some remembered the Soviet dictator as reasonable and pragmatic. For all their fears of communism, they did not comprehend the extent of Stalin's tyranny, his primary agency in mass terror and oppression, and feared that after him things would get worse, not better. People who flocked to the State Department and the CIA during the first years of the Cold War were often educated at Ivy League universities. They scrambled for historical analogies to explain to themselves the nature of the endless confrontation. Those who had studied classical history in college would often casually compare the West to civilized ancient Athens and the Sino-Soviet bloc to militant Sparta. This analogy, however, pointed to an unfortunate ending: the war between Athens and Sparta led to the decline and ruin of the entire Greek civilization, and to its conquest by external powers.

There were other historical analogies. John Foster Dulles, the new secretary of state, sent a note to President Dwight Eisenhower in May 1953, laying out basic points on how to deal with the Soviet threat. This threat, he wrote, was 'like the invasion by Islam in the 10th century. Now the clear issue is: can western civilization survive?' Dulles was deeply pessimistic about the ability of western Europeans to manage on their own, without the United States. Europeans, he wrote, were tired 'old people' who only hoped 'that the Soviets, like Ghenghes [sic] Khan, will get on their little Tartar ponies and ride back whence they came'. The British and some of their dominions still stood strong; otherwise, the world was prone to 'communist penetration'.[1]

With Eisenhower's election as president, the Republicans took the White House in January 1953 after two decades of Democrat dominance. It was not clear if the new team in power would continue the policy of containment. It was not common practice for American troops to be stationed in foreign lands for years and years. Traditionally, America saw itself more like a cowboy who would come, deal decisively with the enemy, and then ride off into the sunset. Many on the Republican right, including the followers of Senator McCarthy, wanted to end the Cold War quickly, with a big nuclear bang and the roll-back of communism in eastern Europe and China. One American popular magazine published an issue with a futuristic account of what would happen after such a war. On its cover was an American soldier standing over a map where eastern Europe, the Baltic states, and Ukraine were liberated by UN forces. Moscow was occupied too with a UN flag planted there. In this context, Eisenhower looked a better alternative to the highly unpopular Truman. 'Ike' had led the Allied forces during the war against Germany and was the supreme commander of NATO during the Korean War. With his military experience and wise smile, Eisenhower seemed the ideal figurehead to calm fears and provide firm but prudent leadership.

Eisenhower chose not to respond publicly to McCarthy and other demagogues. Instead, he found another way to end the calls for a roll-back. In the summer of 1953, he staged a top-secret strategic exercise in a solarium of the White House, with the participation of high-up government officials, the military, and intelligence experts. The three groups played out three Cold War scenarios. Team A, led by Kennan, defended the original idea of containment. Time, it argued, was on the Western side, not on the side of communism. The United States should wage the Cold War mainly through propaganda and financial means and avoid aggressive, provocative policies. The two other scenarios assumed that time would work against the West. Team B proposed that any aggressive act by a communist power, such as North Korea, should lead to the declaration of a general war against the Soviet Union. Team C advocated a military build-up and war against Moscow's satellites, and, if necessary, against the Soviet Union itself, with the aim 'to reduce progressively Soviet power to the level which no longer threatens US security'.[2]

Eisenhower and most officials present concluded that Kennan's strategy was optimal. Many complained that the United States could not continue to militarize its economy, as it had done during the Korean War. John Foster Dulles admitted that the American people could not match the resilience of the Russians. The key to American Cold War strategy, he said, was to pool manpower and resources with allies. 'To go it alone,' he concluded, 'would be a folly and would eventually "bust" us.' Eisenhower jotted down his impression of the discussion: 'Global war as a defense of freedom – almost contradiction in terms.'[3] Eisenhower was financially conservative and believed that the US budget should be balanced, and defence costs that had ballooned during the Korean War should be reduced. He had travelled to Moscow in July 1945 and had even stood next to Stalin during a parade in Red Square. He instinctively felt that the Russians did not want war and were not as strong as others feared.

The exercise seemed to give the United States a balanced

strategy. Still, there were many contradictions. One problem was how to project a sense of American superiority to a domestic audience, particularly to those who had voted for Eisenhower but also listened to McCarthy. Eisenhower believed that a powerful nuclear arsenal, and its deterrence effect on the Russians and the Chinese, would reduce the need to have American boots on foreign soil. In November 1952, the United States tested the world's first thermonuclear weapon. In February and March 1954, the Americans successfully tested several thermonuclear devices of colossal power, obliterating several coral reefs in the Pacific. Each device was capable of annihilating a huge metropolitan city the size of New York, London, or Los Angeles, with deadly radiation killing everything for hundreds of miles around. In a public speech in January 1954, Dulles promised that the United States would respond to any future communist aggression, akin to recent actions in Korea, with 'maximum retaliation'.

American media strove to put a lighter touch on the macabre prospect of living with nukes; the newly invented bikini swimwear, designed to allow more tanning, was even named after one of the atolls destroyed by atomic tests. Yet the prospect of a radioactive suntan failed to reassure the American public. A streak of existential anxiety appeared in American educated elites, normally so optimistic. Could the price of freedom be the risk of nuclear incineration and radiation? And what if the Soviets developed similar weapons? Robert Oppenheimer's prophecy that the nuclear powers would live the life of 'two scorpions in a bottle'[4] was beginning to come true. The tension between deterring the enemy and calming nuclear fears at home would continue to bedevil American political consciousness for the rest of the Cold War.

Nuclear danger created another dualism in the relationship between the United States and its elites. In western Europe, France and West Germany began to integrate their economic resources, a development that would lead to the birth of the European Common Market a few years later. The Eisenhower administration approved and encouraged this integration. Yet, many in western Europe abhorred Dulles' doctrine of 'maximum retaliation'; nobody wanted to live on a nuclear battlefield. It was clear that its centre would be in Germany but the British Isles were to perish as well. In Britain, a popular movement sprang up to ban the bomb. Tens of thousands of people protested against the presence of US bases and atomic tests. The authorities considered the marchers pro-communist, yet they were mostly people who had nothing to do with communist ideology.

In the Middle East and Asia–Pacific, the Eisenhower administration sought to build alliances, just like in Europe. The expansion of American influence outside Europe was a response to American fears that the former colonies would begin to build their statehood and modernize themselves using the Soviet communist model. The administration also became obsessed with credibility. Eisenhower and Dulles spoke darkly of the 'falling domino' in Asia: if the United States let any of its allies in Asia or elsewhere fall to communism, then communist forces would start chipping away one bit of the free world after another. Who would then trust American guarantees of security in Europe? This was yet another manifestation of Cold War paranoia.

Unfortunately for the White House, the disintegration of European colonial empires in Asia led to very different leaders and strategies than those that had emerged at the end of the war in a post-Hitler Europe. By siding with the French and the British, Washington put itself on the wrong side of the barricades, against the most determined advocates of decolonization. In Indochina, Malaya, Burma, Egypt, Syria and Iraq, leaders of national liberation movements began to regard the United States as allies of their colonial masters. Seeking an alternative, they turned to the Soviet Union for assistance. In Vietnam, Ho Chi Minh had once been an admirer of Woodrow Wilson, before later discovering Marxism-Leninism as a source of ideological and political inspiration. In 1954, communist armies created by Ho and his comrades defeated the French military in Vietnam. The Eisenhower administration had invested billions into a French-dominated Vietnam, and now decided to fill the vacuum again. The Americans were arrogant, convinced they would do much better than the French; they convinced themselves they did not have colonial goals and could show Indochina the road to a better, democratic, capitalist modernization. They were, however, wading into a quagmire, sinking American resources into the jungles of Vietnam.[5]

Stalin's Successors

In the Soviet Union, Stalin's death did not empower the communist revolutionaries (they all had been killed by the dictator), but rather the scheming operators who had been following his orders in abject terror. Poet Osip Mandelstam described them as 'the scum of chicken-necked bosses ... half men'.[6] This new Soviet leadership did not even realize how much fear they evoked in the US State Department and in American society. They quickly buried Stalin, and desperately improvised policies of survival. While Dulles in Washington kept citing Lenin as a warning to Americans that history was on the side of the Soviets, the Kremlin potentates were not confident about it at all. Minions of Stalin, they acted in his huge shadow, unable to inherit his supranatural authority – the product of revolution, war, and terror. For them the Soviet Union and its eastern European dependencies were a minefield, where any wrong step could set off an explosion, and neither Lenin nor Marx could give them guidance on what to do next.

To begin with, they changed their rhetoric. The phrase 'peaceful coexistence' suddenly became their mantra. Georgy Malenkov, the new head of Soviet government, declared that 'there are no issues that cannot be settled peacefully'. Soviet actions spoke louder than words. After a brief consultation with the Chinese leaders, the Kremlin's new masters decided to reach an armistice in Korea. In July 1953, the Korean War came to an end. The giant demilitarized zone, roughly along the 38th parallel, remained a permanent scar across the peninsula, dividing it into two states, yet the burning furnace of military confrontation was shut down. Leaders among the Kremlin's highest ranks began to discuss how to improve tense relations with Iran and Turkey. Still, questions remained: how could the Kremlin move towards peace without showing weakness, making fateful mistakes, or losing control? And what if the United States, with so many nuclear bombs and B-29 'Superfortress' bombers in the vicinity, started a pre-emptive war against the Soviet Union or China?

Figure 2.1
A memorial event in Beijing after Stalin's death, March 1953.

There was a great sigh of relief in the Kremlin in August 1953, when Soviet physicists successfully tested the first 'Layer Cake' bomb, which was many times more powerful than the Hiroshima bomb. The problem, however, was that Soviet aircraft could not reach and then return from the United States. The only aircraft they had were copies of the American B-17 'Flying Fortress' that Stalin had ordered Soviet manufacturers to come up with after the Second World War. The Soviet version could fly across the Arctic Circle and reach North America but would have no fuel for the return journey. At the end of the year, the Soviet leadership set a new goal: to develop an intercontinental ballistic missile that would be able to carry a big payload, the size of a hydrogen bomb, to the western hemisphere. Just like the Soviet atomic project, the missile project had been Stalin's brainchild. It was born of German technology and developed with the help of captured German scientists. As with the bomb, it relied on Russian scientists being brilliant at improvising and having access to colossal resources. The irony was that by the time the huge missile was to be tested, the Soviets would no longer need it. Researchers in a secret nuclear lab figured out how to build a much smaller thermonuclear bomb that would have the yield of many millions of tons of TNT, and could easily be converted into a missile payload. In November 1955, a Soviet bomber dropped the first Soviet thermonuclear bomb over the Kazakh steppe. An enormous mushroom cloud heralded the Soviet Union's emergence as a true nuclear power.

For the first two years after Stalin's death, Soviet foreign policy remained the domain of Vyacheslav Molotov, known as 'the iron Vyachi' or 'the iron ass' for his ability to wear down his negotiation partners. Notably, he was the only one in the new leadership who had worked with Lenin. Although Stalin had imprisoned his beloved wife, Polina, Molotov defended Stalin's legacy, at home and internationally. In 1955, however, he was unceremoniously and unexpectedly pushed aside by the least educated and most impetuous member of the new leadership, Nikita Khrushchev. Among the new occupants of the Kremlin, Khrushchev stood out as a man who worshipped the revolution and, although he never could finish a text by Marx or Lenin, took up communism as his religion. A peasant's son, he owed his fantastic ascendancy to social turmoil, the downfall of old elites, and Stalin. The dictator had often treated Khrushchev unfairly; he sometimes used him as a court jester, and even made him dance to folk music during his parties. Khrushchev, however, turned out to be a shrewd politician, with stamina and audacity. He engineered the arrest of the much-feared head of the secret police, Lavrenty Beria, then elbowed out the feckless Malenkov, and questioned Molotov's authority in foreign policy.[7]

Much of what Khrushchev would do in the following years would be coloured by his strange sense of justice and newfound hatred for Stalin. He had committed many crimes against humanity and against his comrades on Stalin's orders, yet when he came to power and was able to read the records of interrogations of victims, he was shocked by the severity and scale of Stalin's methods. It turned out that Stalin had killed the old revolutionary elite, along with so many others, in a bid for absolute tyranny. Khrushchev decided it was his duty to restore the revolutionary communist cause and remove the

Stalinist stain; Lenin was his hero. In February 1956, at the Communist Party Congress, Khrushchev was to jolt the Party and the world communist movement with his 'secret speech' where he emotionally denounced Stalin's crimes. Stalin's 'cult of personality' had to go; only then could the revolution be revitalized and spread throughout the world.

There was no Cold War strategy inside the Kremlin, no task forces like in the White House, no clever memoranda like Kennan's. Rather, the Soviet rulers improvised changes, and as Khrushchev began to prevail over his rivals, those changes became emanations of Khrushchev's will. At a closed meeting in July 1955, the Soviet Party elites were stunned to hear Khrushchev's polemic against Molotov. The new leader did what young Stalin had done in the previous rounds of Party infighting. Khruschchev spoke with startling frankness about a series of errors that Stalin and Molotov had committed in 1945–50. Among them were pressures on Iran and Turkey that had driven the governments of those countries to ask for help from the Americans. 'We started the Korean war,' said Khrushchev to the gathering of military officials, ideologues, and Party officials, 'and even now still have to sort things out. Who needed that war?'[8] This statement was so provocative that it was redacted from the published version of the official transcripts of this meeting. It was clear that Khrushchev had become the top decision-maker in the Soviet Union on foreign policy and security matters. He had strong ideas about what had gone wrong in the past, yet he needed new ideas of how to proceed in the competition against the West. How could the Soviet Union reduce tension with the United States and its allies? How could the

Soviets cut down military expenses, and invest more into modernization, while improving abysmal living standards? How could communism win an economic and technological competition with capitalism? Khrushchev fervently believed he could find a path to victory.

In the realm of security, there was an old idea from Maxim Litvinov, a top Soviet diplomat of the 1930s, to create a 'neutrality belt' in Europe between the Soviet zone of influence and the Western zone. Very briefly, in 1952, the Kremlin considered a new deal with the Western powers for German neutrality. The idea of a neutral and demilitarized Germany was attractive to the Kremlin because it would have meant the end of NATO and the withdrawal of American military forces from Europe. Then the crisis struck. In June 1953, the Soviets almost lost control over East Germany when crowds of workers went on strike and turned against the communist puppet government. Moscow had to send tanks to put down the revolt. The Soviet leaders had to acknowledge that the idea of a neutral Germany would not work, even in propaganda. And the Americans, as well as the West German government located in Bonn, would not hear a word about 'neutrality'. They wanted Germany to be 'free and unified' and a member of NATO. Ultimately, the Soviet leaders were reconciled to the fact that they were stuck with the weak and dependent German Democratic Republic. They would support that rump German state by any means, rather than lose Germany altogether and withdraw their troops from the heart of Europe.

While Moscow failed to negotiate the Germany problem, it was more successful in promoting the idea of neutrality elsewhere. In the spring of 1955, Khrushchev forced Molotov to agree to the withdrawal of Soviet troops from Austria. In return, the government of Austria, formerly a part of Hitler's Reich, agreed to stay neutral and never join Germany again. In May, the Soviet, American, and British governments signed the Austrian State Treaty and pulled out their troops. Another country that had accepted neutrality, even under Stalin, and had escaped the worst, was Finland. Khrushchev decided to close the Soviet base in that country, in return for the Finnish confirmation of neutrality. The idea behind new Soviet foreign policy was simple: to dismantle the Soviet threat to western Europe to which Stalin's policies had contributed so much. Simultaneously, the Soviet leader and his minister of defence, Marshal Georgy Zhukov, began to cut down the millions-strong Soviet army. This, Khrushchev argued, would strengthen the bourgeois pacifist sentiments in western European societies. The Soviet leader hoped that after Austria and Finland's neutralization, perhaps Norway, Denmark, and other NATO members would ask the US troops to go home. It would also complicate US plans to integrate the West German state into NATO and arm it with nuclear weapons.

During his last years, the Soviet dictator had treated eastern Europeans just like his minions at home. Initially, Stalin's successors proceeded the same way, but with different instructions: to stop the crash course of militarization and mobilization that the Kremlin had ordered during the Korean War. The collectivization of the peasantry, persecution of Churches, and preparations for war were called off in order to prevent an explosion of popular discontent. This U-turn, however, only contributed to confusion and triggered unrest, above all in East Germany. Even after this setback, Kremlin leaders continued to move away from the policy of terror and tanks. In May 1955, at a meeting in Warsaw, the leaders of the Soviet Union, Poland, East Germany, Czechoslovakia, Hungary, Romania, Bulgaria, and Albania signed a collective defence treaty modelled after NATO's North Atlantic Treaty. Even though it was an involuntary alliance, the Warsaw Pact was a step towards greater sovereignty for other eastern European countries. Security remained the Kremlin's priority. The joint military command of the Warsaw bloc remained in the hands of Soviet marshals, directed from Moscow.

Stalin's biggest mistake in Khrushchev's eyes was his attempt to subdue the Yugoslav communists and remove their leader Josip Broz Tito from power. Under Stalin, in 1949–52, many communists in eastern Europe were eliminated after being suspected of Titoism. Suddenly, Khrushchev showed up in Belgrade, notably without Molotov, and apologized to the Yugoslavs for the Soviet Union's past treatment of them. The Soviet leadership wanted Tito to return to the communist bloc. The Yugoslav leader and his associates, however, could not forget the poor treatment by the Kremlin master; they had had a taste of independence and had no desire to return to their subordinate status. Soviet hopes to have bases on the Adriatic coast came to naught. They did install one, however, in Albania, a tiny Balkan member of the Warsaw Pact, headed by Enver Hoxha.

Stalin's other sin, in Khrushchev's view, was his mixed treatment of Mao's China. The new Kremlin acknowledged that the communist leadership of a giant country deserved the highest respect and must be treated equally, not only in words, but in deeds. When Khrushchev became Party leader and commander-in-chief in early 1954, his first trip abroad was to Beijing; he brought with him as 'gifts' to the Chinese people the promise to finance and build 156 industrial and other economic projects. In essence, it was what Mao had expected to receive from Stalin and never did: a massive amount of assistance to industrialize and modernize China. During the next five years, the quantity of Soviet material supplies to China exceeded the Marshall Plan in scale. The Chinese scientists and engineers, educated in the West, collaborated with Soviet colleagues to plan colossal enterprises, building railways and dams. Soviet support helped to transform many aspects of China's society, including education, culture, science and art. Thousands of Soviet specialists in every field worked in China. Tens of thousands of Chinese students studied at Soviet universities and got training in Soviet labs. The 'friendship higher than the sky and deeper than the sea' promised by the 1950 Sino-Soviet Treaty of Friendship was finally flourishing.

'Peaceful Coexistence'

Could de-Stalinization – the relative liberalizing of Soviet politics and policies after Stalin – have set the stage for the end of the Cold War? Some Soviet and Western historians have toyed with such a possibility, yet I remain sceptical. The new willingness of the Soviet side to turn a new page did not amount to a worldview change; the Kremlin was not ready to give East Germany and eastern Europe back to capitalists. Still, the positive change was striking. The Soviet leadership and diplomats began to attend informal meetings, including cocktail parties, with Western diplomats. Soviet women could again marry foreigners. In contrast to Stalin, Khrushchev liked to travel abroad and stopped discouraging others from doing the same. Even Soviet international tourism to Western countries, blocked by Stalin, resumed, albeit on a rather limited scale, reserved only for the elites. The times of glum Soviet xenophobia, Kremlin self-isolation, and spy mania were gone. Or so it seemed.

Good intentions came into conflict with the fundamental realities of the Cold War. Was there a way to assuage the fears and diametrically opposed concerns of both sides? In February 1954, Molotov made a surprising declaration in Berlin: the Soviet Union was ready to participate in 'a European agreement on collective security' that would include European members of NATO, eastern Europe, and the Soviet Union – but not the United States. Another surprise soon followed: Molotov proposed that Moscow could join NATO. The Americans, backed by their allies, scoffed at those offers as another propaganda ruse meant to undermine delicate Western talks to add West German military to the American, French and British defence forces. Indeed, this was one of Moscow's aims, yet at the same time the new Soviet leaders were ready to negotiate something other than the division of Europe. It was a first step towards accepting a permanent US role in the collective security of Europe.[9] Two decades later, at the time of détente, similar proposals would lead to a major success: the convocation of the Conference of Security and Cooperation in Europe and the signing of the Helsinki Final Act.

Some Russia-watchers, like Kennan, and Charles Bohlen, a Russian-speaking US ambassador in Moscow, urged American leaders to take the signals from the Kremlin seriously. They realized how much times were changing. Yet their voices were drowned out by the anti-communist chorus in Washington.

In July 1955, a group of top Soviet leaders went to Geneva to meet with their American, British, and French counterparts. It was the first such meeting in ten years. Dulles was against it: he still dreamed of 'rolling back' the Soviets, driving them out of eastern Europe. Any meeting with Russian communists, he believed, only gave their brutal regime a veneer of international legitimacy. The British and the French goaded the Americans into attending. The ghosts of Yalta and Potsdam were in the room, yet expectations this time were decidedly low. The very fact that both sides in the Cold War had relearned to talk to each other, instead of brandishing nuclear weapons and exchanging threats, seemed like a great achievement. The media wrote about 'the Spirit of Geneva', as if this meeting of top leaders had given the Cold War a human touch.

The summit also produced surprises and misunderstandings. Eisenhower unveiled a carefully prepared surprise: he offered to reduce mutual fears of a surprise attack by declaring 'open skies' and allowing each side's aircraft to fly over the other side's military installations and key transportation nodes. The proposal looked fair, but was uneven, given the vast superiority of US aircraft capacities. The Soviet delegation felt ambushed by this offer as none of their spies in Washington, London, or Paris had warned them about it. The 'open skies' proposal presented the Kremlin leaders with a stark dilemma: it could encourage mutual trust but might also expose Soviet vulnerabilities. Khrushchev immediately rejected the idea as a form of espionage in Soviet territory. At this moment,

Figure 2.2
Nikita Khrushchev and other Soviet leaders celebrate the 4th of July with the American diplomatic community in Moscow, 1955.

Western leaders realized who was really in charge in the Soviet delegation. Khrushchev, who was at such a forum for the first time in his life, found Eisenhower an affable man who clearly wanted peace. He remembered his 'chivalry' in 1945, when Eisenhower, instead of rushing his troops forward, had allowed the Soviet army to take Berlin. His hope in Geneva was that the United States would remove Cold War restrictions on trade with the Soviet Union, and Soviet industries would benefit again from American imports and technologies. He was disappointed: the Americans were not going to depart from the strategy of containment. As Khrushchev watched Dulles passing notes to Eisenhower, he deduced that Dulles was the real Cold War mastermind, not the president. This misunderstanding would later lead to a diplomatic debacle between Khrushchev and Eisenhower in 1960.

During the conference, Eisenhower met with his wartime partner Marshal Zhukov, who had conquered Berlin in 1945. The two military leaders, in contrast to the stringent public rhetoric on both sides, agreed that the use of nuclear weapons might lead to catastrophe. 'One can imagine what would happen to the atmosphere,' Zhukov said, 'if during the first days of war the US dropped 300–400 bombs on the USSR, and the Soviet Union, for its part, dropped the same number of bombs on the US.'[10] Thirty years later, such a simple insight would set Ronald Reagan and Mikhail Gorbachev on the path towards the severe reduction of armaments and the de-escalation of Cold War tensions. In 1955, this did not happen. Both sides felt they would still have to build up their military potential much more. Moreover, the military continued to act as if nuclear weapons were the best means to achieve victory over the other side. The Americans considered developing many more nuclear arms, and bombers, and encouraged the West German state to militarize. The Soviet leaders, deeply unsure of themselves, wished to be treated as equals. The meeting gave them a much-needed shot in the arm. As the Soviet delegation were flying back home from Geneva, Zhukov told Khrushchev that with the Americans 'we should keep our powder dry'. Khrushchev was of the same opinion: the Geneva meeting, he recalled, 'convinced us once again that we were not headed towards war, and our enemies were afraid of us in the same way as we were afraid of them'.[11]

The last statement could have paved the way to a step-by-step reduction of Cold War tensions. Yet the mercurial Khrushchev, a proponent of revolution and war, jumped to the opposite conclusion. After Geneva, his diffidence gave way to overconfidence. Geneva confirmed his belief that history was in favour of Soviet communism over American capitalism. And he, once a poor peasant, could lead this process. He was also thinking of the forthcoming Party Congress in February of that year. In preparations for this event, Khrushchev had to juggle many balls. He had to decide what to do with Stalin's ghost; he wanted to offer a better deal to the Party and the Soviet people; and he had to figure out how to avoid a war that everybody in the Soviet Union continued to fear. We already know his solution to Stalin's 'cult of personality'. As for the latter issue, Lenin had theorized in 1916 that as long as capitalism and imperialism existed, world wars were inevitable. Khrushchev, with the help of his propagandists, revised Lenin's words and concluded that 'the socialist camp now has resources to stop the imperialists'. He believed that the Soviet Union should use this time of peace to demonstrate its economic power, technological prowess, and superiority to the world. This was far from a strategy to end the Cold War, but it was a map to live in peaceful coexistence with the United States.

Contradictions bedevilled the external policies of Moscow, just as they did those of Washington. One issue was balancing newfound confidence and old insecurities. In the United States, Dulles feared 'communist influence and penetration' everywhere. Similarly, Khrushchev and the new Soviet leaders combined bombastic pronouncements with fears that Soviet society and eastern Europe were vulnerable to 'western influence and penetration'. Stalin had taken care of this problem by securing his empire with double barbed wire around the borders of the Soviet Union and between the communist satellites and their Western neighbours. What would happen if, as Khrushchev promised, the communist camp stopped being xenophobic and instead opened itself to the world? And what would the communist authorities propose as a counterbalance to the mighty American dollar and the allures of consumerism? Khrushchev continued to convince himself and his colleagues that the majority of Soviet citizens were patriotic and loyal. Yet the Soviet secret police, now reformed into the Committee for State Security (KGB), reported differently.

Soviet self-confidence also suffered when it came to the state of the Soviet armed forces and defence industries. Khrushchev, Zhukov, and other senior leaders knew how economically and technologically backward the Soviet Union still was in comparison with American and western European economies. The Soviet military, a bloated army of peasant conscripts, was vastly inferior to that of the United States. They also knew that the strength the Soviet army projected to the outside world was less impressive behind the veil of secrecy. This sense of inferiority was the real reason behind Khrushchev's rejection of the 'open skies' proposal. During an air show in Moscow in 1955, the same squadron of strategic Soviet bombers flew repeatedly over the stadium to create the image of a massive air force. The same year, the US Air Force received new B-52 'Stratofortress' bombers. Each American plane could now refuel in mid-air, flying along Soviet borders, armed with two nuclear bombs of high yield, to deliver them on order to any part of the Soviet Union. The Soviet aircraft industry could not even remotely match this. Had the Americans learned how weak Soviet strategic forces really were, they could have been emboldened to deliver a strike. It was prudent to keep much of the Soviet Union closed to foreign intrusion and secretive, as before. But this, as Khrushchev knew very well, would continue to feed Western fears and the Cold War. American intelligence declared 'a bomber gap' existed in favour of the Soviets, a myth that would help the US Air Force to get more B-52 'Stratofortress' bombers. Soon there was a huge armada of these large planes, carrying nuclear bombs, being regularly refuelled in mid-air, and patrolling the borders of the Soviet Union at all times.

The shift to 'peaceful coexistence' also posed grave problems for the stability of the Soviet alliance in eastern Europe. Moscow's promises of more autonomy for its satellites relied on a scenario in which the communist regimes in eastern Europe would stand strong on their own two feet. This scenario was stunningly unrealistic. Eastern Europe was in dire straits; extreme industrialization and militarization created acute discontent among workers and the middle classes. The changes after Stalin's death threw the Polish, Czechoslovak, Hungarian, and other governing cliques, which had emerged from the previous period of bloody purges and mass repressions, into immediate crisis. They had been employing Stalinist methods of governance: terror and war-like mobilization. As the Kremlin blew hot and cold, they followed suit, and lost the last of their authority. Western 'roll-back' rhetoric troubled the waters even more. The CIA and its propaganda stations Radio Liberation and Radio Free Europe employed anti-communist émigrés and defectors, who told their countrymen, over the radio waves or via leaflets flown by balloons from the West, that they would soon be 'liberated'.

This political instability came to a head after Khrushchev's reconciliation with Yugoslavia and his anti-Stalin 'secret speech'. Eastern European rulers felt caught like flies in a trap. Suddenly, they were no longer disciples of the Great Leader, but accomplices to his crimes and follies. In Polish and Hungarian societies, with their long tradition of resisting Russian imperialism, the explosion was just a matter of time. Traditional institutions, like the old political parties and the Catholic Church, had been subdued and infiltrated, but still existed. The spark of rebellion, however, came from the milieu that Moscow and the pro-Soviet regimes had been trying to build and cultivate: the cultural intelligentsia, students, and masses of industrial workers. In Poland and Hungary, they flooded the squares and streets. The communist rulers, divided and squabbling among themselves, were caught unawares by the storm. As a result, the summer and autumn (particularly October) of 1956 became in some ways another 'spring of nations' for eastern Europe. (The previous one took place in Europe a century before, in 1848, when national revolutions shook monarchies and empires.)

In June 1956, workers in Poland's industrial city of Poznań went on strike: economic demands soon became political, seeking to end Poland's dependency on Moscow's fiats. The Stalinist rulers used the military and tanks to crush the strike. The use of force against the 'proletariat' by the 'workers' and peasants' state' provoked an unprecedented political and ideological crisis. The factional strife inside the Polish ruling party ended with the ascendancy of Władysław Gomułka. For much of his life he had been a loyal Stalinist, yet in the eyes of millions of Poles he had two advantages over his contemporaries: his Polish working-class background and an aura of political victimhood. The latter was born of the purges of Titoists in 1948–53, when Gomułka's colleagues expelled him from the Party and imprisoned him. In an ironic twist, the turmoil of 1956 propelled him to the top, not as a leader of the revolution, but rather as its tamer, who calmed the Poles with reforms and concessions. The Polish leaders decided to send home all Soviet advisers in Poland, including Marshal Konstantin Rokossovsky. This meant that the Polish army was on its own and could, in the event of a national revolution, fight the Russians. In Moscow, it felt like a trip back in time to the 19th century, when Polish revolts had shaken the Russian empire to its core. Without Poland, the Warsaw Pact would certainly implode, and what would then happen to the Soviet troops in East Germany? Indeed, what would happen to all Soviet geopolitical gains?

In October 1956, every day counted. Khrushchev, accompanied by Zhukov, flew to Warsaw to confront the newly defiant Polish leaders. He was met with a morose reception. The Polish communist leaders told him they had no intention to leave the Warsaw Pact, yet any Russian meddling would only complicate their task of rebuilding the trust of the Polish people. The Soviet delegation returned to Moscow in a pensive mood. Khrushchev and other members of the leadership, including Molotov and Malenkov, weighed up their options: should they bet on Gomułka's loyalty to the communist cause and the Soviet bloc and risk losing control over the Polish army? Or should they use military force and lose the prospect of socialist Poland for ever? For a moment, the Politburo leaned towards military intervention in Poland.

While the Kremlin rulers deliberated, another political volcano erupted, in Hungary. Huge demonstrations of students, workers, and middle-class people in Budapest and other cities demanded political change. Stalin's statue was toppled. The movement propelled Imre Nagy, a politician who had the same profile as Gomułka, to the top. A loyal Stalinist, he had been eased out of the ruling circle by colleagues during the 'Titoist' purges, and was an ethnic Magyar, which qualified him now to become a popular leader. In contrast to events in Poland, however, the Hungarian mutiny turned out to be very violent. The mob hunted down and slaughtered secret police officers. Soviet leaders did what they had done in 1953 in East Germany and sent Soviet tanks to intimidate the crowd. The Hungarians, however, instead of dispersing, rose up in a national revolution against the Russians. The Hungarian army joined the people. Suddenly, power ended up in the hands of the armed people, and their fury turned against the secret police officials and other servants of the Stalinist regime. For a moment it looked like the Hungarian revolution had succeeded.

These revolutionary events in Poland and Hungary presented Soviet leaders with a dilemma: whether to ditch their new policies and return to Stalin's methods or lose eastern Europe altogether. The latter would have meant a crushing defeat in the Cold War. While they fell quite short of brilliance, the Soviet leaders had enough acumen to make tough decisions. Security interests were at the forefront of their minds: the prospect of pulling Soviet forces back – 500 kilometres eastwards – from their current stations in Berlin, Prague, Warsaw, and Budapest. Also, much more than under Stalin, they had to assert their authority and credibility inside the country and towards allies. Those things were as important for communist leadership as they were for American democratic leadership. In 1941, when Hitler attacked, Stalin faced losing the only communist state Lenin had built; he expected his lieutenants to arrest him. Fifteen years later, when Poland and Hungary exploded, Khrushchev must have felt the same about his colleagues. This time he was carrying responsibility for the whole 'socialist camp' and more. He knew he would be blamed for this debacle: the 'secret speech' had been his initiative. Instead of leading to a better, more popular communism, Stalin's denunciation had opened the floodgates.

What happened in Hungary and Poland also affected Soviet credibility and the chances for communism to succeed in the countries of the Middle East, Asia, and Africa. The winds of decolonization blew stronger every day in the Third World, as the regions outside the West and the Soviet bloc began to be called at that time. In December 1955, Khrushchev and the Soviet minister of defence Nikolai Bulganin travelled to Afghanistan, India, and Burma, and came back convinced that these newly independent countries saw the Soviet Union as an economic and political alternative to the West. The reputation of Soviet industrial development was at its peak, not only among the left but also among many Western economists. The Soviets offered India's Jawaharlal Nehru a generous package of investment, including the construction of a large steel plant in Bhilai. In the eyes of the Eisenhower administration, the Soviet Union was breaking out of American global containment and winning the struggle for hearts and minds in the Third World.[12]

Enter the Middle East

The East–West struggle in the Middle East had seemed to end with Stalin's retreat from Iran. In 1953, the British and the Americans had scored another victory there. MI6 and the CIA plotted against and then deposed Mohammad Mossadeq, the nationalist prime minister of Iran. Mossadeq had been educated in Europe and, despite his aristocratic background and frail health, became the first genuinely popular elected leader in the country. He had won national popularity when he resisted Stalin's pressure to grant oil concessions along the Caspian Sea, and again later when he nationalized the British oil company Aramco in Abadan, on the Persian Gulf. For the British, he was a dangerous populist who could open the gates for communists. The Soviet Union had an arm in Iran, the People's Party (Tudeh), with many followers among intellectuals, students, bourgeoisie, and in the army. The British convinced Eisenhower that Mossadeq must be removed. The plot was to elevate the young Shah, a vacillating and dependent figure. The coup worked brilliantly, and Mohammad Reza Pahlavi became the key regional ally of Washington and London for the next twenty-five years.

In early 1955, buoyed by the success in Tehran, the British and the Americans created the Baghdad Pact, an alliance with Turkey, Iran, British-ruled Iraq, Egypt, and Pakistan. The pact was meant to contain Soviet communism and provide Britain with a means of indirect influence in the Middle East. Yet the pact ended up a victim of the rising storm of Arab revolutionary nationalism. The main vehicle of this nationalism, from now on, would turn out to be the

Western-trained military – in Egypt, Syria, and Iraq. The very same force on which the Western powers counted to contain communism transformed into the force that wanted to undermine Western influence in the Middle East.

In Egypt, the nationalist officers had overthrown the old dynasty in 1952. And two years later, the young and charismatic Gamal Abdel Nasser became the new ruler of Egypt and asked the United States to provide credit for, and construct, a high dam at Aswan, to solve the dual problems of floods and irrigation in Egypt. The Americans mistrusted Nasser, who had fought against the Allies on the German side during the Second World War and was known for his sympathies towards Mossadeq. Western intelligence also learned that Nasser had begun to purchase heavy weaponry from Czechoslovakia, a Soviet ally. Performing a delicate balancing act between promoting decolonization and support of the British, Washington dragged its feet, and even made an offer, but ultimately declined to help. Nasser was furious and in July 1956 he nationalized the British–French-owned Suez Canal, aiming to use the navigation revenues to fund his Aswan project. This move caused a geopolitical earthquake in the Middle East.

The Suez crisis was a golden opportunity for the Soviet leaders. Once again, they believed the forces of history were working for them, as Marx and Lenin had promised. For Khrushchev it was also a chance to outdo Stalin and Molotov, who had been suspicious of Third World 'bourgeois' nationalists like Mossadeq and had failed to take a foothold in the Middle East. Stalin and his lieutenant had believed that such leaders would sooner or later betray Moscow for the Americans. As the future would show, this prognosis was

Figure 2.3
Dwight Eisenhower and Gamal Nasser. Egypt's nationalization of the Suez Canal in 1956 brought US power to the Middle East.

not entirely wrong, but for now Khrushchev decided that supporting Nasser was a fair gamble. In August 1956, he dispatched his young foreign minister Dmitry Shepilov, who had replaced Molotov, to an international conference in London, to discuss how to settle the dispute over the Canal. Well-educated and much more amiable than Molotov, Shepilov acted in 'the Spirit of Geneva'. His original instructions were to seek a negotiated settlement of the Suez crisis in cooperation with the United States. He was supposed to convince the Western powers that the Soviet Union did not want to swallow up Egypt and capture the Suez Canal.

Eisenhower and Dulles, however, abhorred the Soviet 'penetration' of the Middle East, seeing it as a mortal threat to the containment doctrine. They both denigrated and exaggerated Soviet chances of exporting their model of modernization in the Third World. Washington saw Soviet-style industrialization as impressive, but the non-market economy was anathema to the Americans. The US leaders continued to view Asia through an Orientalizing lens, assuming its countries could be tempted by the Russians to spurn the benefits of American-style trade and capitalism. Eisenhower and Dulles already viewed Syria as a Soviet client and conspired with the British to overthrow its government. They also detested the charismatic Nasser and his capacity to play on different chessboards: as an anti-British nationalist with Washington, as a non-aligned leader in the Third World, and now as a partner of Moscow. Dulles saw the new Soviet line, more flexible and open to cooperation with non-communist nationalists, as much more dangerous than the old Stalinist policy. It was for him a classic Leninist attempt to drive a wedge between the Western allies and exploit 'contradictions between imperialists'. Egypt was the most important country in the Middle East and, together with Syria, could give the Kremlin command of the region. Washington rejected the Soviet proposals outright.

Khrushchev began to lose patience, the main flaw of his mercurial personality. He cabled an instruction to Shepilov to drop accommodation and embrace conflict: to declare, before leaving the London conference, solidarity with Nasser and denounce the 'blatant pillage and highway robbery' of the British and French. Shepilov ignored the instruction and left London without banging his fist on the table. Back in Moscow, he was excoriated for insubordination. Khrushchev's assessment of the British and French imperialists, perhaps backed by excellent intelligence, turned out to be on the mark. UK prime minister Anthony Eden and his French colleague Guy Mollet, on the other hand, were of the opinion that it was Nasser who had committed highway robbery. The British feared that the loss of their control over the Suez Canal would mean that Soviet-controlled nationalists in Egypt would stifle the Mediterranean trade route and oil supply from the Gulf. In October 1956, the British and French leaders conspired with Israel's prime minister David Ben-Gurion and plotted a daring joint military operation to reclaim the Canal. The Israelis, concerned by Nasser's nationalism and Egypt's armament, started mobilization, and on 29 October Israel invaded Sinai and moved towards the Canal. Using the regional war as a pretext, London and Paris sent an armada with troops to Suez, allegedly to protect the Canal. On 31 October, the world woke up to the news that the British and French air forces were bombing Alexandria and had landed in Port Said.[13]

Eden believed that Cold War logic would force the United States to side with their European allies. Three years earlier Eisenhower had given the green light to the US–British secret operation to overthrow Mossadeq, which had helped the British to regain control over Iran's oil. The British leader badly miscalculated. This British–French–Israeli act of aggression exploded in Eisenhower's face just days before the US presidential elections; he felt double-crossed and furious. 'I think it is the biggest error of our time,' he said to a friend in the US Senate, 'outside of losing China.'[14] For the American strategy in the Middle East, the attack on Egypt was a sheer disaster. The world viewed it as a replay of European imperialism and old colonial games. The British and French had violated the earlier pact with Washington to keep the Middle East demilitarized and safe for the exploitation of its oil resources.

All the Arab countries, including oil-rich Saudi Arabia, rallied to Egypt's side against Israel and the European powers. Any hopes of getting rid of the radical pro-Soviet regime in Syria also had to be discarded. Britain's haste and folly opened the Middle East to even more 'Soviet penetration', serving as a perfect pretext for an alliance between Moscow and radical Arab allies. Adding insult to injury, the Americans were on the same side as the Soviets against their NATO allies during the votes in the UN Security Council and at the General Assembly, demanding an end to the conflict. The British and the French twice vetoed proposals for a ceasefire.[15]

Hungarian Rhapsody

Western historians later speculated that the British–French invasion tipped the scales in Moscow, as Khrushchev and his colleagues at the Politburo deliberated what to do about Hungary. On 28 October, Khrushchev said: 'the English and the French are stirring trouble in Egypt. We should not be seen in the same company.' On the 30th, the Soviet leadership published a declaration ending the Soviet diktat to other members of the Warsaw Pact and stating respect for their sovereignty and independence. At the meeting called by Khrushchev, all senior officials, including even Marshal Zhukov, spoke in favour of pulling Soviet troops out of Hungary. Surprisingly, Moscow was ready to start 'consultations' to withdraw their troops from the territory of other members of the Warsaw Pact. Not until 1989 would the Soviet bloc again come so close to revolutionary change.

On the day of the British–French intervention in Egypt, Khrushchev's mood changed: 'If we depart from Hungary, it will give a great boost to the Americans, English, and French – the imperialists. To Egypt they will then add Hungary.' The news from Budapest, and scenes of the mob lynching Hungarian officials, sealed Khrushchev's determination to strike back. He suddenly saw the Hungarian revolution as a 'fascist revolt'.[16] This was the moment of truth. Had the Soviet leaders let Hungary leave their sphere of influence, it would have been a fantastic gift to the Americans. Khrushchev's authority and credibility would have been irrevocably ruined – not only in Moscow, but also in the whole communist camp. Besides, after denouncing Stalin, he could no longer act unilaterally on the matters that concerned all communist parties. He had at least to pay lip service to following advice and asking for consent.

When the crisis exploded in eastern Europe, China's approval turned out to be key. After 1954, the Soviet leadership were particularly attentive to their Chinese partners, supporting them in all respects. At the peace conference in Geneva on Indochina in 1954, Molotov invited Mao's foreign minister Zhou Enlai; this was the debut of communist China on the stage of great powers. In 1955, Zhou went to Bandung, Indonesia, to attend the founding conference of non-aligned countries that refused to join anti-Soviet alliances in Asia. Around the same time, Kremlin leaders backed Beijing during the 1954–55 Taiwan Strait crisis, when the Chinese army seemed to be gearing up for an attack on Taiwan. Soviet economic aid to China grew exponentially. In short,

China became the biggest Soviet ideological, political, and economic investment abroad.

In October 1956, Gomułka and the Polish leadership asked the Chinese Communist Party (CCP) to intercede on their behalf, complaining about Moscow's 'big-power chauvinism' and an impending Russian invasion of Poland. Mao saw this as an opportunity to snatch from Khrushchev the status of main leader of the communist camp. Later Mao recalled that 'the CCP categorically rejected the Soviet proposal [for invasion of Poland].' The Chinese leader signalled to the Soviet Politburo that China 'was ready to send a delegation to Moscow with prime minister Liu Shaoqi at its head' to participate in discussions. When the Chinese arrived, however, Hungary, not Poland, was under scrutiny. At the Politburo, in the presence of the Chinese delegation (Liu was accompanied by young Deng Xiaoping, a future Chinese leader), Khrushchev and his Soviet colleagues bent over backwards to demonstrate that they had discarded Stalin's playbook and respected the sovereignty of the Soviet Union's allies and satellites.

After a sleepless night on 31 October, Khrushchev turned to the Chinese for their consent to intervene in Hungary, and they granted it. Mao was satisfied to have the final word. Times really had changed. Stalin had granted Mao a sphere of revolutionary responsibility in Asia. Now Soviet leaders asked Mao's consent on managing eastern Europe. The Soviet leader and his Politburo colleagues ordered the military to prepare for the invasion of Hungary, to crush the revolt. Meanwhile, in the new spirit of equality, Khrushchev and his colleagues rushed to receive consent from other partners of the Warsaw

Pact. Khrushchev and Malenkov also flew to Yugoslavia to inform Tito; their plane got into stormy weather and almost crashed. Despite misgivings, Tito gave his consent. Gomułka, who met with Malenkov on the Soviet–Polish border, also agreed. On 4 November, Soviet tanks and troops poured into Hungary. After a few days of bloody fighting, it was over. The revolution of workers and students was trampled. Two hundred thousand Hungarian refugees fled to Austria.

Unexpectedly, Egypt survived the assault. On 6 November, the British and the French succumbed to UN pressure and pulled back their troops. Some scholars believe that it had something to do with dollar diplomacy: in early November, when the Eisenhower administration denounced the British–French–Israeli invasion of Egypt, there was a run on the British pound, which had only recently become convertible to the US dollar. No doubt it was America's denial of support that caused the British–French fiasco. The outcome was Nasser's triumph and a huge blow to British and French imperialism. France had already disastrously lost its war in Indochina and became embroiled in a bloody and costly battle against the National Liberation Front in Algeria. Eden, his reputation tainted, stepped down. Harold Macmillan replaced him at 10 Downing Street with the goal of patching up the special relationship with Washington. In France, the republic collapsed in May 1958, and a new regime emerged with Charles de Gaulle as the leader. It was the biggest crisis in NATO's history.

The events of 1956 put an end to the uncertainty that marked the course of the Cold War after Stalin's death. After a drift towards neutrality, the dividing lines hardened up again in Europe. The United States could do nothing to stop the brutal suppression in Hungary; the rhetoric of 'roll-back' proved to be hollow, and the Hungarians paid a bloody price for having listened. In western Europe, Washington had to mend a fractured NATO. In the Third World, the economic Cold War raged on with the Soviets suddenly on the winning side. In the Middle East, the vacuum left by the British–French defeat gave birth to the 'Eisenhower doctrine': the US government pledged to help the governments of the Middle East, by military force if necessary, to fend off attacks by the Soviets and their Egyptian and Syrian allies. During the next two decades, this policy would turn Washington into the main protector of conservative Arab monarchies as well as the state of Israel.

In Moscow, the period of vacillation, debate, and searching for new ways came to a halt as well. The harder line that said the USSR had to stand up to imperialists prevailed. The brief moment of ideological and cultural thaw in Moscow lasted until November 1956. Then came a wave of KGB arrests of students, intellectuals, and those who had taken the denunciation of Stalin to heart and begun to speak out. While celebrating the anniversary of the Bolshevik revolution in November 1956, after a few shots of vodka, Khrushchev bragged to Western journalists: 'We will bury you!' By reducing the Marxist view of the inevitable end of capitalism to a crass funereal image, the Soviet leader gave an invaluable gift to Western propaganda. His words would help Western governments to prop up the idea of a Soviet threat for years to come.

CHAPTER 6
The Wind from the East

Sputnik

In January 1957, China's foreign minister Zhou Enlai came to Moscow, on his way back after a tour of eastern European countries. Zhou was a first-generation communist who had lived in Europe, and surpassed the Kremlin masters in education and revolutionary experience. He was a perfect servant to Mao's ambition for world communist leadership. The guest came to lecture the hosts. The Soviet leadership, Zhou said, had committed 'three mistakes': there was no comprehensive analysis of the international situation, no self-criticism, and no consultation with countries who were on their side. The Chinese now saw themselves as the teachers, and the Soviets as their pupils, who lacked experience, tact, and political maturity. Khrushchev had to plead humility and even praised Stalin, whom he had earlier trashed. This only made him look weaker. In the eyes of Zhou and other Chinese revolutionaries he was unfit for the job, and the 'collective leadership' around him was not much better.

In June 1957, growing irritation with Khrushchev's impulsive style of leadership led the majority of the Politburo, including the grumpy Molotov, to attempt to depose him. The deposition no longer meant automatic arrest and death, and some even proposed to have Khrushchev in charge of agriculture. Khrushchev survived only by the skin of his teeth: minister of defence Zhukov and the KGB head refused to accept the Politburo's vote. They sided with Khrushchev against the 'oligarchs' and helped to convene an emergency plenary meeting of Party officials. This turned the tables on the plotters and Khrushchev triumphed. Molotov, Kaganovich, and Malenkov were branded as 'the anti-Party group' and sent into retirement. The rest stayed on, but one by one they were demoted and dispatched. Nobody was shot or imprisoned: a sign of different times after the denunciation of Stalin. This unexpected triumph turned Khrushchev into a leader by default. He packed the Politburo with loyalists who did not dare to criticize him. And he did not wait long to fire Marshal Zhukov: anybody who could use the army to save the leader could do the same to depose him.

Khrushchev's survival made him the main political beneficiary of the greatest triumph of Soviet science and technology. On 4 October 1957, at the giant testing ground of Leninsk, in the middle of the Kazakh desert, the first Soviet intercontinental ballistic missile (ICBM) was successfully launched. Constructed by the secret firm of Sergei Korolev and meant to deliver a nuclear payload, the missile carried a harmless ball of steel with a transmitter. The Soviets called it Sputnik. Korolev convinced the Soviet leader it would be a good investment in Soviet prestige, yet nobody anticipated the stunning global effect that followed. Nothing since the Red Army victory over Nazi Germany demonstrated so powerfully what communist rule could achieve in a relatively backward country. The 'beep-beep' signals from the satellite circling the Earth across North America triggered American vulnerability, and with a vengeance. 'There was panic on the Potomac,' recalled one of Sputnik's designers.[1] An American correspondent wrote: 'For a generation, it has been part of the American folklore to think that Russians are hardly capable of operating a tractor. Not since Pearl Harbor has the United States suffered such a jolt.'[2] The Americans' high-tech power was now truly challenged. When the American military tested their first ballistic missile, 'Vanguard', it exploded on the launch pad. The media wrote about 'Flopnik' and the Cold War's Pearl Harbor.

Only a few people knew that Sputnik had also nearly flopped. The missiles designed by Korolev's corporation were unreliable behemoths and malfunctioned in many ways. The designers could not even make sure that the missile payload would return to Earth intact. And a Soviet-made transistor radio inside the Sputnik orb turned out to be flawed and was fixed just before the launch. Still, as Stalin liked to repeat, 'victors are above judgement'. A month after the first metal orb, Korolev launched the larger Sputnik 2, with a dog called Laika in it. American journalists and pet-lovers lamented the fate of the innocent animal while Khrushchev reaped the glory of the Soviet missile project after eleven years of blood, sweat, and tears – much as he had enjoyed the fruits of the nuclear project one year earlier. He was now the leader of a thermonuclear superpower with a means to deliver a weapon of retaliation across the globe.

In November 1957, Khrushchev hosted a congress of sixty-four communist and 'workers' parties in Moscow for the anniversary of four decades of communist rule in Russia. All communist leaders came, except Yugoslavia's Tito, who broke ranks with the Kremlin again after the KGB arrested Hungarian leader Imre Nagy, who was later executed by hanging after a secret trial in Hungary. The Moscow meeting confirmed the quiet death of the Cominform, formally disbanded in 1956. From now on, the leaders solemnly promised, the communist world would be guided by 'collective leadership' rather than revolving around Moscow. Still there were two 'suns' at the conference: Khrushchev and Mao. The Soviet leader boasted that the Soviet economy would catch up and overtake that of the United States within fifteen years. Brushing off the events in Hungary, he bragged that Soviet power had forced the British–French imperialists to give up on Egypt. His loyal associate Mikoyan told the Party elite that what decided the fate of Egypt was the Soviet threat that it would use its nuclear power. Mao Zedong came to Moscow for the second and last time in his life and offered his own assessment of international relations. With a false modesty that concealed his soaring ambitions to be the next Stalin, Mao declared that 'the East wind is prevailing over the West wind'. The communist camp had emerged victorious from the trials of the 1950s, he said, and reached another turning point similar to the communist revolution of 1917. Then the Chinese leader covered ten important developments that proved his point: they included the victory of the Chinese revolutionaries, the Korean War, and Sputnik.[3]

Mao also spoke about the unity of the communist camp, and then suddenly suggested, in contradiction to his earlier grievances, that the Soviet Union should continue to lead.

'There is a Chinese saying which goes, "Even a snake needs a head to crawl."' Mao also publicly sided with Khrushchev against 'Molotov and his clique', who had tried to depose the Soviet leader a few months earlier. Mao's rhetoric elevated Khrushchev, but in reality the Chinese leader posed as the man who stood above Khrushchev and who appointed the communist Pope. In his own circle, Mao did not hide his condescension towards the Kremlin leader, who he thought lacked the right credentials to lead the world communist movement.[4] Mao also declared that China would catch up and surpass the United Kingdom within fifteen years. Back in China, he went further. In January 1958 he unveiled 'The Great Leap Forward', a revolutionary mobilization campaign to drive peasants into communes and quadruple the production of steel. Words of caution from Soviet economic planners and advisers were dismissed. After the UK, Mao wanted to catch up with the Soviet Union, then the United States. The main partner of the Kremlin became its main rival.

The east wind was blowing stronger indeed, although not as strong as Mao and Khrushchev were claiming. Technological inferiority and lack of money continued to hobble the communist camp, and the 'Sputnik effect' only concealed the structural problems. Moscow and Beijing continued to focus on ideological slogans, pomp and personal ambition in lieu of a strategy. Khrushchev, however, was grateful for Mao's support and blinded by his flattery. He promised to grant China even more economic and military assistance. This included new projects such as the creation of a joint naval defence on the Pacific coast and a joint flotilla to stand against the United States. He also incautiously promised to give

China all the secrets of the atomic bomb and even to send a working 'specimen' to Beijing. Very soon, these promises would come back to haunt him.

The Berlin Crisis

The shock of the Suez crisis continued to reverberate in the Middle East for a long time. The Eisenhower administration moved to shore up the breach left by the British and the French, restoring the containment perimeter to the south of the Soviet borders. Against Nasser and his admirers, Washington promoted King Saud of oil-rich Saudi Arabia. American policies continued to be based, however, on the same flawed assumptions. Washington analysts viewed Arab nationalism, especially its project to restore an Arab realm from Casablanca to the Persian Gulf, as a passing phenomenon, or, as some put it disparagingly, a fairy tale. Two hundred years of Western cultural and colonial presence in the Middle East, one American document concluded, made the Middle East too weak to resist Soviet encroachments, as its 'indigenous institutions and religions lack vigor'.[5] The exaggerated estimate of the Soviet threat to the Gulf and the resulting US protection of oil-rich sheikhs against Arab nationalism would define American objectives in the region for decades.

In 1958, the Eisenhower doctrine faced its first test. In Iraq, a military coup by the anti-Western military, headed by Abd al-Karim Qasim, overthrew the pro-British monarchy. The king and pro-British officials were massacred. Eisenhower ordered the US Marines to land in Lebanon and prepare for the worst. Khrushchev immediately recognized the Qasim junta and reacted to the American move with a frantic message containing nuclear threats. Once the Cold War settled in the region, its bipolar logic would have an impact on the Middle East until 1991.

Even as the West suffered blow after blow in the Third World, it grew stronger economically and politically, especially in Europe. NATO refashioned itself as a political body, not only a defense structure. The main driver of Western unity was no longer security fears and geopolitical needs to find a strong protector, but increasingly economic integration, mutual trade, and financial investments. The Marshall Plan created new opportunities for western European countries to cooperate among themselves. A network of 'wise men', including France's Jean Monnet and Robert Schuman, West Germany's chancellor Konrad Adenauer, and Paul-Henri Spaak, developed a strategy for Europe based on the principles of supranationalism. They started with the idea of bringing together the French ore mines and German coal and metal complex under transnational jurisdiction. Their efforts were fuelled primarily by memories of French–German rivalry and the two world wars. Monnet and his associates wanted to prevent the resurgence of this old rivalry, to create a lasting balance. The Americans thought this would help contain the Soviets and encouraged it. In 1951, the French–German coal and steel community was joined by Belgium, Luxembourg, the Netherlands, and Italy. Over the next five years, economic and trade integration proceeded apace. It became a major factor behind the 'economic miracle' in West Germany: a boom of industrial production, followed by the rapid recovery of the whole economy, the disappearance of poverty and unemployment, and the rise of living standards beyond what Germans had ever experienced before.

On 25 March 1957, the leaders of France, West Germany, Italy, and the Benelux countries met in Rome and established the European Economic Community (EEC). They also created Euratom, an agency focused on developing peaceful nuclear energy. The Federal Republic of Germany became an equal member of the community, a great achievement for the state that had emerged only recently from the ruins of the Reich. Some historians argue that the EEC initially worked to strengthen the sovereign states, its members, and that the rise of a transnational superstate happened much later. What counted, however, was the unifying idea of a 'United States of Europe'. The integration effort among the six countries was completely unprecedented in Europe's history. Napoleon and Hitler had each briefly conquered the continent, yet theirs were empires that enforced order, exploited resources, and fought against democratic forces. This time, a voluntary economic realm grew by invitation, forged by common interests and based on liberal norms and values.[6] The leaders of western Europe learned to resolve their conflicts and problems like never before, and their countries gained enormously from this effort. Even in the United Kingdom after Suez, business circles increasingly shifted their focus and interests from the Asian and African colonies to the EEC.

It took some time for Khrushchev and communist leaders in eastern Europe to realize that Western integration was an even more existential challenge than NATO and American nuclear weapons. Vladimir Lenin had once written that a 'United States of Europe' was a pipedream under capitalism; only a socialist revolution would make it possible. Now the pipedream became the new reality, making a mockery of the

Leninist theory of inescapable contradictions between imperialist powers. Moreover, how could communists explain why the United States did not oppose the emergence of a European economic giant? And why did Washington open American markets to western European exports instead of waging a trade war?

Meanwhile, the 'socialist economic integration' within the communist camp did not develop as expected. After 1955, Khrushchev and his colleagues pushed Soviet economic managers to include East Germany, Czechoslovakia, Poland, and other countries of the Warsaw Pact in their supply chains. Yet in the absence of a market, private companies, and convertible national currencies, socialist integration remained a bureaucratic phantasm, with consistently suboptimal results. The Soviet economy, despite all reforms, continued to run on Stalinist tracks, primarily as a security-driven phenomenon. Whatever the economic value of involving East German, Polish, and Czech industries, Moscow could not afford to be too dependent on supplies from its allies. What if a war broke out and those countries were 'lost'? For Moscow, the safest bet remained autarchy, that is to say, reliance on one's own resources and producers for almost everything. And given that security interests always prevailed, socialist integration was consistently trumped by economic nationalism. The Poles, for instance, complained that their coal went at such a low price to East Germany and Russia. They did their best to sell their products and services outside the Soviet bloc, to make 'hard' foreign currency. In the Soviet Union, people complained about their living conditions while so much assistance was given to Egypt, China, and eastern Europe 'for free'. The outcome of socialist integration was affirmation of economic nationalism.

Geopolitics remained central to everything the Kremlin did. After the revolts of 1953, the Soviet leadership 'forgave' East Germany all war indemnities and no longer demanded that the German socialist state cover the costs of Soviet troops on its territory. The Stalinist leader of the GDR, Walter Ulbricht, whose career almost came to a quick end after Stalin's death, learned to become the tail that wagged the dog. Every Soviet ambassador in the GDR discovered that they criticized Ulbricht at their peril. The East German outlasted them all, because he knew that Khrushchev could not afford to lose socialist Germany.[7] After 1955–56, East Germany cost the Soviet economy and budget more than it added; there was a negative balance in trade as well. When Molotov and others criticized Khrushchev for this, Mikoyan responded: 'If we stop [placing orders in] East Germany and Czechoslovakia, then the entire socialist camp would start crumbling. Who needs such a camp? . . . The real dilemma is: to feed the GDR workers or place orders; otherwise we shall lose the GDR.'[8]

The more resources Moscow spent to 'feed' East Germans, however, the more the East Germans looked to the fast-recovering West Germany. And, unlike anywhere else in the Soviet bloc, they were free to take the U-Bahn from East to West Berlin. In early 1953, when tens of thousands had begun to flee from the 'workers' paradise' because of crash industrialization and repression, Ulbricht had asked the Soviets to close the border between East and West Berlin. Moscow said no. Stalin and then his successors were in no mood to violate the four-partite agreement signed with the

Western Allies after the Berlin blockade of 1948–49. And it would mean a humiliating and highly symbolic defeat to admit that socialism could not catch up with capitalism in the homeland of Marx and Engels. Soviet propaganda continued to say that Germany's division was exclusively the fault of the Americans and their allies. In 1954–57, fewer people fled to the West, and the two parts of Berlin developed a symbiotic relationship. There was significant daily labour migration from east to west, but people returned home. They took advantage of higher salaries in the West and cheaper goods in the East. On the black market, they could get as many as six to seven GDR marks for one West German Deutsche Mark.

This symbiosis was short-lived. What triggered a new Berlin crisis was a combination of the lagging economic prospects of the GDR and the soaring ambitions of Khrushchev. In the wake of the Sputnik triumphs, the Kremlin leader wanted the socialist German state to catch up with and surpass West Germany. The failure to achieve this goal stood in the way of his bigger goal to catch up with and surpass the US economy. In May 1958, Ulbricht sent Khrushchev a memo: he explained that the GDR could not compete with West Germany. During the last ten years, he complained, East Germany had lost almost 2 million young, educated, and skilled workers. How to buck this trend and demonstrate the 'superiority of socialism'? Ulbricht asked Khrushchev for 2 billion roubles in credit to rebuild cities and infrastructure still in ruins after the war, to build housing for workers, and to modernize the economy.[9] In other words, ten years after the Marshall Plan, he demanded the same deal from the Soviet Union. He could also have added that it was what the Soviet Union was delivering to China.

This was a request that Khrushchev could afford neither to reject outright, nor to grant. In addition to massive assistance to China, Moscow had to invest a lot into research and development of ballistic missiles, atomic submarines, and other strategic military arsenal, to follow up on the 'Sputnik effect'. Furthermore, they had to find means for generous aid to India, Egypt, Syria, and a growing number of countries in Asia and Africa which Khrushchev considered 'of socialist orientation'. And the Soviet leader ran out of luck just at the moment when he began to make his most bombastic promises. The Soviet economy, which had been recovering and expanding at a robust rate, began to slow down. There was a shortage of credit, particularly dollars, to purchase Western equipment and accelerate the construction of industries and infrastructure. Soviet goods remained of subprime quality and did not sell abroad. Dubious experiments in agriculture failed to yield the expected harvests. It was almost a law of communist economics: the more impatiently the leaders, driven by their politics, pushed to accelerate development, the more problematic the outcomes of their haste were.

Short on money for his ambitious projects, Khrushchev had to be careful with Soviet gold and bank coffers. Some of his bankers quietly criticized him for his profligacy. He decided to pay Ulbricht not in money but in international legitimacy: he would try to get Western powers to recognise the GDR. The Kremlin's new stance was that a future peace treaty should be reached with two existing German states. The Western powers, however, viewed West Germany as legitimate and the GDR as a temporary occupied zone. In November 1958, the Soviet leader made a declaration, addressing Western powers, that the Soviet Union could not wait for more than six months to sign a German peace treaty. If the West refused, then Moscow would sign a separate treaty with the GDR. This would mean cancelling the 1949 agreements on West Berlin. Western troops would have to leave, and the Western sectors would become a 'free city' – a kind of home rule territory, not part of either of the two German states. Initially, Khrushchev even wanted to declare the 1945 agreements on Germany null and void; he argued to his advisers that Western powers had long violated them. The foreign minister Andrei Gromyko and other colleagues talked him out of this dangerous idea. The Western powers took Khrushchev's declaration as an ultimatum and refused to accept it. The outcome was the Berlin Crisis, which had the potential to trigger a war in the heart of Europe, and consequently World War III.

There were other factors that contributed to the Berlin Crisis. West Germany, integrated into NATO, had grown from an irritant into a serious threat for the Soviet alliance and foreign policy. The Federal Republic claimed sovereignty over all lands that had been within the borders of Germany in 1937. In 1955, Adenauer travelled to Moscow and established diplomatic relations with the Soviet Union. Yet Bonn refused to deal with other countries if they recognized the GDR. Khrushchev viewed himself as a master of killing two birds with one stone. He decided to put paid to West German revanchism, and West Berlin was a good place to start.

Another major consideration was Khrushchev's desire to exploit the USSR's newly acquired thermonuclear potential and the 'Sputnik effect' to achieve his geopolitical goals.

Much like Eisenhower, he understood very well that, whatever nuclear doctrines one had, the number one rule was not to use nuclear weapons first. This understanding, however, did not prevent the Soviet high command, politicians, and even scientists taking a flight of unrestrained imagination into all things nuclear. They simply could not afford to plan less than their American counterparts. A wise British analyst, former ambassador to the Soviet Union, wrote: 'On both sides they therefore planned for a wide range of contingencies, for local and all-out [nuclear] war, for the offence as well as the defence. Since they could never be sure of their opponents' intentions, they inevitably assumed that they were irremediably malign. And . . . they planned for victory.'[10] In the United States, the RAND Corporation became a virtual factory that produced highly rationalistic scenarios for nuclear escalation and domination. A host of brilliant mathematicians, sociologists, and political scientists, among them Bernard Brodie, Thomas Schelling, and Herman Kahn, churned out tract after tract on how to wage and win a nuclear war. The effect was terrifying. It was the threat of nuclear war in the background that made the Berlin Crisis so prominent in the political imagination of the Soviet, as well as Western, leaders. The problem was that the Soviets had a vastly superior position in Berlin, while the Americans and their allies there were surrounded by hostile territory.

Khrushchev convinced himself that, in a war of nerves where it really mattered which side would be first to give in, Moscow would prevail without a fight. This was the basis of his 'nuclear education' that led the Soviet leader to use nuclear threats liberally, in full confidence that it would not start a war. West Berlin seemed to be a perfect place to test those policies and prove that Khrushchev could do better than Stalin had with his economic blockade of 1948–49. Khrushchev explained to Polish leader Gomułka that ten years earlier 'we did not have the hydrogen bomb; now, the balance of forces is different. Then, we could not reach the USA . . . Today, America has moved closer to us – our missiles can hit them directly.'[11] Adding to the Kremlin's sense of haste, the Adenauer government did not conceal its ambitions to obtain nuclear weapons from the United States. The Eisenhower administration was ambivalent about it. The main goal of the US strategy then was to reduce the costs of defending western Europe, and instead empower NATO allies to defend themselves.

On a Tightrope

Khrushchev wanted to respond to Mao Zedong's challenge. The Soviet leader had taken to heart Mao's words about 'the Eastern wind' and decided that the time had come to press the United States on settling the German question once and for all. Shortly before his ultimatum on Berlin, the Soviet leader had been subjected to a chilling criticism from his Chinese partner. In July 1958, a cable had arrived in Moscow from the Soviet ambassador in Beijing; he was in a panic. Mao Zedong had unexpectedly vented his rage against an idea proposed by the Soviet military: to set up a joint 'cooperative' of Soviet–Chinese coastal long-wave radio stations to direct a flotilla of Soviet nuclear submarines in the Pacific. Those submarines were still in the testing phase, but a delegation of Soviet navy officers planned to arrive in China to do reconnaissance work.

Mao, in the presence of his top military leader Marshal Peng Dehuai and foreign minister Zhou Enlai, criticized the Soviet ambassador, Pavel Yudin. 'You [Russians] have never had faith in the Chinese people,' Mao railed, 'and Stalin was among the worst. The Chinese were regarded as Tito the Second; [the Chinese people] were considered as a backward nation.' Mao accused Stalin, Mikoyan and now Khrushchev of wanting to colonize China. He rejected a defence 'cooperative' with the Soviets and said that instead China wanted to build its own fleet of 200–300 submarines.[12] In reality, the proposal of a joint fleet that Mao now ranted against was one that the Soviet and Chinese military had begun to discuss just a few months earlier. His accusations were as unfair as they were offensive to Soviet ears. Mao spoke of new colonialism at a time when the Soviet budget and industries were groaning from the burden of assistance to their Chinese ally. The mask of humility dropped: Mao Zedong was doing what Stalin had done many times to his minions. He blew hot and cold, to cut his Soviet ally down to size. Khrushchev dropped all his business and rushed to Beijing.

During meetings that took place in the former imperial palace of Zhongnanhai, Khrushchev seemed to have placated Mao. They spoke about international affairs, and Mao rejected any talk about 'peaceful coexistence' with the United States. He bragged that he did not fear a nuclear war with America. 'I tried to tell him that two [American nuclear] missiles would turn all Chinese divisions into dust,' Khrushchev recalled, 'but he did not want to listen and probably considered me a coward.' In August 1958, without a word to China's Soviet ally, Mao ordered the People's Liberation Army to shell the offshore islands controlled by Taiwan. He was determined to demonstrate that he, not Khrushchev, was the toughest guy in the communist bloc, and was ready for brinkmanship with the Americans, even without nuclear bombs in his pocket.[13] Back in Moscow, the Soviet leader mused over Mao's behaviour; after a few weeks, he sent an official message to Eisenhower that the Soviet Union would stand by its commitments as China's ally: this meant, if the US resorted to nuclear weapons against China, Moscow would use its nukes against the Americans. It seemed like Khrushchev had begun to follow Mao's cue.

This new and disturbing turn in the Sino-Soviet relationship contributed to Khrushchev's November ultimatum on West Berlin. In a new competition in brinkmanship with 'imperialism', Khrushchev was determined to prevail. He would demonstrate to everyone that he did not need Mao's approval to be the head of global communism.

The story of a crisis usually has two particularly interesting aspects: how it begins and how it ends. The Berlin Crisis was an exception; it was fascinating at every twist and turn. It resembled a seemingly endless roller-coaster ride. And it seemed to simply fizzle out after three exhausting years. For Europe, it was perhaps the most tense time during the entire Cold War. Khrushchev was the man who unleashed the crisis and set its conditions. For the United States and its allies, those conditions meant: either the West pulls out of Berlin and makes a peace settlement on Germany, recognizing it as a divided country; or the West faces a nuclear war. Khrushchev was genuinely convinced that the Americans would choose an inconvenient peace over nukes. The Eisenhower administration had behaved with restraint towards China, and the Americans had even initiated secret contact with the Chinese in Warsaw, Poland. He expected the same reaction to his Berlin ultimatum. In January 1959, Khrushchev sent his right-hand man Mikoyan to Washington, to find out what Eisenhower and Dulles would do. The top Soviet troubleshooter returned to Moscow with an encouraging message: the Americans did not mind talking.[14]

Mikoyan misread the tea leaves. Eisenhower was not against a compromise on West Berlin, but not under the point of a nuclear gun. After Sputnik, there was a lot of anxiety in America. At school, students were used to 'duck-and-cover' drills in expectation of a nuclear blast. The White House wanted American strategic superiority to be reconfirmed to assuage West Germany. At the same time, Eisenhower had taken Mao's behaviour for what it was: posturing and braggadocio. The US president did not itch for a nuclear stand-off. In August 1958, he had ordered the US top brass to contain the People's Liberation Army without recourse to nuclear weapons. This had taken the US military by surprise and forced them to scramble for new plans in case of a full-fledged Chinese invasion of the islands.[15]

Germany and Berlin, however, were an entirely different matter. There the Americans were prepared to fight, and to go nuclear. A secret plan called 'Live Oak' tasked the American, British, and French troops, in the event of another blockade of West Berlin, to force their way across East Germany to the besieged city. It was obvious to everyone involved in this planning that Western forces would be overwhelmed by the Soviets. All European members of NATO continued to reduce their armed forces and did not want to return to mass mobilization. This left one option for the West: to use tactical nuclear arms. If the Soviets responded in kind, then an all-out nuclear war would happen. Eisenhower, who knew the Russians well enough, believed that Khrushchev would not go so far as to provoke this. He and Khrushchev had seen the terrible effects of war with their own eyes, unlike the elite 'wizards of Armageddon' from the RAND Corporation.

Khrushchev hardly ever read Brodie, Schelling, or the other prophets of nuclear escalation and domination, but he instinctively grasped their logic: he wanted to play and win a game of chicken against the Americans. He secretly deployed to East Germany a few Soviet middle-range missiles, which could reach Bonn, Paris, and London. He also enjoyed scaring British and French ambassadors in Moscow with small talk about the probable consequences of atomic strikes against London and Paris in the event of war over West Berlin. And the Soviet leader enjoyed receiving Western peacemakers, such as British premier Harold Macmillan, who flew to Moscow to dissuade the Soviet leader from his dangerous intentions. Charles de Gaulle, who became the French president, seemed to be ready for talks as well. Encouraged by the West's wobbly response, Khrushchev switched to a 'floating deadline' on West Berlin. He would be prepared to wait a bit longer for Western statesmen to consider and negotiate his terms.

Khrushchev believed that the outcome of his ultimatum would be a meeting and a deal with Eisenhower. At the same time, he was extremely nervous about how he would perform. He had a chance to rehearse when Vice President Nixon came to Moscow in July 1959, to open the first

American exhibition. The American government and companies displayed the most alluring aspects of American life as part of their ongoing economic, scientific, and cultural competition with the USSR. Khrushchev visited the exhibition with Nixon, and when the leaders entered a pavilion with a US-made model kitchen, they engaged in verbal sparring about whose country was number one. Nixon was bulldozed by his opponent's braggadocio and stamina. The 'kitchen debate' revealed, however, Khrushchev's desire to be treated as an equal, and his impatience.

In September 1959, Khrushchev practically invited himself to America. Under the pretext of attending the UN General Assembly, he obtained from Eisenhower an offer to come to the United States on a state visit. By that time, Dulles, who would have squashed such an invitation, had resigned and died from cancer, and the president decided it was better to give 'Mr K' the red carpet rather than risk another fit of fury. For the Soviet leader this visit was as important as a prom for a teenager. A former mine worker and Stalinist agitator, Khrushchev knew more about how to work a hammer than a knife and fork. He had never worn a tuxedo. And he could hardly tell a glass of champagne from a shot of vodka.

Khrushchev arrived on board a large Soviet-made Tu-104, just converted to a civilian aircraft from a strategic bomber. His plan for the visit was simple: hope that something would work out with Eisenhower or, in case of failure, pretend that he just came 'to discover America'. Wherever he went, he touted Soviet superiority. This turned out to be one of the most memorable state visits in American history. Eisenhower authorized Khrushchev to travel from coast to coast,

Figure 2.4
Khrushchev and Vice President Richard Nixon vie for superiority at the model of the American kitchen, American exhibition in Moscow, July 1959.

suspending Cold War restrictions for communist leaders and diplomats. 'Mr K' toured California by car and train, then went to Iowa, and returned to New York. The Americans' goal was to show off their prosperity and change the guest's mind from stand-off to something less dangerous. Khrushchev brought his entire family: his wife Nina, son Sergei, and daughters Julia and Rada. A horde of journalists followed him and treated him like a media star, a status that he enjoyed.

The man who had promised to overtake America in fifteen years was fascinated and curious, but also predictably upset and frustrated by what he saw. His inferiority complex made him constantly misbehave, making scenes and giving rebuffs to perceived insults. Fortunately, his meeting with Eisenhower went smoothly. Khrushchev was put up at Blair House, which was a sign of respect, and invited to Camp David, the president's country residence. Eisenhower even agreed to look into the problem of West Berlin, without any specific commitments. He also promised to attend a four-partite summit in Paris, and accepted an invitation to come to Moscow and Leningrad on a state visit in 1960. Soviet propaganda put the best spin on the trip and hailed the 'Camp David Spirit'. Just like other spirits, it evaporated quickly.

Historians still argue about what happened next. Khrushchev returned to Moscow in optimistic mood: his prom had gone well. He began to fantasize about the end of the Cold War and to translate his fantasies into policies. He had long grumbled that the military and the defence industries were 'metal-eaters' that stood in the way of his dream of socialist abundance and prosperity. He wrote to his colleagues that a large standing army should be scrapped: an army of volunteers and a deterrent of nuclear ballistic missiles would be enough. In January 1960, Moscow announced plans to cut 1.2 million soldiers in three years. The bulky Soviet army had already shrunk from 5 million to 3 million after 1953. The new reform, if implemented, would have cut Soviet armed forces back to the size they were before the Second World War. Some senior military officers resigned in protest; others were disgusted, yet did not dare to confront the irascible leader. In February, Khrushchev told his colleagues at the Politburo about a great bargain: the Soviet Union would agree to destroy its ICBMs and nuclear weapons if the Americans eliminated their military bases with strategic bombers on the Soviet periphery. Then NATO and all US alliances in Eurasia 'would fall into a precipice'. The minions listened to Khrushchev's daydreaming with inscrutable faces.

The four-partite conference on Germany and Berlin was scheduled, delayed, and finally took place in May 1960 in Paris. As Western leaders talked about strategy, they agreed that Khrushchev's demands were unacceptable. Their extensive consultations did not elude Soviet intelligence. In Moscow, industrial managers and Soviet intelligentsia counted on détente, relaxation of tensions with the West, more trade, more exchanges, and Western technologies. They expected that this would lead to liberalization, more opportunities for innovation and initiative. The military and the vast majority of the Party and state apparatus, however, saw that Khrushchev's foreign policy gambles were unrealistic and dangerous. His domestic economic reforms only added to the chaos. His experiments in agriculture had engendered crop failures, problems with supply chains, and food shortages.

Khrushchev was walking a tightrope. While betting on his agreement with the United States, he undercut his support among the military. His critics, such as Molotov, were still Party members and were expecting his plans to fall apart. And there was a challenge from China. When Khrushchev showed up at the tenth anniversary of the People's Republic in October 1959, Mao had had enough of hearing him talk about his American visit and calling Eisenhower 'my friend'. He was also incensed to learn that Khrushchev had quietly withdrawn a promise to send China a prototype atomic bomb. At the meeting, Khrushchev quarrelled with his hosts about Taiwan and India. Chinese troops had ambushed Indian army forces along the border in the Himalayas, largely because of India's support of the independence of Tibet and the Dalai Lama. Instead of standing by his Chinese ally, Khrushchev tried to mediate, which angered the Chinese. Mao stayed mostly silent, watching his lieutenants attack Khrushchev like a pack of dogs; one of them called the Soviet leader a 'time-server'. This was a far cry from 'the head of the communist camp'. Quick-tempered Khrushchev shouted back and left Beijing in a terrible mood, wondering how to manage the unity of the communist camp while pursuing the end of the Cold War. From that time on, 'China was always on his mind', recalls Khrushchev's foreign policy aide. Once a key partner and investment, it was now an intractable problem.

Up the Wall

On 1 May 1960, the Soviet leadership stood on Lenin's tomb to watch the rally of international communist solidarity in Red Square. The military reported to Khrushchev that they had shot down a US high-altitude spy plane over the Urals. It was an insult for the Soviets to be spied upon on their great holiday. But the downing of the plane was also a great feat of Soviet technology. The U-2 was a marvel of hi-tech that had overflown Soviet secret objects from a US base in Pakistan since 1956. It imposed 'open skies' on the Soviet Union unilaterally from thirteen miles above the Soviet ground. Now the Soviets regained their sovereignty. Khrushchev gloated. But what to do about his forthcoming meeting with Eisenhower, at the summit on Germany in Paris? Without consulting anyone, the Soviet leader designed what he believed was an optimal plan. His idea was to let the Americans prevaricate about this flight. He would then drop a bombshell: the U-2 pilot, Gary Powers, had survived and was being interrogated. (This was true.) Khrushchev believed Eisenhower would not take responsibility and would pass the buck to the CIA head Allen Dulles. This, in Khrushchev's imagination, would then force his 'friend' the president to distance himself from the hard-core cold warriors.

The trap snapped – but caught Khrushchev himself. Eisenhower was an old-school gentleman who publicly admitted his personal responsibility for authorizing the U-2 flight. He also promised to send such missions again, to enhance American security. This was a terrible reputational blow to the Soviet leader, and for the rest of his life he could never forgive Eisenhower for this 'betrayal'. His credibility was suddenly at stake. Mao Zedong watched on in Beijing. Such was, in a nutshell, the reason for Khrushchev's unexpected scandalous behaviour in Paris, where, in the presence of Western leaders and world media, he demanded an apology from Eisenhower. Nobody had ever treated the US president like this. When Eisenhower coldly refused, Khrushchev shunned him and turned his trip into a propaganda charade. The Soviet leader dropped even the barest attempt at manners: he behaved like a deranged bull, to the horror of Soviet diplomats, and the quiet satisfaction of the Soviet military.

The Cold War was back and raging. Collateral damage of the Paris debacle included any dreams of détente and demilitarization among Soviet elites, and the future of Berlin. The biggest casualty, however, was Khrushchev's great bargain. He had launched the Berlin Crisis to kill many birds, now instead his failed scheme threatened the two greatest Soviet investment projects: the relationship with China and the future of East Germany.

Could the Cold War have ended in Paris in May 1960? Of course not. We cannot seriously assume that the greatest confrontation of the century, where the stakes were even higher than in the Second World War, could have been decided with a few amiable chats and a few clever compromises. And still, human history is not only the summary of immutable structures and clashing ideologies. The intentions of top leaders mattered. Contingency and chance always play a big role. Eisenhower, the post-Suez cabinet of Macmillan, and the new leader of France Charles de Gaulle were actually willing to negotiate with the Soviet leaders. All of them fully understood the impossibility of a thermonuclear conflict. And after many years of tension and fear, people had begun to grow tired of the same menacing headlines about Berlin, as well as news of everyday barrages of strategic bombers and various accidents. Moreover, millions of people in Western countries had grown increasingly aware of the lethal dangers of radiation from endless ground tests of thermonuclear weapons. In March 1958, just months before Khrushchev improvised the Berlin Crisis, the Soviet Union announced a unilateral moratorium on such tests. The United States and Britain (by that time a nuclear power) responded by suspending their tests too for a year. The endless sequence of radioactive mushroom clouds came to a halt. What a relief for millions of infants born that year, including myself!

A different combination of events and a bit more luck could have led to 'the Spirit of Paris' and perhaps an earlier European détente. In Moscow, state functionaries, economic managers, and academics had prepared a host of draft projects of cooperation, just like their predecessors had done in July 1947. They ended up in the dustbin of history, much like the proposals of their predecessors after Stalin rejected the Marshall Plan. The forces that had propelled the global conflict for over a decade continued into the next decade. NATO and the Warsaw Pact members continued to prepare for a nuclear war, Germany remained divided, and the anti-Soviet consensus in Washington remained the cornerstone of American global leadership.

The Cold War acquired huge momentum in 1960. Eisenhower was the first president to be aware of the growing power of the national security state – a new sort of empire that rested on huge military expense, hundreds of military bases across all oceans, and the mission of spreading liberty and democracy where it had never had roots. Sputnik made the US increase its nuclear deterrence forces even more: the American strategic triad consisted of an armada of strategic bombers, transcontinental ballistic missiles, and a nuclear submarine fleet. At the end of his presidency, Eisenhower got his military bureaucracy to produce 'the single integrated operational plan' (SIOP) for a nuclear war against the Soviet Union: 3,200 nuclear warheads would strike cities in the USSR and China in the first wave, killing up to 450 million people instantly. Even without Soviet retaliation, the radioactive fallout would circle the globe, making many Americans sick and leading to many more deaths. When the president saw the plan, he was disgusted and horrified. So would be his successors. The young pilots, officers, and technicians who manned and operated the lethal elements of the technical Armageddon had no such doubts; they had been kids during the Second World War, and few of them had ever met the Soviet military, as allies or adversaries.[16]

Before leaving office, Eisenhower warned the nation about the tendency of 'the military-industrial complex' to supplement national interests with its own interests. He thought privately that Congress was also part of the complex. This warning was lost in the midst of domestic pressure pushing for an arms race. The Democratic front-runner John F. Kennedy blamed the Eisenhower administration for allowing a 'missile gap' and being almost 'asleep' while the Soviet and communist tide was rising. He even accused his presidential rival Nixon of debating with Khrushchev about TV sets and kitchen utensils; the Russians could only be persuaded by force: more missiles, not more refrigerators! Ironically, had the U-2 flight ended successfully in May 1960, Eisenhower would have had more ammunition against such absurd claims. There were only a few strategic missiles in the Soviet Union, and all of them rather unsuitable for rapid retaliation. Two years later, the story of Soviet missile deployment in Cuba would provide more evidence of the vast superiority of the US.

Much of this was obfuscated by Soviet secrecy, but also by the wind of history, which blew now not only from the east, but from Africa, changing that entire continent in 1960. Before 1960, there were only a few African sovereign states. Suddenly, convinced by the Suez fiasco and the benefits of the European Economic Community, both the UK and France decided to cut drastically their imperial expenses, which led many of their African colonies to declare independence. A host of Western-educated young politicians, among them Kwame Nkrumah, Léopold Senghor, and Patrice Lumumba, became elected as leaders of new African nation-states. The United Nations accepted seventeen new members, which changed its balance for ever: the US and its allies no longer held the voting majority. Few realized this at the time, but this multiplication of sovereignties would add fuel to the Cold War engines during the next two decades. In recent years one scholar coined the term 'global Cold War' to shift the focus from Washington, Moscow, London, and Berlin to Africa, as well as Indochina and Latin America.[17]

As decolonization reached its peak, it began to have unintended consequences, including conflicts and wars. Before long, it looked like huge areas of Africa were up for grabs, just like Europe had been in 1945. The original Cold War protagonists, above all the United States and the Soviet Union, did not waste any time. In Washington and the European

Figure 2.5
Patrice Lumumba, first prime minister of independent Congo, became the first high-profile casualty of the Cold War in Africa, 1960.

capitals of former colonial empires the old fear of losing ground to communism reared its head. Indeed, many of the newly independent states, such as Ghana and the Republic of the Congo, led by Nkrumah and Lumumba respectively, leaned towards Marxism-Leninism and were influenced by various strands of socialism. For American policymakers and analysts this was enough: as far as they were concerned, anyone who read Lenin and denounced imperialism like Lenin was effectively in Moscow's orbit. Just like a decade earlier in Greece, Turkey, Iran, and Indochina, American fear of losing to communism fuelled the Cold War. Only now the stakes were global.

Khrushchev had already offered economic and technological assistance to the first independent countries of Africa, like Ghana under Nkrumah and Guinea under Sékou Touré. And in the summer and autumn of 1960, after gutting his European diplomacy with his boorishness, the Soviet leader switched his focus entirely to the Third World. In October 1960, the Soviet leader appeared in New York again, travelling by the best luxury cruiser his country had. The ship had been built twenty years earlier in Amsterdam. The Soviet premier acted as the chief defender of the post-colonial world and spent a month living inside the Soviet UN Mission on Manhattan; this time he was denied authorization to travel outside the island. He relished using American media to bash Eisenhower and, as he put it to his Kremlin colleagues, 'fight imperialism' in the vicinity of Wall Street. In one of the most memorable episodes, he took off his shoe and threatened to bang it against the desk while denouncing a Philippine representative as 'a lackey of imperialism'. More moderate Third World leaders were shocked by his poor manners. But many revolutionaries applauded. Among the latter was Fidel Castro, the leader of the victorious anti-American revolution in Cuba. The famous embrace of 'Mr K' and Castro in Harlem, New York, started the most dangerous partnership of the entire Cold War.

Once again Soviet bluster concealed severe limitations in resources. In Ghana, Guinea, Mali, and later in Nigeria and other African countries, the expectations in terms of Soviet aid were unrealistically high, and Soviet engineers and technicians encountered steep natural, financial, and infrastructural obstacles. Moreover, in contrast to the United States and United Kingdom, the Soviet Union lacked merchant navy or cargo planes to deliver assistance to Africa.[18]

The Soviet Union clashed with the West over Congo, a fabulously mineral-rich country. Congo collapsed into civil turmoil after the Belgian colonial authorities pulled out in the summer of 1960. In the resulting vacuum, the country's future direction and leadership depended completely on the money and weaponry provided by great powers and their agents. The Soviet Union backed the elected prime minister Lumumba, expecting him to be another Nasser. The US officials sided with his rival, the Congolese top military officer Mobutu Sese Seko. The CIA chief Allen Dulles considered Lumumba's removal an urgent task.[19] Ultimately, the contest was resolved in favour of Mobutu. The Soviet leaders and military watched helplessly, unable to project power so far away from their frontiers; the African leader was captured by separatists and murdered. Khrushchev raged at the United Nations secretary-general Dag Hammarskjöld, a Swede, whom the Soviet leader called 'an American lackey', and whom he held complicit in Lumumba's downfall. The Soviet government set up a new 'university for friendship of peoples' in Moscow and named it after Lumumba. This new institution seemed to revive the Comintern's traditions of the 1920s and was dedicated to training African, Asian, and Latin American youth for 'anti-imperialist struggle'. The curriculum was not entirely theoretical; some hidden sections, linked to the KGB and Soviet military intelligence (the GRU), provided training for guerrilla warfare. The Soviets learned this from the struggle for West Africa: if they wanted to help their clients and friends in Africa, they needed technical means, transport, and bases to do so.[20]

The struggle for the soul of post-colonial Africa was not

strictly bipolar. The French, British, Belgian, and other former colonial powers in Europe pursued their policies, seeking to convert their former colonial possessions into spheres of economic and trade influence. London did it best by creating the British Commonwealth, and France tried something similar. The Soviet Union was not the only communist power present in Africa: Poland, Romania, and East Germany sent their officials, journalists, and military to the continent, to enhance their international prestige and legitimacy. And China openly contested Moscow's leadership in Africa.

Mao Zedong needed external revolutionary exploits to compensate for the dismal failure of his Great Leap Forward and made a bid for leadership in the communist and postcolonial world. In April 1960, Mao directed his propaganda to start openly challenging Khrushchev's international leadership. He claimed he was a better disciple of Lenin than Khrushchev, particularly in the fight against imperialism and colonialism in the Third World. Furious, Khrushchev lost his patience: he convened a communist forum to denounce the Chinese and hastily withdrew 1,500 advisers from all spheres of China's economy, science, and culture. The blow magnified China's economic troubles, and many Chinese viewed it as a betrayal by 'the senior brother'. The rivalry between the two top communist leaders began to turn into a split between the two countries.

In November 1960, Khrushchev convened another congress of communist and 'progressive' leaders to demonstrate that he, not Mao, was in control of the anti-Western camp. Ulbricht took advantage of this occasion to tell Khrushchev that East Germany was running out of time. The Berlin Crisis and economic opportunities had made tens of thousands of German citizens flee to West Berlin and from there to West Germany. Without a separate peace treaty and with an open border, the GDR economy was losing ground to its Western twin rival. It could even go bankrupt if Western countries were to impose economic sanctions. The East German leader asked again for dollar credits and Soviet gold. Khrushchev pretended to be shocked. He mocked Ulbricht for 'having his hands in [Soviet] pockets' and wondered why hard-working Germans could not manage better on their own.[21] He was fully aware, however, that the Berlin Crisis had reached a deadlock and, like Stalin in 1948–49, searched for an exit. He asked Ulbricht for more time. The young and inexperienced John F. Kennedy had just won the US presidency. Perhaps, Khrushchev thought, another round of pressure would lead to a peace treaty.

CHAPTER 7
Russian Roulette

'A Pampered Boy'

Forty-three-year-old Kennedy brought to the White House a unique combination of dynamism and vulnerability. He had a brilliant team of Harvard-trained men, business technocrats, and neo-Keynesian gurus of economic growth. He embodied inherited wealth, glamour, combat experience in the Second World War, and generational change. At the same time, he was the first Irish Catholic president in a largely Protestant country, his father was a bootlegger and Nazi appeaser, and in 1960 he had won the election by the tiniest margin. JFK had secret flaws. He took strong painkillers because of a war injury to his spine. He was a careless playboy. Not alien to nepotism, he appointed his brother Bobby as attorney general. The Kennedys had a complicated connection to organized crime. Kennedy's father had helped him get a Senate seat and had sent him abroad to gain international experience. Yet he could not prepare him for the extreme pressure that awaited him in the Oval Office as the US–Soviet brinkmanship game continued to escalate.

Kennedy's predecessors, such as Truman, Marshall, Acheson, Dulles, and Eisenhower had left a legacy of Cold War experience, victories and failures, to learn from. Kennedy also inherited the national security state, with all doctrines and battle orders in place. Kennedy, however, wanted to make up his own mind; in fact, he was a bit too cerebral for his own good. The young president was fascinated by Khrushchev and intimidated by his energy and unpredictability. Kennedy's advisers criticized the 'all-or-nothing' nuclear rhetoric of the 1950s and talked about a 'flexible response' to Soviet invasion. But the president knew he might have to press the nuclear button, a prospect which he abhorred. He needed something to demonstrate his credibility, yet his term began with a fiasco: the CIA carried out an operation to overthrow the revolutionary regime of Castro in Cuba.

On the night of 17 April 1961, a group of US-trained Cuban émigrés ('contras') tried to land in the Bay of Pigs, the most remote and deserted part of Cuba's coast. They and their American sponsors were convinced they would overthrow Castro's dictatorship, with broad support from the population. The contras discovered to their surprise that the area was fully lit: Castro had turned the deprived region into a resort for workers and peasants. Neither the émigrés nor the CIA that had trained them knew about this development. This mishap concealed a much greater misreading of Cuban history. The Cubans took the Bay of Pigs inroad as another US-sponsored attempt to restore 'control' over the island, a culmination of an uneven relationship that went back more than a century and made many people resent the firm embrace of Uncle Sam. The United States was to Cuba what Russia was to Poland or Hungary: imperialist, expansionist, and intolerably patronizing.[1] The contras were routed and imprisoned. The Cuban revolutionaries triumphed over the northern giant, just like Hungary in October 1956 had seemed to drive the Soviets out. Except it took the Soviet tanks just a week to return with a vengeance. Cuba stood its ground and humiliated its superpower neighbour. It was logical to expect retribution.

After the Bay of Pigs fiasco, Kennedy sent Allen Dulles into retirement and suffered a huge loss of credibility. He expected, imprudently, to overcome this by facing down Khrushchev at a summit meeting. The US ambassador Llewellyn ('Tommy') Thompson liaised with Khrushchev, who agreed to meet with Kennedy in Vienna. After the Paris debacle, any Western politician should have thought twice before agreeing to this. Kennedy took a chance: he wanted to show respect and hoped to impress on Khrushchev the need to manage an increasingly dangerous game of brinkmanship in the Third World and the nuclear arms race. He also expected to have a one on one with Khrushchev and talk him out of his idea of a separate peace in Germany. For Khrushchev, however, this was a perfect moment to press his new opponent. He viewed Kennedy as the pampered son of a billionaire, not ready for a serious confrontation. The Soviet leader dreamed of 'another Roosevelt' with whom he could do business, and this was another source of his irritation with JFK, who was too weak for this historic role. As Kennedy's prestige plummeted because of Cuba, Khrushchev scored another space triumph to follow the orbital successes of the Sputnik missions: in April 1961, Korolev sent the first cosmonaut, Yuri Gagarin, around the Earth, followed by a successful landing.[2]

Khrushchev prepared an ultimatum for JFK: a deal on West Berlin or a unilateral abrogation of Western rights there. He confessed to his colleagues that the outcome of his gamble was uncertain. Kennedy, he said, was 'under the influence of various groups' and could not act as an independent actor. Still, it was worth a try, as there was a 'ninety-five per cent' chance that the US would not start a war. Mikoyan interceded with his usual cautionary note that the US 'might start military actions without using atomic weapons'. Yet he did not want to stand between the leader and his gamble. Once Khrushchev decided on something, Mikoyan later recalled, he moved like a tank. It was impossible to stop him.[3]

The leaders met in Vienna in early June 1961. At the first meeting with the Soviet leader, Kennedy struck a conciliatory note. He told Khrushchev he would not object to more 'socialist' Yugoslavias or Indias, as long as they would remain non-aligned and not disrupt the balance between the superpowers. He even confessed that the Bay of Pigs was his mistake. He seemed to offer to make a global truce in the Third World. Khrushchev, however, had come to bully, not to negotiate. For two days the two leaders lectured each other on the history and nature of the Cold War: Kennedy emphasized the nuclear danger of 'miscalculations'; Khrushchev dismissed it and responded that no capitalist containment could stop the world's march to socialism and communism. Then Khrushchev pressed Kennedy on West Berlin. To his surprise, in contrast with Eisenhower, Kennedy stood firm and refused even to discuss any changes. The Soviet leader then restated his ultimatum. The USSR would not start a war over Berlin, he told Kennedy, but if the United States was going to unleash war, then let it be now, before the development of even more destructive weapons. Those words were shocking even for the members of the Soviet delegation and they were dropped from both Soviet and American records of the conversation.[4]

The meeting ended in another debacle, even greater than the one in Paris. Instead of a bridge to partnership, the Vienna summit paved the road to more brinkmanship and an intense arms race. There were other important issues to discuss, like a ban on testing nuclear weapons, but the Soviet leader brushed them aside. Kennedy rejected the new Berlin ultimatum and returned home dejected. He mobilized reservists to demonstrate his determination to wage a war in the centre of Europe.

Back in Washington, Acheson urged the young president to keep the course until the Russians backed off. Privately, Kennedy felt cornered. Khrushchev was cornered too, yet publicly kept pushing. On 1 August 1961, he finally gave his consent to Ulbricht to close the border between East Berlin and its Western sectors. He passed the baton to the East Germans: 'Do it when you can . . . If you shut the border, then the Americans and Western Germans will be glad . . . Everyone will be glad. Besides, they will feel [your] power.'[5] On 13 August, the Berliners woke up to find their city divided by barbed wire, all means of transportation cut off. After months of hectic work, a double concrete wall was erected around West Berlin, with a no man's land filled with mines and traps, and policed by East German troops who had the order 'shoot to kill'.

It took almost nine years for Moscow to admit that the

flight of people from their 'workers' paradise' to the West could only be stopped by walls and guns. Khrushchev stubbornly refused to acknowledge that the Wall cancelled out his promises of communist superiority over capitalism. He convinced himself that it was a temporary measure to buttress the East German economy. He also liked to think that West Berlin would wither away without East German migrant labour, and the Federal Republic of Germany would be forced to abandon its policy of confrontation and choose to trade and cooperate.[6] The Soviet leader was wrong on two counts: the Wall would stand until 1989, and West Berlin would thrive as a beacon of freedom and consumerism for millions in East Germany. He was correct on the gradual evolution of West German policies.

Kennedy, tormented by the idea of having to use nuclear weapons, was hugely relieved. 'It is not a nice solution,' he would later say to West Berliners, 'but a wall is a hell of a lot better than a war.' Kennedy surmised that Khrushchev had found a way to get himself off the hook. And the US president could now practise usual containment gestures with more confidence. He sent to West Berlin General Clay, the man who had stood up to Stalin in Germany in 1948. At the same time, the White House did not share the anguish of West German politicians, including the mayor of West Berlin, Willy Brandt, who demanded the US impose sanctions on East Germany or even remove the wall by force. Robert Kennedy used an informal channel with a Soviet military intelligence official to signal to the Kremlin that he was satisfied with the new status quo. In October 1961, Clay overreacted when East German border guards asked US servicemen for their documents at Checkpoint Charlie, the control post between the American and Soviet sectors of Berlin. It was a violation of the 1949 agreement, and the Americans brought in the tanks. In response, Soviet tanks were positioned on the same street, at a distance of less than a hundred metres. After a swift secret exchange of messages through an intelligence channel between Kennedy and Khrushchev, the tanks were removed. American, British, and French military personnel could continue to go to the Soviet zone whenever they liked – unlike the Germans.[7]

The Wall on its own could not put an end to the dangerous stand-off that had been escalating since 1958. A big factor was the Americans' view on nuclear war and its consequences. In the United States, the government discussed whether it was possible to build giant nuclear shelters for millions, then allowed this idea to be commercialized: people were supposed to buy individual shelters. In the Sino-Soviet bloc, fears of war were routinely dismissed by fanfares of communist propaganda. But the biggest source of tension was Khrushchev's conviction that he must now act in the same way the Americans had acted when they had the upper hand. The Soviet premier did not give up on his brinkmanship at all. In January 1962, he told his colleagues that one must calibrate the pressure on the West – it should be like filling a vodka glass up to the brim without spilling over. During 1962, all of this would be turbocharged by the intense nuclear race and the struggle in the Third World.

Blundering on the Brink

The Cuban Missile Crisis was the most memorable moment of the Cold War. In May 1962, Khrushchev decided to send nuclear missiles to Cuba. He would say to his colleagues: 'Our whole operation was meant to deter the USA, so they don't attack Cuba.' The operation was executed in total secrecy, and only on 14 October did a high-altitude U-2 spy aircraft take pictures of near-complete Soviet bases and installations on the island. The discovery of Soviet nuclear weapons less than 300 miles from Miami, Florida triggered a storm. Strategists in their sober language called it 'a security dilemma'. What looked like the only credible deterrent against aggression for Khrushchev was a shocking and intolerable threat for the Americans. The closest analogy was if Soviet troops had left Hungary in 1956, but the US still sent their nuclear missiles and troops. Khrushchev, however, had a different analogy: in 1960 the US had installed its nuclear missiles as a deterrent in Turkey, a NATO ally. The Soviets put up with those missiles that could reach their command centres in Moscow in less than half an hour. Now, Khrushchev reasoned, the Americans should swallow the same bitter pill.

Some scholars have recently claimed that the Cuban stand-off was not as close to a thermonuclear war as people thought, because neither Kennedy nor Khrushchev wanted such an outcome. This is a wrong and dangerous assumption. The crisis over the Soviet missiles in Cuba was the ultimate and most perilous test of wills that took place during the Cold War. It is also clear that had Kennedy and Khrushchev continued to butt heads instead of negotiating, this crisis could have ultimately triggered a worldwide conflagration. Wars, crises, and gang fights have something in common: they are the product of interests, but also of strong emotions, arrogance, and fear. Both sides want to project toughness, superiority, and credibility. Both sides fear they will lose if they don't strike first. The young thugs in *West Side Story* are driven by the same emotions that made the ancient Greeks fight and die at the gates of Troy or Napoleon push his troops to reach Moscow. The Cuban Missile Crisis was defined by flawed logic and little rationality.

Cuba was not as important as Germany in an economic and political sense. But it was not a chance playground for the superpowers' rivalry either. Cuba had a special place in the imagination of millions of Americans: they considered the island 'almost' part of their country, holidayed there, and believed they had once 'liberated' the Cubans from despotic Spain. The Cubans saw it very differently. At the end of 1959, they cheered the small army of young *barbudos* led by Fidel Castro, who overthrew the corrupt regime of strongman Fulgencio Batista, supported by the Americans. Like many self-declared 'revolutions', it was likely that this high-pitched nationalism would quickly succumb to dire economic realities and dependency on the United States. Initially, the Soviet response was reluctance and caution. Some Cuban revolutionaries around Fidel – his younger brother, Raúl, as well as Che Guevara – were communists. But so what? Many times Stalin did not lift a finger to help foreign communists if it did not suit his interests. Under Khrushchev, the Kremlin had been unable to do anything to save Lumumba's government in Congo. How could it rescue Cuba, a US appendix, from the American grip? The Cuban revolutionaries pushed hard. They knew that the United States would crush them, like all previous threats to America's absolute hegemony in the Caribbean. They deliberately doubled down: nationalized US assets, incurred

American sanctions, and turned to Moscow for assistance. And suddenly, this approach worked.

The failure to get a deal with Eisenhower and Kennedy in Germany made Khrushchev search for another way to have the Americans over a barrel and force them to accept 'a new correlation of forces' in the world. The Khrushchev–Castro meeting in New York sealed Cuba's fate: the island was now under the Soviet wing. For the Soviet elites and citizens, Cuba became an instant success, as a revolution in an exotic place seemed to validate the fading Soviet communist cause.[8] The Soviet leader was now under pressure to do something not to lose Cuba, scrutinized by his own people and by a hostile Beijing. He proclaimed that a new correlation of forces could prevent imperialist wars. But how to create a correlation that would prevent American invasion inside the United States' traditional geographic sphere of influence? Much to Khrushchev's frustration, Soviet strategic build-up turned out to be much more modest than the USSR's impressive early victories in the space race. In October 1960, haste and arrogance led to a disastrous explosion of an intercontinental missile that the Soviet military hoped to produce in quantities. Almost the entire collective of designers and engineers died in the blast. Khrushchev boasted publicly that the Soviet Union was 'producing missiles like sausages'. In reality, the United States did it more successfully by deploying hundreds of Minuteman land-based ICBMs and sea-launched Polaris missiles, rapidly increasing their huge strategic predominance.

The Americans could deliver the first strike against the Soviet Union almost without incurring any risk to its own population. And Washington had learned that the Soviet side was much weaker than it claimed. By October 1961, US aerial and space intelligence already had hard evidence that the Soviet strategic arsenal was puny by comparison. Seeking to reassure the nervous American public and allies, the Pentagon announced US superiority. News of this announcement came during the Party Congress in Moscow in October 1961, where Khrushchev reported on his victories and denounced his critics, including in China. For balance, Soviet nuclear scientists detonated in the Arctic Novaya Zemlya islands the largest thermonuclear device ever exploded in human history: it was over fifty megatons – this after the yield was reduced by half because there was no convenient site in the Soviet Union to have an explosion of such magnitude. The detonation wave from 'Tsar Bomba' (as the West called it) circled the globe several times. It was as if Khrushchev was engaging in a kids-in-a-sandbox quarrel with the Americans: you have more toys, but mine is the biggest. 'Let the sword of revenge hang over imperialists!' he exclaimed jubilantly at the Party Congress. He knew, however, that there was still no reliable missile to deliver his toy to the United States. Khrushchev's missile-rattling increasingly looked irresponsible even to his own military, who grumbled that Stalin had been much more prudent and calculating in the face of superior US might.

During a visit to Bulgaria in May 1962, Khrushchev asked his minister of defence how many minutes it would take for American missiles stationed nearby, in Turkey, to reach Moscow. The missiles in question were fifteen Jupiters, deployed by the Eisenhower administration (along with another thirty Jupiters in Italy) to fend off 'the Sputnik

Figure 2.6
Soviet scientists and the military inspect the 100-megaton Tsar Bomba, tested in October 1961.

effect' and guarantee the security of the NATO allies.⁹ Each missile was fitted with a 1.4 megaton warhead, capable of destroying the Soviet capital. Khrushchev did not record the answer of his minister but the technical data points to less than half an hour of flight time. During that time the Soviets could not even prepare Korolev's missiles for retaliation. Something clicked in the Soviet leader's mind: Berlin, China, Cuba, missiles, American superiority, and his own prestige were all connected. On 24 May 1962, at the Politburo, Khrushchev shared with his surprised but cowed colleagues his new proposal: to send to Cuba a division of intermediate and smaller-range ballistic missiles, the reliable type that the Soviet military had deployed and used for a few years, to protect 'the island of liberty' against inevitable American aggression. There was no discussion; Khrushchev brushed off the concerns of the prudent Mikoyan, and smartly made all his colleagues sign off on the official directive. The die was cast. Raúl Castro and Che Guevara, who arrived in Moscow in early July, were surprised but delighted at the offer from Khrushchev to receive a nuclear guarantee similar to what the United States granted to NATO allies. The Cuban risk-taking led to a much bigger Kremlin gamble. Everyone understood it was a historic blow to American prestige in the hemisphere that the United States had claimed in the Monroe Doctrine of 1823 as being under its protection. A week later a group of Soviet military officers landed in Cuba to reconnoitre places for missile bases.

Soviet military command was also enthusiastic and eager to get even with their adversary. From the start, the Soviet General Staff secretly planned to send to Cuba all the necessary troops and equipment to make the Soviet presence there sustainable: bombers, nuclear-tipped cruise missiles, nuclear tactical rockets, and 44,000 troops – an impressive arsenal of deterrence. An armada of eighty-two Soviet ships sailed off with top secret cargos across the Atlantic, in an operation that had no precedent in Soviet naval history. The codename Anadyr, after the river in the Arctic near Alaska, was meant to delude Western intelligence. Once in motion, the operation acquired the force of an avalanche; even Khrushchev probably could not have stopped it once begun. Those who knew about Operation Anadyr supported it wholeheartedly.

When Khrushchev said the Soviet Union would lose Cuba if it remained unprotected, he was not making it up. The invasion of the Bay of Pigs was just the most visible episode of CIA efforts to depose the Castro regime by the hands of those who had fled from revolutionary terror to Florida. The CIA had supported a list of successful coups around the world, including Iran, the Philippines, and Guatemala; assassination was an acceptable method. Cuba was not just a single thorn in the American side: the Cuban revolutionaries planned to spread guerrilla war all across Latin America, asking the KGB for assistance. When Moscow rebuffed them, they turned to China. The Soviet leaders were upset by the recklessness of their new clients and worried even more about their safety. Khrushchev's son-in-law Alexei Adzhubei, a journalist who interviewed Kennedy, reported that the US president wished he could treat Cuba with the same resolve as the Soviets had done with Hungary in 1956.[10]

The secretary of state, Dean Rusk, had said to the US Senate that Cuba might become a Sino-Soviet bloc missile base. Yet almost nobody had taken him seriously. In the summer and early autumn of 1962, the gaze of the Kennedy administration was firmly fixed on Berlin, where, after a few quiet months, another hurricane was expected.[11] The Americans just could not imagine that the Russians would dare to do to them in their own hemisphere what they had done to the Russians in Europe and Asia. Besides, Moscow had never been known to send nukes outside Soviet territory (apparently the CIA failed to detect the Soviet missiles in East Germany). Marxist-Leninists, American analysts insisted, did not improvise; they moved according to predictable patterns. This was wrong in the case of Stalin, and egregiously wrong with Khrushchev. In September 1962, as the first Soviet military personnel and munitions arrived, American intelligence picked up many details that pointed to a major military presence in Cuba, yet nobody saw the forest for the trees. The CIA even decided to suspend overflights for a while, in part because of clouds.[12]

Khrushchev aimed to disclose the missiles after the US midterm elections, yet his plan fell apart after the first U-2 overflight of Cuba. Oleg Penkovsky, a British spy in Moscow, gave the Americans blueprints of Soviet missile bases, and they matched exactly with the pictures the U-2 brought back. The main problem was the inexplicable assumption of the Soviet top command that it was easy to camouflage missiles behind tall palm trees. At every stage, the Soviet deployment in Cuba suffered from haste, improvisation, and sheer blundering. The military, after looking closer at Cuban vegetation, warned their superiors in Moscow that camouflage of missiles was impossible. Yet the planners stuck to the original plans and did not want to argue with Khrushchev.[13] CIA analysts told Kennedy about the missiles on 16 October: his worst nightmare had come true. Khrushchev had set him up. The US's only order of battle in case of 'clear and present danger' of Soviet arms was an all-out nuclear response. The world was now really on the brink.

The next thirteen days of that October have been extensively analysed, mostly from an American perspective. The focus tends to be on how Kennedy and his advisers managed the crisis. The president did two things right. First, he asked his friends in the US media to give him a week to deliberate (today, in the era of instant news and leaks, such a request would make no sense). Second, he convened a special committee that included the most important officials and military staff, and asked them to provide several options, without telling them in advance his own stance. In doing so, Kennedy let the passions of his entourage and the military cool off, and delayed the public uproar that would most certainly have demanded to attack Cuba immediately. There were a number of trigger-happy men among Kennedy's generals; some of them had bombed German and Japanese cities in 1942–45 and approved the use of atomic bombs on Hiroshima and Nagasaki. The discussions that Kennedy held with his advisers, government, and the military are some of the most studied in history, helped by the fact that they were secretly recorded and nobody, except the president, knew of this recording. The transcripts of these tapes are widely available online today. Here is one segment, for instance:

> JFK: Can we get a little idea about what the military thing is? Well, of course, one, would you suggest taking these [missiles] out?
>
> [Secretary of Defense] McNamara: The Chiefs [of Army, Navy, and Air Force] are strong in their recommendation against that kind of an attack, believing that it would leave, uh, too great a capability in Cuba undestroyed. The specific number of sorties required to, to accomplish this end has not been worked out in detail. The capability is for something in excess of seven hundred sorties per day... The Chiefs have also considered other alternatives extending into the full invasion, uh, you may wish to discuss later...[14]

Kennedy began by siding with the hardliners who wanted a pre-emptive attack on the Soviet missiles, only to accept the merits of a more moderate option. A crucial factor was assurances from the former ambassador in Moscow, Llewellyn

Thompson, who knew Khrushchev well and was convinced he would not start a war. Just as he himself had gained time, Kennedy decided to allow the Soviet leader time to contemplate the consequences of his actions. This was his third good decision: to let his adversary change his mind.

On 22 October, the Soviet embassy and intelligence informed Khrushchev that next morning Kennedy was going to make a major address to the nation. It was already late evening in Moscow, but the Soviet leader convened all his colleagues and the top military leaders for an emergency meeting. The session lasted through the whole night. We owe its recording to two officials. Here is one of the most dramatic excerpts:

> [Khrushchev]: The tragic thing is – they can attack, and we will respond. This could escalate into a large-scale war.
>
> One scenario: they will begin to act against Cuba. [To prevent this we can] declare on the radio that there already is an agreement concerning Cuba.
>
> They might declare a blockade, or they might take no action.
>
> Another scenario: in case of an [American] attack, all the equipment is Cuban, and the Cubans declare that they will respond. And another: do not use strategic weapons, but use tactical weapons.[15]

All the scenarios were meant to deter an American attack, not to provoke it. Mikoyan, however, pointed out to Khrushchev that if the Americans had learned that Castro now had nuclear weapons in his possession, they might be so upset that they would deliver a strike to take those weapons out.

Instead of an invasion, Kennedy announced a 'quarantine' – another word for a blockade – of Cuba by the US Navy. In the West, the common reaction to Kennedy's announcement of Soviet nuclear missiles in Cuba was tinged with horror and expectation of apocalypse. Those Americans who had built nuclear shelters rushed to stock them with food and medicine. Many tried to travel across the border to Canada or Mexico. American women sent urgent letters to Khrushchev – and to his wife Nina, with appeals to restrain her husband. The populations of the Soviet Union, China, and to a lesser extent eastern Europe were the happy exceptions to this universal moment of doom: the communist censors successfully created a parallel reality. Still, even Soviet diaries reflect expectations of imminent war. Khrushchev somewhat regained his self-confidence. In the next few days, he dictated several secret messages to the US president, blowing hot and cold, reshuffling an old pack of grievances and ideological statements, and often just blabbering.

The most acute phase of the crisis lasted for five days, and during this time chances of accidental use of nuclear arms multiplied by the minute. At that time the chain of nuclear command was much less strict, and there were no technical means to preclude an overzealous local commander from using nuclear weapons on his own. The head of the US Strategic Air Command (SAC) General Thomas Power said: 'The whole idea is to kill the bastards! At the end of the war if there are two Americans and one Russian left alive, we win!' His interlocutor told him it would be better to make sure there is a man and a woman among the American survivors.[16]

A similar character later appeared in Stanley Kubrick's black comedy *Dr Strangelove*, perhaps the greatest film about

Figure 2.7
Stanley Kubrick's *Dr Strangelove* became the best black comedy about the Cold War, 1964.

the Cold War. Some Soviet marshals, for instance Khrushchev's war buddy Andrei Grechko, subscribed to the same logic of 'winning' the nuclear war. In Cuba, Soviet generals, junior officers, and soldiers, convinced a nuclear war was imminent, pledged 'to carry out any order from the Party and the Soviet government'. Khrushchev was appalled that things might get out of hand and ordered that any nuclear missiles in Cuba must not be used without Moscow's explicit authorization. Nuclear warheads were kept under lock and key in separate storage, at a distance from the deployed missiles. Yet some dangerous details remained under the radar: there were tactical nukes, called Lunas, that the Soviet military in Cuba could use in case of a US landing. There were also four Foxtrot-class Soviet submarines that were sailing towards Cuba as part of Operation Anadyr with rather vague instructions on what to do with their nuclear-tipped torpedoes if the Americans attacked.

The constant low-altitude flights of American aircraft over Soviet bases in Cuba and ships on the ocean had everyone on edge. Thousands of Russian military personnel in Cuba were convinced they would soon perish, fighting next to their Cuban comrades-in-arms. Looking back, a single spark into this tinderbox would have been fatal. Kennedy instructed all branches of the military to report to the Situation Room before taking any actions, yet he could not control everything; nor could Khrushchev. In two confused letters to Kennedy, Khrushchev proposed a trade-off: no missiles in Cuba in exchange for the US non-invasion pledge and removal of missiles from Turkey. On 26 October, an extremely agitated Bobby Kennedy met in Washington with Soviet ambassador Anatoly Dobrynin and accepted Khrushchev's expanded deal: in addition to the missile withdrawal, the US would give a pledge not to invade Cuba. He said he could not make this deal public, for fear of negative American reaction.

Before the talks could reach fruition, however, other events forced Khrushchev's hand. Early on 28 October, he learned that Soviet-manned surface-to-air missiles had shot down a U-2 and killed its pilot. Soviet intelligence reported that an American invasion of Cuba was imminent. Adding to the pressure was Castro's cable from Havana with advice to the Soviet leadership to strike the Americans first, before the reverse happened. He compared the situation to Hitler's attack on the Soviet Union in June 1941 and implied it should not be allowed to happen again. Khrushchev never trusted

Kennedy's ability to restrain his military. Reading and perhaps misreading the intelligence, he hastened to stop the clock of brinkmanship, as time was ticking.

This happened on Sunday 28 October 1962, at 6a.m. Moscow time. Soviet international radio announced the decision of the Soviet government to remove 'all Soviet offensive means' from Cuba. This caught Soviet elites, the military, diplomats, and the Cubans completely by surprise. It also surprised numerous international actors, including the UN secretary-general, who scrambled to find a peaceful exit from the crisis. The Kennedy administration managed to secure Turkey's and even Italy's consent for the removal of missiles stationed on their territory.

Khrushchev's rushed decision cost him a lot. Castro never forgave this 'betrayal', the Chinese called the Kremlin leader a coward and appeaser, and the Soviet political and military elites blamed him for taking them into a mess only to beat a humiliating retreat. It is widely assumed that the Cuban gamble and this rushed, undignified retreat united Khrushchev's colleagues in their determination to get rid of him.

Much of November 1962 passed in tension. The Americans were not exactly forthcoming and helpful. Kennedy encouraged his media friends to create a narrative where he was a cool, heroic leader, while Khrushchev had 'blinked'. The administration pressed Moscow to pull out all weapons that had been deployed in Cuba; the Soviet leadership tried to placate Castro, who refused to let the missiles leave the island and then flatly banned any American inspectors. Khrushchev sent Mikoyan to the United States and then to Cuba to negotiate an exit; the seasoned politician did all this

Figure 2.8
Castro visits the USSR after the Cuban Missile Crisis, 1963.

troubleshooting stoically. The US administration demanded that all Soviet forces leave the island along with the missiles, and did not care what problems this caused the Soviet leader. Finally, by the end of November, in extreme haste and under stress, the Soviet troops left Cuba with all their weaponry.

The long shadow of the Cuban Missile Crisis led to an earnest search in the United States for rules and limitations on nuclear tests and exercises. Most leaders and opinion-makers still had personal experience of the Second World War and were also aware of the great role of accidents and triggers that had started the First World War in 1914. The Korean War also offered mixed lessons: they had to build up military power but also limit its use to avoid the descent into a global catastrophe. A memorable new acronym was coined: MAD, standing for mutual assured destruction, which captured the new situation where the United States could attack the Soviet Union only as an act of suicide, to disappear in the nuclear flames a few hours later. The same was true for any initial strike by the Soviets. It was not such a revolutionary idea. In 1946, Bernard Brodie had written essentially the same thing. Politically, however, it was a huge development: the US leadership publicly acknowledged what previously only a few in Washington and Moscow had privately realized. This meant that the thermonuclear revolution finally began to change the politics of security, contradicting the instincts and habits of centuries of military history. The very idea of the futility of a nuclear war and inevitability of a catastrophe begged for self-limitation and invited the parties to the negotiating table.

Is There an Exit?

The saga of the Cuban crisis has gone from a fairy tale about heroic Kennedy to a tale of folly, full of chilling moments of carelessness and blundering, and calls for prudence. Those who called for the first strike are criticized, and those who kept cool heads and prevented Armageddon came to be praised for saving humanity from genocide. Among them Kennedy, the American military with access to nuclear weapons, Soviet submarine commanders, and even Khrushchev. This is a story without heroes, however. It is more honest to conclude that humanity was extraordinarily lucky. People usually learn lessons from crises when it suits their interests and forget those lessons when danger passes. Inside the Kennedy circle, the sobering realization of mortality in October 1962 was subsequently overridden by the need to project global leadership and to win the elections in 1964. Kennedy did not live to see those elections. During the early phase of the electoral campaign in Dallas, he was shot by a sniper and died. When it came out that Lee Harvey Oswald, the disgruntled assassin, had resided for a while in the Soviet Union, both sides squashed what could have become another dangerous scandal.

The lessons of Berlin and especially the Cuban crisis had a significant impact on Western and Soviet policymakers for three decades, until the very end of the Cold War. Crisis management required quick and safe communication channels. Those channels included a hotline, the first secure phone connection between the Kremlin and the White House. Unbridled nuclear brinkmanship stopped. Khrushchev stopped pressing for a 'free city' in Berlin and a German peace treaty. After intense negotiations, in 1963 the United States, the Soviet Union, and the UK reached a nuclear test ban on the ground, under water, in the atmosphere, or in space. This was the first tangible act to limit the arms race, and created a precedent for other talks and agreements. As many historians agree, the twin crises, in Berlin and Cuba, set the stage for European détente, and pushed some countries in NATO and in the Warsaw Pact to distance themselves from the superpowers in search of security.

At the same time, very few people at the time imagined that the conflict would end one day. All thoughts went in a different direction: how to regulate the confrontation and how to set safety rules. The idea of arms control, first floated by Oppenheimer and the American nuclear physicists in 1945–48, now became legitimate in the American policymaking community, and even began to win hearts in the Kremlin. Nuclear arsenals remained key to the superpowers' sense of power and legitimacy, and mutual nuclear deterrence, and the Pentagon and the Soviet General Staff continued to demand weapons for any war scenario, from a total thermonuclear war to a regional nuclear-free conflict. And yet something important happened. As the youngest designer of Tsar Bomba told me, 'the [Cuban missile] crisis marked the peak of the confrontation, [where the protagonists] took the measure of each other, and realized that a compromise was the only option.' The climbers reached the peak and stared into the abyss. Khrushchev said to an Indian diplomat on 26 October, as he still peered over the brink: 'History tells us that in order to stop a conflict, one should begin not by exploring the reasons why it happened but by pursuing a ceasefire.'[17]

After almost two decades, it was becoming clear that the USSR and the US needed each other. The Soviets started to see American leaders once more as human beings. When Soviet television aired the funeral of Kennedy, many Soviet women wept at the sight of Jackie with her orphaned children. Yet this did not mean Soviet citizens were ready to lose the Cold War. Competition with the United States provided the same glue to the Soviet Union that 'the Russian threat' offered to American interventionism. While the Americans feared 'the Russians', many ethnic Russians, as well as ethnic Ukrainians, Jews, and others, willingly adopted a Soviet identity – more ideological and synthetic – that superseded national feelings and cultural memories. This Soviet identity was boosted by pride over real achievements: the nuclear status, Sputnik and space exploits, and Soviet-made aircraft; and in the cultural sphere the Bolshoi ballet and other virtuosos. There was also Soviet sport. In the Olympics of

Figure 2.9
Détente possible? Dean Rusk, Khrushchev, US Ambassador in Moscow Lewellyn Thompson, Andrei Gromyko and Soviet Ambassador in Washington Anatoly Dobrynin, in Pitsunda, the Soviet Black Sea resort, with their wives.

1956 and 1960, the Soviet team scored more gold and silver medals than the United States and anyone else. Multi-ethnic Soviet teams excelled at football, hockey, and ice-skating. Moreover, Soviet elites continued to believe that communism made their country a superpower and would eventually make them live well. Though Khrushchev's antics and pie-in-the-sky promises were ridiculed, intellectuals, students, and common people alike remained more optimistic than pessimistic. The horrors and ghosts of the past were behind them; the future was beckoning.

The time of Vulcan was an era of breathtaking growth of lethal capacities: nuclear missiles, then nuclear-powered submarines, and supersonic bombers armed with nuclear weapons. The people who made it possible were scientists and engineers, not communist fanatics and financial capitalists. These years of nuclear mushroom clouds also became a time for unprecedented influence of scientists and analysts. The darker side of scientific discoveries was compensated for by dreams of great breakthroughs for humanity: eternal and cheap energy, computers, robots at the service of humans, boundless harvests, and – in the imagination of fiction writers – colonization of other solar systems. The negative aspects of those promises, such as environmental concerns and nuclear fallout, gathered rallies yet had still to get to the agenda of politicians. Much of what happened in that era was done for simple reasons of prestige or, as Vladimir Lenin put it, the question of 'who would prevail'. The nuclear and missile race logically led to the space race. Envious of Soviet success, Kennedy started the Apollo program that would take Americans to the Moon by the end of the 1960s.

It was a time when, both in the West and in the East, science and technology captured hearts and minds, becoming the central subject of science fiction and mass culture. Radioactive bikini tans gave way to literature and films where humans conquered other star systems and even galaxies, only to decide what kind of social relationships would prevail there. Scientists not only invented the dreadful arsenals of the Cold War but held out the promise of creating universal scientific recipes to eradicate disease and poverty, defeat social inequality, and bring about eternal peace. The ideologies of scientific rationalism exacerbated the rivalry between the US and the USSR, as each rival advanced its universal recipes for transforming the world.

These technocratic dreams turned out to be short-lived. The world and the future of mankind remained in the hands of politicians subject to nationalist passions. The globalization of the Cold War also brought along new actors, guided not by scientific rationalist utopias but by nationalist and revolutionary zeal. Mao, Nasser, Castro and Che Guevara, Franz Fanon and the Algerian radicals, Nkruma, and Touré, to name only the most famous ones, made a hash out of the designs of Washington and Moscow. Most consequential for the next phase of the Cold War were the independent actions of the Communist Party of Vietnam, led by Ho Chi Minh. In 1954, in an attempt to settle the Cold War in Asia, Moscow and Beijing had forced the Vietnamese communists to accept a temporary division of their country into North and South, with the Americans helping to set up a dependent regime in the latter territory. As the focus of the East–West confrontation returned to Europe, in 1960 the Vietnamese communists decided that they should take the matter into their own hands. Against Khrushchev's advice, they launched a revolutionary guerrilla war to reunify their country, even if they were to have to fight alone, without Soviet and Chinese assistance, against the American power. Nobody at the time could have imagined that they would succeed.

The next two decades were the time of Janus – the Roman god of beginnings and endings. Images of Janus are two-faced: one face gazes at war, another contemplates peace. In the mid-1960s, after huge relief followed the spike in nuclear fears over Berlin and Cuba, the focus shifted to the Third

World, and many in Europe began to imagine the end of the Cold War. Détente was in the air. Instead, the arms race continued, and Asia, Africa, and Latin America saw new wars, interventions, and bitter rivalry between the West and the East. After a decade of hopes for a more stable and peaceful order, the world seemed to have careened back to the familiar bipolar conflict. Janus remained true to his nature.

PART THREE
The Time of Janus, 1963–1980

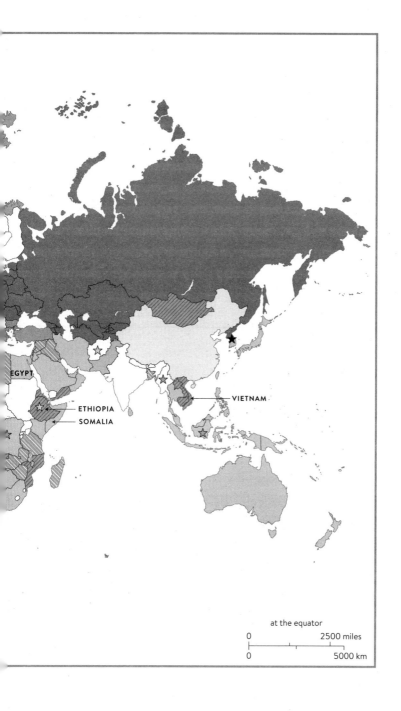

CHAPTER 8
Vietnam and the Origins of Détente

Quagmire

On Friday 22 November 1963, when Kennedy was assassinated, Soviet leaders lost the partner who could have been 'the second Roosevelt'. The purgatory of the Cuban crisis had created a strange bond between Kennedy and Khrushchev. His successor, former vice president Lyndon B. Johnson, had other priorities than a partnership with the Kremlin. His main focus was on the 'Great Society', a set of far-reaching domestic reforms that marked the peak of American state-led liberalism. Johnson's Great Society, boosted by a booming economy, was the peak of America's desire to demonstrate to the world that the United States, not the Soviet Union, could eradicate poverty and end discrimination. Thanks to his thirty years of experience in Congress, Johnson managed to get a record amount of money for social programmes. A hard-nosed Texan politician, Johnson achieved what had eluded Roosevelt, Truman, and Kennedy – he carried out quasi-socialist programmes that provided, for the first time in US history, a real safety net for the poor, the needy, the unemployed, and the old. The Great Society also tore down the walls of segregation and discrimination against Black people.

In 1965, the new immigration law ended the old discriminatory quota system and opened the United States to émigrés from the Third World.

When it came to foreign policy, one of Johnson's top priorities was to contain communism in Vietnam. The Americans had turned their attention to Indochina in 1953–54, after the loss of China and the end of the Korean War. At that time, the French colonial regime in the region was crumbling. In 1954, the French army had lost the war against Vietnamese communist forces led by Ho Chi Minh and General Vo Nguyen Giap. A peace conference on Indochina had met in Geneva: the French and the Americans confronted the Soviets and the Chinese. The conference reached a compromise: Indochina was divided into three supposedly sovereign states: the Kingdom of Cambodia, the Kingdom of Laos, and Vietnam. The latter was temporarily divided along the 17th parallel: the communists ruled in the north, and the French-protected 'state of Vietnam' was in the south. But national elections, promised at Geneva, never took place. Washington feared that communists would win the ballot. For many in the US government, above all Eisenhower and John Foster Dulles, the communist regime established in 1954 in Hanoi risked leading to more of the same across Asia. The Eisenhower administration chose to take over from the French, arrogantly expecting to get things right in South Vietnam. The main base for the Americans in the region had hitherto been Thailand; now they decided to build up another anti-communist state around Saigon. Bao Dai, the last emperor from the Vietnamese dynasty, a French-educated man, was weak and compromised: he had been a figurehead for the

French for too long. The ambitious and US-educated Ngo Dinh Diem deposed the emperor and proclaimed, with the support of Washington, the Republic of Vietnam (ROV).

Supporting the ROV was a self-inflicted nightmare for Washington. There were a few analogies for this kind of set up, such as South Korea, the Philippines, Iran after 1953, and Guatemala in 1954, but it did not work out in South Vietnam. The US-backed South Korea survived with American intervention, and the demilitarized zone later worked to protect the South from Northern aggression. The ROV was much more vulnerable, geographically and politically. Crucially, this was the first time the US was operating in a context where there was a strong indigenous communist force that had broad national support. There were numerous guerrillas (Vietcong) in the South. The Hanoi communist regime could send military reinforcements and arms to those guerrillas across the 17th parallel by using numerous jungle trails across the neighbouring Laos and Cambodia. South Vietnam continued to exist on American subventions, an unviable satellite that could not be sacrificed. JFK inherited this burden from Eisenhower and passed it on to Johnson.

In 1954, the Soviet Union and China had stepped in to achieve an international accord between France, the US, and Hanoi's communist government. The Soviet idea was to avoid another conflict like the one in Korea. For the Vietnamese communists, however, the Geneva accord was 'a stolen victory' and they never put up with it. In Hanoi in the North, they created a communist state, using the Soviet model. Vietnamese communists avoided the error of Kim Il Sung: they did not stage an invasion and did not give the United

States an opportunity to offer a legitimate defence of a half-baked 'nation'. Instead, Ho Chi Minh's younger successors Le Duan, Pham Van Dong, and others resorted to guerrilla war, inspired by Mao in China, and Algeria's National Liberation Army, to destabilize the US puppet state and delegitimize the American use of force in Vietnam. They overruled the cautious Ho and launched an operation to reunify the country. The rivalry between Mao and Khrushchev worked to their advantage. Had the communist world been united and stable, Moscow and Beijing would have contained the Vietnamese allies. After all, none of them needed the US to build up its military presence in Indochina. Khrushchev, despite his fiery rhetoric in support of 'anti-imperialist forces' in 1960–62, recommended that Hanoi hold fire. In Beijing, however, Mao supported the 'national liberation struggle' of Hanoi both on ideological grounds and because the Vietnamese communists followed his advice. Mao's line prevailed.

A leading Cold War historian has called the American involvement in Vietnam 'a folly from the beginning'.[1] The escalation of US interventionism in Indochina in general, and in South Vietnam in particular, was relentless and unstoppable. In his book *The Quiet American*, the British writer and intelligence officer Graham Greene illustrated a paradox of American Third World interventionism: the Americans arrived with the best intentions but caused more devastation. For many locals it was not clear what was worse: to be overrun by communists or protected by Americans. The Republic of Vietnam under Diem was totally dependent on American financial and military aid. This denied the Vietnamese leader any nationalist credentials. As American ideas on how to

VIETNAM AND THE ORIGINS OF DÉTENTE

Figure 3.1
Actress Jane Fonda's controversial visit to North Vietnam during the war, 1972.

modernize Vietnamese society and protect it from communists backfired one after another, Diem struggled to escape the constant monitoring of his American sponsors. He could never find an alternative to communist nationalism in order to make South Vietnam a viable national project. He alienated nearly everyone: the middle classes, students, Buddhists, and peasants. In November 1963, the head of the ROV was overthrown and murdered by his own generals.[2]

The American war in Vietnam was never declared. In fact, the US Congress did not make a single declaration of war after 1942. Instead, it delegated authority to the US president, who became by default the person to decide on issues of war and peace. On 10 August 1964, there was a congressional resolution that referred to the 'deliberate and repeated attacks' of the North Vietnamese on the US Navy in the Tonkin Gulf. Whether those attacks or 'incidents' on 2 and 4 August really took place remains a matter of controversy to this day. North Vietnamese forces did strike a US vessel, but the second attack probably never took place. The resolution gave President Johnson, as commander-in-chief, the authority to take action to protect American forces and 'prevent further aggression'. Beneath the Tonkin Gulf incidents lay deeper reasons for war.

The US leadership had already convinced itself that full American military power was the only way to check Hanoi's military encroachments and to preserve the ROV. Johnson was sucked into the conflict by commitments made by his predecessors, Eisenhower and Kennedy, and suffered from personal insecurity: his foreign policy experience was minimal, but he knew how quickly and dramatically his authority could be lost on the battlegrounds of the Cold War. He asked Kennedy's circle of advisers (who had been described as 'the best and the brightest') to stay on after his assassination, and relied on their advice. Despite their brilliance and credentials, they repeated all the mistakes from the French colonial war and inherited from Eisenhower the fear that Asian countries might start falling to communism like dominoes. And they were doubtful that the swift use of US military power would overwhelm the Hanoi-controlled guerrilla forces. They did learn one important thing, however: they avoided crossing the 17th parallel, for fear of provoking China again into joining the conflict. The result was a paradox: the White House failed to contain Vietnamese communism but ended up restraining American power. In the end, 2.5 million Americans served in this war: 58,300 of them paid the ultimate price. Over 1 million Vietnamese military and 2 million civilians died in Vietnam from both sides.

There were strong doubts in the White House, but no systematic discussion of different options. This only ensured the perpetuation of the sunk cost fallacy, i.e., the reluctance to give up on the thing into which they had already invested so much. It meant that every time the next step was considered, the most prudent voices lost to those who argued that more bombing and more troops on the ground would fix the problem and bring victory. Early on, there were no strong domestic and international factors to push the United States into this war. Yet once Johnson chose to go to war, it was increasingly difficult to turn around. Thanks to a potent mix of arrogance, exceptionalism, and fear of losing credibility by abandoning their allies, American Cold Warriors could not accept that their crusade made no sense, and they were facing an unwinnable war, or, even worse, a defeat.[3] The national security state and the Cold War domestic consensus continued to support the escalation of the war until 1968. Only then did everything begin to unravel.

Pragmatism or Adventurism?

On 16 October 1964, Khrushchev was ousted from power in a palace coup by his colleagues, who had had enough of his mercurial and risky policies. The 'troika' of the new Soviet leadership consisted of one Russian and two Ukrainians. Premier Alexei Kosygin, a Russian from Leningrad, was an impressive technocrat and expert on the Soviet economy. The new Party head Leonid Brezhnev was a bureaucrat with a modest intellect but considerable political skills. His previous job had been to oversee the missile-industrial complex, but he was an advocate of peace through strength, and hated Khrushchev's nuclear blackmail and brinkmanship. Nikolai Podgorny, the head of the legislative body known as the Supreme Soviet, was a bland apparatchik. Both Brezhnev and Podgorny were the result of a negative selection set in motion by Stalin's constant purges and Khrushchev's removal of political rivals: by the mid-1960s the Soviet elite was full of badly educated careerists, sycophants, and mediocrities. Mikoyan, the last Old Bolshevik in the Kremlin, was soon eased into honourable retirement. The favourite pastimes of the Soviet leadership were hunting, drinking, and dominoes. They knew very little about international affairs, had never lived abroad, and were incapable of strategic thinking. Their objectives were neither revolutionary nor grandiose. Brezhnev's chief motivator was vanity, not ideology. He wanted to build up the nuclear-missile arsenal to reach equal status with the United States but hoped the USSR would never find itself in the same situation as during the Cuban Missile Crisis. The new leadership also wanted to repair the fractured communist camp, above all the Sino-Soviet alliance.[4]

Khrushchev's removal from power allowed the Politburo to start discussing his policy mistakes. His adventures in the Third World became an object of ridicule. One of his critics wrote: 'Comrade Khrushchev declares carelessly that Stalin failed to penetrate Latin America, and that he [Khrushchev] managed to do it. But only a gambler may assert that under modern conditions our state can grant real military assistance to any country on that continent. Missiles will not do in this case: they will burn to the ground the country that requires assistance – nothing else.' In Africa, the critic wrote, Moscow wasted money and assistance on those leaders who claimed 'socialist orientation' – yet the same leaders soon switched to the Western side or pragmatically milked both sides for their own profit. Those were fair observations, yet quickly forgotten. Before long, the new Kremlin masters returned to costly commitments in the Third World.

They did not want to 'conquer the world', as Americans incessantly warned. Ideologically they were captives of the lodestar that defined Soviet international behaviour: the revolutionary-imperial paradigm. Lacking personal revolutionary credentials, the Soviet leaders wanted to demonstrate they were loyal to Leninism and so reluctantly pursued Lenin's 'internationalist mission' worldwide. Some of them also absorbed the concept of imperial grandeur inherited from the Russian empire. And the more they cared about the centrality of the Soviet Union in the world, the more they had to invest into a growing network of clients and satellites around the globe. They just could not see a better way to enhance Soviet global status. Their view of the United States was a peculiar mix of inferiority complex and the desire to be equal. So long as the Americans pursued global hegemony, the Soviet Union needed its own global 'empire' to match the that of United States.[5]

Vietnam was not Khrushchev's war. He remembered what had happened in Korea and had repeatedly warned his Vietnamese comrades not to provoke the Americans. He had preferred a negotiated neutrality. After Khrushchev was gone, his successors were also reluctant to support the North Vietnamese militant drive for reunification. When Johnson sent American troops to fight against the Vietnamese communist state, the Kremlin was taken by surprise. Initially, there were voices of caution: why mess with the Americans again? But as American bombs began to fall on North Vietnam, indiscriminately killing civilians, caution gave way to outrage. The fundamental trap of the revolutionary-imperial paradigm also worked: the Kremlin had to support Hanoi, as the Soviet Union was in an open rivalry with China over revolutionary credibility and influence in the Third World. Most men in the Politburo, above all Kosygin, also believed that assisting Vietnam would help the Soviet Union reconcile with China and restore the unity of the communist camp. Party elites viewed the Sino-Soviet split as something historically wrong, ideologically inconceivable, and attributed it to Khrushchev's gross behaviour and lack of tact. 'We are communists and they are communists,' Kosygin said at the Politburo about the Chinese. 'It is hard to believe we will not be able to reach an agreement if we meet face to face.'

It took the Soviet leadership some time to realize that, so long as Mao stayed in power, no reconciliation was possible. The Chinese agreed to let the Soviets ship military aid to Hanoi through their territory, but only by train, not by air – and, it turned out, only to avail themselves liberally of that equipment, which 'disappeared' along the way. In 1966, Mao launched the Great Proletarian Cultural Revolution, his new bid for greatness. The Maoist revolution unleashed the blind energy of China's youth and shattered the Party elites, defeating Mao's rivals. China became almost ungovernable, with no state apparatus worthy of the name, hardly able to conduct foreign policy. And the main external target of this revolution was no longer American imperialism, but rather 'Soviet revisionism' – Mao's new line by which he accused the Kremlin of alleged betrayal of Leninism and revolution. Kosygin bravely made a stopover in Beijing on his trip to Vietnam in an attempt to find a common language with the Chinese leadership. It was a fiasco. He returned to Moscow humiliated and sobered. The Politburo decided to continue to assist Hanoi no matter what, even though many in the North Vietnamese leadership leaned towards Mao in his feud with Moscow.

As the United States was getting mired in Vietnam, the Soviets had their fair share of shocks and challenges. This time, these were not the result of their own missteps, but rather of a new phase of post-colonial political dynamics in the Third World. The first cohort of anti-imperialist leaders, many of them European-educated intellectuals, were quickly replaced by military strongmen, also trained by former colonial masters. In 1965, Indonesia exploded in violence and the father of the Non-Aligned Movement Ahmed Sukarno was overthrown by the head of the army, General Suharto, who turned to the CIA for support. About 300,000 communists, most of them ethnic Chinese, perished in the resulting massacre. Even though Sukarno had leaned on Beijing against Moscow, in the Kremlin this was viewed as the biggest loss for 'the progressive forces' in Asia. An even greater blow, this time directly to Soviet prestige, was the Six-Day War in June 1967. Israel delivered a pre-emptive strike on Egypt and Syria, destroying their Soviet-made air force and capturing the West Bank, the Gaza Strip, Sinai, the Golan Heights, and East Jerusalem with its holy places. The defeat suffered by Soviet Arab clients was so unexpected and shocking that the Politburo was in session day and night. After a decade of triumphant engagement in the Middle East, Soviet investments there seemed to be lost. In an emotional backlash, the Kremlin for the second time broke off diplomatic relations with Israel (Stalin had first done this in January 1953). This time the Soviets refrained from any nuclear threats. The Kremlin must have learned that Israel had secretly built its own atomic bomb.[6] Khrushchev's era of nuclear threats and brinkmanship was over.

As the Six-Day War still raged on, Kosygin flew to the United States to attend the UN Assembly and demand Israeli withdrawal and restitution for the Arab states. He and Johnson decided to meet separately to discuss the Middle East conflict, in the small town of Glassboro, midway between Washington and New York. This was the first US–Soviet summit since the debacles in Paris and Vienna. The US administration sided with Israel and did not want to push Tel Aviv to abandon the conquered territories without some kind of peace guarantee. Kosygin was not an experienced negotiator and was reluctant to veer from the instructions agreed by the Politburo. Still, the talks went on more positively than might have been expected, given mutual mistrust and the fluidity of the Middle Eastern crisis. The Americans indicated for the first time their serious interest in talks to limit the strategic arms race. They were especially interested in a ban on developing anti-missile defence systems, which could only become the driver of an endless competition between 'offence' and 'defence'. Johnson was also keen to keep things quiet in Europe, while the American military was committed in Vietnam. Even though he was unhappy about the US bombing of North Vietnam, Kosygin invited Johnson to visit Moscow and Leningrad the following year. Their meeting was a pragmatic contrast to the dismal failure of the previous summits.

One of the advocates of arms control talks with the Kremlin was secretary of defense Robert McNamara, one of the authors of the concept of mutual assured destruction (MAD). Both sides already had the capacity to destroy each other and the world. To race further would be a waste and destabilizing. The best one could hope for was to accept the status quo in a kind of mutually established nuclear control regime. The former head of the Ford Corporation, McNamara viewed the arms race through a technocratic lens, as an issue that could be resolved rationally. His cost–benefit analysis showed that the US triad of strategic bombers, nuclear submarines, and Minuteman missiles had reached the optimum level, exceeding the potential targets in the USSR. American nukes could annihilate everything worthy of destruction in the Soviet Union, China, and eastern Europe, even if the Soviets launched a surprise attack. Why then deploy more missiles? Rather, it made sense to reach an agreement with the Soviet Union that would stop the build-up and keep it at its current 'reasonable' level.

It was not the first attempt at using Western rationality to shape the Cold War, but perhaps it was the most emblematic one. There were two problems with McNamara's analysis: technological advancement and human psychology. American and Soviet labs continued to work on new and expensive ways to destroy the enemy, including anti-missile systems and multiple payloads on one missile that could strike many targets. Even more importantly, the logic of mutual assured destruction was counterintuitive: it ran against all human instincts and customs, and so was difficult to accept. Kosygin and other Soviet leaders did not understand why they should leave themselves and their country vulnerable to incoming American missiles. And many in Congress, not to mention the American public, were not ready to accept the new philosophy of nuclear doom, which went against American optimism and sense of superiority. This new reasoning, in the opinion of many critics, favoured the Soviets, who were the weaker side in the conflict, and nullified numerous Western advantages. Moreover, it implied a 'moral equivalence' between the 'good' Americans and the 'evil' communist empire. This was intolerable for American patriots as it undermined the core of American identity.

Discussing Détente

In western Europe, NATO members supported the US, but public opinion in their countries turned against the war in Vietnam. The news of bombing of civilians and use of chemicals and napalm inspired outrage and led to a democratic peace movement that embraced anti-American slogans. In West Germany, where older people had gone along with Nazi aggression, the new generation turned against the war – as well as against their parents. The radical Western youth did not feel much sympathy for the bureaucratized and imperialistic Soviet Union and redirected their unspent radical romanticism towards the Cuban revolutionaries, the North Vietnamese guerrillas, and the Maoist Cultural Revolution.

Among western European politicians, accustomed to the protective cocoon of NATO and the shield of US nuclear superiority, the Vietnam War triggered security worries of a different kind. US military command had to redeploy more and more American brigades from West Germany to Indochina. What would the US do next time a crisis in Europe broke out? Would they act as rationally as they had under Eisenhower and Kennedy? Would the Americans use their nukes against Moscow to protect Hamburg, if West Germany were overrun by Soviet tanks? And what would they do if the Soviets deployed, as was clearly their intention, hundreds of intercontinental missiles to strike Washington, New York, and Los Angeles? NATO allies in Europe were concerned that the Americans would 'decouple' their own survival from the defence of Europe. Most western European leaders still remembered the Second World War and they were starting to realize that they would not be able for ever to outsource their security to the United States. They had to take European affairs into their own hands.

In 1966, the Belgian foreign minister Pierre Harmel proposed a strategy exercise: four teams of experts from European countries that were part of NATO worked on four papers on the future of the alliance. The Harmel Report, presented in December 1967, offered a distinct western European agenda on how to tame, if not exit, the Cold War. The first team concluded that the division of Europe and Germany was 'unnatural' but could not be ended by force. The final goal of NATO, the report argued, should be a lasting European order that would necessarily involve the Soviet Union and eastern Europe. This, however, could only be achieved through 'a climate of détente', not the militarized containment practised in the 1950s. The experts argued that détente necessitated talks between the West and the East. Eastern European countries such as Poland had gained more sovereignty and independence from Moscow, and were actively pushing for the end of the Iron Curtain. Crucially the report stated that 'economic and technological exchanges for the Soviet Union and Eastern Europe occupy an important place in breaking down communist rigidity and in furthering the process of détente'. The Americans were not happy with this view but the European allies defended their stand. Détente, they argued, was compatible with NATO unity, as long as it would not come at the expense of Western freedoms and values. As the Harmel Report concluded, 'each Ally should play its full part in promoting an improvement in relations with the Soviet Union and the countries of Eastern Europe, bearing in mind that the pursuit of détente must not be allowed to split the Alliance.'[7]

French president Charles de Gaulle went beyond the Harmel doctrine and tested NATO unity. Wanting to distance himself from the United States and enhance France's independent role in Europe, he touted 'a Europe from the Atlantic to the Urals', without the Americans. He emphatically stated that the Soviet Union was 'Russia', a great power that should be a member of a post-Cold War European order, a new version of a Concert of Europe, just like imperial Russia had once been. De Gaulle made a trip to Moscow to promote his vision and, most dramatically, he pulled France from the military structures of NATO. The French 'defection' caused dismay in Washington and was welcomed in Moscow. NATO headquarters moved from Paris to Brussels, where it stays to this day.

De Gaulle's nationalism, as well as the anti-American

youth radicalism, ran against the general European mood. No security order in Europe could function without American power. Decades later, western Europe still could not defend itself against the Soviet Union. And there would have been huge economic and financial consequences if America had left Europe to become isolationist again. Most importantly, it would have imperilled the trans-Atlantic liberal order, which was important for western European prosperity as it gave Europeans access to American markets. And what would have happened to the European Economic Community? By the end of the 1960s, France and West Germany enjoyed a positive trade balance. Once desperate to get US dollars, they now had a surplus. The economic interdependence between NATO members reinforced the foundation of NATO and withstood the political wind from Paris. Even de Gaulle recognized this reality, and France stayed in the political organization of NATO, continuing to be a reluctant American ally.

In November 1967, Kremlin leaders celebrated the 50th anniversary of the Bolshevik revolution. They were optimistic. The Soviet economy had improved and continued to grow considerably. Millions of young professionals, engineers, and skilled technicians, educated post-Stalin, joined the workforce, and felt they lived better than their parents. Poverty began to recede, and even peasants, who had long lived like serfs, started buying fridges and TV sets. They were now free to move out of collective farms, send their children to school in the city, and benefit from social mobility. The Soviet economy profited from expanding economic and technological contact with the West as the USSR bought Western technical patents and entire new plants and factories. In 1965, Italy's largest car-making corporation, Fiat, agreed to build a huge plant on the Volga, and the Americans did not object. For technocrats and economic managers in the Soviet Union, this was a harbinger of further such projects to come.

The Soviet military-industrial complex also continued to surprise the world with its achievements. After operating in fits and starts, it finally began serial production of reliable intercontinental ballistic missiles, most of them built in Dnepropetrovsk, Ukraine. At the same time, the Americans stopped the deployment of Minuteman missiles and other strategic systems – they remained at the same level as in the early 1960s. This meant that for the first time the Soviet strategic arsenal could reach the American level, something that had previously been inconceivable. The Soviet momentum for détente, however, was not created by this achievement or by economic interests. It grew out of Kremlin politics. An unlikely coalition emerged in favour of détente: its members were not typical 'doves' and included even some admirers of Stalin. Soviet foreign minister Andrei Gromyko supported détente because he wanted to bring back the time when the Big Three decided the world's future. The new KGB head Yuri Andropov realized that without access to Western technologies the Soviet Union would not overcome its lingering backwardness and in a couple of decades would no longer be a superpower. Both thought that it was possible to reach an understanding with the West without dangerous gambles and while steadily accumulating strength.

There were also much less prominent supporters of détente. In the educated Soviet elites many admired Western science, technology, culture, and consumer goods. They believed détente would help to get rid of Stalinist xenophobia and open Soviet society to the world. The Sino-Soviet split helped détente advocates to hold the line against more orthodox politicians. Mao's warmongering and the folly of his Cultural Revolution discredited those in the Soviet Union who wanted to go the Chinese way. The target of Soviet propaganda in the late 1960s, Maoist excesses reinforced pro-European, pro-Western, humanist sentiments in the Soviet elites.

Still, those who championed negotiations and détente were a distinct minority in the Soviet Union. The bulk of officials, military, KGB, and Party elites had been brought up on a xenophobic diet and Stalin's tenets of inevitable war with the capitalist West. They supported the hard line. Most of the population, living in an information vacuum, feared a new war, yet at the same time slavishly repeated the official patriotic mantra of strength and vigilance. Détente needed a powerful political sponsor.

An Unlikely Peacemaker

Leonid Brezhnev became such a sponsor and a crucial convert from hard line to détente. Having fought in the Second World War, he was colonel-general at the age of thirty-eight. In June 1945 he participated in the victory parade in Red Square. By nature, Brezhnev was conservative, more like a Party bureaucrat than a ruthless communist believer. He lacked Stalin's evil mania and Khrushchev's stubborn energy. He had not truly been exposed to Western politics, culture, and ideas. He was convinced, like countless others in the Soviet establishment, that the enormous power of destruction accumulated by the Soviet Union was all in the service of peace, progress, and stability. And yet, remarkably, he ended up looking at the leaders of major Western powers, above all the United States, as potential partners, not enemies, as he recalled Stalin's cooperation with Western powers in the anti-Nazi coalition in the early 1940s. He held a naive faith that the Cold War could come to an end if he met with key leaders of the West and agreed to preserve peace and punish aggressors. In this he was in sync with the feelings of millions of Soviet citizens who were tired of want, unpredictability, violence at home, and fear of war.[8] A status-quo Soviet bureaucrat at home, Brezhnev turned out to be an architect of peace abroad. A two-faced Janus planted inside the Kremlin.

First Brezhnev had to prove his credentials as a Cold Warrior. This happened in 1968, when the Soviet leadership agonized over what to do about the 'Prague Spring' – as Czechoslovakia had a new leader: Alexander Dubček, a reform-minded communist who embraced liberalization and 'socialism with a human face', with the enthusiastic support of Czech society. When Dubček abolished censorship, the Kremlin leaders shuddered. While Soviet bureaucrats paid lip service to ideology, the regime was rigidly based on total control over ideas and mortally feared free debate. Even under Khrushchev, the KGB arrested 'dissidents' who dared to tell foreign journalists that the Soviet Union was not a paradise of workers and peasants, that national minorities were persecuted, and that the Soviet constitution was not observed. If anyone could say and write what they wanted, what would happen to the Party, the Soviet Union, the entire communist bloc?

Czechoslovakia was peaceful, and Dubček enjoyed huge popularity. For the orthodox thinkers in Moscow, it only made the problem worse. How to stop this quiet 'counter-revolution'? Use military force in the heart of Europe against a small and friendly Slavic country? Brezhnev was instinctively against it. Even those intellectuals who harboured no illusions about the brutal nature of the Soviet regime believed there would be no invasion of Czechoslovakia. Yet the leaders of important Soviet bloc countries, above all Poland's communist leader Gomułka, East Germany's Walter Ulbricht, and Hungary's János Kádár, feared the prospect of a neutral Czechoslovakia. What would then happen to the Warsaw Pact? For some supporters of détente in the Kremlin, the Prague Spring was also a danger. KGB chief Yuri Andropov was convinced: the end of censorship today would produce a revolt like that of 1956 in Hungary tomorrow. Too many influential people, and not only in Moscow, feared a domino effect across the entire bloc, just like their American adversaries in Asia a decade earlier. As always in the Cold War, paranoid fears fed on geostrategic stakes and vice versa. Czechoslovakia was a strategic corridor between West Germany and Ukraine that the Soviets could not afford to lose.

The Prague Spring happened in a vastly different international context than the Polish and Hungarian revolutions of 1956. The United States was bogged down and distracted in Vietnam. Western democratic politics was unstable. Mass dissent rocked American society: campuses saw countless anti-war protests. The student movement converged with a powerful civil rights movement. Cold War liberalism was now split, and many American liberals sided with the civil rights protesters. The anti-communist consensus seemed to have gone up in smoke where it had been rock-solid only a few years earlier.

On 4 April 1968, Martin Luther King was assassinated. Over one hundred American cities experienced violent riots, whole neighbourhoods went up in flames, and troops and tanks were brought in to restore order. Western Europe was also witnessing a revolt as young people embraced the counterculture of sex, drugs and rock and roll. Politically they were inspired by Marx, Mao, Ho, Castro, and Che Guevara. In West Germany and West Berlin, students revolted against police and began to ask why so many ex-Nazis had not been purged. In May 1968, students at the Sorbonne University began to build barricades in Paris, and were supported by French trade unions. Briefly the French capital was paralysed. De Gaulle never recovered from this blow. Suddenly, the West looked inwards and was torn asunder. It was hard for Western politicians at that moment to focus on the Cold War and Czechoslovakia's peaceful revolution.

Brezhnev was agonizing over what to do: the Czech leader whom he called 'Sasha' Dubček was his old protégé; they had chats in Russian. The Soviet leader did not want to ignite a crisis in the centre of Europe. And yet he feared being blamed for losing eastern Europe. He tried to convince Dubček to abolish some reforms, but the Czech leader refused. During these talks, the Soviet leader struggled for sleep and became addicted to strong sedatives. As the pressure from hardliners was becoming unbearable, in August 1968 the Politburo sent the Soviet army to occupy Czechoslovakia. Other eastern European armies joined: 250,000 soldiers in total. It was the biggest military invasion in Europe since the Second World War. The Czech reformist leaders were brought to Moscow and forced to capitulate to Soviet political demands. The Czechs were appalled by the invasion, but their resistance was non-violent. Thousands of them fled to the West. One student, Jan Palach, immolated himself in protest. In the West, the Soviet Union was once again a clear villain, and anti-American radicals in Europe concluded that the Russians were the same reactionary force they had been in the era of the tsars. The French and Italian communist parties declared that they now represented 'Eurocommunism' as distinct from the Soviet totalitarian version.[9]

In the Soviet Union, the impact of 1968 was even deeper than that of 1956. In Moscow, only seven brave dissidents walked out in Red Square to protest the invasion and were quickly arrested. The vast majority were on holiday and indifferent. Yet deep down, the Prague Spring was a mortal blow to the idea of communist utopia. The events of 1968 killed the dreams of those in the educated elites who had hoped to follow the Czech example. The Soviet intelligentsia, particularly literary and artistic figures like Mstislav Rostropovich, Vassily Aksenov, and Lev Kopelev, but also representatives of other fields such as scientist Andrei Sakharov, felt completely alienated from the domestic regime and many began to think of emigration. These developments would have a huge impact on the outcome of the Cold War and on the fate of the Soviet Union.[10]

At the time, however, the Kremlin seemed to be a clear winner. The Cold War balance was preserved, indeed even improved. The unity of the eastern European bloc was reaffirmed. The Warsaw Pact countries, the communist leaders of Poland, Hungary, and East Germany, had joined the invasion. The only exception was Romania, whose leaders, although perfectly Stalinist, had secretly asked the Americans to protect them against a possible Soviet invasion of their country. Romania, however, was lonely and isolated inside the bloc. The only big casualty for Moscow's diplomacy was the upcoming summit with the US president, but Johnson was already in a tough spot: the domestic crisis and Vietnam meant he would not run for re-election. Brezhnev emerged from the crisis with stronger credentials for leadership than before: he proved he was able to preserve the unity of the Soviet camp and defend its frontiers. This gave him the credibility to become a champion of détente.

Brezhnev, though, was not the right person to initiate something new and radical. He needed a Western partner to take the initiative. That would turn out to be the future chancellor of West Germany, Willy Brandt, and his adviser, Egon Bahr; they were to advance a new course that would come to be known as *Ostpolitik*. As mayor of West Berlin, Brandt had been appalled that the Americans did not want to do anything to prevent the division of the city in 1961. In 1965, as the leader of the Social Democratic Party, he argued for 'building bridges' to East Germany and eastern Europe in general. The keys to this, however, were in Moscow. Brandt and Bahr came up with a simple formula: change through trade and rapprochement. The more trade, economic and cultural exchange with the Soviet bloc countries, the sooner these regimes would mellow. This premise did not contradict what George F. Kennan, the American father of containment, had envisaged.

Other developments helped the two potential partners to meet and launch the talks. One was the arrival of Richard Nixon in the White House. The new Republican president was intensely disliked in Moscow as a bedfellow of Joseph McCarthy and an extreme anti-communist. Khrushchev had celebrated Kennedy's victory over Nixon in 1960. Before he assumed high office, Nixon deliberately created an impression that he was mad enough to use nuclear weapons to win the 'war'. And in February 1969, the new American leader ordered a huge bombing campaign in Vietnam and expanded it to Cambodia. The rain of bombs on the small country exceeded the amount dropped by the Allies on Germany during the Second World War. The Politburo feared that this indicated an escalation of war in Asia, with possible reverberations in Europe.

Another development occurred in the Soviet Far East. China's behaviour caused even greater anxiety in Moscow. Mao Zedong directed the energy of his Cultural Revolution against the Soviet Union. From 1965 on, tens of millions of Red Guards across China chanted, 'Death to Soviet revisionists'. The Soviet embassy in Beijing was under siege, subjected to the slow torture of constant drums and loud threats. Mao declared that the Soviet Union had severed Outer Mongolia from China. He also complained that imperial Russia had annexed Chinese territories from Lake Baikal to Vladivostok. In October 1964, China had tested its first atomic bomb in the desert of Lop Nor. And in June 1967, despite domestic turmoil, the first Chinese thermonuclear bomb was detonated. There was growing tension along the Amur and Ussuri rivers that demarcated the Sino-Soviet border. Crowds of Red Guards shouted angrily in loudspeakers across the river at the 'revisionists'. And in March 1969, Chinese military forces ambushed Soviet border guards on Damansky (Zhenbao) island on the Ussuri river; there were casualties on both sides. The Chinese claimed the island was theirs. The Soviets responded with massive artillery fire. A wave of panic swept over Moscow's political leadership and military command. What to do if millions of Chinese were to start crossing the Soviet border? Suddenly, the worst nightmare in the Kremlin was not a crisis in Europe but a war with another nuclear communist power along along one of the longest frontiers in the world.

CHAPTER 9
Brezhnev's Peace Project

Ostpolitik

In October 1969, Brandt became chancellor of West Germany, leading the coalition of Social Democrats and Free Democrats. This was the first defeat for the conservative CDU and CSU, who had adhered for two decades to a policy of *Westbindung*, or alliance with the United States. Brandt immediately contacted the Soviet leadership through a secret channel operated by a KGB operative working under cover. The head of the KGB, Andropov, saw *Ostpolitik* as a big opportunity. He viewed West Germany as a source of technological modernization for the Soviet Union. At first Brezhnev and his colleagues remained cautious. Was Brandt really interested in peace and cooperation? The memory of the Nazi–Soviet pact of 1939 between Hitler and Stalin haunted everyone. Bahr began to fly to Moscow regularly for secret consultations.

It was a complex task, after many years of enmity. Yet Brandt and Bahr won Brezhnev's trust. Brezhnev's foreign policy adviser recalled that it was their great fortune to deal with Brandt, 'a man of crystal integrity, sincerely peace-loving and with firm antifascist convictions who not only hated Nazism but fought against it during the war'. The Moscow Treaty was signed in

August 1970. It was Brezhnev's first great diplomatic success. Both states agreed that they 'have no territorial claims against anybody nor will assert such claims in the future'. West Germany legally abandoned claims to the lost territories to the east of the Oder–Neisse Line which had become part of Poland and the Soviet Union. It was a brave and huge step for Brandt, given that millions of German citizens had been resettled from those territories in 1945 and some still dreamed of returning to their ancestral lands. The Moscow Treaty opened the doors for the Soviets to West German technology and credit. In the following years, German banks funded the largest peaceful enterprise of the Brezhnev tenure: the construction of thousands of

Figure 3.2
Breezy *Ostpolitik*. Leonid Brezhnev, Willy Brandt, and Egon Bahr tour Crimea, 1971.

kilometres of oil and gas pipelines from Siberian oil fields into eastern Europe. The treaty unlocked Brandt's other diplomatic initiatives. In December 1970, West Germany signed the Treaty of Warsaw with communist Poland, recognizing the new borders and easing Polish insecurity.

Ostpolitik worried the US administration. Fortunately, Brandt had strong credentials in Washington, as well as in Moscow. He managed to convince a suspicious Nixon that he was not interested in weakening NATO. The reluctant Americans decided it was better to join the process and shape it from within. They sat down to talk with the Soviets and settled the status of the contested city of West Berlin. This was a particularly desirable goal for Brandt. The four-power treaty, signed in September 1971, also involved the UK and France and confirmed their right to station troops in Berlin, but refrain from the use of force. It was also a masterpiece of subterfuge: the Wall was not mentioned, and the status of West Berlin remained highly vague. Legally, it was neither a part of the Federal Republic nor a free city like Khrushchev had wanted. The agreement did not help those in East Germany who wanted to cross the Wall: it remained one of the most dangerous frontiers in the world, where many defectors were killed by East German border guards almost every week. Still, the isolation of West Berliners became less acute. Most importantly, the treaty greatly reduced the danger of a new international crisis over the divided city.

The last and perhaps most difficult piece in the *Ostpolitik* puzzle was to engage the East German regime. Walter Ulbricht was the man who had leaned on Khrushchev to agree to the Wall; he was a master of playing a weak hand to force the superpower to comply with his wishes. The East German secret police, the Stasi, had a much better intelligence network in West Germany than the KGB, and even had a spy who worked in Brandt's inner circle. Ulbricht resented having Brandt and Brezhnev talk over his head and did everything he could to undermine their plans. *Ostpolitik* wouldn't work in the GDR as long as he was in power. In May 1971, younger colleagues, led by Erich Honecker, eased Ulbricht out of the leadership, with Soviet consent. The two German states signed a 'Basic Treaty' only in December 1972: they now recognized each other and it was even possible for Germans from the West to visit their relatives in the East during state-organized tours. The treaty elevated the East German regime's international status, as it became a member of the United Nations. *Ostpolitik* also allowed transfers of money and goods across the FRG–GDR border, which was of great help for the perpetually stuttering East German economy. There was a special 'money for people' secret deal: the Federal government in Bonn secretly paid a ransom to the East German regime so that relatives of West German citizens trapped in the East could emigrate.

The conservative parties in West Germany, as well as British and American media, sharply criticized Brandt's policies as concessions helping to legitimize the totalitarians of the East. When Brandt kneeled in Warsaw at a monument to a Jewish ghetto eliminated by the Germans in 1943, his critics jeered. The controversy over the Moscow and Warsaw treaties in the Bundestag (the West German parliament in Bonn) was acute. Millions of German voters, refugees from the lost territories, resented the treaties. But the ratification of the treaties – achieved, some say, with the help of Soviet bribes – removed the biggest obstacle to European détente. Germany became the main engine of this process, backed by powerful economic interests. Even the conservatives gradually had to adjust and accept it.

The China Joker

Richard Nixon was a crucial and surprising convert to détente. As a very conservative Republican, he had built his career on anti-communism. In 1968, when he ran for president, he benefitted from all the upheaval in the United States. Many Americans saw the Vietnam war as unwinnable, and their own society heading towards another civil war. The liberalism of Johnson's 'Great Society' programme was collapsing amid polarization and violence. There was bloodshed during the Democratic convention in Chicago, Martin Luther King and Robert Kennedy had been assassinated, and there were constant protests against school desegregation. Nixon successfully appealed to the fears of the 'silent majority' of Americans and won. He knew, however, that Vietnam remained a giant albatross around his neck. The Vietnam War had destroyed Johnson, and now could destroy him too. In 1970, when Nixon ordered the bombing of the Ho Chi Minh Trail in Cambodia and Laos, and then the ground invasion of Cambodia, university campuses across America erupted with anti-war protests. In May 1970, the Ohio National Guard opened fire at Kent State University, leaving four students dead. Students called Nixon a 'baby killer', just as they had recently called Johnson. The best scenario for the White House was an armistice that would allow American troops to go home without losing face. Nixon was cynically prepared to leave South Vietnam to its fate. After many months in Paris at a negotiating table with the Hanoi emissaries, however, the Americans failed to obtain a face-saving deal for the United States. Nixon felt he should capitalize on his hardliner reputation and approach the enemy in a different way.

His national security adviser Henry Kissinger had a strategy. A German-Jewish émigré, Kissinger had taught the history of diplomacy at Harvard, and also made his way into the world of think-tanks and foundations. He was an insider in the national security establishment but had an unconventional approach. He viewed the Cold War through the prism of realpolitik, the art of foreign policy honed by such European 19th-century statesmen as Prince Clemens von Metternich and Otto von Bismarck. For the disciples of this art, the use of power was more important than principles, and treaties and sovereignty were never written in stone. Kissinger's ambitions were sky-high: he wanted to restore what the old establishment had wasted in the jungles of Vietnam, 'to reclaim for the United States its position as the dominant player in world affairs'. In 1969, and Nixon contemplated a 'triangular diplomacy' – a new strategy to achieve a face-saving exit from Indochina. The strategy had two parts. First, manage the growth of Soviet power using various means, including negotiations and détente. Second, bring Mao's China back into international affairs as an American partner. This was a striking revision of the old strategies of containment of communism, without totally ditching their essence. One may say that Kissinger offered a more realistic way to contain the USSR just as American power became gravely limited.

He promised that, with a skilful combination of sticks and carrots, he would be able to manage the rise of Soviet power around the world.[1]

In February 1969, Kissinger met with the experienced and affable Soviet ambassador Anatoly Dobrynin and offered to set up a secret backchannel from the White House to Moscow. No publicity, and even the State Department would be excluded. Kissinger ended up as the sole signal-sender to Moscow; he also decided on how to spin Soviet messages to Nixon. At some point, Nixon made what he believed was an irresistible offer: he would come to Moscow. The Soviet leaders were bemused but pleased with this new mode of communication with the White House. They were not, however, in a hurry to respond to Nixon's offer to hold a summit. And they certainly did not want to sacrifice their Vietnam allies for a deal with the Americans. 'The Russians squeeze us on every bloody move,' Kissinger complained, 'and it has just been stupid.'[2] Simultaneously, Nixon sent signals that he wanted to come to Beijing. This approach, surprisingly, took time. Chinese diplomatic cadres had been decimated by the purges, and foreign minister Zhou Enlai did not have a lot of agency.

Nixon became impatient; his presidency was also threatened by inflation and recession. In August 1971, he surprised the world by announcing the end of the gold standard. The US dollar's convertibility to gold and fixed exchanges between the dollar and other currencies were a pillar of the capitalist order after 1945. Along with the Marshall Plan, this system had contributed to the rapid recovery of global trade and American allies. The military costs of the Vietnam War and consistent trade deficit in the American economic relations with western Europe and Japan, however, made this system untenable. It was a real shock for America's allies; it took years to compensate for the financial volatility it caused.

The US leader needed major foreign policy success before his re-election campaign. 'Just make any kind of a damn deal,' the president told Kissinger. 'You know it doesn't make a goddamn bit of difference. We're going to agree to settle it anyway.'[3] In April 1971, Nixon learned that Mao had consented to meet with him. A strategic reappraisal was taking place in Beijing. The Chinese military were very concerned about revolutionary disarray and the Soviet military concentration in the Far East after border clashes. The presence of well-armed Soviet troops along the Amur and Ussuri and in Mongolia made the prospect of war very real. Chinese strategic wisdom says it is better to be a monkey on the mountain watching how two tigers fight in the valley. China, however, found itself in the position of a much weaker tiger. Mao and his colleagues were also vexed with the Vietnamese communists, who had turned to the Soviets for assistance and advice, after two decades of receiving massive aid from China. The Chinese leaders could no longer press Hanoi to end the war, but Vietnam no longer stood between China and America.

Nixon prudently decided to send Kissinger to Beijing on a secret reconnaissance mission. Kissinger was overjoyed to perform this historic mission: the first US official to enter China since the Americans had 'lost' the country in 1949. He even made sure to be in the pilot's cabin. Kissinger's meeting with Mao in July 1971 became the first gem in his exceptional international career. The ageing revolutionary was no longer in his prime, but was eager to explore what the Americans could offer, particularly against 'Soviet aggression'. Kissinger's 'China opening' became a world sensation. Nixon then announced on television that he was going to Beijing 'soon' to further the cause of world peace.

Suddenly, all the pieces of the US triangular diplomacy clicked into place. Inside Mao's circle, the enemies of rapprochement with the Americans felt ambushed. Marshal Lin Biao, a likely successor to Mao, tried to defect to the Soviet Union; his plane mysteriously crashed on the way. Zhou Enlai, who was in favour of the opening to the Americans, now had Mao's ear, at least for a while.[4] Until this moment, Brezhnev, despite his primacy in the Soviet leadership, had been hesitant to go against his colleagues, who preferred helping Hanoi fight the Americans over 'appeasing' Nixon in Moscow. In August, however, Brezhnev decided to invest his political capital into a rapprochement with Nixon. Brezhnev was shocked by the news of Nixon going to China. He was certain that the Chinese, dangerous and cunning as they were, wanted to entrap the United States in an anti-Soviet cabal. He was determined to fend them off. Besides, Kissinger had taken to asking Dobrynin to send messages from the White House 'personally to Secretary Brezhnev'. Vanity was the Soviet leader's major weakness.

Nixon travelled to Beijing in February 1972. He met Mao, but all talks were conducted by Zhou Enlai. Nixon told the Chinese that American power in Asia was directed only against the Soviet threat, which was in China's interest. Nixon also made a crucial concession on Taiwan, something that probably only he, as an arch-Cold Warrior, could do. The joint Sino-American communiqué stated: 'The United States acknowledges that all Chinese on either side of the Taiwan Strait maintain there is but one China and that Taiwan is a part of China.' The Chinese side offered little in return. Nixon's visit received a lot of coverage around the world, particularly his stroll on the Great Wall and his dinner with Zhou, where he learned to use chopsticks, but it was not the start of a strategic partnership between the two countries. Still, it made an impact. For Japan, South Korea, Taiwan, and Southeast Asia, Nixon talking to the Chinese was a strategic earthquake. And its waves rocked the Kremlin.

Soviet–American détente was the result of changes of heart and fundamental strategic rethinking. It was also the result of luck. Just like with China, Kissinger's triangular strategy failed to get Moscow's assistance in helping the United States to exit Vietnam 'with honour'. North Vietnamese leaders kept demanding that the Soviets send them more military assistance, while completely ignoring their calls for moderation. Still, the American approaches produced other important and lasting outcomes. The opening of China would lead later to a collaboration between the leaders of the capitalist world and the most populous communist country – a phenomenon that would continue for forty years and would outlast the Cold War. With the Soviets, it was arms control and reducing the nuclear threat which became a cornerstone for Moscow–Washington relations. This achievement, however, would not last long.

The Arms Control Mantra

During the 1970s, arms control became almost synonymous with US–Soviet détente. For two decades the world learned a host of acronyms to follow the progress or setbacks of this process: SALT (strategic arms limitation talks), ABM (anti-ballistic missile), ICBM (intercontinental ballistic missile), SLBM (sea-launched ballistic missile), MIRV (multiple independently targetable re-entry vehicle), and their Russian equivalents. The agreement to hold bilateral talks on strategic missiles and bombers had been reached in 1967 in Glassboro. Despite the invasion of Czechoslovakia, the strategic arms limitation talks opened at the end of 1969 in Helsinki. The Americans had a natural advantage: as an open society, they had a vast community of experts, journalists and scientists who had developed a theoretical milieu and jargon of nuclear-strategic studies. The US military complex and nuclear forces remained behind a wall of secrecy, yet the numbers and some characteristics of American missiles and bombers were discussed openly. Even the data on the Soviet build-up of missiles and weaponry, grossly exaggerated at first, became remarkably accurate thanks to space and electronic intelligence.

The Soviets had none of this. Blanket secrecy, zealously protected by the military and the KGB, amounted to total censorship, and knowledge was fragmented. Soviet diplomats knew very little about Soviet missiles and their capabilities, and what they did know came from American open sources. The military understood nothing about international affairs and assumed that nuclear weapons were the means to achieve victory in war; they saw compromise with the Americans as betrayal. Missile designers were consigned to their closed world of secret labs and were not supposed to think about the larger implications of their work. There were, however, several think-tanks in Moscow related to the Academy of Sciences, where experts dealt with international security and carefully studied Western security discussions. In the end, the SALT negotiations, by mutual consent, were based on US data only; the Soviet negotiators accepted this, never disclosing their data or even the in-house names for their missiles. The Soviet idea of strategic arms was decidedly simplistic, without the plethora of doctrines and complex schemes that characterized American strategic culture. The Kremlin and Soviet military just thought that their growing strategic nuclear arsenal entitled them to an equal superpower status with the Americans, which meant sharing the central role in world affairs. The rest was unclear.[5]

American theoretical and informational superiority notwithstanding, both sides had to learn a lot and both had a limited understanding of how to tame the nuclear race. As a British veteran of diplomacy aptly wrote, 'The generals of the nuclear age suffered one immense handicap. They lacked even their predecessors' dubious advantage of being able to plan (often wrongly) on the basis of what they thought they had learned in the previous war.'[6] The same was true of the Americans, despite their bravado and sophisticated jargon. In the Brezhnev Politburo, nobody except for Gromyko and Andropov read about or even thought about security in the nuclear age. Fortunately, there were some scientists who had learned from their Western counterparts, access to their publications and periodic meetings having been made possible by scientific exchanges since the late 1950s. Those scientists formed, as one scholar put it, 'epistemological communities' of experts, the first of the invisible coalitions that would overcome Cold War polarization.[7] Some of those scientists, whose work was central to atomic and missile development, enjoyed Brezhnev's trust.

The hardest issue was to agree on limitations of anti-ballistic weapons. Both the Americans and the Soviets had failed to build a shield against a nuclear attack; the Soviet designers had come to the same conclusions as McNamara in 1969: it was better to reach a certain number of ballistic missiles and then stop and accept the reality of mutual assured destruction. The Soviet military resisted this counterintuitive logic to the end.

The opponents of Nixon's visit in Moscow had other strong arguments. Only recently, in November–December 1971, Washington and Moscow had almost come to direct confrontation, because they backed their respective clients, India and Pakistan, which slid into a brief but calamitous war over East Pakistan (Bangladesh). In the Middle East, the Soviet-backed Egypt was in a low-fire war of attrition with US-backed Israel. And in April 1972, just a few weeks before the scheduled arrival of the US president to the Soviet Union, the North Vietnamese launched another offensive against South Vietnam. Nixon ordered a massive carpet-bombing campaign. Kissinger had to rush to Moscow to answer Brezhnev's concerns and guarantee that the forthcoming summit would be very fruitful. The Politburo hawks were inclined to disinvite the US leader, but Brezhnev was determined to have his summit no matter what.

Nixon finally came to Moscow in May 1972, to sign the agreement on offensive missiles (SALT I) and the ABM treaty to limit anti-missile defence. The Soviet defence minister Andrei Grechko loudly objected: how could one trust the Americans? Brezhnev convened the council of the highest military leaders and said to his war buddy: 'If we make no concessions, the nuclear arms race will go further. Can you give me . . . a firm guarantee that in such a situation we will get superiority over the United States?' Grechko waffled. Brezhnev concluded: 'Then what is wrong? Why should we continue to exhaust our economy, increase military expenses?' The marshal reluctantly dropped his objections, and the treaties were finalized hours before they were officially signed by Nixon and Brezhnev in the Kremlin.

The ceremony of signing the SALT I agreement and the ABM treaty took place in the splendid St Catherine Hall in the Kremlin on 26 May 1972. This was a milestone of diplomacy: the first time in the Cold War when the two adversaries agreed to trust each other to keep a ceiling on their most formidable strategic weaponry. They also agreed on a sort of nuclear concordat, making both sides equally vulnerable to nuclear annihilation. This was the first crowning achievement for US–Soviet arms control communities. The main protagonists had opposing views. Nixon, who had too much to drink on his visit to Beijing, lost his moorings in Moscow completely. He still had doubts about Soviet credibility, but felt that his foreign policy breakthroughs would secure his re-election later that year. Brezhnev was delighted: this was the pinnacle of his career. Two years later, the Soviet leader recalled how he took the surprised Nixon for a one-on-one meeting, out of the earshot of the Politburo and other Americans. Those few minutes, Brezhnev said, were crucial for building trust with the American leader. He accepted what Kennedy seemed to have offered to Khrushchev in 1961: to build a partnership despite their different social systems. There would be a relationship of two equals and no interference in internal affairs. 'A whole series of political and economic agreements had been reached on this basis.' Brezhnev pressed the reluctant American leader to sign a document that had this basic understanding in writing, a mantra of peaceful coexistence.[8]

Naive? Simplistic? Only in hindsight. At the time, the Moscow summit seemed like the dawn of a new era. Many hoped this might put an end to the Cold War. There was a widespread belief, in the West and in the East, that after decades of wasteful and dangerous confrontation the US and the USSR would cooperate and their industrialized economies could even converge. The idea of 'change through trade and rapprochement' was particularly influential. Nixon brought with him to Moscow a group of American corporate leaders, who had been lobbying for decades for a chance to cultivate the huge Russian market. Those in charge of Soviet industries and banks coveted a chance to get American investments and long-term credits. The Soviet leaders even consented, after twenty-seven years of stubborn refusal, to pay back what they owed the US for the lend-lease they had received during the Second World War. They refused, however, to pay the debts incurred by the Russian rulers during the First World War. For a brief moment, it looked as if Soviet citizens would finally drink Pepsi cola and get access to 'made in the USA' products. Few thought about what the Soviets would offer American consumers in return, aside from caviar, vodka, and Siberian furs. It was the high noon of détente.

Summitry and the Idea of Europe

Nixon took full advantage of this peak of détente. In November 1972, he was re-elected as president by a landslide. Earlier he had sent to Congress a package of economic and trade agreements with the Soviet Union, expecting it to be ratified without problems. And in January 1973, Kissinger signed peace accords in Paris with Hanoi that gave the Americans a face-saving pretext for withdrawing American troops. Immediately, the US government cancelled the military draft, eliminating the main reason for students' discontent. Anti-war protests ceased, although the spirit of radicalism that spread among the American educated elites did not go away. The leaders of the doomed

Figure 3.3
Brezhnev is greeted by Kissinger and Nixon in San Clemente, 1973.

Republic of Vietnam affixed their signature as well; they understood that the Americans had let them down. Indeed, the Hanoi communist leaders did not wait long, and began their offensive at the end of 1974. Saigon fell in April 1975, sending millions of Vietnamese fleeing to find refuge across the world, via Thailand and Hong Kong. The Americans evacuated a few of them and abandoned many more to their fate.

Nixon did not enjoy the fruits of his new strategy for long. The break-in at the headquarters of the Democratic Party at the Watergate Hotel, ordered by his staffers, caused a scandal and then a constitutional crisis in the summer of 1973. Nixon denied his involvement, but his cover-up was revealed by investigation, which led to his resignation in August 1974. Neither Nixon nor Kissinger ever took responsibility for the calamitous fall of the Republic of Vietnam.

Brezhnev was also eager to reap the fruits of détente. He directed Soviet diplomats to do their best to convene a European conference on security, which he believed would cement his peacemaking. This idea had originated in February 1954 but had been dismissed by Western statesmen who viewed it as a Soviet attempt to split NATO and drive America out of Europe. Yet even then Soviet leaders wanted to end the Cold War and were looking for an architecture of European security that could replace the division between two blocs and include the Soviet Union. In 1969, in the wake of the invasion of Czechoslovakia, Brezhnev embraced the European project wholeheartedly. Moscow reached out to the Finnish president Urho Kekkonen, who, after some hesitation, agreed to host a conference in Helsinki. In return, Moscow turned a blind eye to Finland's increasing integration into the European Economic Community and promised the Finns preferential trade deals, including cheap gas.

Kekkonen thought Western countries would reject his invitation but the Helsinki initiative gained irresistible momentum. The mood in Europe favoured détente. Historians agree that the turmoil of 1968, from Paris to West Berlin, drove western Europe towards détente.[9] The European security conference gave even the smallest countries of the continent, such as Malta and Liechtenstein, an equal vote with the great powers. The project received support in France and West Germany, and eastern European communist governments were also in favour as they wanted to boost their legitimacy, weakened by the invasion of Czechoslovakia, and had their own economic interests that overlapped with Moscow's designs. After intense talks in Geneva, an agreement was reached to convene a conference of foreign ministers of thirty-three European countries in Helsinki in July 1973. While they shared an interest in economic cooperation, there were also many differences. The Soviets primarily wanted recognition of borders, status quo, and non-involvement in internal affairs. The Western countries, many of them members of NATO and the European Economic Community, promoted permeable borders, free travel of people and ideas, and other civil rights. Normally, the Soviet and eastern European communist governments would have rejected these demands as a threat to their political and ideological control. This time, however, Western diplomats and journalists who covered the process were surprised to see that Soviet diplomats put aside their usual objections and ended up accepting the Western agenda almost without caveats and restrictions. The answer to this riddle was Brezhnev's vanity and impatience. The Soviet ruler wanted to have his conference as soon as possible, to form the crowning achievement of his political career. The KGB and the diplomats who took part in the talks played along.[10]

In the spring and summer of 1973, Brezhnev travelled to West Germany and then to the United States, accompanied by a host of Soviet industrial managers and trade experts. In Bonn, the Soviets signed off on a host of new contracts. West German–Soviet trade and economic relations were starting to take off: Deutsche Bank began to credit the rapid growth of the Soviet oil and gas empire; the pipes for the pipelines were made in the Ruhr. Brezhnev's American visit was not so fruitful. In Washington, no major agreements materialized. Nixon was already under fire because of the Watergate scandal. And American corporations complained about the Cold War legislation that made it difficult to receive longer-term credits and insurance to deal with Soviet markets. Still, the Soviet leader felt more satisfied and confident than before. The Sino-American alliance he feared did not materialize. Brezhnev adored American cars, gadgets, and cowboy apparel. And he could not believe that an American supermarket he saw was genuinely well-stocked for all people at all times. 'They got it prepared for my visit,' he said with a smirk to his subordinates. The Soviet leader, experienced in the Russian practice of staged achievements, refused to believe that modern capitalism had long fulfilled and surpassed communist dreams of mass consumption.[11]

Brezhnev was also eager to implement the Soviet–American partnership in troubled parts of the world. When Kissinger flew to Moscow in May 1973 to prepare for the next

Figure 3.4
Pipes, not missiles... The Soviet gas pipelines from Siberia to central Europe became détente's lasting product.

summit, Brezhnev took him to a hunting lodge: his favourite hobby was to kill boars. There was a lot of drinking involved, but it was a great place for one-on-one conversations, with only a trusted Soviet interpreter, Viktor Sukhodrev. Brezhnev, as Kissinger related to Nixon later, told him: 'Look, you will be our partners, you and we are going to run the world... The President and I are the only ones who can handle things.' Brezhnev then allegedly said: 'We have to prevent the Chinese from having a nuclear program at all costs.'[12]

It is unclear what Brezhnev, probably quite tipsy at this point, meant. The Chinese had already had a nuclear programme for years. Was he contemplating a joint, Soviet and American, pre-emptive strike to disarm the Chinese revolutionaries? There was a curious precedent for this idea in 1963, when Kennedy's emissary Averell W. Harriman broadly hinted to Khrushchev that the Americans would not mind doing it. Then, the Soviet leader had indignantly rejected this offer. Brezhnev could have known about it and ten years later decided to broach it again. Kissinger, who never forgot about trilateral diplomacy, interpreted it as a Russian desire to get the American green light to attack China. With Nixon's consent, he passed this information to the already paranoid Chinese. In his memoirs, Kissinger later asserted that the Soviet Union considered a surprise attack against China.

One Russian–British historian noted that Brezhnev often spoke about 'us, Europeans' when he addressed the United States and NATO members.[13] This was an important reminder that, after all, the Soviet leaders continued to consider their country a European great power. The Soviet Union, whatever one thinks of it, was an ideological structure based on European Marxism-Leninism. Most of its educated elites were embedded in Russian culture, which was European. Brezhnev's 'European' identity rubbed up against the Americans' idea that they themselves were protectors of Europe in the name of a liberal democratic order. The Russian-Soviet idea of Europe that Brezhnev represented was contradictory. Nobody in the Kremlin believed any longer in the communist future of the continent. Rather, the Soviet advocates of détente hoped that the Soviet Union would become part of a new world order centred in Europe. But what kind of order? The Kremlin's imagination, no longer fuelled by revolution or ideology, gravitated to a concert of great powers like in the 19th century. Brezhnev and his comrades viewed the USSR as the second pillar of European security and stability, equal to the United States. Theirs was a profoundly conservative utopia, one which would be dashed by powerful economic, political, and cultural forces that were to transform the world. A new Europe would indeed emerge, but it would be liberal democratic, and radically different from the one Brezhnev and his lieutenants imagined.

CHAPTER 10
A Partnership of Rivals

The Shoals of the Middle East

Brezhnev wanted to test his idea of a joint US–Soviet 'action for peace' in the Middle East. Nasser's successor in Egypt, Anwar Sadat, had bet on war against Israel to escape the shadow of his charismatic predecessor. Sadat had grown tired of his military dependence on the Soviets. He also mistrusted the Kremlin and suspected the Russians would deter him from having his 'victorious war'. In July 1972, Sadat demanded that Soviet advisers leave Egypt. In essence, the Egyptian leader emulated the North Vietnamese by taking Soviet weaponry but refusing to listen to Soviet advice. Soviet leaders and military were confident that another war would lead to another Arab disaster: 1967 had taught them that no matter how many Soviet arms the Egyptians and Syrians had, Israel would win.

Eager to prevent this humiliation, Brezhnev decided to warn his 'friend' Nixon personally. In June 1973, the Soviet leader stayed overnight in San Clemente, Nixon's country house in California. Brezhnev, dependent on sedatives, could not sleep. In a complete breach of protocol, late one evening he asked a shocked Nixon to hold a night meeting. The idea was to talk without Kissinger, whom the Russians suspected of being on Israel's side. During this extraordinary meeting, Brezhnev proposed a joint US–Soviet settlement of the Israeli–Arab conflict as a matter of urgency. Otherwise, he warned, another Israeli–Arab war would break out soon.[1]

This awkward signalling was yet another indication that Brezhnev wanted to leave the Cold War behind and end costly geopolitical games with a superpowers' settlement. It was, however, not something Nixon and Kissinger wanted to do, for domestic and international reasons. The US strategic goal remained the same: to reduce Soviet influence in the Middle East, not to legitimize it. The ghost of falling dominoes in the Middle East continued to haunt Americans, particularly after being forced to leave Indochina. And Kissinger was trying backchannel diplomacy again, this time to mediate between Sadat and the Israeli government. Kissinger, who had just assumed the post of secretary of state, while remaining a national security adviser, was dead set against a mediated peace settlement in the Middle East, unless it was his own doing.

The sixth of October 1973 was the eve of Yom Kippur, the holiest day of the Jewish calendar. On that day, Sadat and his Syrian ally Hafez al-Assad delivered massive two-front surprise attacks on Israeli positions. The US and Israeli intelligence services failed to predict them. The Egyptian army successfully crossed the Suez Canal. For a brief period, the Arabs were triumphant. Israel lost many tanks and its air superiority was not absolute, because Egypt had received advanced Soviet anti-aircraft missiles. Faced with existential danger, the Israeli government contemplated the use of its nuclear weapons. The crisis, and fear to see the Soviet client winning, forced Nixon, already embattled by Watergate revelations, to reverse the previous American policy of appearing neutral in the Arab–Israeli conflict. He ordered a massive air delivery of weapons to the Israelis. Thus resupplied, the Israeli army reversed the course of the war. The overextended Egyptian army was surrounded; Cairo and Damascus suddenly stood defenceless. Sadat changed from an arrogant nationalist to a supplicant: he assaulted Brezhnev with pleas to save him and get a ceasefire by any means possible.[2]

Brezhnev was caught in a bind. The Syrian dictator Assad had warned Moscow in advance that the war was coming. The Soviet leader knew he had no veto over that decision. Sadat and the Arabs were clients who depended on Soviet assistance, yet they had a 'just cause' of reclaiming their territories, Sinai, and the Golan Heights. An open Soviet collusion with the United States at that moment would have scuppered Soviet influence in the Middle East. In other words, the Soviets could not force their Arab clients to give up on their war, just as they could not force the Vietnamese communists. The truth was that Sadat wanted his victory, and only the prospect of defeat could bring him to his senses. Sadat kept the Soviets completely in the dark and did not listen to Soviet warnings that the tide of war might turn soon. And now he wanted to drag Moscow into a world conflict, make Brezhnev sacrifice détente and his partnership with Nixon, in order to rescue the Egyptian leader from the consequences of his own folly. Brezhnev refused to follow Sadat's (and Khrushchev's) playbook. Later Kissinger acknowledged 'our political strategy put [the Soviets] in an awful bind' in the Middle East, but 'they haven't really tried to screw us'. The Americans, however, did not respond in kind. Nixon was binge drinking, reacting to the meltdown of his presidency. This left Kissinger in charge of US foreign policy. And Kissinger was determined to let Israel win decisively. Any loss of Israeli territory for him would have meant a victory for the Soviet Union. And any gain of Egyptian territory by Israel would mean Soviet defeat and a signal to the Arabs to turn to Washington for help. Kissinger dashed to Moscow and negotiated a ceasefire agreement with Brezhnev within twenty-four hours. Desperate to save Egypt, the Soviets did not even push for territorial concessions from Israel.[3]

On 22 October 1973, the UN Security Council approved a joint US–Soviet resolution for a ceasefire. Kissinger, however, played a double game: he signalled to the Israelis that their army could continue to pummel the Arabs for another day, while the US procrastinated. The crisis could have escalated again. The Israelis kept pushing forward in defiance of the UN resolution. Brezhnev collapsed in his hunting lodge after several sleepless nights. Gromyko, Andropov, and the Soviet military then drafted a letter to Nixon wherein they proposed a joint military effort to stop the Israelis. Otherwise, the Soviets reserved the right to act unilaterally. It was certainly a bluff, yet it caused Kissinger to panic: while Nixon was drunk or sleeping, the White House put US nuclear forces on 'DEFCON 3', the highest level of alert since the Cuban Missile Crisis. The Soviet military wanted to retaliate, but Brezhnev and the rest of the Soviet political leadership reacted soberly: they ignored the American alert. The Israelis stopped after all, and the talks began.[4]

Contrary to the views of many Western writers, the Yom

Kippur War did not undermine détente. In fact, it confirmed cooperation between the superpowers as a much preferable option to unilateral action. The prospect of Egypt's and Israel's collapse created high stakes for both sides, and a runaway dynamic, similar to the Cuban crisis. This was stopped only because Brezhnev and Nixon wanted to preserve their partnership and détente. The backchannel talks between Kissinger and ambassador Dobrynin were enormously helpful for troubleshooting. And the joint US–Soviet resolution was a radical departure from Cold War patterns. Brezhnev appreciated it. He continued to support his 'American friend', even as Nixon's presidency was in its inglorious coda. Nixon's resignation in August 1974 was a great shock to his Soviet counterpart: Brezhnev could never fathom the reasons for his partner's downfall and ascribed it to a conspiracy of 'anti-détente forces'.

The aftermath of the war brought more international fame to Kissinger. Sadat sent the Russians packing and turned to the American statesman as a mediator. Kissinger's shuttle diplomacy mapped out the contours of the historic 'land for peace' agreement between Israel and Egypt – a deal that would come to fruition in 1978, after the master of triangular strategy had left the White House. The Soviet Union was cut out of this deal and humiliated. It seemed for a moment that Janus turned its peaceful face to the Middle East. The other face, however, was just changing colour. Egypt ceased to be a champion of pan-Arab nationalism and socialism, and became a breeding ground for a new scourge of the West, Islamic fundamentalism. A group of fanatical officers would conspire to assassinate Sadat as a traitor in 1981.

Human Rights

The concept of human rights was not at the core of ideology and propaganda during the early Cold War. Yet since the start of the great confrontation, the antagonists fought for the heart and soul of mankind by posing as global champions of supreme human aspirations and interests. In 1948, both Washington and Moscow approved the United Nations' Universal Declaration of Human Rights, viewing this document from opposite angles. A prominent historian of human rights concludes that this declaration was 'less the annunciation of a new age than a funeral wreath laid on the grave of wartime hopes' of better humanity.[5] The United States quickly retreated from the language of human rights. They waged the Cold War as a crusade for 'freedom and democracy' against Soviet 'totalitarianism'. But American Cold War ideology and propaganda downplayed or even ignored institutionalized racism, segregation, and discrimination at home. On the other side, Soviet diplomats and propagandists presented the Soviet system as the only system that could bring about 'real rights': social justice, full employment, equality, and freedom from want and fear. Capitalism, the Soviets claimed, was the enemy of the working class and the force behind imperialism and colonialism. American democracy was a sham that concealed the rule of Wall Street and Jim Crow.

One may be surprised to find that the outcome of the hearts-and-minds battle was not clear cut for contemporaries, despite the realities of Soviet terror and gulag camps. Soviet propaganda, however, had a lot of sway around the world. It was not just a big lie: it was a myth. Like all myths, it fed on realities elsewhere. The flaws of Western societies and European colonial empires were not imaginary. American post-war prosperity, the Marshall Plan, and democratic openness contrasted with the societies behind the Iron Curtain. Yet communist states could negate this disadvantage. The closeness of Soviet society, tight censorship, and absence of tourism were the main assets for Moscow; they helped to preserve a mythologized image of Soviet Russia that Churchill famously called 'a riddle wrapped in a mystery inside an enigma'. The Soviet Union had numerous willing promoters, fellow travellers among the leftist intellectuals in the West, who continued to subscribe to Marxian anti-capitalist ideas and imagined the Soviet lands to be the opposite of what they criticized.

Totalitarian myth began to erode after Stalin's death. The revelations of Stalin's horrendous crimes, along with the Soviet invasion of Hungary in 1956, caused splits and defections in the ranks of Western sympathizers and critics of capitalism. But then Soviet propaganda got a new boost with the Sputnik effect, when Moscow vigorously supported anti-colonial nationalism in the Third World, and when the Americans blundered into the war in Vietnam. The watershed came only in 1968, the year of rebellions of students in the West, and of the Prague Spring. Within just a few years, the Soviet Union lost its aura of progressiveness and most of its Western sympathizers. In Poland, Jewish students who still thought as Marxists encountered state anti-Semitism and many of them were forced to emigrate. Suddenly, amidst the bloody war in Vietnam, the West gained new ammunition to attack Soviet communism and even deny it legitimacy. And human rights became the sharp spear-end of this attack.

This remarkable transformation had a preface in Moscow: a tiny gathering of dissidents in Red Square protested against the Soviet invasion of Czechoslovakia and unfolded banners that said: 'For your and our freedom.' The protesters were Moscow intellectuals, 'human rights defenders', who demanded that the government follow the Soviet constitution and enact political freedom. The KGB quickly arrested the group. Yet it was the start of a much more profound shift in Soviet society. Numerous Soviet intellectuals who after Stalin had begun to root for 'socialism with a human face' realized that it was all an illusion as long as the Party was in control. The crumbling of the communist myth among writers, scientists, and other intellectuals created a fertile soil for cultural dissent, Russian and non-Russian. Dissidents viewed the Soviet Union as an oppressor of nations, including Russia. The most illustrious of the human rights defenders was nuclear physicist Andrei Sakharov, the father of the first Soviet hydrogen bomb, who was stripped of his state clearance for his political activities. The best-known promoter of Russian anti-communist nationalism was the writer Alexander Solzhenitsyn, who brought to light the horrors of Soviet camps. And the most active and fearless group consisted of Russified Jewish intellectuals, who decided to break not only with the communist project, but with the Soviet Union – and to emigrate.[6]

The human rights defenders and Jewish intellectuals caught the attention of Western journalists stationed in Moscow. A brilliant group of men (women were still not sent to report from the Soviet Union), they considered Moscow 'the Everest' of international reporting and became very involved with public Soviet dissent. American and British journalists, some of them of Jewish descent, came to admire the heroism of dissidents and Jewish people who discovered Zionism and wanted to emigrate. The secret police continued to surveil foreigners and their meetings, yet journalists took risks to meet with courageous non-conformist intellectuals and dissidents. They ended up looking at the Soviet Union through their eyes. And with those journalists' assistance, a tiny network of dissidents made their message heard across the world.

The reporting from Moscow led to strong public support in the West for Jewish emigration from the Soviet Union. In June 1970, a group of Soviet citizens plotted to hijack a Soviet aircraft to fly to Israel. Most of the plotters had grown up in the Baltic states, where Zionism had had deeper roots until 1940–41. They, like the Moscow intellectuals, were galvanized by Israel's victory of 1967 and all the revelations about the Holocaust. The KGB arrested the plotters. The leaders were sentenced to death; others received long prison sentences. The 'aircraft affair' caused an international uproar: Western media and Jewish organizations presented it as a case of Soviet anti-Semitism. Soviet discrimination against 'people of Jewish nationality' had indeed been multifaceted since Stalin's post-war campaigns. This time, however, it was a broader issue that united many in the United States: those who sympathized with Israel, the new generation of educated American Jews, who were proud of their Jewishness, and allied liberal civil rights activists across the US and on university campuses. What brought them all together was the fact that the Holocaust was starting to be seen as the central event in modern European and world history.

All this threatened Brezhnev's détente. The international uproar surprised and upset the Soviet authorities. They commuted the harsh sentences of the Jewish would-be plane hijackers. The KGB chief Andropov came up with a way to avoid similar scandals: allow the limited emigration of Jews from the Soviet Union. Those with Jewish backgrounds who had sensitive jobs, particularly in the military-industrial complex, were refused their exit visa – they became 'refuseniks': blacklisted, unable to find jobs. And those who received the coveted 'yes' to emigrate were asked to pay a 'diploma tax' to compensate for the costs of their state-funded higher education. One way or another, it was a mess: a blow to the mythology of 'the happy family of peoples' who resided in the Soviet Union. Wasn't everyone supposed to feel happy to live in the motherland of communism? And why were Jewish people the only ones allowed to emigrate? Still, Brezhnev approved this wave of Jewish emigration, so long as it remained quiet and helped to proceed with détente. In addition, the new policy helped the KGB to get rid of the most vocal domestic critics of the regime, some of whom were Jewish. The secret police gave them a choice between emigration to Israel and possible imprisonment. Israeli officials, eager to attract as many educated Soviet Jews as possible, quietly provided invitations and false credentials for all would-be émigrés.

The issue of Jewish emigration made headlines in America alongside reports about heroic Soviet dissidents. The campaign in support of Soviet Jews helped to regain the moral high ground, and resonated with millions of US citizens whose ancestors came from eastern European countries and Jewish shtetls. Soon a broad political alliance emerged in the United States: a growing coalition of politicians as well as religious, cultural, and other groups rallied to demand freedom for Soviet Jewry. The same people demanded to place human rights at the forefront of the US foreign policy agenda. The crusade against détente and for human rights marked another phase in the American cycle of attraction to and alienation from the Russians. The failures in Vietnam and the Watergate scandal had undermined American idealism and the country's sense of exceptionalism. Americans needed to reinvent their national greatness and global mission. As at several times in the past, the Americans supported a crusade that helped them restore their sense of moral superiority – over Soviet communism, over the Russians, and in the world at large. Promoting human

Figure 3.5
The US campaign for the emigration of Soviet Jews led to a clash between human rights and détente, 1973.

rights helped the American political elites to overcome the Vietnam syndrome – i.e. the loss of confidence, stemming from that conflict, in America's right to use force abroad and promote its way of life globally – and become once again a shining beacon of freedom and democracy for the whole world. Indeed, 'the human rights revolution' was a new and highly successful transnational ideology for the entire West.[7]

In American politics more generally and in Congress specifically, Jewish human rights activists and liberals found themselves on the same side as Republican religious conservatives and Cold Warriors of all stripes: all of them regarded Nixon's détente with the Soviet Union as morally wrong. They did not want to grant legitimacy, nor American credit and goods, to the Soviet regime. Senator Henry Jackson, the ambitious frontrunner for the Democratic Party's presidential candidate, was laser-focused on human rights and criticizing the idea of détente. He introduced an amendment to the US–Soviet trade package which stated that any country that wanted tariff-free commerce with America had to grant its citizens the right to emigrate. That was a stake through the heart of the Soviet project of economic and technological cooperation with the United States. The historical irony was that it happened at the same time as Brezhnev ended the emigration exit tax and let Jewish emigration grow from a few hundreds to almost 30,000 people a year; the Soviet leader also 'recommended' the KGB restrain its harassment and persecution of dissidents and nationalists. Another irony was that at the same time the United States wanted to expand its trade and contacts with China, a country with a much more repressive regime and much worse record of human rights abuses.

Human rights politics was a sudden threat to the Nixon–Kissinger strategy of foreign policy. Congress and human rights activists looked to replace the 'carrot'-based policy offering American credit, technologies, and goods with a 'stick', punishing the Soviets for their authoritarian regime. There was no way the Soviet Union would accept Jackson's humiliating deal. The Jewish question left Brezhnev squeezed between his willingness to pursue détente and his conservative policies at home. He could not afford to change his domestic rules under US pressure, particularly after he and Nixon had pledged to respect each other's political systems and treat each other as equals. During his confidential conversation with Kissinger in May 1973, Brezhnev had begged the Americans to understand the dynamics of Soviet politics. 'Do you know what your people are doing?' he had asked him. In the eyes of the Russian majority and more conservative Soviet elites, Jewish people were already the privileged group: the best educated, living in the big cities. 'No one else receives an exit visa,' Brezhnev concluded, 'and [if] you people keep humiliating us, you're going to create the worst [wave of] anti-Semitism ever in the Soviet Union.'[8] Kissinger tacitly agreed with Brezhnev's logic: the only realistic way to help Soviet Jews was through secret diplomacy, not public declarations. Yet he and Nixon, whose authority had been destroyed by Watergate, could do nothing to stop Jackson and his supporters. As the US president resigned in August 1974, Congress approved the US–Soviet trade bill with the Jackson amendment.

The Brezhnev Politburo and Soviet officials grossly underestimated the challenge that the Jewish question posed for them. And they remained blind to the power of the 'human rights revolution'. The chief Soviet diplomat Gromyko viewed human rights activism as a passing distraction for realist statesmen (this was what Kissinger thought as well). The focus of Soviet policies of détente remained, as before, on security and economic interests. After Nixon's resignation, Brezhnev immediately invited his successor, Gerald Ford, to a summit meeting in Vladivostok. Brezhnev went out of his way to make up for the loss of his erstwhile partner in the White House. He urged Ford to consider not only limitations, but reductions of nuclear weapons. And he was serious, ready to confront his own military to make it happen. The détente process weighed heavily on the Soviet leader; his health became extremely fragile as years of dependency on sedatives took their toll. Brezhnev collapsed on the last day of the summit. He recovered, but his mental and emotional state were changed. Kremlin medicine could help him only so much. From 1975 on, he acted as a sick leader who could no longer steer the huge vessel of the Soviet state and its foreign policy.

In the summer of 1975, the Politburo discussed the draft of the Helsinki Final Act, the key document to be signed by thirty-three European countries, including the Soviet Union, as well as by the United States and Canada. This was Brezhnev's dream coming to fruition. Many Politburo members, however, were horrified to find out that Soviet diplomats had made concessions on key points of the Western human rights agenda. All 'three baskets' of the Act, dedicated to security, economy, and human contacts, adopted Western formulas of political freedoms at the expense of the traditional Soviet interpretations. Some Politburo members professed horror, but

Gromyko and Andropov knew Brezhnev wanted to have his conference. They provided irrefutable arguments for Brezhnev's trip to Helsinki. The Conference on European Security and Cooperation, Gromyko claimed, was like the Congress of Vienna of 1815, where the Russian tsar led the original Concert of Europe. With a nod to the KGB, he suggested that 'we remain the masters of our own house'. On 1 August 1975, Brezhnev, visibly aged and with slurring speech, added his signature to the Final Act. He was happy as a child to see his dream fulfilled.[9]

Was it really Brezhnev's triumph, or a fatal error? Historians, always wise in hindsight, claim that the new European norms helped to erode Soviet legitimacy and led to the end of the communist regimes in eastern Europe and in the Soviet Union itself. The Soviets hoped to boost their sovereignty by having international legitimacy, yet in the end got increasing pressure to subordinate their sovereignty to international norms generated in the West. The Helsinki process would later influence Mikhail Gorbachev's choices and strategy of exiting the Cold War.[10] There is a touch of triumphalism in this narrative, but also some truth. Still, we know today that Brezhnev's ambition to have a 'Concert of Europe' backfired, and his belief in a bilateral partnership with Washington proved to be elusive. The Final Act became indeed the foundational text of a new Europe, yet not what the Soviets had hoped to see. Human rights, enshrined in the document, became a scripture of internationalist liberalism. It was increasingly adopted by Western government institutions and instrumentalized by a proliferating number of transnational and non-government organizations.

Across western and eastern Europe, intellectuals turned away from Marx, Lenin, and Mao and began to preach human rights and minority rights. The KGB's games with dissidents also boomeranged. Calibrated emigration helped to reduce the ranks of domestic dissidents, but Sakharov stayed in Moscow and set up the Helsinki Watch Group to monitor Soviet violations of human rights. Solzhenitsyn also refused to emigrate and published, in the West, the most important anti-communist book of the decade, *The Gulag Archipelago*. In October 1975, Sakharov received the Nobel Peace Prize. Solzhenitsyn had become a Nobel laureate for literature five years earlier. In February 1974 the KGB arrested him and forcibly deported him to the West. Many other dissidents chose an Israeli visa or emigration to the West. But they were not silenced. Instead, many of them found employment at the US-funded Radio Liberty in Munich. People who were known at home by a small circle, whose writings were typed up and passed from person to person at great risk, now had a powerful platform to speak to millions of Soviet people, who had short-wave radios at home. It was a much more serious challenge to the Soviet propaganda machine than the US could have ever produced on its own.

Visible Cracks

In July 1975, the US and Soviet spaceships Apollo and Soyuz successfully docked 200 kilometres above the Earth. Three American astronauts and two Russian cosmonauts greeted one another in two languages. On the ground, however, the golden age of Soviet–American cooperation was about to end. After Watergate, US foreign policy could not be separated from politics and kept autonomous from Congress. The host of Democrats elected to Congress in 1974 lashed out at realpolitik, denounced the CIA's covert operations and assassination attempts, and wanted, in cooperation with journalists, to make the national security state more transparent. In both political parties, pro-détente voices became silenced by critics and advocates of the human rights agenda.

In the presidential campaign of 1976, President Ford ran for re-election and was already in trouble for granting a pardon to Nixon, whom many wanted to see in the dock. Under a barrage of criticism, Ford stopped using the word 'détente', a symbolic and significant change in American political discourse. His opponents included another Republican, the governor of California, Ronald Reagan, and Henry Jackson, who ran as a Democrat. They argued that the détente policy was in Soviet, not American interests, and helped legitimize Soviet 'colonization' of eastern Europe and expansion in the Third World. A little-known Democratic governor of Georgia, Jimmy Carter, did very well by promoting a new idealist agenda of human rights, morality and transparency in foreign policy. While Ford refused to meet with Solzhenitsyn, who had been deported from the Soviet Union, Carter promised to consult with Soviet dissidents in conducting diplomacy with the Soviet Union. In November 1976, Carter was elected as the next president. In January 1977, in his inauguration speech, the new president said: 'Our commitment to human rights must be absolute.'

The success of détente until 1975 owed largely to the political and economic turmoil in the West, the US failure in Vietnam, and the rise of a new politics that attacked the conservative pillars of American society. It was also the era when mutual assured destruction and nuclear war were at the forefront of public consciousness. A cohort of senior statesmen in France, West Germany, and the United States decided for different reasons to treat the Soviet Union as a partner in the post-Cold War order. And Brezhnev, despite all his limitations, turned out to be a surprisingly responsible and willing partner. By 1975, however, another crop of leaders came to view détente as a flawed project. Now those who wanted to end the Cold War wanted to do so based on liberal values and norms, not through compromises and deals with the Soviet regime. And those who had never supported détente began to emphasize its contradictions and frustrations; they argued for a return to the 'moral clarity' of the Cold War, as a choice between 'freedom and totalitarianism'. Anything else, they said, jeopardized American identity, the unity of US-led alliances, and the West as a whole.

Carter criticized détente, but he also strongly wanted to negotiate and reach agreements with Moscow. He promised 'a fresh start', even though he also refrained from using the word 'détente'. Acting on best intentions but unwisely, he decided against using the secret diplomatic backchannel so vital earlier. And he listened to détente critics, especially the experts who argued, quite falsely, that Nixon and Kissinger had made unjustified concessions to the Kremlin, and that now the Soviet strategic arsenal was bigger and mightier than the American one. Those experts proposed 'deep cuts' on the biggest missiles, which happened to be mostly Soviet. The Soviet leadership, however, was not in the mood to adapt to the constantly changing American leadership and policies. Brezhnev was not capable of dedicating more than a couple of hours a day to state affairs; day-to-day policy increasingly fell to his duo of trusted lieutenants, Andropov and Gromyko, who were, respectively, the main interpreter of international affairs and the chief of national security bureaucracy. It was a significant problem, because in the Soviet system only the head of the Party, who also had the role of commander-in-chief, could come up with bold policy innovations.

Combined, these factors turned Carter's well-intentioned diplomatic debut into a debacle. The new secretary of state, Cyrus Vance, who replaced Kissinger, came to Moscow to propose the recommended deep cuts on nuclear arms, including the biggest Soviet ballistic missiles, each of which could carry ten warheads. The Americans, who had nothing similar to cut, only promised they would not deploy some of their systems. Brezhnev, briefed on this, was scandalized. Earlier, he and Kissinger had negotiated a complex formula of mutual concessions; now Carter was offering something that was completely unacceptable to the Soviet military. Notably, the Americans offered no incentives as part of their new package.

The Kremlin rulers suspected the worst. Vance was a well-meaning person yet he was received so poorly in Moscow that he later said it was like 'a wet rag in the face'. Brezhnev read him the riot act about violations of the spirit of détente and of basic agreements between the two superpowers. Human rights were a key cause for Soviet anger. Carter had begun his presidency by sending a letter not to Brezhnev, but to the Soviet rights defender Sakharov. In response, the KGB arrested three dissidents who, together with Sakharov, formed the Helsinki Watch Group in Moscow. Others were forced to emigrate. Carter doubled down by inviting to the White House another dissident, Russian anti-communist Vladimir Bukovsky, whom the Soviet press referred to as a 'hooligan'. The Americans occupied the moral high ground, but it was a highly inauspicious start. Brezhnev coldly informed Carter that he would not be ready to meet him until the arms control treaty was agreed on mutually acceptable terms. Without Brezhnev's personal input, the talks stalled or proceeded at a bureaucratic (snail's) pace. Brezhnev and Carter met only in June 1979. By then the US–Soviet rivalry reared multiple heads in many areas – above all in the Third World.

The Crisis of Arms Control

A leading Cold War scholar has described the late 1970s as the years when détente was 'defeated'.[11] But détente was untenable in the long term because the United States and the Soviet Union could be partners only briefly when the interests and ambitions of their top leaders overlapped. Cold War thinking, despite Nixon and Brezhnev's bizarre partnership, remained strong on both sides. Many in Moscow and certainly in Washington continued to view the international power struggle as a zero-sum game, where each side could either win or be defeated. Most of the Soviet military and Party-state elites had continued to believe that might made right. Some in the United States agreed. So long as Brezhnev endorsed détente, Soviet hardliners preferred to give lip service to 'the great struggle for peace'. In the United States, with its competitive system and the fiascos of foreign policy, the idea of winning the Cold War was unavoidable. The Americans were accustomed to victories, not defeats. The failure in Vietnam and the chaotic evacuation from Saigon in April 1975 had magnified the national identity crisis. In American binary thinking, if the United States was losing, then the Soviet Union had to be winning. American moralism, exceptionalism, paranoia, and domestic politics prevailed. Claims of Soviet superiority and plans to 'conquer the world' became new certainties, and those certainties necessitated new policies. American hardliners did not imagine the Soviet threat, but they grossly exaggerated it.

The best example of this mindset is the story of the 'Committee on the Present Danger' (CPD), a group of veterans of the Cold War who viewed détente as a Soviet plot to gain superiority, and bashed Kissinger's strategy. One of the members, Paul Nitze, was the author of the most alarmist and militant version of containment of the Soviet threat, adopted in 1950. Harvard historian Richard Pipes, another member, viewed the Soviet regime as immutably aggressive. Richard Perle, Senator Jackson's assistant, regarded arms control talks as 'a Soviet trap'. Their message to the Americans was that Kissinger and the CIA were naive and underestimated the Soviet danger. Many of them would later join the Reagan administration.

In May 1976, pressured by the anti-détente camp, Ford agreed to have another strategic exercise to evaluate Soviet power and intentions. This was the first such exercise since Eisenhower's 'solarium project' of 1953. The CIA and government officials formed Team A: they concluded that the two superpowers were roughly equal and that Moscow was not interested in actively promoting communism around the world. Team B consisted of the CPD experts and concluded that the Soviets were superior, wanted to defeat the United States and were prepared, if necessary, to wage a nuclear war.[12]

Today nobody takes the conclusions of Team B seriously. True, the Soviet military-industrial complex was at its peak in the 1970s. Several millions of scientists, designers, and qualified workers worked in Moscow, other major cities, and almost fifty 'closed cities' built exclusively around secret installations and labs. Yet the Soviet Union was not the superior and aggressive juggernaut the American Cold Warriors imagined. American journalists reported from Moscow that the Soviet society and economy suffered too many problems. This was a welcome message, but it was ignored. The evidence from Soviet memoirs and archives gives a complicated picture: the KGB kept expanding its operations around the world and continued to bank on the post-Vietnam surge of leftist, socialist, anti-Western sentiments in Latin America, Africa, Asia, and Europe. One expert in the Party's International Department even recalled in an interview: 'The world was going our way.' At the same time, the ideological spirit that animated Soviet expansionism was already hollowed out, replaced by a chauvinist, jingoist mentality. There was none of the early revolutionary and anti-imperialist fanaticism that had fuelled the earlier struggle. Much of what the KGB did, particularly in the Third World, was used to pander to Brezhnev's vanity by sending 'good news' up the bureaucratic pipeline.[13]

In terms of the military, the CIA's views were closer to the mark. Soviet military and missile designers continued to operate in conditions of technological and financial inferiority compared to their American colleagues. American military systems and particularly control and communications were better, more precise, and more efficient than their Soviet counterparts. In the 1950s, American hardliners had shouted about 'Soviet superiority', but at least back then they had no access to space intelligence. This time, however, plenty of intelligence existed, including much gained via human sources, recruited agents inside the KGB and the GRU, and yet the myth of 'Soviet superiority' came back with a vengeance. Such was the power of worst-case scenarios. There was no McCarthyism this time, yet the advocates of détente ran the risk of being accused of gullibility and lack of vigilance.

These exaggerated fears greatly complicated and slowed down the arms control negotiations. Everyone knew that the negotiated treaty (what would become SALT II) would be scrutinized in Congress by many critics and enemies. As a result, the American side asked for foolproof verification methods, including inspections of Soviet missile bases carried out by the US military. The Soviet military were adamantly against this, ever paranoid about revealing their secrets. The two sides got bogged down in technical details of how to read radio signals and telemetry, and monitor compliance with the treaty in any other way. This was the work of a few classified experts, not the public. In the West, public expectations and support for arms control started to flag.

Liberal Capitalism's Hardships

The 1970s was a decade of many ambiguities, especially in terms of the international economy, trade, and finances. After two decades of robust economic and trade growth, crucially backed by US power and money, Western countries surpassed the levels of prosperity and mass consumption they had enjoyed before the world wars. Yet the end of the gold standard in 1971 introduced a decade of weak growth and high inflation. The most acute phase of this started in 1973, as a result of the Yom Kippur War and the US support of Israel. Infuriated by another Israeli victory with American assistance, Saudi Arabia and Arab sheikdoms in the Gulf declared an embargo on oil exports to the United States and other countries who supported Israel. Since the 1960s, the Gulf petrostates had been part of the Organization of the Petroleum Exporting Countries (OPEC), but could never work effectively as a cartel. This spontaneous embargo caused the biggest global energy crisis of the century. The price of oil quadrupled, from $3 to $12 per barrel, causing severe and lasting shocks to Western economies and the rest of the world. The end of 'cheap energy' in the US caused long queues for gasoline and calls to do without Christmas lights, before the economy absorbed the shock. This new situation, just like the ignominious American exit from Vietnam, seemed to mark the decline of American and Western power. From that time on, Cassandra cries of 'US decline' became a standard feature of Western debates. Some propagandists and even KGB experts in Moscow gladly translated those debates for the Brezhnev leadership.

Despite these shocks, capitalism was becoming truly global while the United States, and broadly speaking the collective West, held most of the levers and assets. From Latin America to the Middle East, globalization continued to spread. The tide was in favour of international capitalism, not the Soviet

Union and communism. This globalization put paid to the hopes of leftist and socialist-leaning economists that the collapse of colonial empires would bring about a more just and fair economic order. The opposite happened: the western European, Japanese, and North American producers and exporters of sophisticated products and services had more and more edge and leverage over those in the global south who traded raw materials. The global market and trade worked in the same way as in any context of unregulated capitalism: it enriched the global metropolitan city and exploited the global periphery.[14]

Thinkers from the Third World, like Argentinian economist Raúl Prebisch, proposed to reduce the fatal inferiority of the global south by developing local industries that could 'substitute' for expensive imports from the developed West. Such schemes worked on paper better than in reality. The global market served the interests of the elites in the global south who exported raw materials and invested their wealth in the north. They were not interested in change. The aftermath of the OPEC embargo and oil shock of 1973 demonstrated the power of capitalist hierarchy, with the United States on top. This shock only confirmed the global centrality of the US dollar, despite the end of the Bretton Woods system. Kissinger's meetings with the Saudis and the Gulf sheikhs helped get oil flowing again. OPEC agreed that oil trading should continue to be denominated only in US currency. As foreign holders of huge amounts of US bonds and stocks, the petrostates had to import US goods and to invest petrodollars back into the US economy.

In the decades to come, the colossal money earned by the

Saudi Arabian royal family and the sheikhs of the Gulf generated rapid development of the Gulf states – turning them from desert landscapes into oases of conspicuous consumption. Flush with petrodollars, Western financial institutions began to lend to Third World countries at very low interest. As détente took hold in Europe, a lot of money was offered by Western banks to eastern European governments such as those of Poland, Hungary, and Romania, who were eager to increase their ties outside the Soviet bloc. In just a few years, this would produce fatal dependencies of whole regions on Western banks.

The Soviet Union was also a beneficiary of this economic shock, albeit a marginal one. The Soviet budget reaped tens of billions of US dollars in increased oil prices. Some of this money was invested into industrial plants built with the help of West German, French, and American companies. Yet the impact of the oil windfall on Soviet economic modernization was limited. A large portion of revenues went into the construction of Soviet oil and gas pipelines; the Soviet Union embarked on the road of becoming the largest supplier of energy for Europe. Its dependence on Western technologies and materials, including large-size gas pipes, grew considerably.

The systemic failures of Soviet agriculture, especially around the production of protein, made Moscow import increasing amounts of grain, to feed cattle and to make cheap bread available to people. It became an endemic form of dependency. In 1977, the Soviet Union had to purchase urgently over 11 million tons of wheat to avoid food disruptions. It was a painful demonstration of woeful inefficiency: decades after the Soviet Union collapsed, the same fertile lands of Ukraine and southern Russia would produce enough grain for domestic consumption and also to feed millions of people abroad. Economists later concurred that much of the Soviet oil revenues were 'eaten' in this way. A considerable part of this money also went into maintaining the Soviet 'external empire': Moscow sent a lot of crude oil to its satellites, to meet their energy needs and as a substitute for the hard currency that the Soviets never had enough of; this helped sustain the budgets of the communist regimes of eastern Europe, Cuba, Vietnam, and other countries of 'socialist orientation'. The petrodollars also encouraged the Soviet military and KGB to expand their operations in other parts of the world, such as Africa, where they wanted to compete with their American adversaries.

Soviet Pessimism

Soviet society did not convulse like the West in the late 1960s and early 1970s. Everything looked quiet, as if half asleep. Yet Western observers and journalists noticed a change from Soviet optimism in the 1960s to a new pessimism. Life became much better during the first decade of Brezhnev's rule: no more famine, no more workers' revolts over the absence of basic goods in stores. What was the reason, then, for this pessimism? It came from a growing gap between promises and performance. Soviet people had been accustomed to queueing to buy bread and other products. Now, basic products were available. And yet the queues in shops became longer and longer. And they were different: they were usually for quality food and quality products that Soviet consumers wanted, but which were always in short supply. People in Soviet cities behaved increasingly like consumers in Europe, but in the absence of private trade and retail markets, the Soviet planned system was bound to frustrate Soviet consumers. Moscow became the hub for the best supplies, so millions of Russians had to go to Moscow, travelling by train and bus, to buy the sausages and cheese they could not find in their provincial stores. Everyone envied Muscovite standards. The Muscovites, in turn, envied the Poles, the Czechs, and the Hungarians, who had decent restaurants and cafés, and even some elements of nightlife and mass culture that were missing in frugal, spartan Moscow. Naturally, the eastern Europeans envied those who lived across the Iron Curtain in the West.

This consumerist envy boded ill for the Soviet Union and its camp. Earlier, the Russians had felt pride in their space exploits, the Bolshoi ballet, and socialist experiments. Increasingly, they felt inferior to everyone around them, even the people on the western borderlands of the Soviet Union, such as Ukraine's Lvov and Odessa, as well as the Baltic republics, who had better access to coveted Western imports and mass culture. Soviet youth felt this inferiority most acutely. Western rock music took young people by storm and Soviet censorship was unable to block Western cultural influences. One scholar, who was born in Leningrad and later became an anthropologist in Berkeley, noted that Western goods and mass culture did not foment anti-Soviet dissent. Rather, it made everything 'Soviet' unpopular among the youth, synonymous with shoddy, dated, and decidedly uncool. Young people no longer wanted to be associated with the Soviet experiment: they wanted to exist *vnye* – outside it.[15]

In the early 1970s both global secular faiths, the American dream and the Soviet communist model, revealed their limitations and problems. In many countries in Asia, Africa, and Latin America, attempts to find a third way yielded disappointing results. Many began to combine communism and capitalism into the concept of the 'global north' that only played games with the Third World, which was now called the 'global south'. After some landmark successes, American and Soviet aid, not to mention small Chinese programmes of development, produced more frustration, miscoordination, and corruption than tangible results. Most of the countries that aspired to jump from the bottom to the middle of the supply and production chains remained largely where they were. In a few places in Asia, such as Taiwan, Singapore, and South Korea, this realization turbocharged home-grown strategies of development that combined some practical elements from market capitalism and discarded American and Soviet ideologies of development. Their strategies would have spectacular success as the decade progressed.

In 1974, American sociologist and economic historian Immanuel Wallerstein published the first part of his study *The Modern World-System*, which put a new spin on the economic theories of Riccardo and Marx. The world economy, Wallerstein wrote, has its core in the West, where most of capital, skilled labour, and other capitalist and trade assets are concentrated. The south remains on the periphery. Most interestingly, Wallerstein wrote about the Soviet Union and its allies and clients as occupying the 'semi-periphery' of the capitalist global system, not an alternative economic world based on socialist distribution and the absence of exploitation. Instead of weakening global capitalism, the communist countries struggled and competed with each other to find a place in the 'world-system'. According to Wallerstein, the Soviet Union industrialized itself without Western investment, by using the resources of its population, ruining the peasantry and applying political coercion and regulation. This road of development, however, could produce only second-best products and enduring dependence on Western technologies. Soviet assistance to China, and Soviet projects in India and Egypt only proved the rule. Market dynamism, competition, and investments remained the main drivers of prosperity.

CHAPTER 11
The Destruction of Détente

A Latin American Cold War

Latin America never had a deficit of revolutionary energy. Many young radicals were inspired by the Russian revolution, as well as the Mexican revolution, and more recently, by that of Cuba. In October 1967, however, dreams of violent revolutionary change suffered a symbolic blow, when the Bolivian military caught and executed Che Guevara. An Argentinian doctor who became a great revolutionary and a comrade-in-arms of Fidel Castro, Che Guevara was very keen to export the Cuban revolution across Latin America. But the Cuban revolution would not be exported. This was, in part, due to the mobilization of ruling elites in many Latin American countries: the few who possessed land, water, raw materials, and money. It was also because of those countries' militaries with strong connections to the United States and a strong tradition of *pronunciamento*: overthrowing democratically elected governments and forming terrorist juntas. For a long time, the United States tolerated and even encouraged this; a widespread, racist view among American foreign policy elites was that 'Latinos were not ready' for democratic self-governance. In the words of one eminent historian, while

Figure 3.6
Fear of 'another Cuba' in Latin America. Police in Chile before the coup against Allende, 1973.

the Americans built 'an empire by invitation' in Europe, in Latin America they 'studied how to execute imperial violence through proxies'.[1]

This background explains in part the tragic outcome of the last attempt to promote socialism by peaceful and legal means. In Chile, the moderate socialist Salvador Allende won democratic and fair elections in 1970. The middle classes were split between the pro-US and pro-socialist parties. The workers voted for Allende. The socialist government established diplomatic relations with Castro's Cuba and began to talk to the Soviet Union about assistance. The radical reforms of this government threatened American-controlled businesses in Chile, especially the export of copper. In Washington, Nixon and especially Kissinger viewed the Allende government as a geopolitical danger. The US president's reaction to Allende's election is described by one historian: '"That son of a bitch," screamed Nixon. When the president noticed his startled ambassador to Chile, he calmed down and said, "Not you, Mr. Ambassador . . . It's that bastard Allende."'[2] The Nixon administration had no doubt that Chile, like Cuba earlier, would fall into the Soviet orbit.

Allende's government, the product of an unprecedented broad coalition of leftist parties and forces, adopted a foreign policy of 'reasoned rebellion' against the US-centred international order, in defiance of American political and economic recipes. The goal was to fight for a 'New International Economic Order' that would make the distribution of wealth fair towards the global south. In 1971, Allende nationalized Chile's copper industries that benefited American interests and the local oligarchy. Very soon after the nationalization,

Chile began to slide into an economic crisis, and then experienced economic collapse. It is not clear to what extent American subversion and CIA covert operations exacerbated the internal crisis in Chile. While Nixon's concerns turned to Watergate in 1973, Kissinger actively conspired with those on Chile's right who held land, water, and resources, along with the military, to encourage an anti-constitutional coup by the military. Much of the disaster, no doubt, was the result of Allende's radical and well-meaning, but misguided reforms that shattered the economy and sowed social unrest. In September 1973, the head of the Chilean army, General Augusto Pinochet overthrew the socialist government. Allende was killed, and the military unleashed a 'white terror' against the left, killing 3,000 and torturing and sending into exile about 300,000 civilians. The Nixon administration turned a blind eye to these atrocities and offered assistance to the Pinochet dictatorship. Economists from Chicago arrived to help revive Chile's economy, and Chilean military personnel were invited to the US for training on how to fight subversion and the communist threat.

Chile's 'peaceful road to socialism' stands out as the defeated twin of the Prague Spring five years earlier. This time, the butchers were not the Soviets but the Latin American right and its American sponsors. Both Chilean and Czech idealists were victims of Cold War geopolitics and demonstrated to the global south the power of the bipolar forces and their respective zones of influence. For Castro and communist Cuba, it was a crushing blow to their hopes of revolutionizing Latin America. The overthrow of Allende happened just days after the fourth summit meeting of the Non-Aligned

Movement in Algeria, where seventy-seven members discussed the prospects of the New International Economic Order – which meant a non-US order. The CIA-backed coup cast a pall on expectations of a peaceful road to a fairer, gentler international set-up. Détente, many concluded, was only for big powers, not for the rest. Fans of Che Guevara everywhere felt vindicated in their insistence that the only answer was revolutionary violence.[3]

In the Soviet Union, the downfall of Allende caused much shock and was mourned by millions. Another lesson of Chile was that Brezhnev's détente did not really make the promotion of socialism around the globe much easier. In fact, the opposite was true: across Latin America powerful anticommunist forces viewed the warming of relations between Moscow and Washington as a mortal threat to the status quo. There was a transnational coordination of forces among the military and secret services to hunt down and eliminate leftist activists. South America, especially the Southern Cone, seemed to be a graveyard of the left. The secret services of the Latin American dictatorships, of Chile and Brazil especially, collaborated as part of the infamous Operation Condor which targeted leftist leaders and activists across the Americas and carried out assassinations. Military dictators had encouragement from Washington, at least until the Carter administration came to power. And they argued that their policies were essential to contain communism, and thus aligned with US national interests.[4]

The last peaceful socialist experiment in Chile also pointed to a major rule of the Cold War: its battles were ultimately decided by a combination of military force and economic power. Cuba managed to break out of American orbit with the help of the Soviet Union, and it took the tremendous shock of the missile crisis to make this shift. Allende's dream of a peaceful rebellion against US economic dominance led to his brutal end. During the 1970s, the power of American credit and investment in Latin America would be consolidated, and justified by new economic nostrums, soon to be called neoliberalism.

African Temptations

Moscow swallowed the loss of Egypt, then the loss of Chile. And yet the Cold War right in the United States was convinced that the Russians were on the march across the Third World. To be fair, the growth of the Soviet navy and capacity for aerial transportation fed these exaggerated fears. During the early 1970s, the Soviet flotilla patrolled the Mediterranean, side by side with the US Sixth Fleet, and began to venture outside the natural bottlenecks of inner seas into the Pacific, the Atlantic and the Indian oceans. Soviet seamen took over Cam Ranh base in Vietnam, abandoned by the US Navy, and built another base in Somalia, dangerously close to the Persian Gulf. American strategists grew worried. The Soviet Union was not a maritime trade power. Did it build up its navy to disrupt capitalist trade routes, especially to stop the tankers that brought Arab oil to the developed economies? Had the Soviets done this, Western prosperity would have ground to a screeching halt. Military and KGB officials toyed with such schemes, yet at no point after the Berlin blockade did the Soviets attempt to do anything along these lines. They certainly did not want to shut down the

Suez Canal in 1956 or later. The Soviets built their navy in the 1970s for the same reason imperial Germany had done so in the 1900s: to qualify as a great power with global access. The American reaction, however, was predictably the same as that of the British to the Kaiser's navy: fear, worst-case scenarios, fuel for confrontation.[5] And inevitably, the potential to project Soviet power into Africa and Asia created a temptation in Moscow to do just that.

The biggest temptation occurred after the revolution in Portugal in April 1974 that overthrew the Salazar semi-fascist dictatorship and brought socialists to power. Kissinger panicked: since the Second World War and throughout the Cold War the Portuguese territories in the Atlantic and in Africa had been crucial nodes in the US and NATO global transportation network. Washington feared communists coming to power in Lisbon. It did not happen and Portugal, now democratic, remained a member of NATO. Then Washington's worries shifted to Africa, where the Portuguese colonies declared their independence. The largest and most important of those colonies was Angola, comparable to Congo in territory and valuable resources, including oil. Just like Congo under Lumumba in 1960, Angola broke into a civil war among various factions, which had contested an anti-colonial struggle since the early 1960s. The balance of power had shifted since the time when Khrushchev failed to rescue Lumumba. Now the most popular group, the Popular Movement for Liberation of Angola (MPLA), led by Agostinho Neto, worshipped Marxism-Leninism, and had long-term connections to Moscow, as well as other communist administrations, including in Beijing, East Berlin,

Warsaw, and Havana. The KGB and the military also had the technical means to deliver military aid to the MPLA in its struggle against other factions. One of those factions, the FNLA, enjoyed American support. Another, UNITA, received aid from China.

Kissinger signalled to Moscow not to get too deeply involved in the strife in Angola. This, he correctly argued, would add fuel to the critique of détente in the United States, presented as a return to Khrushchev's revolutionary tactics. This was a moment when the US Congress investigated CIA subversion in the Third World: many congressmen wanted to prevent 'other Vietnams' and voted to stop funds for any cloak-and-dagger operations in the global south. In Moscow, American warnings only caused irritation. The Americans never asked anyone what to do in the Third World. And they repeatedly rejected Soviet offers of cooperation, clearly determined to ease Moscow out of the Middle East, Africa, and Latin America. Brezhnev, among others, viewed American signals on Angola as another case of duplicity. Some Soviet experts remembered well the humiliation the Soviet Union had suffered in Congo in 1960. They feared that the Americans, who supported other political forces in Angola, would have the upper hand again. They were determined not to allow it. The Soviet navy set up a base in Luanda. Still, the Soviets proceeded cautiously in their support of the MPLA. And they made sure that the property and operations of oil companies in Angola remained untouched.[6]

The Castro leadership in Havana was less cautious. Five hundred Cuban military instructors, then the special forces, and then the regular troops arrived in Angola on Soviet planes and by boat. It was another spectacular case (after North Korea, North Vietnam, and East Germany) when a client badgered the Soviet Union into doing something risky, creating a point of no return. The tail wagged the dog. Later, Soviet officials close to the Kremlin explained that there was no political decision made to bring the Cubans to Africa to wage a proxy war. Rather, the Cubans somehow convinced the Soviet military to allow them to do it. Of course, the Cubans depended totally on Moscow's logistical aid, yet they were not mere clients. The Soviet military could not say 'no' to their allies, whose anti-American passion they shared. And the Soviet leadership did not stop this Soviet–Cuban military symbiosis, because Moscow had a big chip on its shoulder after Khrushchev's withdrawal of forces from Cuba in 1962. Furthermore, the Cubans had accused Moscow of a lack of revolutionary resolve in the Third World. Brezhnev, along with other Soviet functionaries, felt he had to placate the Cubans. The Soviet–Cuban military cooperation transformed the civil war in Angola into a Cold War by proxy in Africa.[7]

The American Cold Warriors saw the writing on the wall: the involvement led to Soviet expansion in Africa proceeding in leaps and bounds. Worst of all, the Cubans succeeded beyond belief. First, they helped the MPLA to drive their rivals out of Angola. Then they played an even more prominent role in October 1975, when a new front opened in the south: South Africa sent forces of mercenaries against Angola's government. Pretoria hoped to play a Cold War card: by going against a Marxist regime, the autocratic apartheid regime expected to win plaudits in Washington. The Cubans routed the mercenaries in a pitched battle. Washington saw

Figure 3.7
Angola's independence brought the Cold War back to Africa, 1975.

the Soviet–Cuban victory in Angola as the first domino to fall: after Angola, Marxist-Leninist guerrillas prevailed in Mozambique. Namibia and Zimbabwe could be next. Kissinger wondered why Brezhnev allowed all this to happen. Angola armed Kissinger's enemies in Washington: it looked like his promise that he would be able to manage the Soviets did not hold for Africa.

The answer to Kissinger's question was simple and not encouraging: the Soviet leader delegated policy initiative to his subordinates. In fairness, the Soviet leadership tried to restrain Castro's commanders. And they encouraged MPLA leader Agostinho Neto to make a settlement with other factions. The defeat of South African forces and the CIA-trained FNLA was a huge boost to the Marxist guerrillas in Mozambique and elsewhere above and below the African equator. Once in Africa, the Cubans did not intend to leave. The Soviet military, who had recently had to leave Egypt, found new operational theatres. Other Warsaw Pact countries, including Poland and the GDR, followed their example. The longer this intervention lasted, the greater the damage to détente. Many Soviet activities in Africa were committed out of inertia and a desire to increase credibility and project power. In the end, the Soviets expanded their activities in Africa without any clear design or strategy – until too much was invested.

In the US, Carter's national security adviser Zbigniew Brzezinski, CIA officials, and the military were alarmed by Soviet military activism in Africa. Where would the Soviets and Cubans go next? The answer came soon: the Horn of Africa. In 1974 the ancient monarchy in Ethiopia was deposed; in the autumn of 1976 a militant pro-Marxist regime was established, led by ambitious warlord Mengistu Haile Mariam. The revolutionary dictator used the Lenin–Stalin playbook to establish his power through terror and conflict with neighbours, particularly with another 'Marxist-Leninist' regime, Somalia, which was led by strongman Mohamed Siad Barre. The bone of contention was Ogaden, a desert land that was a historical part of Ethiopia but was populated by Somalis. Both sides turned to Moscow for support. Barre used the fact that he was a Soviet ally in Africa and had allowed the Soviets to build a naval base on the Red Sea. Brezhnev initially tried to mediate the territorial dispute and tried to reason separately with both dictators. The mediation failed, and from August 1977 Soviet sympathies gravitated towards Ethiopia. To make matters worse, the Somalian dictator then invaded Ethiopia and expelled the Soviet military from his country. Barre immediately turned for support to Beijing and Washington. The scandalized Brezhnev could not forgive this affront, coming shortly after Sadat had expelled the Soviet military and advisers from Egypt. Again, Soviet credibility and pride were at stake. The Soviet military started a large-scale airlift to deliver military assistance to Ethiopia. Castro, eager not to be left behind, sent a contingent of Cubans to fight against the Somali military in Ogaden to defend Ethiopian territorial integrity. Like earlier in Angola, the Soviet–Cuban coalition scored a victory.

The Horn created a dilemma for Washington as well. For many, the loss of Ethiopia to the Soviets was one loss too many. Brzezinski depicted Moscow's collection of African dictatorships as a global strategic threat, especially for the crucial Middle East oil reserves and maritime routes. The Soviets, Brzezinski explained to Carter, were a relentlessly revisionist power, and they followed in the footsteps of the Russian empire. 'Détente perished in the sands of Ogaden,' he quipped. The United States, he argued, had to respond strategically. In order to contain Soviet encroachments, Brzezinski and secretary of defense Harold Brown proposed to play the 'China card'. Brzezinski repeated Kissinger's feat by flying to Beijing. He offered the Chinese a military alliance against 'the northern Bear' whose expansionism now threatened both China and the United States.[8]

China Switches Camps

The approach to China was part of a turbocharged triangular diplomacy, with different objectives and outcomes compared with Kissinger's manoeuvres a few years before. Kissinger had used his opening to China to affect Soviet behaviour, yet he had also managed Soviet fears and employed a backchannel to the Kremlin for constructive negotiations. Brzezinski wanted to shift the balance of power in America's favour and check perceived Soviet expansionism in Africa and the Middle East with one smart geopolitical move. Instead of parallel talks with Brezhnev, there was only growing rhetoric of Soviet human rights violations. Kissinger's strategy had led to cooperation and détente. Brzezinski's approach destroyed trust between the superpowers and was the final nail in the coffin for détente. Secretary of state Vance opposed playing the China card. Carter, however, sided with Brzezinski and Brown.

There was a new leader in Beijing. Mao had passed away in September 1976, and after a swift and brutal succession struggle among his subordinates, Deng Xiaoping had assumed control over the army and the Party. Some in China's senior Party leadership, nostalgic for the halcyon days of the Sino-Soviet alliance, began to warm up to the idea of rapprochement with the Soviet Union. Deng nipped it in the bud. Instead, he eagerly embraced the US offer of partnership. The new leader contemplated the first steps in what would become a breathtaking new course for China – using American and Japanese capitalism for modernization. Deng's new course emerged out of cultural shock: he travelled to Japan for the first time and was stunned by the economic miracle he saw there. Likewise, the rapid progress in South Korea and Taiwan, in contrast to the economic misery of China, where peasants lived on a bowl of rice per day, wounded Chinese pride. His conclusion was simple yet remarkable for an old diehard communist such as himself: those who allied with the Soviet Union remained underdeveloped and poor; those who got close to the United States modernized and prospered. In December 1978, the Chinese leader went on a state visit to Washington. He came with a broad set of proposals: America should help transform China into a developed country, just as it had other American allies. On 1 January 1979, the two great countries finally established diplomatic relations, broken off thirty years before. Simultaneously, Beijing refused to extend the Sino-Soviet treaty that Stalin and Mao had signed in 1950.

Carter expected that 'the normalization' of US relations with China would 'drive the Soviets up the wall'. In the Kremlin, the news about the American attempt to play the China card caused even more dismay than Washington's weaponization of human rights. This went against Brezhnev's understanding with Nixon and Ford. All his warnings about the perfidious Chinese had been in vain. Somehow, people around Brezhnev did not connect the dots, and failed to see that the US–Soviet partnership was in serious peril because of Soviet activities in Africa. In part, such misunderstanding was the logical result of the disruption of the usual channels of communication. In the past, with savvy Kissinger, anything could be talked about in the spirit of frankness. Now, both Moscow and Washington acted in parallel, stepping on each other's toes. In the Kremlin, Brezhnev and his associates thought that the president was a pawn in the hands of his advisers. Gromyko remarked privately to Vance that 'Brzezinski has already surpassed himself' in making statements that 'are aimed at nearly bringing us back to the period of the Cold War'. This suggested that for Gromyko détente was a new era of great power collaboration and not an iteration of the Cold War. Dobrynin, in his political report to the Party leadership in the summer of

1978, called Brzezinski a 'Rasputin' of the Carter administration. The Soviets expected that the next US presidential campaign would only intensify the rhetoric of confrontation.

They were right. Carter, despite his good intentions and interest in reducing the nuclear threat, felt he was drowning in domestic and international troubles. Some of those troubles were caused by his own policies. There was an impression that his administration had two faces: Secretary Vance favoured détente and talks with the Soviets while Brzezinski was a hawk like Dulles who saw Russian geopolitical threats from Africa to Japan. Carter listened to both men, and some of his speeches began to look like a compilation of their conflicting judgements. He also lived up to his promise of absolute commitment to human rights. Later critics accused Carter of weaponizing human rights against foes and friends alike. Among the friends were the anti-communist dictatorships of Latin America, and pro-Western autocracies of the Middle East, such as Iran. For those in Moscow the human rights discourse added to the impression of a confused American policy. What did Carter want? Détente, confrontation, or a moral crusade? When Carter met Deng Xiaoping in Washington in January 1979 to restore diplomatic relations with China, he dutifully raised human rights concerns, such as the absence of freedom of travel for Chinese citizens. Deng allegedly quipped: 'How many Chinese nationals do you want? Ten million? Twenty million? Thirty million?'[9] He of course knew that 100 years earlier the US government had issued the 'Chinese Exclusion Act' to stop Chinese labour immigrants. And now Carter was sanctimoniously defending the rights of their great-grandchildren!

There were also deep structural problems at home, which were outside Carter's power to tackle. The American economy was transforming after the energy shock, and suffered from 'stagflation', a pernicious combination of high inflation and almost zero growth. The earlier splits, shocks and failures like Vietnam and the Watergate scandal sowed deep mistrust of political institutions among Americans. As a person, Carter projected morality and kindness, yet for millions of Americans, he could not effectively restore prosperity and project power.

In the climate of deteriorating leadership in Washington and Moscow, with the return of zero-sum outlooks and a lack of negotiations, any rapid change, power vacuum, or conflict became fuel for mutual mistrust and hostility. The first such case was China's war on Vietnam in January 1979. It was Deng's idea to 'teach the Vietnamese a lesson': the Chinese were not happy with Hanoi's ingratitude and the move of the Vietnamese armies against the regime of the Khmer Rouge in Cambodia. Mao's China considered this genocidal regime its ally, one of very few. Besides, as some Chinese historians believe, in this way Deng consolidated his power and credentials in order to yank China from Mao's communism and put the country on a different path, towards a Party-steered capitalism. The United States looked at it with apparent approval. The Soviet leaders and people shuddered, thinking again of millions of Chinese threatening the longest border the Soviet Union had. The seasoned Vietnamese troops quickly repelled the Chinese forces. Still, the war signalled a monumental change that some later considered the end of the bipolar Cold War system. China began to openly play on the other side, with the United States.

The Islamic Earthquake

Another geopolitical earthquake occurred in Iran. Since 1953, it had been considered one of the biggest successes of anti-communist containment, helped by the CIA and a few million dollars. The United States sponsored and groomed the Shah's Iran as an anti-Soviet bulwark in the Middle East that protected the oil-rich Gulf. Washington was delighted: Mohammad Reza Pahlavi's regime was conducting 'correct' American-style modernization in an Islamic country, under US instructions and with US advisers. During the 1960s, things appeared to go relatively smoothly: the Iranian secret police, SAVAK, created with American assistance, terrorized the Iranian pro-Marxist intelligentsia and middle classes through arrests, torture, and assassinations.

After 1973, the Shah, his coffers flush with petrodollars, accelerated what he called 'the white revolution': a path to modernization and secularization of the country, with numerous American advisers in the wings. The Shah also bought huge amounts of US armaments and inflated his ego by acting as the main policeman of the Persian Gulf, to the great displeasure of the Arab petrostates. He even toyed with developing nuclear weapons. The Shah's course brought about new tensions and political realignments that neither the Shah nor the Americans expected. People from the countryside moved to live in Tehran and other cities: some joined the Westernized urban classes, but many more continued to listen to traditional Muslim clergy and the ayatollahs. The Shah was far removed from Islamic conservatism, but also from the liberal expectations of the middle and upper urban classes. The SAVAK henchmen arrested and tortured leftist students, but did not prevent other students from going to mosques, where they fell under the influence of increasingly fundamentalist Shia imams and ayatollahs.

Mohammad Reza Pahlavi also suffered from a serious legitimacy problem. Many remembered that the Shah had got his power thanks to a coup that had overthrown a truly national leader, Mossadeq. One of the last nails in the coffin of the Shah's authority was Carter's human rights focus. Suddenly, the Shah's main patron and sponsor was sending him contradictory messages, and urging him to soften his autocratic regime and its terrorist methods. Still, the Iranian revolution, like all great revolutions, erupted unexpectedly, when the tide of demonstrations and rallies clashed with the Shah's military and the latter refused to shoot the protesters. In January 1979, the Shah left Iran and went into exile. Fearful of repercussions, Carter refused to let him enter the United States. He said to his national security adviser Brzezinski that he 'did not want the Shah to be here playing tennis while Americans in Tehran were being kidnapped or even killed'. This remark turned out to be prophetic a few months later, when Carter was forced to let the Shah come to New York for cancer treatment.[10]

The revolution took everyone by surprise. Washington and London acted on anti-Russian reflex, just like in 1953. They expected that the Soviets would take over Iran. Marxism remained popular among Tehran's students and exiles living in the West. The Iranian communist party (Tudeh), however, had long been suppressed. Moscow's experts in the Middle East were sceptical about the chances of bringing Iran into the Soviet orbit, and there is no evidence that the KGB and the GRU sent any meaningful instructions to their secret agents and agents of influence in Iran. Instead, a new and completely unexpected third force triumphed: political Islam. The leader of Iran became Ayatollah Ruhollah Khomeini, who had lashed out at the Shah's regime as 'un-Islamic' from his exile in Paris. In February 1979 he returned to Tehran and was met by a million-strong weeping crowd of followers. Khomeini declared jihad, a holy war, against the United States as 'a greater Satan'. He called Soviet communism a more modest 'Satan'. Islamic vigilantes, including students, brutally eliminated the Shah's ministers and officials. They also overwhelmed Iran's Marxists. Their main target, however, was the Americans and their agents.

Today it is easy to see these events as the birth of a post-Cold War world where Marxism-Leninism was losing its global reach. This world no longer revolved around binaries

Figure 3.8
Iranian revolution: women in an anti-US protest, 1979.

such as communism vs imperialism, or democracy vs totalitarianism. Islamic fundamentalism made its powerful debut. Yet nationalist pride, power games, and geopolitical fears remained immune to change. And for contemporaries, new revolutionary changes were a cacophony of uncertainties. The Soviet–Cuban military in the Horn, the US building an alliance with China, the Islamic revolution – all of these generated old fears, not new insights. And in Washington and Moscow, people tinkered with a familiar Cold War puzzle and traded the same old currency: geopolitical paranoia. Each side counted their adversary's gains while discounting their own. In the White House, Brzezinski warned about an 'arc of insecurity' from Iran and Iraq to Yemen and the African Horn. This arc looked menacing on the map, as it enveloped the oil-rich Gulf. In Moscow, inside the Soviet international security bureaucracy, another arc of insecurity spread out immediately beyond the Soviet borders in the south and in the Far East, from the dangerous frontiers with China, now a US partner, to revolutionary Iran. And there was one country in between that had been for years an oasis of neutrality and calm, but which now suddenly erupted with revolutionary instability: Afghanistan.

Even today, after the failure of the American occupation and 'state-building' in Afghanistan from 2001 to 2021, some consider Afghanistan as not a real country, but a craggy conglomeration of mountainous borderlands between Iran, India, Pakistan, China, and Central Asia. Indeed, this country, when viewed from the outside, could appear to be a vacuum of power, ruled not by a state but by custom, a subtle balance between different tribes, the largest of them the Pashtuns. The British, who had made two disastrous attempts to conquer it during their own 'cold war' against the Russian empire in the 19th century, ultimately decided to keep Afghanistan as a neutral spot on the map. The Russians, for all their expansive energies in the 1880s and later, came to the same conclusion. The Americans, not known for such prudence, viewed Afghanistan, like any other country of the Third World, as a potential domino in the geopolitical game. Fortunately for Afghanistan, it was spared Cold War pressures until 1978.

Then came the coup of a group of officers in Kabul who launched the Saur (or April) revolution and turned to the Soviets for weapons, arms, and advice. The Kabul revolutionaries were late-comers, years after the uprisings of Nasser in Egypt and other nationalist militaries in Syria, Iraq, and elsewhere in the Middle East. They sought to make up for lost time by rash and violent reforms that included secularization, nationalization of land, and unveiling and integrating women. Many of them were murderous romantics, some composed poetry, and admired Joseph Stalin. For the increasingly sclerotic Brezhnev leadership and bureaucracy, this revolution was like a bolt from the blue. Their new revolutionary clients acted like creatures from the Soviet past that most of the Soviet officials would rather forget. They could not, however, spurn them and their revolution. The Party, the KGB, and the military sent their representatives and instructors to Kabul, Herat, Kandahar, and other Afghan cities. It was the same script as in Angola and Ethiopia, but without the Cubans. And Afghanistan was even less conquerable and amenable to modernization than those countries.

During 1979, Soviet advisers in Afghanistan discovered a new, formidable enemy: Islamic fundamentalist groups.

Those groups operated from bases in Pashtunistan, an enormous heathland, part of which was in Afghanistan and part in Pakistan. Before long, the Pakistani secret services, in collaboration with the CIA, began to arm and train refugees from the revolutionary regime. In March 1979, a violent mob in Herat killed a number of Soviet advisers and their family members. The leader of the Afghan revolutionary regime immediately called for Soviet military intervention. There was even talk of inviting Cuban troops. The Soviet Politburo was startled. The proximity of Afghanistan to Central Asia made instability there dangerous. In the 1920s and 30s, when the Soviets had ruthlessly built communism in Central Asia, thousands of locals had rebelled, resisted, and ultimately been driven across the frontier, into Afghanistan. There were reasons to fear the turmoil spilling back into Soviet lands. And the Iranian revolution suddenly made the entire neighbourhood a geopolitical prize. What if the Americans, kicked out of Iran, came through the back door in Afghanistan? Gromyko, Andropov, and others in the Politburo agreed that to 'lose' Afghanistan would be unacceptable.[11]

There was one person who disagreed. It was Leonid Brezhnev, who was either sick or hunting so did not attend the Politburo meeting. His position became apparent the next day, when the same speakers made a U-turn and began to talk about how disastrous Soviet military intervention in Afghanistan would be. Andropov summed it up when he said: 'We can uphold the revolution in Afghanistan only with the aid of our bayonets, and that is completely impermissible to us.' Gromyko explained: 'All that we have done in recent years with such effort in terms of détente ... arms reductions, and much more – all that would be overthrown. China, of course, will receive a nice gift. And the non-aligned countries will be against us.' He got to the main point: what would happen to a summit meeting that had been scheduled for June in Vienna, between Brezhnev and Carter?[12]

A disastrous Soviet intervention seemed to have been averted by sensible arguments. In effect, only Brezhnev remained the last enemy of the invasion and the last prop of détente. It was, however, a remarkably fragile prop.

The Last Prop

The European interest in détente remained stable and strong, particularly from France and West Germany. In Paris, Gaullist foreign policy continued after de Gaulle died in 1970, and every new French president prioritized relations with Moscow and Brezhnev. In West Germany, Social Democrat Helmut Schmidt continued Brandt's *Ostpolitik*. The new chancellor was smart and ambitious. Under him, economic relations with the Soviet Union and eastern European countries kept expanding. He spoke of *Weltpolitik*, where the Federal Republic could act as a key member of NATO, but also a leading promoter of global economic order and a defender of human rights. Yet it was Schmidt who inadvertently triggered a NATO security debate in October 1977, when he spoke about 'disparities of military power in Europe' and urged for armaments to be reduced in the centre of the continent, particularly in the two German states. The call for arms reductions concerned the deployment of the new generation of Soviet intermediate-range nuclear missiles, known in the West as SS-20s. These were designed as missiles that could be used to target western Europe, especially West Germany.[13]

Schmidt repeatedly tried to warn the Kremlin leadership that western Europeans did not understand the reason for this deployment, particularly after the Helsinki Final Act. A vigorous and comprehensive nuclear initiative, and a frank discussion, could have helped. Yet Moscow ignored Schmidt's warnings, Soviet diplomats behaved as if nothing was happening, and the deployment continued. The Soviet marshals considered the SS-20 missiles to be a replacement for the outdated rockets of Khrushchev's era, and saw them as a legitimate response to the numerous US submarines docked in western European waters and ports. Brezhnev was the only person who could tell the Soviet military to stop the deployment, but he did not. In the increasingly sclerotic, ageing Politburo, the issue was left unattended, and tension began to grow.

Soon western European politicians and military leaders spoke of a 'Euromissile crisis'. Worst-case scenarios resembling those of the early 1960s circulated in the media. The Harmel Report remained the foundation of NATO strategy, yet the argument now was that the pro-détente track needed to be rebalanced with an additional deployment of American missiles. Schmidt, playing the first fiddle, asked the Carter administration to deploy modernized Pershing missiles and cruise missiles to boost NATO confidence and security. At the start of 1979, Carter was too weak domestically, criticized by hardline Republicans, and could not reject the invitation from Europe. Earlier, the new Soviet missiles had meant a threat to western Europe. Now, if new American missiles were to be deployed on the continent, it meant a return to the times before the Cuban Missile Crisis. The 'Euromissile crisis' was slow in the making, yet its psychological effects were largely the same. One side's deterrence made the other side cry intimidation.

Such was the setting for the long-delayed Soviet–American summit in Vienna that took place in June 1979. A lot had changed since Khrushchev met Kennedy almost two decades earlier. No more fiery polemics about whose system would prevail, no more threats of war. The hordes of military experts and scientists had finally fixed all tricky verification problems, compromised on an asymmetrical balance of forces, and prepared a multi-volume text of the treaty known as SALT II for signature by Carter and Brezhnev. Instead of sharp cuts, the treaty disappointingly codified what each side already had and only tried to put a ceiling on further deployment. The European missiles, the biggest controversy at the time, were not part of the document.

The summit was anticlimactic after years of expectation. Brezhnev was a shadow of himself; he moved like a zombie, and read from small cards with very big letters, prepared by his entourage. He quickly grew tired, and then two KGB bodyguards carried the incapacitated Soviet leader like a pair of giant robots. After signing the treaty, Carter suddenly reached out to Brezhnev and embraced him, adding a kiss on the cheek. This kiss would later be used by Carter's critics against him, to devastating effect. It was, however, a gesture of genuine affection and desire to continue détente. Carter's dream was to continue talks, to move away from nuclear build-up, and reduce the number of strategic

Figure 3.9
Carter's kiss to Brezhnev turned out to be a goodbye to détente, 1979.

nuclear arms. He handed the Soviets a working paper that proposed something along these lines. The Soviet ambassador to the US, Dobrynin, who was intimately immersed in US–Soviet talks, observed in his memoirs that these were good proposals. Brezhnev was moved by Carter's emotional gesture and readiness to continue talks. Later at the Politburo he muttered that the US president was 'quite a nice guy, after all'.[14]

Historians and other commentators endlessly debate whether the summit could have prevented the end of détente. Many say that it was already dead, killed by American domestic politics and the Euromissile crisis. It is too easy to judge something as inevitable in hindsight, given that six months later the Soviet Union launched a 'special operation' to assist the friendly regime in Afghanistan. I would argue that it was Brezhnev's vanity (again) and the tragic events in Kabul that were fatal to détente. In September 1979, the Soviet leader met and embraced the leader of the Afghan revolution Nur-Mohammed Taraki and declared he was his friend and a good fellow. Just a few days later that good fellow, back in Kabul, was overthrown and later strangled in prison by his second-in-command, Hafizullah Amin. When Andropov reported this to the Soviet leader, Brezhnev was visibly shocked. What was going on in Afghanistan? Who was Amin? That was enough to tip the balance. From late October, Brezhnev began to mention Afghanistan regularly in his diary, normally reserved for trivialities, medicine, and hunting. At one point Brezhnev wrote: 'Amin is executing many cadres.' The new Afghan leader was an avid emulator of Joseph Stalin. Brezhnev delegated the decision on intervention to Andropov, Gromyko, and Minister of Defence Ustinov, and ultimately that troika decided that Amin might betray the Afghan revolution and that he had to be removed from power. The Politburo, presided over by the feeble Brezhnev, rubber-stamped the decision to send troops to back up the regime change in Kabul on 10 December.[15]

By then it had become clear that NATO countries would approve the decision to deploy US Pershing and cruise missiles by the autumn of 1983 if there were no deal on SS-20. Did it matter? The Soviets at the last moment sought to fend it off with a peace offer: to remove some Soviet troops and tanks from East Germany. Too little, too late. The NATO new resolve then confirmed the Soviet momentum for the Afghan invasion. For the Soviet leaders, it was just another phase in the resuming great power competition. Andropov and Ustinov promised Brezhnev that 'the introduction of a limited contingent' of Soviet troops to Afghanistan would be a brief, surgical operation: Amin out, and a more reliable politician installed, and then the Soviet troops would be going home.

If anyone in the Politburo expected a quick exit, it was an exercise in self-delusion. The war in Afghanistan started with the brutal assassination of Amin by the KGB *spetsnaz* (special forces), which shocked the West. Carter famously declared that he learned more about the Soviets in a few days than he had ever learned before. He declared a new doctrine, taking the Gulf under US military protection. The American enemies of détente drove a stake through its corpse. The Soviet Union would wage an unwinnable war in Afghanistan for the next nine years, losing 15,000 people, and causing the deaths of 1.2 million Afghans.

No Time to Relax?

Fifteen years of détente had allowed people to relax only up to a point: crises, wars and revolutionary convulsions were often looming in the background. A world of material plenty never guarantees happiness and calm. Still, a fragile stability reigned in Europe, which meant that people could stop worrying about another war and go about their lives. They could study, work, build, and go on holidays. The West Germans, the French, and the Italians forgot about wartime rationing and hunger; they bought refrigerators, washing machines, and cars to go to American-style superstores. Even in eastern Europe, things looked better than they had. The Czechs and Slovaks chafed under the regime imposed in 1968. But the Hungarians and Poles improved their living standards. In Poland, the new leader Edward Gierek began to borrow money from Western banks and import Western technologies and consumer goods. The average Polish worker got a free flat from the state for his family, with cheap electricity and gas, plumbing, and central heating. The Poles even opened private cafés and held rock music festivals. Some in Prague and Moscow joked that Poland was 'the merriest barracks' of the communist camp.

The three ghosts that used to haunt Europe – imperialism, extreme nationalism, and revolution – seemed to have disappeared. The overseas colonies largely became independent, and the violence, terror, and wars associated with colonialism and decolonization subsided. Internal post-colonial hotbeds of violence, such as Northern Ireland, became rare and local. Africa, the Middle East, south and east Asia were now masters of their destiny, or so it was proclaimed. Although post-imperialist trauma was strong in France and some other European countries, it was being healed by rapid economic growth. For the first time in centuries, the European economies did not flourish by openly plundering other peoples and continents but grew primarily because of intensive inter-European and trans-Atlantic trade, technological developments, and expanding consumer markets. Revolutionary fury also became a distant memory, the Portuguese revolution of 1974 being an exception. In West Germany and Italy, radical students turned to Maoism because they were frustrated by the conformism and consumerism of the masses. Other intellectuals, unable to wake up workers and white-collar professionals, became obsessed with sexual and political identities. The fascist and militarist regimes in Greece and Spain stood out for a while like aberrations, and then collapsed not into chaos and communism, but parliamentary democracy. Instead of revolutions, people went on holidays. Mass tourism, a sure sign of stability and well-being, grew apace on both sides of the Iron Curtain in the 1960s and 70s. It was standardized and not very imaginative, yet allowed millions for the first time to escape from the doldrums of their work and everyday life.

In the United States, the period between 1964 and 1980 was a time of great achievements and even greater troubles. The American economy remained the largest in the world and pioneering in technology and science: the US victory against the Soviets in the race to the Moon demonstrated it. And yet after decades of nationalist unity, inflated by anti-communist fears, most Americans felt disoriented, polarized, atomized, and often angry at their political leadership. The Cold War had once helped to sweep many social problems under the rug; then, suddenly, all those problems erupted simultaneously. Institutionalized segregation and racism, economic and social discrimination of against women, anti-Semitism, religious bigotry – all were deep-seated features of American society, and all now came under severe attack. For a few years it looked like the United States was losing the Cold War morally and ideologically. Looking back, the United States had lived through an extraordinary period of change and civil violence, unseen since the 1930s. The trouble brought about impressive reforms: civil rights legislation, the 'Great Society' programme, the new immigration law of 1965, the economic and social liberation of women; it all began to change the face of America, and would continue to do so for the next decades. Throughout the revelations of atrocities in Vietnam, the shame of

Watergate, the clashes of anti-war students and Black demonstrators and rioters with the police and the army, American democracy remained vibrant. This did not mean the United States stopped being racist, bigoted, unequal, parochial, and imperialist. Crucially, however, it revealed itself again as a vital and fascinating society that went through a never-ending social experiment in self-invention.

Millions of Soviet citizens learned about it and were impressed. The drama of 1968, with the assassinations of Robert Kennedy and Martin Luther King, was reported on Soviet TV and in numerous books. Soviet propaganda presented the American turmoil as a battle between 'progressive forces' and 'the imperialist state', but the Soviet audience paid more attention to human drama and individual stories. Responding to this demand, the leading Soviet journalists stationed in the United States began to publish highly personal, highly readable, books about the America they saw. The people who produced those books and films no longer fulminated against American imperialism; they demonstrated and explained its complexities. By the 1970s, most Soviets, even in the countryside, had acquired TV sets, and were glued to their screens watching programmes about American life. They could see US highways, the villas of the super-rich, the high-rises of American cities, and the amenities of suburban life.[16]

Most revolutionary for the Soviet image of America, however, was the scale of the peaceful protests there against racism and segregation, the unimaginable freedom of going out in the streets, despite police dogs, water cannons, and other means of state repression. I later heard from the wife of an adviser to Brezhnev and Gorbachev: 'We admired *that* America [of the protesters], we followed its drama in movies and read its translated literature.' During détente, the Soviet government stopped jamming Western radio stations, created during the early Cold War as tools of propaganda. The result was extraordinary: virtually all Soviet middle-class people obsessively listened to Voice of America, the BBC, and other Western radio stations. The anti-Soviet dissidents listened to Radio Liberty, with its sharp anti-Soviet message. Most Soviet citizens, however, had an internalized 'firewall' to reject open attacks on their country and system. Western reports about heroic dissidents, like Sakharov and especially Solzhenitsyn (whose short stories were read by millions), had a much broader impact than constant reports on KGB harassment of Jewish refuseniks. And the message that went farthest was rock music for the youth. The adults, however, appreciated dramatic reports on American domestic politics. I recall, for instance, my father, a Soviet TV engineer, and his friends following the drama of the Watergate investigation. It was unbelievable to hear that Nixon, who had bombed Vietnam and then signed treaties with Brezhnev, could be sued, investigated, indicted, and removed from power. It was a lesson in democracy, the division of powers, and freedom of speech, even though it was not clear how it could be applied to Soviet reality.

One message that the Soviet journalists sought to convey about America was the 'soulless' nature of American society, so immersed in material consumption, in contrast to the 'spiritual' and 'communal' nature of Soviet society. This contrast, however, only irritated many Soviet readers, who coveted basic consumer goods. They combed the publications about 'the rotten West' in search of specifics, such as models of cars and kitchen amenities. When a Soviet journalist described his visit to a topless club in the US and decried its vulgarity and commercialism, a typical Soviet reader devoured the details and ignored the didactic message. They wanted to see, taste, and savour the fruits forbidden to them. The urban youth learned whatever they could glean about the hippie movement, sex, and other manifestations of youth culture. The list of Western rock records banned or 'not recommended' for Soviet youth clubs was the list of the most popular bands among the youth. Almost everyone could afford a magnetic tape recorder and could listen to Western music in the privacy of their homes and in the countryside. In a growing youth subculture, no longer controlled by Soviet authorities, 'Lennon defeated Lenin' by a landslide.[17]

At the very start of the decade, the echoes of Khrushchev's promise to catch up to and surpass the United States within twenty years disappeared from state propaganda, but still reverberated in society. My eighth-form geography teacher asked for volunteers to make a presentation on the United States. With my classmate, I volunteered and we enthusiastically did our homework. Our presentation revolved around the idea of how the Soviet Union would catch up. We read the glitzy journal *America*, distributed by the US Embassy, and listened to Western radio. Our report inadvertently demonstrated the power of American industries, science, and technology. Twenty years earlier, we would have been arrested; ten years earlier, we would have believed that the Soviet Union would catch up; in 1973, we simply made comparisons and left our classmates to draw their own conclusions. The teacher wrote a report to the KGB, but nothing happened to me, and two years later I was accepted as a student of history at the Moscow State University. It was a strange time, when the regime restrained its power for repression, the greatest result of Brezhnev's détente. Dissidents and dissident-like children of high-placed communist apparatchiks taunted the secret police agents, despite evident risks. The secret police still lurked everywhere, and yet an increasing number of people lived as if it were not so.

Soviet public opinion was indifferent to Party-imposed clichés. It was obsessively Americano-centric and hungry for news and experiences outside the Soviet borders. At the top were the 'Americanists' and other experts on international relations, who worked in newly opened institutes of the Soviet Academy of Sciences. Those institutions were fruits of détente. The previous groups of experts in the 1920s and 30s focused on the prospects of a world revolution; the new institutes were modelled after Washington think-tanks and gathered knowledge which hopefully in the future could be used to reform the Soviet Union. Intellectuals who no longer wanted to make their career inside the Party after the Prague Spring congregated in such places, which they called 'oases of free thinking'. The KGB monitored them but tolerated their special status. Some people from those institutions would play an active and essential role ten to fifteen years later in the discussions and reforms of the Gorbachev era.[18]

Anatoly Chernyaev, one of the 'free thinkers' of the Party and a speechwriter for Brezhnev, enthused in his personal diaries during Nixon's visit to Moscow: 'These May days of 1972 will be counted as the start of an era of convergence [of capitalism and communism] – in its truly revolutionary sense of the word, the one that would save humanity.' Chernyaev spoke about the rapprochement and mutual understanding which could prevent a nuclear conflict between the hostile superpowers, and even end the Cold War. His expectation was romantic and naive. Détente, as we have seen, brought about only a superficial, top-level rapprochement. And in the United States, the idea of the Soviet threat remained entrenched. While many Soviet citizens developed a much more diverse, humanized, and positive image of the Americans, the Americans adhered to their Cold War stereotypes about 'the Russians'. Most strikingly, during the 1970s those stereotypes became more negative than even in the 1940s and 50s.

How come? The answer seems easy: the Soviet Union remained a dictatorship, ruled by a secretive Politburo clique, with the KGB persecuting heroic dissidents and freedom-loving Jews. It was also an empire that squashed the national aspirations of people in the Baltic states, in western Ukraine, and in Georgia. The reader can continue this list and conclude that a lasting partnership with such a regime was unthinkable. Yet in human history, nothing is so simple and clear. The above statements are, of course, true, but the resulting picture was nevertheless constructed by American media, propaganda, and, above all, the need to sustain American self-mythologizing.

American journalists, many of them young and talented, reported on changes in the Soviet Union through the prism of dramatic changes at home. They saw their country as being in a state of dramatic change, while the Soviet Union was stuck, conservative, and regressive. The only groups there that wanted change were human rights defenders, intellectuals, and Jewish people. Soviet dissidents, as well as the lack of reforms, led Western, primarily American journalists, towards a new take on the Soviet Union. They discovered that this was not so much a totalitarian society that ruthlessly transformed and shaped the future. Instead, it was 'an eternal Russia', a backward and brutal country on the margins of European civilization. 'The longer I lived in Soviet Russia,' wrote American journalist Hedrick Smith in 1975, 'the more Russian it seemed to me and hence the less likely to undergo fundamental change.' Hopes for convergence between Russia and the West, young Western journalists wrote, were an illusion. The only feature of the Soviet Union that deserved admiration were its dissidents and their heroic struggle. American images of Brezhnev's Soviet Union made a U-turn and went back to the images of the pre-modern empire of the tsars.[19]

The new look was quite old: in the 1940s, when the Cold War began, Kennan, Bohlen, and British diplomats had thought of Stalin's dictatorship in the same terms. But it was not simply an American reaction to the cycle of Russian history, with its bouts of reforms and reaction. Kennan felt 'love for Russian people'; the journalists of the 1970s had 'love for dissidents'. The human losses in revolution, war, and violence only made them condemn 'the Russians' themselves, for their slavish obedience. The Russian people, wrote Smith, 'find comfort in the stability and order that it provides. Fearing what seems to them the chaotic turbulence of Western liberal democracies, most of them do not want democracy for Russia.'[20] This conclusion was linked in American reporting to mocking Soviet state socialism, which could never deliver goods to its consumers. In a word, Russian society was backward not because of its past, but because it remained wedded to its past. It was permanently inferior to the West, slavish and pliant, unable to enjoy the fruits of freedom and democracy. In the 1950s, Kennan advised the Americans to let Russians move to democracy at their own pace. But Russians were now seen as not truly convertible to liberal democracy, so they were bound to be adversaries for ever.

After the time of Janus, the last phase of the Cold War and its overwhelming, mind-boggling conclusion are best represented by the Roman goddess Minerva. This was the goddess of war, but also of wisdom and commerce. German philosopher Georg W.F. Hegel wrote that 'the owl of Minerva takes flight only at dusk'. He meant that the human mind understands the most profound causes of change only in hindsight: we are always caught by surprise, and it takes time for us to understand what just happened.

PART FOUR
The Time of Minerva, 1981–1991

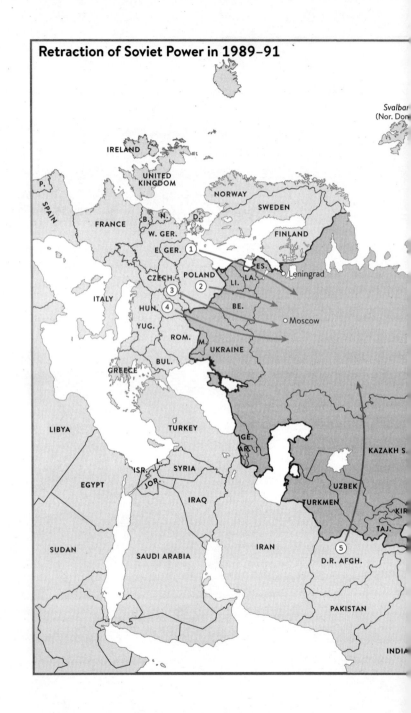

CHAPTER 12
Another Round

Reagan's Wisdom

In January 1981, Ronald Wilson Reagan stood on the porch of Congress taking an oath as the 40th president of the United States. In less than a decade the Cold War would come to a sudden happy end for the United States, as if it were one of the Hollywood movies Reagan had acted in before entering politics. The end of the long twilight struggle between the two superpowers, the two ways of organizing economy and society, was one of the greatest surprises in human history. The Soviet Union in the early 1980s was a military colossus, bristling with nuclear missiles, submarines, tanks, and more than enough weaponry to destroy the world many times over. Later many would say that it was a colossus with feet of clay.

The Reagan administration, and some of its Western allies, thought very differently in 1981. They could not predict that the formidable Soviet military would get bogged down in Afghanistan, just like the Americans had in Vietnam two decades earlier. China, who aligned with the United States against the USSR, was populous, but militarily weak, exhausted by the excesses of the Maoist revolution. When a Soviet dissident, Andrei Amalrik, predicted that the Soviet

Union might not survive until 1984 few paid attention. The Republican Reagan and his administration sincerely hoped to contain the Soviet juggernaut, like in the early 1950s, and used decades-old policies to do it: moralist propaganda, an anti-communist 'crusade' in the Third World, and a massive military build-up.

It seems clear now that the Soviets could not win in Afghanistan, and that they could not win a new round of the arms race against the United States. Many will also remember that Polish workers rose in 1980 and formed Solidarity, a free trade union, which many Poles came to believe crushed the back of the communist dragon. The Soviet economy also was 'in a crisis' – or rather faced many economic, demographic, and political problems. And in 1985, fifty-four-year-old Mikhail Gorbachev inherited this mess. A graduate in law from Moscow University, he belonged to the post-Stalin generation and came to power with the firm belief that deep reforms were inevitable. Many in the Soviet elites hoped that Soviet power would grow more formidable under Gorbachev's command.

Gorbachev at first tried to wage the same old battles, but quickly decided to try something new and came up with sweeping new ideas and proposals. In 1986–88, he and his free-thinking advisers pulled the giant country out of its stasis and put it on track towards liberal freedoms and economic reforms. And then came 1989 with its most spectacular images of the sudden fall of the Berlin Wall and peaceful revolutions in Poland, Czechoslovakia, Hungary, Bulgaria, and beyond. So heady was the euphoria, the whirlwind of freedom, that even mature historians and strategists completely changed their minds. Before 1989, some of them thought that a truce between superpowers was the best one could aspire to, something like a long peace. After 1989, however, Western liberal democracy had not only won but also was thought to have led to 'the end of history'.[1]

To paraphrase what Churchill said about Russia before 1917, the giant ship of the Soviet state was already near the long-expected harbour: the end of the Cold War and reconciliation with the West. And then it capsized and began to sink. In December 1991, the Soviet superpower fell apart, and its largest chunk, the Russian Federation, inherited its nuclear weapons, status, and the permanent seat on the United Nations Security Council. Many at the time concluded that all this was predetermined: wasn't it exactly what George F. Kennan, the author of containment doctrine, had promised? The long-expected mellowing and melting of the Soviet empire had finally occurred. The triumphalist endgame of Cold War history was impossible to resist. The great clash between American liberalism and Soviet communism ended in Germany, in Europe, where it had begun forty years earlier. This is fundamentally what all Western history textbooks have been saying ever since.

No one predicted how rapidly and surprisingly the Cold War would end. Not even Kennan himself, who scribbled in his private notes in 1946 his vision of the future: the Soviet threat to the West could be removed by a 'gradual mellowing of Soviet policy under influence of firm and calm resistance abroad'. Yet this mellowing, he warned, would be 'slow and never complete'. A more radical option was 'internal dissension which would temporarily weaken Soviet potential & lead to [a situation] similar to that of 1919–20'. That

Figure 4.1
The three who won the Cold War? Reagan, Secretary of State George Shultz, and Vice President George H.W. Bush.

would have involved a break-up of the state, and civil war, which Kennan did not consider likely.[2] In October 1990, at the age of eighty-five, Kennan admitted that 'We could not have foreseen today's developments.'[3]

To this day many Americans believe that Reagan 'won' the Cold War. This is not what happened. The conclusion that pressure on Soviet communism helped to win the confrontation is a myth – not very different from the revolutionary myth of Lenin and Trotsky, who allegedly seized power in 1917 on the crest of the great popular revolution. The most important point to explore here, with the help of Minerva's owl, is why and how the Soviet leadership decided to exit the Cold War, and why it doubled down when the Kremlin's power began to shake and crumble. We often know much less about how wars end than about how they begin.[4]

Capitalism Revived

Margaret Thatcher was elected as Tory prime minister of the United Kingdom in May 1979 amidst a national crisis. The country was in a financial deadlock. Many old industries, such as mines, were unprofitable and required state subsidies. Nationalized railways were hit by constant strikes. Oil and energy prices were high because of the Iranian revolution. Thatcher was convinced that the only way to deal with the situation was to restore 'financial discipline', stop caving to unionized labour's demands, and let capitalism and entrepreneurship fix the rest. A child of the Second World War, Thatcher did not want to slash the National Health System (NHS), a significant gain for the British people after years of sacrifice, but she often praised the Victorian values of the early 20th century such as hard work and grit. This was the start of a new global politics that came to be called neoliberalism: emphasizing market reforms over the distributive state without completely removing the welfare network for poorer people.

In Washington, Paul Volcker, the head of the Federal Reserve Bank of New York, the de facto US central bank, faced a similar situation. American capitalism no longer produced most of what the world wanted. 'Made in USA' goods competed with better German and Japanese products. The price of gasoline and energy tripled. American salaries were the highest in the world but they drove inflation. The distributive welfare state grew exponentially after the social reforms of the 1960s. The unemployment rate jumped to almost 10 per cent, and many millions more lived on welfare payments. The total welfare budget of the United States in 1979 was $428 billion – more than three times larger than the defence budget. In a word, expenditures surpassed revenues, and the government began to print money too fast. For many Americans, the state became bloated and lived beyond its means. Meanwhile the American dream was crumbling.

Carter, like Thatcher, viewed these economic problems in moralist terms, but in contrast to the 'Iron Lady', the president dithered and made unrealistic promises. Volcker and other American central bankers took the matter into their own hands. In 1978–79, central bankers hiked interest rates to 7 per cent, and then to 10 per cent to curb inflation. It did not work: wages kept rising, and inflation jumped from 8 per cent to 13 per cent. For many, it looked like the demise of the US dollar as a global capitalist currency. Tens of millions of Americans could not afford to take out mortgages or loans. The price of gold skyrocketed. In August 1979, Carter appointed Volcker to chair the Federal Reserve Board. A few months later, Iranian students took the US embassy in Tehran hostage, and then the Soviets invaded Afghanistan. There was a real sense that America had lost direction and lacked political will.

Volcker's task was to avoid the collapse of the US dollar as a global currency, and he ultimately brought interest rates up to 20 per cent, the highest rate ever. This was a last resort to save American financial stability. One of its casualties was the Carter presidency. Ronald Reagan was elected based on one slogan: 'Are you better off than four years ago?' During the first two years of Volcker's 'therapy', unemployment shot up to 11 per cent, yet Reagan did not flinch. He supported Volcker and turned to a new school of economists based at the University of Chicago. They argued that the way to tame inflation was to stop pumping money into the economy, regain control of the volume of money in circulation, and deregulate the market to let it find a new balance.[5] Thatcher was already implementing such policies in the UK. An important part of the neoliberal revolution was the government's crackdown on trade unions. Thatcher used force to close the unprofitable mines and ignored miners' strikes. Reagan did the same with air traffic controllers, whose strike paralysed US airlines.

From the Soviet side, this looked like American power was in decline and the long-prophesied crisis of capitalism was indeed happening. Yet in 1982 inflation sank to 5 per cent and continued to decline. US banking regulations began to ease, economic recession ended, and economic growth resumed, and then continued for years to come. It was, however, a new kind of growth. The wages and salaries of American workers stopped growing, in fact they declined in relative terms, thanks to inflation. From 1979 on, the income of the middle class remained frozen for the next three decades. This was a capitalism of deregulated financial markets. The United States was no longer obliged to hold gold for all its dollars, and retained all the benefits of dollars as the central global currency. Global capital, including billions of petrodollars from the Arab states, flocked even more than before to the United States, invested into US bonds and stocks. The moribund stock market of the 1970s shot up and continued to grow, with ebbs and flows, to unprecedented heights.

As the United States emerged from the recession of

1980–81, Reagan increased federal expenditure substantially, cut taxes, and tripled the federal debt to $2 trillion. This money went into waging the Cold War against the Soviet Union. The Pentagon and CIA budgets ballooned. Reagan proposed to increase the military budget by $160 billion in six years – an unprecedented amount in peacetime, and the third highest in Cold War history, after the expenditures during the Korean War and the war in Vietnam. It was a sharp break with the economic nostrums of the previous decades. Neither Truman nor Eisenhower would have authorized this profligacy. And yet American finances absorbed this, inflation stayed low, and the American economy continued to grow. For many Reagan critics in the United States, and all Soviet economists in Moscow, it was as an utter surprise. 'Reaganomics' defied gravity. The miracle was to a large extent an exaggeration. Absolute defence spending during the eight Reagan years rose from 4.9 to 5.8 per cent of GDP, from 22.7 to 27.5 per cent of public expenditure. A big deal, but not huge. The myth, however, was powerful: later Americans would believe that Reagan outspent and bankrupted the Soviet Union.

This myth concealed other grave consequences of the US crisis and the medicine applied to cure it. A global financial tsunami, caused by high interest rates and very expensive dollar credits, swept through the world. The countries that did not have dollar reserves from trade, and which had borrowed 'cheap' dollars after the oil shock of 1973, were suddenly in big debt. The balance of trade of Latin American countries was shattered. Low export revenues and growing import costs sent them into a spiral of economic recession.

There was no money to cover state social programmes. The only country that managed better was Chile: after the coup, Pinochet's dictatorship had already crushed the unions and invited American conservative economists from Chicago to teach the Chilean state how to manage its economy. They proposed deregulation and budget austerity. Those who opposed those policies were simply imprisoned and tortured. In the rest of South America, it was much harder to follow this path as long as regimes remained democratic and depended on elections.

In the Third World, the expensive dollar killed the industrialization efforts of many countries; they were deep in debt and back to the old role of exporting raw materials and importing American, European, and Japanese goods. Gone were the dreams of the New International Economic Order, in which the south would get a fairer deal from trade with the north. In fact, nearly every country whose wealth depended on the export of raw materials (except oil) was in deep trouble. There were spectacular exceptions to this rule: the economic miracle of South Korea, Taiwan, and Singapore. Yet the situation overall was very bleak.

Eastern Europe was another victim of global financial turbulence. It was particularly bad for Poland, where the communist regime ran up a $20 billion debt to western European banks, and Romania, where the dictator Nicolae Ceaușescu instituted a megalomaniac project of industrialization. It turned out that nobody in the world was eager to buy shoddy Polish and Romanian products. Meanwhile, the banks revved up their rates and created a situation where the communist regimes of these countries could not pay back their debts. To try to do so they had to impose austerity measures and raise state-fixed commodity and food prices. Unlike the Latin American dictatorships, the communist regimes derived their legitimacy from the promise of a better life for the working class. Polish shipbuilders in Gdańsk, and other workers, suddenly had to pay one and a half times as much for the same basket of goods.

This had a significant impact on the outcome of the Cold War. One scholar expressed it succinctly: 'Volcker and Reagan unwittingly accomplished the feat which Soviet leaders were never able to achieve: getting their empire to pay for itself. After 1980, the American empire became an enormous material asset to Washington, while the Soviet empire remained an enormous material burden to Moscow.'[6] This clarity, however, was like Minerva's owl and came much later. Until the very end of the Cold War, and indeed for many years after it ended, people's gaze was clouded by other developments. Not least by the prospect of a nuclear war.

Nuclear Fears and the Polish Crisis

American baby boomers grew up with 'duck and cover' drills at elementary school. As teenagers they protested the draft that forced them to go to war in Vietnam. During the years of détente, their attention shifted to other causes, but the collapse of détente refocused their minds on the dangers of nuclear war. In 1980, after the Soviets invaded Afghanistan, Carter came up with a new doctrine which said that if the Russians were to decide to conquer the Gulf, American retaliation would be 'by any means available'. Reagan assumed office with a reputation as a Cold Warrior, and his advisers and cabinet members used the language of confrontation, not heard since the Cuban Missile Crisis. In May 1981, Reagan said in a public speech: 'The West won't contain communism, it will transcend communism.' In 1982, speaking to the British parliament, Reagan declared that 'a great revolutionary crisis is happening' not in the capitalist West, as Marx and Lenin had prophesied, but 'in the home of Marxism-Leninism, the Soviet Union. It is the Soviet Union that runs against the tide of history by denying human freedom and human dignity to its citizens.'[7] For veterans of the US–Soviet confrontation, this rhetoric smacked of the early 1950s, the times of 'rolling back communism'. And some members of the Reagan administration passionately believed in their mission to do so. Secretary of Defense Caspar Weinberger wanted to accumulate American military force in order to make the Soviet Union capitulate. CIA director William Casey wanted to throw the Soviets out of Latin America and defeat them in Afghanistan. None of them believed in negotiating with the Kremlin. The communist enemy, they thought, could not change, it could only be destroyed, preferably without nuclear war, mainly by undermining its economy.[8]

Baby boomers were the most educated men and women in American history. They had learned from John Lennon to 'Imagine all the people Livin' life in peace' and feared the worst from the Reagan administration's old-fashioned rhetoric of anti-communism and strength. This was the setting for a widespread surge of nuclear fears in 1981–84. It was a time of public diplomacy, when many Americans citizens wrote to Brezhnev and his successor, Yuri Andropov, pleading for peace. Even children did it: ten-year-old Samantha Smith sent a letter to Andropov. The Soviet leader invited her to the Soviet Union, where she received a red-carpet reception as a child who was advocating for peace in stark contrast to Washington's adult warmongers. American nuclear physicists, political and social scientists, journalists, and historians used international conferences to liaise with their Soviet colleagues and discuss how to reduce the nuclear threat.[9]

In western Europe, many people also listened to Lennon and regretted the escalation of Cold War rhetoric. Accustomed to years of détente, they felt fearful – and rightly so – that their continent would once again become the main battlefield. It all looked like a bad remake of the 1950s and early 1960s. The Euromissile crisis became the focus of their fears. The NATO decision to deploy American nuclear-tipped Pershing missiles and cruise missiles in West Germany was passed before the Soviet invasion of Afghanistan. In 1981, the political context for this deployment changed radically. For the Reagan administration the missiles were a way not only to protect western Europe but press the Soviets into concessions. European governments did not go along with it; they continued to insist on a 'dual track': deployment and negotiations. The talks were to start in November 1981 in Geneva. Western media discussed, like two decades earlier, what the Americans would do in the event of a war. Nobody doubted that this war would be nuclear. Would the US defend Hamburg while putting New York at risk? Strategists argued that the new missiles would enhance American security guarantees to Europeans. Many Germans thought differently and repeated a popular ditty: 'The shorter the range [of missiles], the deader the Germans.'

The Euromissile crisis unfolded in parallel with a dramatic

crisis in Poland. It all began in the summer of 1980, when the communist leadership raised prices for food. In August, shipbuilders in Gdańsk went on strike, and soon the whole country was striking. During a similar crisis in 1970, the Polish leader, Władysław Gomułka, had troops fire at the workers. The new leader Edward Gierek did not use force. He was not a diehard Stalinist and the times had changed as well. Using the Polish army against Polish workers again would have been risky. The Pope also played an important role. The Polish cardinal Karol Wojtyła had been elected as Pope John Paul II in October 1978. Poland's population was 35 million, most of them Catholics, and in addition there were millions of Polish-Americans in the United States. In June 1979, Wojtyła came from the Vatican to Poland on an official visit, and the communist authorities could not control the ecstatic millions who greeted his message: 'Do not fear.' One year later the Poles would put this message into practice. With Polish dissidents providing additional impetus, the wave of Polish strikes led to the first anti-communist trade union behind the Iron Curtain, called *Solidarność* (Solidarity). The Polish authorities did not dare to suppress it by force.

Moreover, the Kremlin also did not want to see further bloodshed in eastern Europe. In July–August 1980, the Soviet capital hosted the Summer Olympic Games, a colossal peace propaganda investment. The United States and some of its allies boycotted the Games because of Afghanistan, but some Western countries and the rest of the world sent their athletes. A lovely teddy bear was the symbol of the Games, representing peace and love. The Soviet authorities did not want to have their propaganda feat besmeared by fresh violence.

By the time Reagan became president, Solidarity had almost 9 million members, just under a third of Poland's entire working-age population. The country had two centres of power now: the communist state and the Solidarity movement. The amazing growth of Solidarity was a major reason why Reagan spoke about revolution stalking the Soviet Union, not the West. Indeed, the Polish crisis left the Kremlin with a familiar dilemma: to invade or not to invade. In October 1956, the Soviet army had not invaded Poland. Conversely, in 1968, the Kremlin had decided in favour of the invasion of Czechoslovakia, because the Soviet leaders had feared losing a strategically vital country. Poland was much bigger, and even more strategically vital as a corridor from the Soviet Union to the Soviet armies in East Germany. The Soviet military were clear with Kremlin leaders that they could not afford to lose Poland: it would mean the collapse of the Warsaw Pact and losing the Cold War. Inside the Soviet Union, many, including the Baltic peoples, Ukrainian nationalists, and Soviet dissidents, tensely watched the drama as a possible prequel to their liberation.[10]

History had taught the Russians that invading Poland would cause enormous resistance and bloodshed. Andropov, who had insisted on the use of force in 1956 and 1968, this time said to his colleagues: 'Our quota for foreign interventions is exhausted.' The Soviet Union could not afford to have a second war alongside Afghanistan. Brezhnev already regretted his decision to send troops to Kabul and was opposed to the Soviet intervention in Poland. The Soviet leadership also faced a financial challenge: if there were another Warsaw Pact intervention, the Soviets would have to pay over $20 billion of Polish debts, and take food from Soviet workers and send it to the Poles. In November 1980, Brezhnev informed the leaders of East Germany, Czechoslovakia, Hungary, and Bulgaria that the Soviet Union would have to cut their supply of oil 'with a view of selling this oil on the capitalist market and transferring the hard currency gained' to help the Polish communists. There was no solidarity among comrades, however. Brezhnev was told that, on the contrary, Moscow should send more cheap oil to its loyal allies, not to the rebellious Poles. Brezhnev was clearly upset by the eastern European recriminations and ingratitude.[11]

The Politburo created a special commission, which decided that the only way to proceed was for the Poles themselves to sort it out. The Polish communist leadership had to deal both with economic chaos internally and with Soviet tanks externally. In the autumn of 1980, and throughout 1981, the Soviet military staged menacing large-scale exercises, making everyone guess at what would happen next. Meanwhile the Polish economy was wrecked by endless waves of strikes and sank deeper into chaos. The Polish Communist Party was on the verge of disintegration, and its new leader found escape from stress in alcohol. Then the Kremlin had a stroke of luck: the commander of the Polish army, General Wojciech Jaruzelski, turned out to be pliable. Jaruzelski and his family had been deported to Siberia under Stalin; he understood the stakes of letting the chaos continue. Convinced that the only alternative was a Soviet invasion and perhaps war in Poland, the general assumed leadership and agreed to introduce martial law, to disband Solidarity, and return the country to order. This choice made Jaruzelski one of the most controversial figures of Polish and Cold War history.[12]

Western newspapers and TV reports throughout 1981 focused on the worst-case scenario. If the Soviets were to invade Poland, and there were to be a war, would NATO get involved? And what would the deployment of American nuclear missiles mean in this dangerous context? The estimates were that it would take only fifteen to twenty minutes for precision warheads to reach the Kremlin and the military headquarters of the Soviet Union. The CIA had a high-placed spy in the military command of the Warsaw Pact, a Pole, who sent very alarming signals about an impending invasion. The Reagan administration and its British allies sought to make it as clear as possible that the consequences of a Russian invasion would be very grave. Foreseeing the crisis, the American Paul Nitze, a Cold War veteran and the author of the worst-case estimates of the Soviet threat, met informally with a senior Soviet diplomat, Yuliy Kvitsinsky. The two had a walk in the woods and emerged with a possible diplomatic compromise on the deployment of middle-range nuclear missiles in Europe. The draft was rejected by both Moscow and Washington. Instead, the hawkish members of the Reagan administration prepared for the talks in Geneva in November 1981 a devious idea that could placate the European peaceniks and was guaranteed to be rejected by the Kremlin. It was called the 'Zero Option': the Soviets were supposed to dismantle all their SS-20 missiles, and then the US would not deploy its Pershings. The idea of the Zero Option was very popular in NATO countries, and became the word of the year.

The Kremlin leadership took it for what it was: an American propaganda trap. Andropov believed that the Americans wanted to exploit all Soviet vulnerabilities, including the creation of a shortage of foreign currency reserves, disrupting the supply of Soviet oil and gas pipelines to Europe, intensifying human rights propaganda, and bleeding the Soviet troops in Afghanistan, in collaboration with China. In May 1981, Andropov invited Brezhnev to a meeting with the KGB cadres. His message was that with Reagan in the White House, a surprise nuclear attack against the Soviet Union could not be ruled out. The Soviet minister of defence Dmitry Ustinov, another powerful Politburo potentate, thought the same.[13] The secret backchannel for informal contacts no longer worked and the political climate was such that the leaders of the US and the Soviet Union could no longer meet face to face.

On 13 December 1981, Jaruzelski declared martial law in Poland. Riot police acted in coordination with the security forces; the entire leadership of Solidarity and thousands of activists were arrested overnight. The Soviet army did not intervene, and the Polish military played second fiddle to the police. Still, they had to open fire in Silesia against the miners. The Catholic Church, fearful of a civil war, preached that Poles should not kill other Poles. The 'revolution' that Reagan had talked about was over, or at least suspended. Reagan was furious and wanted to hit the Soviets hard and save Solidarity. The president wrote in his private diary: 'This may be the last chance in our lifetime to see a change in the Soviet empire's colonial policy re Eastern Europe.' At the same time, the president took the danger of a war in Europe, which would become nuclear, very seriously. Earlier, he had written in the same diary: 'Right now in a nuclear war we'd lose 150 mil. people. The Soviets could hold their loss down to less than were killed in W.W.II.' The American response to the Polish declaration of martial law was limited to economic sanctions.[14]

Fear

After Soviet forces invaded Afghanistan, Carter had feared they would march to the Gulf. Similarly, Reagan was now convinced that the Soviets were preparing to take over Central America. In Nicaragua, a group of Marxists, the Sandinistas, had seized power in 1979 and turned to Cuba for help. The CIA under Casey launched a series of covert operations to help the military in El Salvador and Guatemala eliminate the threat from their revolutionary neighbours and keep the Cubans out. The inter-American Cold War intensified as those associated with the right, who called themselves 'Contras' or counterrevolutionaries, killed those on the left, including socialist-leaning priests, with US assistance. Unfortunately for Cold Warriors, Congress continued to put severe limits on funding such operations abroad due to the legacy of Vietnam. To get around these restrictions, a group of Reagan's officials came up with an unusual plan. They contacted the Iranian regime, the great foe of the United States, and proposed to sell them American armaments and spare parts. The money obtained from these illegal deals was funnelled to the Contras and CIA operations in Central America, against Cuba, Nicaragua, and local pro-Marxist guerrillas.

Niccolò Machiavelli, the Italian Renaissance thinker who theorized cynical power politics, would have approved of this move. Yet it was against the law and stood in contrast with Reagan's lofty moralistic rhetoric. Moreover, the United States was now in the position of arming both Iran and the brutal dictator of Iraq, Saddam Hussein, who launched a war against Tehran in September 1980. My enemy's enemy is my friend, is the familiar saying. The United States helped the two enemies to kill each other in the Middle East and obtained the money to wage the Cold War closer to home, in Central America. $3 billion also went to arm the Mujaheddin ('freedom fighters') in Afghanistan, the Islamic groups that fought against Soviet troops and the army of the pro-Soviet regime in Afghan cities.

In the Middle East, Reagan's core ally was Israel. Other allies were the petrostates of the Gulf, above all Saudi Arabia, and Egypt. The Egyptian dictator Anwar Sadat had turned his back on the Soviets in 1974–78, become a friend of the United States, and signed a peace deal with Israel. In October 1981, however, Sadat was assassinated by nationalistic anti-Israeli officers. Suddenly, the balance of power in the region looked very precarious again. The Soviets armed Syria and the militant Palestinian movement led by Yasser Arafat. In 1982, Lebanon became the seat of war, after Israeli invasion of it led to clashes between Iranian-backed and Christian forces, as well as the Syrian army. A similar Lebanon crisis in 1958 had caused Eisenhower to send in US Marines. In turn, this had prompted Nikita Khrushchev to make nuclear threats, which led to the Berlin and then the Cuban crises. This time, Reagan sent the US Marines to Beirut, the capital of Lebanon, but only as part of a multinational United Nations force.

Leonid Brezhnev died in his sleep in November 1982. His successor was the KGB's Yuri Andropov, a formidable and sharp leader. Very few knew that he suffered from an incurable kidney disease, and that his days were numbered. Andropov, a self-taught Marxist intellectual, saw that the Soviet Union was in trouble. In 1968 he had sent a memo to Brezhnev in which he warned that Soviet science and technology could lose the USSR the position of a superpower within the next twenty years if it did not double its efforts to develop electronics and automated systems. Brezhnev read it and kept it in his safe; a few days later Soviet troops invaded Czechoslovakia.[15] Andropov concealed his reformist zeal for the rest of Brezhnev's term. But as soon as he came to power, he started working on economic reforms, cracked down on endemic corruption, and tried to restore work discipline. His main tools were the Party apparatus and the KGB. It is now easy to dismiss Andropov's measures, as many do, as the attempt of a former Stalinist and secret police chief to save a declining system. Yet at the same time, another former Stalinist and Maoist, Deng Xiaoping in Beijing, was setting China on a new economic course. Andropov needed time to do the same.

The new Soviet leader knew that the ongoing confrontation with the West was the greatest problem for his reformist course. In 1981, he said to the head of the East German secret police that the Soviet Union 'cannot avoid the strains of military expenditures both for us and for the other socialist countries'. Moscow could not give up on Soviet clients, including Vietnam and Cuba, Angola, Ethiopia, Mozambique, Syria, Iraq, and others. Without this burden, Andropov believed, 'we could solve all the other problems in two or three years.'[16] This was a stunning understatement of the challenges the Soviet Union faced. Even the KGB head could not imagine the enormity of the task. Still, his words implied that he was ready to take on 'all other problems', as he saw it. He began to reassess relations with Soviet allies and satellites, and he took steps to restore relations with China.

Andropov knew how troubled the Soviet economy was, yet for him the problem was not the 'crushing' military outlay. The Soviet military and defence industries were remarkably cost-effective; they never exceeded 15 per cent of GDP. Afghanistan remained a quagmire but did not cost the Soviets too much blood and treasure. The main point of vulnerability was the balance of trade: the Soviet Union during the 1970s became very dependent on Western imports, including grain and fertilizer, to be able to feed the Soviet people. For this the Soviet budget needed US dollars and became utterly dependent on oil exports to gain this currency. Andropov clamped down on wasteful imports yet needed fundamental and lasting reforms. And in 1981–82, he could see that the Reagan administration was doing everything it could to deny the Soviet Union inflows of dollar revenues. The Americans applied pressure on West Germany to stop the construction of another gas pipeline. Andropov also complained that American and West German banks 'have suddenly stopped giving us loans'. He was probably the only man in the Kremlin who understood that it was dangerous for the Soviet Union to fall into the same debt trap as Poland had.

As 1983 began, nuclear fears also escalated. At a closed meeting in March with the party secretaries of the socialist countries, Andropov said that new US shorter range missiles, if stationed in West Germany, would take only six to seven minutes to hit targets in eastern European countries, and a bit longer to reach deep inside Soviet territory. 'It is increasingly obvious,' he concluded, 'that the US consider them a weapon of the first strike, capable to paralyse retaliatory actions.'[17] With such weapons, the Reagan hawks could kill the Soviet top leadership before they could decide what to do. At this dangerous moment, some resourceful members of the Soviet military labs came up with a response: 'the Dead Hand' was the codename for a project of computer-managed retaliation in case the top leadership was incapacitated. This project would later be abandoned under Gorbachev for humanitarian reasons. The Soviet leadership decided it was too dangerous to entrust the future of humanity to artificial intelligence.[18]

In March 1983, Reagan confirmed Moscow's worst fears. He gave a speech that the media quickly dubbed the 'Star Wars' speech after the famous movie by George Lucas. He announced a Strategic Defense Initiative (SDI) to invent a shield that would be able to stop incoming ballistic missiles and prevent the destruction of the United States. 'As we in the Soviet Union saw it,' recalled Soviet ambassador to the United States Anatoly Dobrynin, 'Reagan has embarked on a path of breaking the military and strategic parity between the two nations.'[19] It was, however, another remarkable case, following that of Brezhnev, when the personal motivation of a superpower leader had nothing to do with complex strategy. Privately, Reagan was unsettled by visions of a nuclear apocalypse and wanted to prevent it. He just viewed nukes as evil, not a deterrent. This became his sermon, rooted in his religious faith. A close call with death had reinforced Reagan's attitude: he was almost assassinated in March 1981. From his hospital bed, the president had written a letter to Brezhnev, proposing to meet and talk about peace. After Brezhnev died, Reagan sent a similar personal, handwritten letter to Andropov. He called the Soviet ambassador to the White House and told him that he wanted a direct channel to the Soviet leader, no bureaucracy involved. Nobody in the Kremlin, however, could believe that Reagan was sincere. In a speech in March 1983 to Evangelical Christians, Reagan called the Soviet Union an 'evil empire'. Did this mean the US leader denied the USSR its legitimacy and was ready to strike against it?

Still, Andropov was prepared to give it a try. After he received another personal letter from Reagan with an offer to reopen a secret channel of negotiations, the Soviet leader responded positively. As he explained to his East German colleague, the Americans 'are striving for military superiority in order to check us and then declare checkmate against us without starting a war'.[20] The Kremlin leader needed to return to détente and carry out the economic reforms that he had begun to discuss in secret with a few trusted officials. But then fate intervened. On 1 September, Andropov chaired the last Politburo meeting of his life and left for a summer holiday to the Black Sea. He never returned to the Kremlin, because his kidneys failed; he was put on dialysis and was hospitalized for several months until his death in February 1984.

On that same 1 September 1983, Soviet military pilot Gennady Osipovich spotted what he believed was an intruding American spy plane flying over the Soviet Far Eastern borders, Kuril islands and Sakhalin. When the plane continued its course, Osipovich was ordered to shoot down the target. This was not a cynical act of mass murder, as the US president and media presented it later, but an act of frustration after months of deliberate US efforts to collect intelligence in this area by provocative means, in violation of Soviet air and nautical space. The plane turned out to be a regular flight operated by Korean Airlines; all 269 on board died, including 61 Americans, and one US congressman. To make their terrible error worse, the Soviet military lied and denied they had shot down the plane. The Americans, who had intercepted Osipovich's radio conversation with his base, aired the part of the recording where the pilot is ordered to hit the target. Suddenly, Reagan's 'evil empire' became everyday parlance. The blowback only made the Kremlin entrenched and embittered. As he lay dying, Andropov declared that the KAL-007 tragedy was 'a sophisticated provocation organized by US special services' and that there should be no more 'illusions' that the Reagan administration might be moving towards negotiations.

October–December 1983 saw a cacophony of international crises. Reagan and the CIA viewed any revolutionary movement in the Caribbean as an opening for Castro, and a danger that the Soviets would win in Central America. They were right in that the Cubans were active in the Caribbean and Nicaragua. In October, Reagan sent US Marines to overthrow the Marxist government on the island of Grenada, restoring in the eyes of many the old privilege of the Monroe Doctrine. Tensions ran so high that Margaret Thatcher asked the White House for reassurances that Reagan would consult its allies about any use of force in the future.[21] At the same time in Beirut, a suicide terrorist blew up a truck with explosives, killing over 200 US Marines in barracks. Defying calls to withdraw, Reagan continued his mission; in December the battleship *New Jersey* shelled the Syrian positions with

16-inch guns. The Soviet navy that patrolled the Mediterranean watched silently as their Syrian ally was pummelled.

In western Europe, there were countless demonstrations against nuclear deployments. People in the United States were worried as well; on 20 November, ABC aired a film about nuclear war, in which Soviet missiles destroyed the city of Lawrence, Kansas. Religious leaders, and even George Kennan, spoke and wrote against sending US missiles to Europe. Reagan, who watched the ABC film in advance, was distressed and wrote in his diary that everything must be done to prevent a nuclear war. The US hardliners reasoned that the best way to prevent a nuclear conflict was to have a strong nuclear deterrent against the Soviets. In West Germany, in October 1982, Social Democrats lost ground to the advocates of a stronger NATO; Schmidt was replaced by the new chancellor Helmut Kohl, the candidate from conservative bloc CDU/CSU.

Soviet leaders deluded themselves if they hoped that peace protests would disrupt the NATO deployment. On 22 November, American Pershing II missiles arrived at US bases in the United Kingdom and in West Germany. Police dispersed the protesting crowds. In parallel, NATO began its largest military exercise, called 'Able Archer 83', which included an imagined use of tactical nukes. The American military tested its novel electronic command and control means. On the Soviet side the public knew nothing about this, but for the KGB and military it was a trying time. They increased their level of readiness and put their camouflaged SS-20 missiles in a firing position; the head of the General Staff Marshal Nikolai Ogarkov even spent his time during the exercises in a bunker deep under Moscow. The Polish and East

German air forces, allies of the Warsaw Pact, were on high alert as well. In contrast to the Cuban crisis of 1962, when the Soviet military were ordered to keep nuclear warheads separate from the missiles, this time the Soviet military used helicopters to bring nuclear warheads to the missile sites.

The confused and leaderless Politburo reacted emotionally to the Pershings' deployment: it ordered the Soviet diplomats to walk out of the Geneva talks that were by now under way. In December, Andropov told a senior diplomat who visited him in hospital that the US and the Soviet Union were on a collision course for the first time since the Cuban Missile Crisis. 'If we begin to make concessions,' the dying leader mused, 'defeat would be inevitable.'[22]

At the time, I was a junior researcher at a think-tank that studied American policies, and lived in Moscow. It was striking how many Soviet people began to think about nuclear war. The atmosphere was gloomy and Soviet media portrayed Reagan as a warmonger, a trigger-happy cowboy, toying with nuclear weapons. There was a strong sense of Russian fatalism as well: nobody knew what would happen tomorrow. It all brought back the national trauma of the last major war, with Nazi Germany. Even two years later, in 1986, people who lived far from Moscow asked me, by then a young lecturer, the same question: 'Will there be a war with America?' During my research four decades later, I found the private diary of a senior Soviet diplomat who captured the same mood. He wrote in September 1983: 'The Americans are pressing us hard – meaning to deliver a coup de grace to a weaker but insolent competitor . . . They are acting harshly, in gangster style.' He blamed the old Soviet leaders for 'inadequate actions', and castigated the Soviet political and economic system; yet he saw ahead only a perilous stand-off and perhaps 'a big blood-letting'.[23]

The Americans were unconcerned and dismissed the unusual Soviet response to Able Archer, but the British picked up on Soviet anxiety. A British spy in the KGB, Colonel Oleg Gordievsky, passed information to London that the Soviet leadership was 'paranoid' about US and NATO actions, and saw them as preparation for a first nuclear strike. In 1990, when the Cold War was over, American intelligence experts reassessed US actions and concluded: 'In 1983 we may have inadvertently placed our relations with the Soviet Union on a hair trigger.' They also wisely concluded that it was dangerous to say 'never' on such dangerous matters as a stand-off between nuclear superpowers. In their view, 'It is an especially grave error to assume that since we know the US is not going to start World War III, the next leaders of the Kremlin will also believe that ... and act on this belief.'[24]

American officials refused to listen to the concerns of the British until the spring of 1984. Reagan reacted earlier, after receiving the message through Thatcher. The president was a man not of analysis, but of impressions. He was struck by the idea that the Soviets could be as fearful of the United States as the Americans were afraid of them. He continued to think of the Soviet Union as an 'evil empire'. He decided, however, that he had to engage the Russians in secret diplomatic talks and meet with the Soviet leader. His wife, Nancy, supported him. Reagan invited a self-taught cultural historian, Suzanne Massie, to give him private lectures on Russian culture. The tale of the Russian people, deeply religious but held captive by the communist regime, captured his imagination.[25] He just needed a Russian leader with whom he could negotiate based on the principle 'trust but verify'. He had to wait one more year, until Mikhail Gorbachev became the general secretary of the Communist Party of the Soviet Union.

CHAPTER 13
The Advent of Gorbachev

How Would It End?

When the Cold War began, there were several scenarios for how it could end. In the United States, Kennan wrote about a 'mellowing' of Soviet communism and its threat because of Western containment and economic revival. In Moscow and later Beijing, the end of confrontation was linked to the bright future of communism and a universal crisis of capitalism. Neither vision had a clear timeline. One just had to persevere and hope for victory. In 1961, Kennedy urged Americans to bear the burden of a long twilight struggle, year in and year out. Then came the word 'détente', which instilled hope that the great confrontation would gradually diminish and melt, through the streams of human contact, trade, and exchange. German *Ostpolitik*, based on this vision, vaguely hinted at peaceful changes in the East.

Inside the Soviet bloc, the communist dictatorships recognized only one way of discussing the end of the Cold War, though with variations depending on who was in charge. So long as Stalin lived, the dogma was Lenin's 'theory of imperialism'. It said that there would be another capitalist crisis, like in the 1930s, and another world war that would end with an uprising of workers in industrial countries and those countries which had been colonized. Then communism would triumph. Khrushchev repudiated the inevitability of a world war; for him, nuclear weapons and the strength of the socialist camp made Leninist claims outdated. Western imperialists, he reasoned, would eventually recognize the inevitability of the universal march of communism and would no longer be able to stop it. For Khrushchev the key to victory was no longer nuclear confrontation, but economic competition. He did not doubt that his system would win. Later, under Brezhnev, Soviet society and the economy lost their dynamism. People stopped thinking about the 'bright future' and focused on the present and the past.

Soviet intellectuals, however, continued to ask how it would end. In 1954, Mikhail Botvinnik, a world chess champion, sent a long note to a senior Party ideologist with the title, 'Is socialist revolution in the West possible without a third world war?' He approached this question logically. If Western imperialists and capitalists realized they were losing the global conflict, they would not hesitate to unleash a nuclear war. How then could communism win without total annihilation? He suggested a great compromise with capitalist owners and middle classes so that the transition to a new era would happen peacefully. Botvinnik also wrote that the 'class interests' of workers should be set aside, and 'all-human interests' should be more important. Party ideologues viewed this as a heresy and rebuked his ideas, but Botvinnik was too famous to be punished.

Around the same time, the world-famous Soviet physicist Lev Landau spoke about the end of the confrontation with his friends. Landau was brilliant, a mix of Niels Bohr and J. Robert Oppenheimer, and was fiercely anti-Stalinist. For him the Soviet regime was 'a fascist system'. His priority was intellectual and scientific freedom. The Hungarian revolution of 1956 and the Soviet crackdown shocked him: he concluded that the Soviet system could never be reformed. The regime was the dictatorship of bureaucracy, and would never yield power. Landau began to dream about a military coup that would topple the Party. One had to do it somehow, he said to a colleague (the secret police tapped their conversations). 'If our system can be liquidated without a war – by revolution or evolution, does not matter – then there will be no war at all. Without fascism, no war can occur.' Remarkably, Landau was not arrested. In early 1962, however, he suffered a car accident and lost his intellectual capacities after a brain haemorrhage. He received the Nobel Prize at the end of the year.

The third famous Soviet scientist who talked about how the Cold War could end was nuclear physicist Andrei Sakharov. In 1961 he had designed Tsar Bomba, the greatest nuclear bomb that ever exploded. He came from a family of humanist Russian intelligentsia. His grandfather was inspired by Leo Tolstoy's ideas of pacifism and non-violence. Like Oppenheimer, Sakharov was besieged by thoughts that the military and politicians would mishandle the enormous destructive power that he had created. After the Cuban Missile Crisis, Sakharov concluded that the only chance to avoid a thermonuclear catastrophe and universal irradiation was a dialogue between the Soviet Union and the West. He dreamed of a global intelligentsia, bringing together scientists and other educated people in the East and in the West. They could educate politicians and 'help bring about the escalation of peace' that would replace the escalation of the arms race, and war. The result would be détente, reform, and 'convergence' between the two hostile systems.

In 1968 Sakharov wrote an essay based on these views and passed it to Western journalists in Moscow; it was translated into many languages and published around the world. The main condition for Sakharov's scenario was intellectual freedom, but the Soviet regime was not going to grant it. The KGB harassed the dissident scientist, and he lost his official clearance, job, and privileges. Then there was his involvement with the Helsinki Watch Group in Moscow, to monitor the violations of human rights by the Soviet regime. When Soviet troops invaded Afghanistan, Sakharov denounced the invasion, and was exiled from Moscow to a provincial city where he was off limits to foreign journalists.

These three Soviet thinkers were not loners. Their views were shared by many members of the Soviet elite, who were critical of the policies of the Cold War, and worried that their country spent too much on the military and satellites abroad while neglecting domestic needs such as the poverty of the countryside and the endless crisis in agriculture. Some well-educated Party members, who worked as government and Party analysts and in academic think-tanks, shared those concerns. They realized that the Soviet Union and the Soviet bloc would never catch up with the West. Most of them wanted change and believed in democratization. The only issue was how to do it. A minority agreed with Landau and believed the Soviet system had to be overthrown; others

Figure 4.2
Nuclear scientist Andrei Sakharov and Gorbachev both imagined an exit from the Cold War.

believed that reforms could come from intellectuals inside the Party and bureaucracy, and then in the rest of the society. A crucial condition for the spread of such ideas was the Westernization of Soviet elites: many were shaped not so much by the old dogmas of Marxism-Leninism as by Western culture, art, science, and technology. Just like their predecessors in tsarist Russia, they debated what it would take for the Russians to become 'true Europeans', to come to Europe not as conquerors, but as part of a common civilization.[1]

At the same time, there were many others who disagreed. They represented a powerful anti-Western trend, xenophobic and nationalist. They viewed the West as an eternal enemy of Russia and read Russian religious and nationalist authors from the past. The Cold War, they argued, was just another cycle in the never-ending struggle between the West and the East. They were convinced that the United States, NATO, and the CIA were working to destroy the Soviet Union, which was 'a historic Russia' in Marxist-Leninist disguise. Alexander Solzhenitsyn expanded on this view. Although the KGB expelled Solzhenitsyn from the USSR in 1974, he was hostile to the liberal West, and worked in self-isolation in the United States. Gradually, this vision of a never-ending Cold War spread among Russian Party functionaries, and even among KGB officers.[2]

The ideas of Russian dissidents were publicized and discussed in the West. Many liberal-minded people responded to the idea of a peaceful coexistence and rapprochement. The crumbling of détente, the Soviet invasion of Afghanistan, and the nuclear build-up made many wonder if there could be a peaceful, diplomatic, or cultural way of ending the Cold War.

Not everybody, however, feared the prospect of nuclear war. In the early 1980s, NATO and the think-tanks did not offer any realistic scenarios for the end of the global confrontation as their focus was on how to wage and win World War III. Instead, the task was left to novelists. In 1978, a retired British general, Sir John Hackett, wrote a novel in which he described the Warsaw Pact forces invading western Europe. This imaginary war was a triumph of new Western technologies, including microchips, which defeated the Soviet army. The desperate Politburo used a nuclear strike against Birmingham, England; in response, NATO struck Minsk. All of this led to the uprising of the nations oppressed by the Russian empire, such as Ukrainians and Kazakhs, and the war ended after a sudden military coup in Moscow, when a Soviet general, who turned out to be a Ukrainian nationalist, killed the Soviet leader and declared the Soviet Union dissolved.[3]

Against this bleak background, the US president emerged as a visionary. In January 1984, Reagan gave a speech in order to placate a Western public that considered him a warmonger, and also to send a signal to Moscow. He inserted several paragraphs of his own into the draft produced by his speech writers. Those paragraphs contained a scenario for ending the Cold War peacefully. 'Just suppose with me for a moment,' Reagan said, 'that an Ivan and an Anya could find themselves . . . sharing a shelter from rain . . . with a Jim and a Sally.' The Russians and Americans, he said, would have a conversation about their lives and interests, not about geopolitics and weapons. Reagan continued: 'People don't make wars . . . If the Soviet Government wants peace, then there will be peace. Together we can strengthen peace, reduce the level of arms and know in doing so that we have helped fulfil the hopes and dreams of those we represent and, indeed, of people everywhere. Let us begin.'[4]

Nobody knew what would happen in just a few years. Minerva's owl was still nowhere to be seen.

New Thinking

It was impossible to meet the new Kremlin leader and fail to see his charm. In photographs with his Politburo colleagues, fifty-four-year-old Mikhail Gorbachev stood in the same dark coat and astrakhan hat, with the same blank face – and yet he was different. He had something resembling a boyish grin. And he had a twinkle in his eye. It is safe to assume that power corrupts. It remains an enigma why it did not corrupt Gorbachev enough. His career within the Party, his privileges, the wall of security that separated him from the world did not produce a creature of power. Gorbachev turned out to be starkly different from the leaders of the Kremlin before him – and after him. He belonged to a new generation that came of age after Stalin and experienced the ups and downs of the 1950s and 1960s: hopes for liberalization and a better life, then the death of idealism and the triumph of conformism.

Biographers concur that Gorbachev had grown up as a Soviet patriot and inherited Andropov's intention to reform the Soviet system, not to destroy it. 'We owed him everything,' said Gorbachev's wife, Raisa, about Andropov. Like the KGB reformer, Gorbachev viewed the Cold War as a great obstacle to the task of reforming the Soviet Union and making socialism better and stronger. At the same time, he was proud of the USSR's superpower status and felt insecure when Reagan questioned it. And yet there were important differences between Gorbachev and Andropov. Gorbachev did not serve in the army. He had not been through the hard school of Soviet diplomacy and KGB warfare against the United States. He was a provincial leader in the North Caucasus, focused on agriculture and spa resorts. And he had visited western Europe a few times as a tourist. In contrast to Andropov, he was viscerally averse to any use of force.[5]

Gorbachev was not the only one in the Soviet government to desire change and reforms. And after years of détente policy, there were officials, above all diplomats and economic managers, who continued to want cooperation, not confrontation with the United States, West Germany, France, Italy, and other Western countries. During his first year in power, Gorbachev turned to those officials and experts with a new message: foreign policy must help the country's economy grow. In January 1985, the talks on European missiles, interrupted after the incident with KAL-007, resumed. In April, with Gorbachev in charge, the Politburo decided to stop further deployment of SS-20 missiles in Europe.[6]

Gorbachev solicited advice and received it aplenty. Georgy Arbatov, the head of the US Institute in Moscow, sent Gorbachev a ream of proposals on how to correct Brezhnev's mistakes and clear room for Soviet diplomacy. He advised Gorbachev to withdraw troops from Afghanistan, improve relations with China, reduce support for Third World clients, and accept cuts of nuclear armaments. He also wrote that Soviet diplomats and scientists could actively use US opposition to Reagan's rearmament course, above all in Congress. The proposals made sense, but Gorbachev

Figure 4.3
New thinking at work. (From right to left) Margaret Thatcher, Gorbachev, Soviet Foreign Minister Eduard Shevardnadze and Gorbachev's wife Raisa, 1987.

ignored them: he decided he did not need a Kissinger next to him. In July 1985, to everyone's surprise, he replaced the top Soviet diplomat Gromyko with Eduard Shevardnadze, a communist leader from tiny Georgia. Shevardnadze had zero diplomatic experience, but in Gorbachev's eyes he possessed two major advantages over other candidates: he was not part of the Cold War bureaucracy and agreed with Gorbachev that it was time for a fresh start. And with Shevy, as Americans would call him, Gorbachev remained the architect of his own foreign policy.

At the end of his first year, Gorbachev proclaimed the need for 'new thinking'. Nobody knew what it was, yet it became clear that Soviet policies were based on 'old thinking'. The Soviet leader wanted to open people's minds and was prepared to go far. Like Reagan, Gorbachev was not a man of systematic analysis, but he believed in his abilities as a global thinker. He admired Vladimir Lenin and he believed his mission was to bring about another revolution, aimed at reforming the state, the Party, the economy, and society. He viewed Stalin as a villain. In his reading of Soviet and world history, Stalin was guilty of sacrificing 'true socialism' while building a military superpower. Gorbachev and his wife, Raisa, were not alone in thinking so: many Party members had been shocked at the revelations of Stalin's crimes, disapproved of the Soviet invasion of Czechoslovakia, and wanted more freedom to discuss how Soviet socialism could be reformed. For Gorbachev's predecessors, the Soviet superpower had been more important than communist dogma. Gorbachev became the first Party leader who placed principles above power. As he would demonstrate, he was ready to achieve the ideal of 'socialism with a human face', even if it put the USSR's superpower standing at risk.

Gorbachev grasped the enormity of Soviet problems even less than Andropov. He could not even imagine how much the Soviet economy was behind the capitalist West. Nor did he know what to do about it. In his younger years, he had celebrated Sputnik and other space exploits, and was optimistic that Soviet science labs and military industries could produce new miracles, like in the 1950s. He was vaguely aware of developments in electronics and the first steps of the digital revolution, and hoped that with proper focus and funding this would give a new boost to the stagnant Soviet economy. The Soviet Union, however, was chronically behind the West in new technologies. The Soviets lacked the capacity, entrepreneurship, and logistics that had created chip-based electronics in the United States, Japan, western Europe, and later South Korea and Taiwan. Global capitalism meant that the United States had an endless supply of dollars and increasingly powerful microchips for its consumer goods and weaponry. The KGB could steal those chips from Western companies, yet Soviet labs could not replicate them like they had done with atomic weapons decades earlier.[7]

It was logical for Gorbachev to respond to Reagan's invitation to meet and discuss nuclear security. The new Kremlin leader was uneasy about his duty, as commander-in-chief, to use nuclear power, even as a deterrent. The first US–Soviet summit of this new phase of the Cold War took place in Geneva in November 1985. Reagan spent months preparing for the event. So did Gorbachev: he gathered information about Reagan from all foreign visitors, including Nixon, Thatcher, and the French president François Mitterrand. The first meeting was a rhetorical showdown. Gorbachev directed his main attack at the SDI programme that could undermine nuclear parity between the two countries. Reagan stood firm and attacked the lack of human rights in the USSR. The two sides could not even agree on a communiqué, but Gorbachev weighed in to get the text through. The communiqué contained an important message that a nuclear war 'cannot be won and must never be fought'. It was a mantra worth repeating after many years of fear and tension.[8]

Gorbachev was still inexperienced and inflexible. His entourage, especially the military, watched his performance and expected him to be tough. None of them believed it was possible to trust Reagan and the Americans. With his colleagues in the Politburo, Gorbachev called Reagan a 'troglodyte' of the Cold War. He communicated, however, with the US president through a secret channel, returning to the practice that had been disrupted in the mid-1970s. Gorbachev was also eager to break out of the cage of security fears. He faced a catch-22 situation: how can you build trust with your enemy? And can you take the first step, when it could be seen as a sign of weakness? The safest way to proceed was to put Reagan on the defensive. In January 1986, Gorbachev came up with a major peace initiative aimed at Western public opinion. He proposed to talk about nuclear cuts and a nuclear-free world by the year 2000. Propaganda? Of course. Khrushchev had done the same in the past, while continuing his strategic build-up. This time, however, an unexpected catastrophe underscored the real threat.

In April 1986, because of human error, one of the four power blocs of the atomic plant in Chernobyl, north of Kiev, exploded. The radioactive fallout covered northern Ukraine and Belarus, then parts of the Soviet Union, and reached western Europe. It was the biggest irradiation in the history of humankind. The accident showed what a war in Europe, which was studded with nuclear power plants, could do. Just like with KAL-007, the first Soviet response was a denial, but after a few days the flustered Gorbachev had to acknowledge the truth to his country and the world. His reputation was at stake. Privately, over the phone to an adviser, he said with great emotion that Chernobyl showed the insanity of nuclear weapons and nuclear war. He had reached the same conclusion that Botvinnik and then Sakharov had reached decades earlier: it was necessary to replace 'class interests' with 'all-human interests'. This became the core of his new thinking. The top Soviet military, who took part in an enormous operation to secure the radioactive area, felt it was the closest thing to the Second World War that they had experienced.[9]

Perestroika and glasnost

In Geneva, Gorbachev invited Reagan to visit the Soviet Union in 1987. Yet events developed too fast, and so did tensions. Reagan continued to put pressure on the Soviet Union and other enemies. In April 1986, the US used military force against Libyan dictator Muammar al-Qaddafi, who was widely believed to be connected to violence and terrorist activities in Western countries (even suspected to be plotting the assassination of Reagan). Earlier, two US military ships waded into Soviet territorial waters off the coast of Crimea, where Gorbachev holidayed. And the CIA–KGB spy war continued apace. The KGB had a lucky streak: they received information from Aldrich Ames, a treasonous CIA official, on many American moles working inside Soviet intelligence. Those people were arrested and shot. Then the Americans arrested a Russian intelligence officer in New York. In response, the KGB framed an American journalist in Moscow, Nicholas Daniloff, and accused him of espionage. The gradient was towards confrontation, not détente, and it was steep.

Gorbachev then sent an invitation to Reagan to meet without a specific agenda on a neutral territory, which turned out to be Iceland. A deal to end the spy scandal was quickly reached. The Americans and Soviets met in October 1986 in a small waterfront house near Reykjavík. It was hardly fit for a big negotiation team. Gorbachev pursued his earlier proposal to cut strategic weapons by half – but only if Reagan renounced SDI. The Soviet leader continued to view the missile defence programme in the way it would have been considered by, say, McNamara twenty years earlier: as highly destabilizing and ultimately futile. Gorbachev was still in the grip of Soviet fears: what if, from behind their space shield, the US leaders delivered a first strike against the USSR? Reagan, on the contrary, was convinced that his defence idea was the magic wand that would save humankind. After hours of passionate debate, both leaders doubled down. Reagan offered to share the technology of SDI with the Soviet Union. Gorbachev scoffed: Americans consistently did all they could to deny much less sensitive secrets to Moscow. They ended up discussing the total abolition of nukes over ten years and actually agreed it would be a good thing. In the end, however, Reagan refused to stop SDI, and the negotiations floundered. The two leaders then had to explain the failure of the summit to their respective audiences.

The confrontation continued. Moscow and Washington engaged in power games, kicking out and arresting spies. The Nicaraguan guerrillas and Contras continued to kill each other; the Soviets continued to train their clients in Mozambique and Angola; the tension in the Middle East did not abate. The Soviets explored other parts of the world, outside the West, to improve their positions. They attempted to improve relations with China; Deng Xiaoping was responsive but set conditions for the normalization of relations. Those conditions included the withdrawal of troops from Afghanistan and Mongolia, and more. Gorbachev also flew to India and proposed to the Indian leader Rajiv Gandhi a strategic triangle against American hegemony. This did not work out.[10] Meanwhile, the Reagan administration consolidated NATO, continued to deploy new missiles in western Europe, and firmed up alliances with Japan, Saudi Arabia, and South Korea. The economic boom in the United States continued apace.

In 1986 the global price of oil plunged: good news for Western economies and an unpleasant surprise for the Soviet economy, which had grown dependent on high oil prices to keep a balance of trade. Later, Reagan's fans claimed that his Cold War strategy successfully bankrupted the Soviet Union. There is no solid evidence to back this claim. Reagan's personal diaries have nothing on such a strategy. Instead, Reagan expressed concern for how to help American oil industries, 'hit by the nose-diving price of oil'. At the same time, the drop in oil prices affected Soviet calculations. In Reykjavík, Reagan asked Gorbachev to honour a deal to purchase 6 million tons of US wheat. Gorbachev brought up low oil prices – the Soviets did not have the money.[11]

Gorbachev meanwhile launched his economic reforms at home. He called them *perestroika*, which means 'reconstruction' in Russian. A group of Soviet experts prepared far-reaching economic changes that gave extraordinary new rights to Soviet enterprises: to managers of plants, factories, and other economic units. Gorbachev pushed for decentralization. Enterprises were no longer responsible to the central Party and state institutions; they could sell their products, with permission, abroad, except for strategic goods like oil. At the same time, Gorbachev stopped short of crossing two crucial bridges to a market economy. He fudged on the question of capitalist property and profit. Soviet plants and factories would now be 'in possession' of managers and working collectives, who would be able to open cooperatives (commercial shops) and use commercial banks to keep a growing part of the profits for themselves. Communist states in Poland and Hungary had experimented with such a set-up for decades. Yet there was no state regulation or tax system to guide these new economic activities. Gorbachev also refused to free the old state-fixed prices, including artificially low prices for energy and raw materials. He thought like a politician: so far people had received nothing good from his regime, only Chernobyl and problems with buying vodka (Gorbachev was trying to curb Russian alcoholism). They should not get higher prices too.

If the Soviet budget had been flush with petrodollars, it would have been a bit easier for Gorbachev to give something positive to Soviet consumers, such as importing American jeans and Japanese electronics. The fall of oil prices denied him this chance. Still, even with high oil prices, 'Gorbynomics' would have been an exercise in disaster. The state empowered thousands of economic actors, who began to act like irresponsible renters, not owners. They would take advantage of huge, cheap state resources and speculate with them on domestic and even foreign markets. Instead of filling shelves, they emptied them. Instead of filling the state budget, they hollowed it out, along with the economy. An American scholar who compared Reagan and Thatcher's neoliberal policies to Soviet perestroika concluded that, in contrast to Western capitalist policies, Gorbachev consistently shied away from imposing price increases, bankruptcies, and unemployment on the Soviet people. Indeed, Gorbachev went in the opposite direction from his mentor Andropov.

One can add here that Deng Xiaoping in China gambled on economic liberalization but kept it under tight Party controls. Gorbachev did the opposite, which led to a loss of economic discipline, to monetary crisis, high inflation, an angry population, and the failure of his perestroika.[12]

Gorbachev also moved to liberalize the Soviet regime, to give more rights to elites and the people, and not only economic rights. His biographer later marvelled at his audacity. The Soviet leader wanted to overcome centuries of Russian authoritarianism and oppression. But Gorbachev was optimistic and tended to think that people, like him, cared more about principles than about bread and order. After the Chernobyl disaster, Gorbachev and his liberal-minded associates encouraged the media to practise *glasnost*, openly discussing problems and reforms. This word first appeared in the 1860s, when tsarist Russia abolished serfdom of peasants and introduced great reforms. Several generations of intellectuals under the Soviet regime had dreamed of free speech. Gorbachev, as it turned out, wanted to go even further. In 1987 he focused on his economic reforms, and during 1988 he prepared a comprehensive political reform – a major transfer of power from the Party to the elected parliamentary bodies, called the Supreme Soviets. The starting point would be the convocation of a Congress from all parts of the Soviet Union. Meanwhile, the Politburo ordered the KGB to release most political prisoners. Sakharov, the most famous dissident, was allowed to return to Moscow and even be elected to the new Congress. During 1987–88, the Soviet cultural and intellectual environment was changing rapidly. The crimes and dirty secrets of the Soviet past, particularly from Stalin's era, became open for scrutiny. Forbidden novels and films were now widely available. People were euphoric, like deep divers who rapidly rose to the surface and saw the sky and the sun. Fear, the cement of Soviet society, began to crack.

Glasnost affected everything, including discussions of security. Towards the end of Brezhnev's regime, few people had asked questions and information was scarce. The KGB saw any debate, even a small discussion, as potentially subversive. Many Soviet mistakes and risky steps originated not from ideological blinkers, but from xenophobia and ignorance. Now the experts in charge of national security and negotiations were allowed to meet their Western counterparts and raise any questions. Another gift of glasnost was the revelation of previously unimaginable information. The absurdity of Soviet secrecy meant that nobody in the end knew how many nuclear warheads the USSR had, nor how much it spent on defence. This used to be the sole prerogative of the top leader, but because of convoluted bookkeeping even Gorbachev did not know the real numbers. The head of a special panel working on arms control proposals for US–Soviet talks told the Politburo that, to his surprise, the Soviet Union did not have 32,000 nuclear warheads in store, as they had said to the Americans, but 10,000 more. Quite a discovery! It also turned out that Soviet defence expenditure was not 20 billion roubles, as per official data, but 77 billion, 16 per cent of total state expenditure. In 1986, under Gorbachev's pressure, the military reluctantly adopted a new doctrine, based on 'strategic sufficiency'. In practice, it meant they and the military-industrial complex could no longer rely on the permanently open spigot of state funding.[13]

The Soviet leader returned to an old idea of Khrushchev's: reduce the Soviet military burden and redirect resources to domestic needs. He had to tread carefully as he was still surrounded by older statesmen and military leaders who had fought in the Second World War, while Gorbachev had been a boy then, briefly living under German occupation. All the reforms and glasnost helped him to argue that the Soviet Union should try to engage the Reagan administration in peaceful de-escalation. It is impossible to say if Gorbachev borrowed this idea from dissident intellectuals like Sakharov or came to it on his own. The reluctant top brass refused to trust the Americans but found it hard to ignore the arguments of their own commander-in-chief. There was, however, a lot of indignation among the top Soviet military when in the spring of 1987 Gorbachev and Shevardnadze accepted the Americans' Zero Option, which meant the destruction of all Soviet SS-20 missiles. Gorbachev made one extra concession to the Americans: he proposed to destroy a brand-new short-range Soviet missile. This was more than the Americans had asked for, and US Secretary of State George Shultz pocketed this concession without reciprocating. Back in Washington, he said he was happy to accept Soviet concessions and ask for more, as long as 'Gorby' was moving 'our way'.

In May 1987, an incident helped Gorbachev to tame his military hardliners: a Cessna plane, piloted by Mathias Rust, an enthusiastic West German, landed almost next to Red Square. When the astounded Muscovites surrounded him, Rust claimed he came 'with a peace mission'. The Soviet air force and air defence allowed the plane to land safely, mindful of the 1983 episode with KAL-007. This time the USSR was not reviled around the world, but it was ridiculed. An indignant Gorbachev summarily fired the Soviet minister of defence and dozens of other generals who had had long military careers. As one British historian summed up, the Soviet General Staff and Defence Ministry 'had suddenly lost any right of resistance [to Gorbachev's reforms] because of the Rust affair'.[14] After this, Shevardnadze and his diplomats were free to negotiate with the Americans an Intermediate-range Nuclear Forces (INF) treaty, essentially based on the Zero Option. Even the US hardliners had never imagined this negotiation would be possible. And Reagan did not even have to sacrifice SDI. Instead, Shultz promised Shevardnadze that SDI would be delayed, and Gorbachev accepted this pledge.

In December 1987, Gorbachev went to Washington to sign the INF treaty and other agreements. Just a few years earlier the American people had feared and hated the Russians – indeed, some had poured away Russian-made vodka to protest against Soviet atrocities in Afghanistan and the shooting-down of KAL-007. Now thousands greeted the Soviet leader in the streets as a peacemaker. This was the start of 'Gorby-mania', as Gorbachev embodied a new hope for the end of the Cold War. The Soviets agreed to eliminate 1,846 missiles, while the United States was to destroy about 850. There was a breakthrough in the arms reduction talks because suddenly the Soviet leader began to make many concessions, willing to meet American terms. Gorbachev no longer objected to the US 'Star Wars' (SDI) programme. In contrast, Reagan continued to talk about other conditions, including Soviet withdrawal from Afghanistan and human rights. Later, Reagan's fans ascribed Soviet concessions to American pressure. That is nonsense: such pressure had never worked. What really mattered for Gorbachev was the progress of Soviet domestic reforms. Gorbachev and Shevardnadze used the language of 'new thinking' to link the end of the Cold War to the success of domestic reforms. 'Our power lies not in our number of rockets,' Shevardnadze instructed his diplomats, 'but in a stable and strong economy.' And Gorbachev told the Politburo: 'Without a reduction in military expenditure we can't resolve the problems of perestroika.'[15]

However, rather than strengthening the Soviet economy, Gorbachev's reforms destabilized it. The jettisoning of hundreds of missiles won the trust and sympathy of millions in the West yet did not make the Soviet standing any stronger vis-à-vis the United States and its allies. As the 1980s wound down, Reagan and Gorbachev, backed by Shultz and Shevardnadze, seemed to work towards bringing the Cold War to an end. Or did they? As US policies would demonstrate in the following few years, while the Soviet Union was weakening, most of the American policymakers continued to treat it as an 'evil empire' and a potential adversary – while praising Gorbachev for his reforms.

The Union is in Trouble

Reagan arrived in the Soviet Union in May 1988, after a stop in Finland. He hoped to sign a treaty concerning the reduction of numbers of large ballistic missiles, called START I. Yet the task turned out to be too complicated, because the formula 'trust but verify' still required huge efforts, and the military on both sides doggedly defended their interests and advantages. It became clear that the treaty's completion and signing would have to be passed to his successor. Both sides understood this fact and sought to make the summit as undramatic as possible. Reagan met with a group of Soviet dissidents, spoke to Moscow University students, and publicly asked Gorbachev to grant religious freedoms to his people. In fact, Gorbachev was already doing this by authorizing a state-level commemoration of a millennium of Christianity in Russia. Reagan and Nancy were impressed by the ongoing changes. The Soviet leader had a considerable publicity triumph when, during a staged stroll with Reagan across Red Square, a journalist asked the US president if he still thought the USSR was an 'evil empire'. 'No,' Reagan replied. 'You are talking about another time, another era.' Some of his Republican admirers and his vice president George H.W. Bush, thought that Reagan was too warm towards Gorbachev and too romantic about the changes in Russia. The KGB, after all, was still everywhere in Moscow, and handled the cheering crowds who huddled to watch the leaders rather brutally.

While the wheels of US–Soviet arms reductions talks were grinding slowly, history accelerated its course, largely due to Gorbachev's reforms and glasnost. It was the last summit at which Gorbachev's realm and the communist bloc remained relatively calm. Soon after Reagan left Moscow, Gorbachev convened an important Party conference and got the green light for his most audacious series of political reforms. The methods he used to obtain Party consent could be called 'authoritarian plus': Gorbachev used his immense power, but also glasnost (the conference was televised), and political tricks. He scheduled the crucial vote on reforms when the delegates were already tired and ready to go home.

The deliberately vague 'Party resolution' gave Gorbachev a lot of room to decide on the content and scope of changes. By that time, he and his liberal-minded supporters had cowed those in the Politburo who wanted to throttle glasnost and return to a more authoritarian regime. The literary magazines, the most influential source of information for educated Soviet citizens, were liberated from censorship, and became extremely critical of Stalinism. Gorbachev moved deftly: he got rid of the rest of the old guard from the Brezhnev era, and he developed the new, groundbreaking reforms in a closed circle. His advisers noticed that he already had a clear idea of how the Soviet constitution and state structures had to be reformed. As Shevardnadze told me a decade later: 'Gorbachev used Stalin's power to dismantle the Stalinist system.'

The Soviet Union was, however, a dangerous place for liberalization. And not only because the Russian people had never lived in a democracy. Lenin had conceived of the country as a confederation ('the Union') of national republics. His idea was that the Party and its powerful ideology, with the help of revolutionary terror, would control and ultimately fix the problem of nationalism and separatism. Stalin kept this system intact, even though in reality he ruled the Soviet Union as a unitary state. But how could one hold the empire together when the Party was no longer omnipotent and was no longer relying on fear?

Rather optimistically, Gorbachev counted on the fact that the peoples of the Soviet Union had lived together for decades, had one interconnected economy, served in one army, and married across ethnic and cultural lines. As a follower of Lenin, he should have known better. Glasnost affected non-Russians even more than Russians. The Balts, whose states had been annexed by Stalin in 1940 and reconquered in 1945, remembered terror and deportation of their elites to Siberia. Already in August 1988, people in Estonia, Latvia, and Lithuania were starting to agitate to exit the Soviet Union. At the end of the year, the Estonian Supreme Soviet voted to restore the full sovereignty of the republic. This was just the first pebble. The real avalanche of nationalism began in the South Caucasus, the birthplace of Stalin and the most unstable lands conquered by the tsars and the Bolsheviks. A territorial dispute erupted between two Soviet republics, Armenia and Azerbaijan, in the mountain district of Nagorno-Karabakh. It led to violence, ethnic cleansing, and ultimately a war (which continues intermittently to the present day). In Georgia, radical nationalists called for independence from the 'Russian empire' while trying to suppress the autonomy of ethnic minorities inside the republic, the Ossetians and the Abkhazians. The genie of ethnic hatred was out of the bottle.

In the Baltic states, the Politburo helped to set up 'people's fronts and movements in support of perestroika' which soon became legal vehicles for national liberation and separatism. In the South Caucasus, Gorbachev did not want to use force, when his predecessors, such as Andropov, would not have hesitated – and reluctantly sent troops and declared martial law only when armed nationalists began to kill innocent civilians. With all this, the Politburo's attention began to shift from foreign policy and international security concerns to the brewing domestic crises. Gorbachev faced a stark choice: backtrack on liberalization or double down. He chose the latter.

Eastern Europe remained, in the eyes of the West, an outer ring of the Soviet empire, conquered by the Red Army and brutally consolidated by Stalin behind the Iron Curtain. When Gorbachev came to power, he attempted to reform relations between Moscow and the communist dictatorships in the region, and to infuse new life into the sclerotic economic cooperation between eastern European countries and the Soviet Union. Like his mentor Andropov earlier, he soon gave up in frustration. The countries of the region had long since become financially dependent on the West (much like they had always been culturally) and pursued their selfish courses of earning hard currency. Eastern European communist leaders kept begging Moscow to supply more cheap oil and gas. And with the falling oil prices, the Soviet Union found itself in a bizarre situation: the cheaper the oil Moscow supplied to its allies, the worse off it became in terms of balance of payments.

Gorbachev decided to leave eastern Europe alone. He also firmly decided there would be no more military interventions like Hungary in 1956 and Czechoslovakia in 1968. One of Gorbachev's close associates in the Politburo recalled that Gorbachev followed this principle 'to the point of squeamishness' – it was pointless to propose anything that he would consider 'interfering with the internal affairs' of the other countries of the bloc. In 1987–88, many in East Germany and Czechoslovakia expected the Soviet leader to push for glasnost and reforms in their countries; he did not. In spring 1987, Gorbachev and Shevardnadze tactfully asked the East German leader Erich Honecker if there might be a gradual dismantling of the Berlin Wall. After receiving a firm 'no', they did not persevere.

Reluctant to meddle with eastern Europe, Gorbachev became enamoured with a new grand idea: a 'common European home', a proposal to push the Helsinki Final Act of 1975 even further and build a new Europe that would overcome the differences between East and West. At the time, the politicians and economists of the European Economic Community, primarily the French and West Germans, were intensely negotiating the idea of deeper integration. The Soviet leader was trying to jump on the bandwagon. The Western left applauded him as he seemed to be exploring a new way of ending the Cold War. At the end of 1988, Gorbachev gave a speech at the United Nations General Assembly. There he unveiled an even more grandiose plan: a new world order where wars and any use of force must be outlawed. He declared that the Soviet Union would cut its military presence in Europe by withdrawing 50,000 troops and 5,000 tanks. He also renounced the Marxist-Leninist dogma of 'class struggle' between capitalism and communism that had been the ideological bedrock of Soviet foreign policy. This speech made Gorbachev the darling of pacifists, liberals, and many others who had grown tired of the superpowers' showmanship. It was another step towards the 'escalation of peace' Sakharov had written about twenty years earlier. The biggest surprise was that this vision came from the head of the Communist Party, which had one of the bloodiest records in contemporary history. At least one US official, the ambassador in Moscow Jack Matlock, concluded that this speech was in fact a declaration of Soviet exit from the Cold War.

Rapid changes around the world and in the Soviet Union unavoidably had an impact in eastern Europe. Many remembered how earlier periods of change, after Stalin's death and in the 1960s, had spilled over into Poland and Hungary and how revolutionary change in eastern European countries had resonated in the Soviet Union. Poland, always the most troubled part of the bloc, was the first to start moving. Between 1956 and 1980, the Polish state and society had grown out of the Soviet communist model and recouped most of the sovereignty it had lost; the crackdown on Solidarity could only temporarily keep the genie of independence in the authoritarian bottle. Economically, Poland was a never-ending drain for Soviet oil and other resources. The US economic sanctions after the crackdown on the Solidarity movement had not abated. Solidarity leaders quietly entered into a dialogue with the embattled Party leaders, and at the same time signalled to Washington to mix pressure with promises by alleviating Western sanctions. The result of these manoeuvres was a quiet compromise: in 1986 Washington suspended sanctions, and the Polish government amnestied and released political prisoners. Debts to Western banks, however, could not be paid back, and the interest on those debts kept rising, from $24 billion in 1981 to $39 billion at the end of the 1980s.[16] Jaruzelski and other Polish Party leaders realized that they, like the leaders of Latin American countries, had to impose austerity and beg the International Monetary Fund (IMF) for money. For this to work, Jaruzelski had to reach a deal with the opposition. At the end of 1988, he informed Gorbachev of the Party's decision to hold a round table with Solidarity. The

Soviet leader nodded, staying true to his desire to not interfere. The leaders of the opposition also agreed.[17]

Some experts in Washington, including Kissinger and Brzezinski, became concerned that Poland might explode again, and this time violently. What would then happen to Gorbachev and arms reductions? In Moscow, Gorbachev's advisers had similar concerns. In April 1988, Shevardnadze told his deputies at the Foreign Ministry: 'If we do not want a violent anti-Soviet reaction, we should think about withdrawing [our] troops.'[18] In October, Gorbachev's adviser Georgy Shakhnazarov warned him of a probable chain reaction of financial bankruptcies in eastern European countries. He concluded it would be prudent to pull out Soviet troops from Poland, Hungary, and Bulgaria. Soviet forces had to stay in East Germany according to the Potsdam accords among the great powers in 1945 – at least until a new agreement was negotiated. Gorbachev, however, was busy on other fronts. In addition to political reforms and trouble in the South Caucasus, the Soviets were withdrawing from Afghanistan. It was simply too much to tell the Soviet military to begin doing the same in eastern Europe. Internal deliberations continued in the Party and at Moscow think-tanks. The events that took place in eastern Europe in the spring and summer of 1989 would catch Moscow, just like the West, by surprise.

CHAPTER 14
The End of Confrontation

A Tale of Two Squares

Reagan received Gorbachev one last time in the United States, in December 1988. He was leaving the White House, and his successor George H.W. Bush joined the meeting of the two leaders on Governors Island. The Soviet leader was glowing after his triumphant address to the UN General Assembly. Still, when Reagan asked him about the progress of perestroika, Gorbachev blushed, interpreting the innocent question as mockery. While from the Western perspective glasnost was a great success and Gorbachev was a hero, the Soviet economy had gone from bad to worse, and national separatism was already out of control.

Gorbachev expected Bush to become his partner in ending the Cold War, yet the incoming president was not in a hurry. Bush and his team, including Brent Scowcroft, James Baker, and Dick Cheney, considered Reagan's shift from confrontation to negotiation too hectic and not grounded in reality. Bush struggled with Reagan's economic legacy and profligate spending; at the same time, he lacked Reagan's charisma and huge support among the Republican Party. The new administration believed that the Cold War continued so long as

Soviet troops were still stationed in the heart of Europe and Soviet missiles were aimed at the United States. The CIA's Robert Gates publicly stated that perestroika was failing, and Gorbachev was 'an uncertain trumpet'. Gates, Cheney, and others claimed that Gorbachev's new thinking was simply a product of economic necessity, a crafty strategy to gain some breathing space so that Moscow could solve its problems, modernize, and resume its aggressive behaviour. Instead of meeting with Gorbachev early, Bush pressed pause.[1]

As a result, Gorbachev could not show to the Soviet people and their allies that his reforms were synchronized with the start of a new era of international relations. Lofty principles fell short of reality because of scepticism in Washington. The Soviet leader decided to move ahead with his plans regardless. In February 1989, after months of preparations, the last Soviet troops left Afghanistan. The bloody ordeal, a Soviet version of the American war in Vietnam, ended with a similar result: the regime in Kabul was completely dependent on Soviet money and supplies while its enemies continued to receive weapons and money from the United States and Pakistan's intelligence services. Still, with seven years of military involvement now at an end, it was one problem less for the Soviet Union.

The next foreign policy step was Gorbachev's trip to China, where he was keen on political reconciliation after twenty-five years of rivalry. The road to Beijing was long: the Soviets did a lot to satisfy Chinese conditions, above all on Afghanistan and the reduction of troops in Mongolia. There were, however, complications that did not depend on Gorbachev and Shevardnadze. The Chinese demanded

Figure 4.4
Chinese students in Tiananmen Square wait for Gorbachev, May 1989.

that Vietnamese troops pull out of neighbouring Cambodia, where they had put an end to the genocidal pro-Maoist regime. In truth, the rulers in Hanoi did not listen to Moscow's advice on this issue, and it was not clear until early 1989 if this obstacle to the summit in Beijing could be surmounted. Eventually the Chinese relented and the Soviet leader arrived in Beijing with his big team of advisers, ministers, journalists, scientists, and cultural figures.

This trip turned out to be doubly dramatic. The Soviet delegation happened to be there for what looked like a new Chinese revolution: Beijing was full of students and young people who demonstrated and demanded that Deng Xiaoping step down. Many students viewed Deng's reforms as a betrayal of socialist promises and wanted to see China adopt a socialist perestroika like Gorbachev's. Younger reformers in the Chinese leadership, above all Zhao Ziyang, clearly viewed the Soviet leader as a role model. Deng and the Politburo elders were embarrassed by the turmoil but did not lose face: they told Gorbachev that normalizing relations did not mean a return to the Sino-Soviet alliance. After Gorbachev left, Deng and other hardliners put a brutal end to the students' revolution: Tiananmen Square, in front of the Forbidden City, where many students were on strike, was cleared up by troops and tanks, with significant casualties.

This was the moment when the two great experiments, Gorbachev's and Deng's, parted ways. From Gorbachev's perspective, the Chinese reforms were leading to a political explosion and bloodshed. He said to his entourage: 'Some of those present here have promoted the idea of taking the Chinese road. We saw today where this road leads. I do not want Red Square to look like Tiananmen Square.' In fact, Gorbachev's road was not bloodless at all for those who were in the South Caucasus. Thousands of Armenian and Azeri armed militias roamed Nagorno-Karabakh, with tens of thousands of refugees and many victims of violence. In April 1989, the intervention of Soviet troops in the main square in Tbilisi turned Georgia into a hotbed of nationalist mobilization; armed men disrupted railway connections, and violence broke out between Georgians and the Ossetian and Abkhazian ethnic groups.

From Deng's viewpoint, Gorbachev was an 'idiot' who weakened the Party, liberalized the regime, and as a result lost control over the economy. Gorbachev would eventually find a partner and indeed a friend in Bush, but at the expense of fatally weakening his power and the Soviet Union. China's communist leadership consolidated its power and then opened the country to global investments and companies. China's geopolitical role, in between the two superpowers, was a boon. The Bush administration feared that after the Tiananmen Square massacre China would become a Soviet ally again. The US president and his people went out of their way to assure Deng Xiaoping that they wanted to stay partners, even 'friends' of China. After 1992, billions of Western, as well as Hong Kong, Taiwanese, and Japanese, investments would flow into China. The Americans did not offer anything similar to Gorbachev in 1989. And when they began to speak about it, the Soviet Union was already falling apart and therefore not good for business.

In March–May 1989, the Soviet Union experienced a political revolution of its own: millions of Soviet people voted in the first competitive elections behind the Iron Curtain, to send deputies to the Congress of People's Deputies. Several regional Party bosses were opposed by alternative candidates and lost. Instead, some intellectuals, including Andrei Sakharov, were elected. The KGB stood aside. The political shock was profound. The Congress opened on 25 May and lasted for sixteen days: all sessions were aired on state television. Everybody with a TV set was glued to the screen: those sixteen days shook the Soviet Union. People were witnessing the first time the Party had an official opposition since the Bolshevik victory. This was part of Gorbachev's reform strategy. As he said in his speech in Beijing, 'We became convinced that we cannot succeed with reforms unless we dismantle the command-administrative system.' This awkward tongue-twister meant the Party and central economic planning.

Historians can endlessly argue about what came first: the

economic and Cold War pressures that pushed Gorbachev and his circle of reformers to dismantle the old Soviet system, or the idea of a new revolution that led to the weakening of the Soviet Union. My own view is the latter, but it is impossible to convince those who believe in the former. One thing is obvious: the main engine for the multiple endings of the Cold War was in the Kremlin. This was obvious to eastern European communist leaders and the opposition in those countries. Many historians see the events in Poland as the first step in the collapse of communism and the peaceful revolutions of 1989. However, I would argue that the first step was glasnost and the political revolution in Moscow, as it sent a clear signal to the Poles and others that the clock was ticking for communism, not only in eastern Europe, but also in the Russian core of the empire.

In 1988, when strikes had begun to shake Poland again, Gorbachev's adviser had told his Polish Party colleagues that if another crisis were to emerge in Poland, then the Soviets would not intervene. And what if Solidarity were to seize power in Poland? Well, the adviser replied, then Poland would become like Finland, a neutral country. The USSR would have to accept it. The word he used was 'Finlandization'. It meant that a post-communist Poland would not be able to join NATO but would become a neutral country with security commitments to the Soviet Union. The adviser, Georgy Shakhnazarov, thought that Soviet troops would remain in East Germany and nobody would be able to dislodge them by force. Within two years, however, this scenario would be overthrown by the powerful forces that Gorbachev's policies had unleashed.

The End of the Wall

The communist government of Hungary felt the pressure of financialized global capitalism no less than the struggling countries of Latin America and Africa. After oil prices dropped, it was no longer possible for Hungary to pay off its debts by selling cheap Soviet oil. It reached the end of its credit line. Hungary, like Poland, found itself stuck between Moscow's lack of munificence and new capitalist realities. The Hungarian leaders began to negotiate with the IMF and prepare for austerity. For this, they needed to spread the political responsibility, which meant democratizing.[2] This financial tight spot was not the only reason for Hungary to abandon the harbour of the Communist Party system. The new generation of Hungarian communists were hardly communists: they were politicians who looked for bargains and opportunities. After 1956, liberalization had not been an option as they knew it meant the arrival of Soviet tanks. But with Gorbachev now carrying out political reforms and promoting glasnost, this option became quite realistic. The smartest Hungarian leaders of the new generation began to discuss a 'socialist democracy' that would allow freedom of expression.

Soviet leaders had long recognized the perilousness of the Hungarian situation. Hungary was following Poland 'into a trap' of financial dependency on Western banks, said the Soviet prime minister Nikolai Ryzhkov at the Politburo in October 1986. At the same time, Moscow could not offer what the West could: convertible currency.[3] Gone were the days when communist revolutionaries and Stalin's disciples used force against capitalism. They were now on the brink of turning into capitalists themselves. In January 1989, amid all the warnings about imminent changes in eastern Europe, Gorbachev said: 'The people in those countries will ask: What kind of leash will [the Soviets] use to hold our countries? They do not know yet that if they pull strongly on the leash, it will snap.'[4] Gorbachev did not speak about the 'Finlandization' of eastern Europe but mentioned 'the kind of relations we are developing with China'. On the economic side, the Kremlin reformers understood that Poland and Hungary would 'return to Europe'. Perhaps, they argued, it would also mean that Soviet consumers, who received 40–50 per cent of imported goods from eastern Europe, would benefit from the expansion of trade. This was a rather naive calculation, betraying an absence of knowledge in the Kremlin about how global capitalism really worked.

The Hungarians pulled on the leash first. In early 1988, young technocratic leaders replaced the retired ex-Stalinist leader Kádár. A year later, they declared that the revolution of 1956 was a popular revolution and a good thing. In early March 1989, the Hungarian prime minister Miklós Németh informed Gorbachev of the decision 'to completely remove electronic and technological protection from the Western and Southern borders of Hungary'. That was the infamous Iron Curtain from the Stalinist era. Németh argued that the need for such a barrier had gone, 'and now it serves only for catching citizens of Romania and the GDR [East Germany] who try to illegally escape to the West through Hungary'. Of course, Németh added, 'we will have to talk to comrades from the GDR.'[5] The consultations took a surprising turn, however, because instead of going to their East German counterparts, the Hungarian leaders turned to the West German leader to develop a tacit understanding. Earlier, the head of Hungary's ruling party, Károly Grósz, had accepted gratefully a loan of 1 billion Deutsche Marks from Helmut Kohl, chancellor of West Germany. It was *Ostpolitik* again, which meant that Hungary was under German financial protection. For Budapest, this relationship meant more than the old ties of the Warsaw Pact. Honecker and his state were no longer allies for Budapest. The Hungarian leaders were on a fast train towards capitalism and the West.

In early June 1989, it was time for the Poles to pull on the leash. The round table talks resulted in a deal between the Party and Solidarity: the Party would keep the majority in the lower house of parliament (*Sejm*), but one-third of it would be contested in open elections. The upper house (*Senat*) would be elected. On 4 June, the second semi-free election behind the Iron Curtain took place, after the one in the USSR. The result was an utter rout of Party candidates: the Solidarity candidates won in nearly every precinct. The days that followed were full of suspense; many in the West, especially Polish-Americans, feared that the Soviets might pull the trigger and use force to prevent changes. Polish politicians knew better: Soviet intervention was simply not coming. In July, after intense negotiations, the leaders of Solidarity proposed a compromise: Jaruzelski could stay as president, but the prime minister would be theirs. It took a while to fulfil the second part of the deal. Only in August, after many manoeuvres (and a rapid reduction of the Party ranks), the Catholic Tadeusz Mazowiecki became the head of the first post-communist Polish government. Polish technocrats began to prepare for a rapid entry into the global capitalist economy, with guidance from the IMF.

Gorbachev, his Politburo, and the Soviet government had other headaches and priorities, mostly domestic. The Congress in Moscow selected the permanent Supreme Soviet as the top constitutional body, and Gorbachev dedicated his energy to the legislative process: he hoped to get new laws in place to steer the Soviet Union towards a 'mixed economy' with representative government. He opened the Soviet borders: hundreds of thousands could travel abroad for the first time in their lives; many of them were Soviet Jews, who began to emigrate to Israel and the United States for fear that this window might soon shut. Indeed, signs of trouble kept multiplying, and events were overtaking the father of perestroika. The economy worsened by the month, and in July a strike of 200,000 miners shook the country. Gorbachev found himself in the same position as Thatcher in 1984–85, yet instead of an austerity regime, the Supreme Soviet and the government met the strikers' demands – which only added to inflation and the state budget deficit. In the South Caucasus, interethnic violence increased, so much so that Shevardnadze, who was on holiday in Georgia in August, had to engage in local troubleshooting. And the Balts prepared their own surprise: 2 million of them formed a giant human belt ('a Baltic Way') from Estonia to Lithuania, demanding the denunciation of the German–Soviet pact of 1939. Most of them wanted to regain sovereignty and leave the Soviet Union.

In June–July 1989, Gorbachev hectically sought to rebalance his domestic reforms and foreign policy. He travelled with a large team of industrial managers and ministers to West Germany. Then he went to France, where he talked to Mitterrand, and then gave another memorable speech in Strasbourg, at the Council of Europe, painting in more dramatic terms his vision of 'a common European home'. He asked the French president to help him to bring the Soviet Union into 'the world economy'. In practice, this would mean Soviet membership of the IMF, the World Bank, and other institutions spurned by Stalin and reviled by communist propaganda for forty years. The final stop of Gorbachev's European tour was the meeting of the Warsaw Pact in Bucharest. Pressed by Romanian dictator Nicolae Ceaușescu and East Germany's Honecker, who told him that 'Poland cannot be lost', the Soviet leader stated his view: the new Poland was a fact, and other eastern European countries were on their own. Still, Gorbachev and his close circle continued to hope that a bloc of eastern European countries would continue to exist for a while. The Warsaw Pact and NATO had to sort out many problems that had accumulated during decades of confrontation. Number one was the planned reduction of conventional forces and armaments (the talks on this opened in March 1989 in Vienna). Number two was the German question and borders. This was a reasonable expectation: even the post-communist government of Poland realized they had to stay in the Warsaw Pact until the post-Second World War Polish borders were recognized by the West.

Soon after Gorbachev left eastern Europe, Bush arrived in Warsaw. The US president had been widely accused of pausing just as history was accelerating. However, while in Poland, Bush had an epiphany: the changes in eastern Europe were real, and Gorbachev was the person who had made them possible. From Warsaw, Bush went to Budapest before a G7 meeting in Paris. What he saw impressed him. He saw the communist technocrats opening – like in China – their countries to capitalism and democracy. He shed tears when Grósz and Németh invited him to cut the last barbed wire on the Hungarian–Austrian border. It upset him when Lech Wałęsa and other Solidarity leaders said they wanted to get rid of all vestiges of communism. While western European leaders thought that the Cold War was over, Bush and Scowcroft feared that 1956 would repeat itself. What if the Poles and Hungarians went too far, and the Soviet hardliners realized they had to save the empire by sending in tanks? The Bush administration thought it was prudent to keep all the instruments of waging the Cold War intact. Still, Bush sent a note to Gorbachev saying that he wanted to meet with him before the end of the year. His adviser Scowcroft set up a special secret group to monitor such scenarios as a possible coup against Gorbachev.

The peaceful melting of communism in Poland and Hungary, and the dismantling of the Iron Curtain borders, put the East German leadership in an impossible situation. Honecker's regime had long since become financially in debt to West Germany, but this was top secret, even from Moscow. Both Western experts and the Soviet government considered the German Democratic Republic a robust economy, one of the strongest in Europe and in the bloc. Many East Germans, however, wanted out, attracted by freedom and consumerist prosperity across the Wall. In August, thousands of East German 'tourists' flooded Hungary, with the clear intention of crossing over to Austria and then to West Germany. The embarrassed Hungarians at first closed the border with East Germany, but then reopened it – after a secret deal with the Kohl government that promised them additional credit. Over 40,000 East German citizens then rushed to Hungary, triggering a political crisis in East Germany.[6] The Western media treated it as another test for Gorbachev, perestroika, and glasnost. Very few realized that it was perestroika itself that was in crisis, and that Soviet attention remained fixated on the rising trouble at home.

The saga of the GDR implosion became the subject of many books and films. Just like the story of the Poles in 1989, this narrative says that the East Germans rose against communism and they – not Gorbachev or Reagan – ended the Cold War in Europe. Yet these revolutions did not happen separately, they were all part of a common tide. The hundreds of thousands of East Germans who demonstrated in October 1989 against Honecker and the Stasi would not have dared to do it had they not been emboldened by developments in Moscow, Poland, and Hungary. In that month, the KGB and military representatives in East Germany bombarded the Kremlin with desperate messages that they required immediate Soviet intervention. The Kremlin did not respond.

Gorbachev, famously, went to East Berlin for the celebration of the 40th (and last) anniversary of the GDR. He continued to adhere to his policy of non-interference. The Soviet military stationed in East Germany received strict orders: whatever happened in the streets of East Berlin, Dresden or Leipzig, the troops should stay in their barracks. The East German regime had just several weeks left. Younger Party members sent Honecker into retirement and scrambled to improvise a semblance of order. The provisional leader, Egon Krenz, the former security chief, knew that the GDR was bankrupt; it could not pay back its debt to the West. He went to Moscow to ask Gorbachev for help. The Soviet leader, however, could not do it, even if he had wanted to: the Soviet Union was in a financial hole as three-quarters of its foreign currency revenues went to service its growing foreign debts. And now Lithuania declared it wanted to exit the USSR, the first of the Soviet republics to do so. Others waited in the wings. Gorbachev wished Krenz good luck in his new job, encouraged reforms, and consented to a tentative plan to start a controlled opening of the borders with West Berlin and West Germany. On 9 November, the confused East German Politburo discussed this measure, and later gave a press conference, but failed to give an exact description of the reform. At one point the Politburo spokesman blabbered that the access to West Berlin was happening 'right away'. Western journalists present at the press conference interpreted it in their own way: 'The Wall is coming down.' The transmission of this sensational news, received by the millions of East Germans who watched and listened to Western channels illegally, caused a stampede at the border checkpoints and an unexpected and uncontrollable breakthrough of the Berlin Wall. It was the most consequential media scoop of the Cold War and indeed the most felicitous and dramatic communications blunder in contemporary history.[7]

Nobody woke up Gorbachev that night. Some later mocked him for losing the Soviet empire in his sleep. Others, like Colonel Vladimir Putin, a KGB officer in Dresden, were dismayed that Moscow stopped answering frantic calls from the GDR. They could not understand that Gorbachev was determined not to use force in any event, and that he had to refocus on the survival of the Soviet Union itself. But the Soviet leader was also full of bravado, which was bizarre even at the time. When Thatcher crowed at 'the crumbling of the totalitarian socialist system' in eastern Europe, Gorbachev told the British ambassador with aplomb that events 'are going in the right direction . . . Perestroika will reach out to you as well.'[8] Gorbachev refused to see the proverbial writing on the wall. His project to negotiate a 'common European home' between the Soviet Union and the West fell victim to the East Germans' and eastern Europeans' frantic stampede away from communism, towards the West.

It was a stampede for freedom from secret police, and also freedom to savour the forbidden fruits on the other side of the Iron Curtain. Most East Berliners, after crossing the Wall, went to Ku'damm (Kurfürstendamm), a posh street with department stores in West Berlin, to taste the fruits and goods of liberty. West Berliners greeted them with generosity: the West German government began to give each person from the East one hundred Deutsche Marks as 'guest money'. The same search for forbidden fruits was everywhere behind the crumbled Iron Curtain. At the end of 1989, *Playboy* magazine claimed it was 'exporting the American dream' as the first American consumer magazine published in Hungarian. That was the kind of perestroika people wanted, at least at that time. And the Western media, above all the American media, were in control of the narrative. Thatcher's words, not Gorbachev's, would be translated and relayed to hundreds of millions.

After snapping, the leash disappeared. One witness and historian of those revolutions quipped: 'What took ten years in Poland took ten months in Hungary, ten weeks in East Germany, and ultimately ten days in Czechoslovakia.'⁹ The latter refers to the 'velvet revolution' that broke out in Czechoslovakia, where millions of people protested and the communist regime was resigned to its fate. The same happened in Bulgaria, where the regime folded and dissidents came to power without even having enough time to get organized as a political opposition. The last holdover was the regime of Ceaușescu in Romania. His dictatorship was severe even by eastern European and Soviet standards. In the 1970s, the Romanian dictator had begun to conduct an 'independent' foreign policy within the Soviet bloc, boycotting whatever Moscow suggested and building relations with China.

Figure 4.5
Violence in Romania capped the series of peaceful anti-communist revolutions in eastern Europe, December 1989.

This endeared Ceaușescu to Nixon and subsequent US presidents, who turned a blind eye to his horrible regime, and praised his 'independence'. The Romanian dictator, however, fell into the same debt trap as other eastern European and Latin American countries: he had to pay back the IMF and Western banks. He chose to do so by imposing great misery on the Romanian people – food shortages and repression – rather than liberalizing. For a short time, it looked like Romania would be a communist island, with revolutionary waves lapping on its borders.

'The Cold War is Buried . . .'

We have no monument to the outbreak of the Cold War, but at least we have got its gravestone. Visitors to the island of Malta who stray from its better-known historical sites may discover a stone in its southeastern harbour that says: 'George Bush. Mikhail Gorbachev. 2–3 December 1989. End of the Cold War'. This stone commemorates the summit between the two leaders who met here: three ships, the USS *Belknap*, the Soviet missile cruiser *Slava*, and the cruise ship *Maxim Gorky*, were moored in this harbour. The idea of a meeting on ships originated with Bush, who had fought in the Pacific during the Second World War and was fascinated by the meeting between Churchill and Roosevelt in Malta in February 1945, before they flew to Yalta to meet Stalin.

Bush arrived on the crest of Western geopolitical and ideological triumph. He suddenly had a formidable hand to play at his meeting with Gorbachev. Anything looked possible, and it was clear that a new order in Europe, perhaps even a new world order, would be shaped primarily by the

United States. Bush, however, refused to make triumphalist remarks such as Thatcher had made. This was because he still did not believe the Cold War was over. In late September, Shevardnadze had told Baker, and then briefed the White House during his official visit, that the Soviet economy was in terrible shape. The CIA had reported on this for months, but first-hand evidence struck the US leadership. Something extraordinary was indeed going on in the USSR, and this could mean huge instability. Scowcroft knew that empires do not disintegrate easily, particularly empires such as the Soviet one. He advised the president that the revolutions in eastern Europe could tip the balance inside the Soviet Union, and hardliners might overthrow Gorbachev. Bush concluded it would be prudent to help Gorbachev manage the rapid decline of Soviet power and stay in control of his military and hardliners.

There were three issues that concerned Americans most: Soviet assistance to Cuba and Nicaragua, which continued; the Soviet troops stationed in East Germany; and the future of the dreaded Soviet nuclear missiles. A major complication was the Baltic problem: if Gorbachev reacted to Lithuanian separatism with force, the pressure would be hard on the US administration to impose sanctions on Moscow – what would then happen to the other three concerns? It was impossible, however, to ignore the demands of the Balts for independence; they had broad popular support in America.

Gorbachev arrived in Malta from Italy, buoyed by an enthusiastic welcome there: in Milan, he had been mobbed by ecstatic crowds who viewed him as a peacemaker and a hero. Gorbachev came to the summit to declare the end of the Cold War. The sea in the Maltese harbour was choppy, even stormy, so the talks had to be held on Soviet territory, on board the *Maxim Gorky*. The Americans arrived showing signs of seasickness and appearing somewhat tense. In his introductory speech, Gorbachev made a carefully prepared announcement: 'I want to say to you and the United States that the Soviet Union will under no circumstances start a war. The Soviet Union is no longer prepared to regard the United States as an adversary.' It was a hand extended to the Americans to bury the hatchet and negotiate a partnership. The Soviet delegates, however, noted that Bush did not react, as if he failed to notice the meaning of such a declaration. The extended hand did not get a handshake.

Bush instead went through the American demands. He wanted the Soviet Union to stop assistance to Fidel Castro and the communist Sandinistas. This perplexed the members of the Soviet delegation: they believed they had just offered something much more important. Gorbachev, however, appeared to be unflappable and energetic. He beamed with pleasure when Bush said that he wanted to suspend the discriminatory terms of US–Soviet trade, imposed in 1974. He also promised to explore with Congress how to increase American credit to Moscow. He approved Soviet participation in negotiations on free trade. He said nothing, however, about Soviet membership of the IMF and World Bank. Gorbachev hinted that some of his economists had advised him to ask for a big Western loan, about $16–20 billion, to import Western goods and quell the discontent of Soviet consumers. Bush replied that the US had its own budgetary problems, trying to deal with the financial mismanagement of the Reagan administration. During the next two years, the administration refused to offer financial assistance to its troubled ex-foe.

There was also a one-on-one meeting of the leaders on the situation in the Baltic states. Bush reminded Gorbachev that the United States had never recognized those countries as a legal part of the Soviet Union. Gorbachev explained to Bush his problem: he could not just let the Lithuanians go, because this would create a precedent for other republics. The Soviet Union still had to establish a constitutional order instead of a fake Stalinist confederation. Bush replied: 'If you use force – you don't want to – that would create a firestorm.' There was no longer any pretence of equality between the Soviet Union and the United States. Only recently, the White House had employed military force again in Central America, to remove the dictator of Panama, Manuel Noriega, and put him in an American prison on charges of drug trafficking. This contrasted with the Soviets choosing not to use force in eastern Europe, and now Bush was politely warning Gorbachev that he could not exercise force against a separatist republic.

Gorbachev was determined to put his spin on the summit. His resourceful press secretary Gennady Gerasimov had already declared on American TV that 'We now have the Frank Sinatra doctrine'. He was jokingly referring to Sinatra's famous song, with the refrain: 'I did it my way.' In Malta, Gerasimov came up with another punchline: 'We buried the Cold War at the bottom of the Mediterranean.' Millions of Europeans applauded. Soviet citizens, who heard this on TV, received the news with hope. Many of them, however, did not feel immense relief, like people in the West, because they were aware of the dire state of the economy and the ethnic conflicts inside their country. Shevardnadze's assistant rued in his diary: 'Only the well-nourished people in America and Europe can applaud their liberation from the fear of nuclear Apocalypse. This feeling is denied to the country where hunger and misery cloud the light for people.'[10]

After Malta, the US leadership made two crucial moves on the geopolitical chessboard. Bush went to Brussels for a NATO session, a one-on-one talk with Chancellor Kohl. During the previous week the German leader had greatly upset Gorbachev, but also Thatcher, Mitterrand, and some of the western European leaders, when he announced to the Bundestag, without any warning, a ten-point programme. It was a pledge that West Germany would take care of the economy and finances of East Germany. Kohl, however, understood how sensitive his policy would be for Germany's European neighbours. He also declared that he would abide by the principles of Helsinki and the European Economic Community and that 'the future architecture of Germany must fit in the future pan-European architecture'. At the meeting with Bush, Kohl assured him that if Germany were united, it would remain a US partner within NATO. This became a cornerstone of European history.[11]

Another US move concerned China. Scowcroft flew to Beijing, where he assured Deng Xiaoping and other Chinese leaders that nothing that happened in Europe would affect the Sino-American partnership. The Chinese accepted the American reassurances and expressed open contempt for Gorbachev's policies. The Chinese foreign minister said that Gorbachev wanted to build a new order, but he could not manage order in his own country.

Gorbachev returned to Moscow to meet with the leaders of the Warsaw Pact – the bloc that lived on borrowed time. The meeting was an assortment of old figures, like Ceaușescu and Jaruzelski, and new people like the Catholic anti-communist Mazowiecki. One senior Soviet diplomat whispered to Shevardnadze's assistant: 'Half of these people will not be around at the next meeting.' The assistant thought to himself: 'If the next meeting ever happens.' Ceaușescu did not wait long for an exit: on 16 December, workers rose up in Timișoara, Romania. Five days later the Romanian dictator, who had been convinced that the people loved him, had to flee for his life as workers in Bucharest took to the streets. The military turned against him too. For a brief moment, civil war in Romania seemed like a real possibility, and the Americans approached Gorbachev and Shevardnadze asking if Soviet forces could be used to put an end to the bloodshed. The answer was no. Soon the dictator and his wife, Elena, were caught and executed after a drumhead trial. The bloodshed in Romania did not significantly affect the general euphoria around peaceful revolutions in eastern Europe.

When on 16 December Shevardnadze arrived for his first official visit to the NATO headquarters in Brussels, the entire staff came out and greeted him with applause. The Cold War seemed to be ending in the most auspicious way for the West. But was it really the end? Bush, Scowcroft, Baker, the Pentagon, and many in Congress and in Washington think-tanks were uncertain. Communism was collapsing everywhere in Europe, even in the Soviet Union; increasingly, former communists wanted to join the capitalist 'civilized' world. Still, all the revolutionary changes in Europe appeared too miraculous to be irreversible; even the science fiction of the previous years had not imagined anything like it. The Soviet army was still intact, with over 3 million officers and soldiers, 390,000 of them in East Germany, plus tens of thousands of tanks. It simply did not look like the end of any other war. Many people in the Soviet Union and especially in the United States did not have time to reassess reality. Recent changes could be reversed and had to be locked in. This became a refrain for American policy for the next two years.

CHAPTER 15
Other Endings

German Unification and Treaties

The country whose uncertain fate had led to the Cold War in the first place was Germany. During the 1950s, the great success of the Federal Republic and the economic failure of East Germany, along with other factors, had led to the stand-off over West Berlin. The *Ostpolitik* launched by the West German government had crucially helped set the stage for the end of the confrontation in Europe. Without the dedicated anti-fascist Willy Brandt and the two decades of reconciliation and economic cooperation he launched, the events of 1989 would have been hard to imagine. The images created by Second World War enmity would have been impregnable barriers, on both sides. And perhaps Soviet troops would have prevented the East Germans from getting rid of their pro-Soviet regime.

This background must be kept in mind when we look at Europe during 1990. It was not enough for the Soviet side to declare the Cold War over. It was vital to reach a set of agreements to codify the outcomes of the last world war and many revolutions. The treaties of 1990 revolved around one major geopolitical fact: the unification of Germany and restoration of its full sovereignty. Germany had been unified for the first time in 1870–71, by the wars of Chancellor Otto von Bismarck, after German troops had laid siege to Paris. The German Reich, the outcome of that unification, is widely believed to have been a major cause of two world wars. The agency and context of the second reunification could not have been more different. This time the East German people, not the 'iron and blood' chancellor, drove the unification. And the background was the crumbling of communist dictatorships, democratic revolutions, and strides towards Europe's integration.

History, however, is never predetermined. And as 1990 began, there was a lot of suspense. After the fall of the Wall, different scenarios seemed possible. Years later, Scowcroft, national security adviser to President Bush, recalled that the White House saw a danger: what if Gorbachev made an offer to Kohl that the chancellor felt he could not refuse? Had the Soviet leader promptly offered a grand deal – withdrawal of Soviet troops in exchange for Germany's neutrality – what would have happened? In 1952 Stalin had suggested exactly that. Many in West Germany, including Kohl's foreign minister Hans-Dietrich Genscher, would have supported such an option. This would have meant the end of NATO and US military dominance in western Europe. Scowcroft wondered: 'I still don't know why Gorbachev did not do it.'[1]

For two months after Malta, the Soviet leadership was fixated on other issues: Lithuania wanted freedom; at a Congress in Moscow the opposition demanded a multi-party system; and chaos in Azerbaijan required the use of Soviet troops. Only in late January 1990 did Gorbachev convene a group of senior officials to discuss what Moscow should do if

West Germany were to move to take over East Germany. The group members remembered the German aggression of 1941 that cost the Soviet Union 27 million lives. Shevardnadze's brother had died in the first weeks of the invasion. Two of Gorbachev's advisers had fought in the war as officers. The head of the KGB had been evacuated from Stalingrad. The top military had volunteered in the first months of the war. In a different situation, with a different leader, such a gathering might have concluded that the disappearance of the GDR was an existential threat for their country. The discussion, however, was remarkably calm.

Gorbachev did not speak first but let his close assistant (who wrote a memo of this meeting) lay out the only option he envisaged: to cooperate with Kohl and negotiate a settlement with the Western powers. That settlement should finish what had started in Potsdam in 1945, but also must take account of the reality on the ground. Gorbachev thought that the Soviet Union had 'no moral right' to oppose the free will of the German people. At the same time, he said, it was better to stretch the process of reunification for as long as possible. The traumas of 1941–45 had not gone away completely. For four decades the presence of the Soviet army in the heart of Europe was justified as the fruits of victory in the Second World War. Memories of Stalingrad, the Leningrad siege, and Kursk had become part of the identity of the Soviet military, the KGB, and the Soviet people at large. Gorbachev said: 'It is necessary that Germany, and Europe, and the USSR get used to this [reunification] goal.' He also added: 'Nobody should consider that a unified Germany could join NATO. The presence of our troops [in East Germany] would preclude it. And we can withdraw them if [the] Americans withdraw – and they will not do so for a long time.'[2]

The Soviet leadership, like everyone, thought that German unification might take years. Western European leaders, including Thatcher and Mitterrand, also wanted to slow down the process. The quick disappearance of East Germany confounded their expectations. Those who thought that the GDR was a stable state, and that its population's separate identity would prevent reunification, were wrong. Indeed, the flight of young people across the Wall, which often ended in their tragic death, had told a different story. After the Wall fell, the separate existence of East Germans became untenable: the autocracy, border control, their separate identity, and their currency all collapsed simultaneously. This caught both Gorbachev and Western leaders by surprise.

In March 1990 the GDR held elections, and Kohl employed his most powerful tool: the Deutsche Mark. The West German currency reserves were deep, and the chancellor offered a monetary union with the GDR, with a pledge to exchange people's savings in the devalued Eastern mark to the strong Deutsche Mark, one to one. It was the greatest use of money in international politics since the Marshall Plan. Any prospect of a separate East German sovereignty vanished overnight. Gorbachev's position on NATO remained the only obstacle to German unification. On this, Kohl acted in close coordination with the Bush administration. They agreed that they should strike the right balance between bringing a unified Germany into NATO and keeping Gorbachev in power. As a result, ultimatums were counterproductive. Secretary of State Baker arrived in Moscow to tell Gorbachev that the idea of two Germanies or German neutrality was off the table and made a vague pledge that NATO's jurisdiction and military presence would not be extended 'one inch to the East'. That phrase would become a subject of immense controversy in the decades to follow. Gorbachev replied: 'Of course, the expansion of the NATO zone is unacceptable.'[3]

Kohl came to Moscow right after Baker. To his delight, Gorbachev agreed that the Germans had the right to live in a unified state. The Soviet leader, however, stuck to his demand that a united Germany should not be in NATO. The Americans and Kohl decided to give the Soviet side more time. They knew that Gorbachev was running out of options. On 1 July, East Germany would enter the Deutsche Mark zone. From that day on, the Soviet troops and their dependants in East Germany would find themselves in a country where their salaries had no value. When parting with Kohl, Gorbachev hinted at this problem. With tact, Kohl offered him friendship and assistance. 'If you have any problems, I would be ready to meet you at the first sign, at several hours' notice.'[4] The roles were reversed. Now Kohl was making the embattled Soviet leader an offer that he could not refuse.

Gorbachev was embattled domestically, stuck between the Party, the army, and the KGB on one hand, and the republics claiming sovereignty on the other. In March 1990 he assumed the new constitutional post of the president of the USSR, elected by deputies of the Soviet Congress. This, however, did not help him to govern the increasingly fractious country. At the end of May, during a summit with Bush in Washington, he made a decisive step: he hinted that the Germans had the right to choose an alliance, according to the Helsinki principles.

This was an impromptu answer at a press conference, and it took the Soviet delegation, including the top military, by surprise. Just a few weeks earlier, at the Politburo, Gorbachev had fulminated and had not wanted to give a green light to NATO expansion. In parallel, Soviet government officials began to talk to Kohl, his advisers, and West German bankers about possible assistance to prevent imminent Soviet bankruptcy. Economics trumped geopolitics and historical memories.

On 15 July, Kohl came to Moscow for a one-on-one meeting with Gorbachev. The leaders agreed to work out a treaty that would cancel their mutual demands and obligations. Gorbachev accepted that a unified Germany would stay in NATO and promised that Soviet troops would leave German soil after four years. Meanwhile, Kohl agreed that the Soviet army in East Germany would be tacitly funded from the German budget. The talks continued in the North Caucasus, Gorbachev's homeland, in a cordial atmosphere; teams of bureaucrats and experts finalized the agreements. Gorbachev was jubilant: he viewed it as a major diplomatic result.

This was the third time the Germans and the Soviets had reached a bilateral treaty of great significance. The first treaty was signed in Rapallo, Italy, in 1922, when the two countries also cancelled each other's debts, settled grievances, and agreed on secret military cooperation. The second was the Nazi–Soviet pact of 1939, made in Moscow, which opened the gates to the Second World War. This time, the treaty would not impair in any way the emerging architecture of Europe, built on Western institutions. After many decades of wars and estrangement, there was a lasting foundation for partnership between Russians and Germans, and not at the expense of peace in Europe and the world. The meeting and the resulting treaty paved the way to German unification and NATO membership.

There were other important treaties in the making during 1990. One was the Treaty on the Final Settlement with Respect to Germany, which involved 'two plus four': the two German states and the four powers that had occupied Germany after 1945. This document formalized the restoration of one German state with full sovereignty within the borders established after the Second World War. In Vienna, diplomats were in a rush to finalize the Treaty on Conventional Armed Forces in Europe (CFE). The goal of this was to achieve a sharp reduction of armies on the continent. Each bloc, the Warsaw Pact and NATO, was asked to share the permitted level of armaments among its member countries. The number of tanks on each side was reduced to 'only' 20,000 tanks; 6,800 combat aircraft were permitted, and 2,000 attack helicopters. Any kind of military exercise had to be transparent and observed by the other side. Each side could at any time ask to inspect what the other side was doing and they would be obliged to comply. Last but not least, there was another multilateral agreement under discussion – a Charter for a New Europe, modelled after the Helsinki Final Act. It was a grand attempt to promulgate common norms, principles, and values. The document was negotiated by a commission that included thirty-five countries of Europe, as well as the United States and Canada. Its preamble said:

> Europe is liberating itself from the legacy of the past.
> The courage of men and women, the strength of the will

of the peoples and the power of ideas of the Helsinki Final Act have opened a new era of democracy, peace and unity in Europe.[5]

A new era of convergence and harmony? Many understood that the year between November 1989 and November 1990 marked a triumph of the West and the Western liberal order created during the Cold War. The treaties were to lock this in. The unified Germany intended to keep the US bases and troops on its territory, although not on the territory of the former GDR. The formal equality of the CFE concealed a new geopolitical reality because Poland and other eastern European states were eager to join the West as soon as possible. And the Soviet army, which had accumulated a vast superiority over NATO in armaments, would now have to destroy a huge number of tanks, motorized vehicles, artillery, and other equipment. The post-communist governments of Hungary and Czechoslovakia were already demanding that Moscow start to pull out its forces from their territory. The Polish government did not do the same only because it was waiting for a comprehensive settlement that would mean the Polish–German border was recognized internationally.

Gorbachev was prepared to overlook all of this in the name of the future, a common European home, and new thinking. In September, he called Kohl and asked him for emergency financial assistance to the value of 12 billion marks to help Soviet economic reforms. Kohl agreed. The next two months were a sprint of international conferencing and signing ceremonies. The Final Settlement was signed first, then on 3 October 1990, Germans celebrated their unity. Then on 9 November, the first anniversary of the fall of the Wall, the Soviet Union and Germany signed a treaty that included all that Gorbachev and Kohl had agreed upon. And on 18 November, key leaders, including Bush and Gorbachev, met in Paris to sign the Charter for a New Europe and the Treaty on Conventional Armed Forces in Europe.

For Gorbachev, Shevardnadze, and those who supported perestroika and new thinking, the Paris summit was as important as the one in Malta. It was a kind of a peace gathering that symbolized another end of the Cold War. Yet many senior military and KGB officers viewed the past year as a geopolitical catastrophe. In the months leading up to the Paris meeting, top Soviet military officials made a frantic effort to save the Soviet military equipment slated for destruction under the CFE terms. They ordered the shipment of 21,000 of the newest tanks and armoured personnel carriers, as well as 20,000 artillery pieces, from East Germany and eastern Europe to Soviet Central Asia – outside of the treaty's geographical scope. The Americans spotted these shenanigans from space satellites and complained to Shevardnadze. The Soviet foreign minister wrote a letter to Gorbachev, decrying the military's cheating and threatening to resign. The Soviet Union stood on the brink of bankruptcy, he wrote, and 'our partners' in the West, instead of supporting the Soviet state as they did, could have toppled it – not by tanks and aircraft, 'but by simple refusal to finance us'. The military, however, stuck to its guns. The minister of defence, Dmitry Yazov, who was wounded in 1942 at Leningrad and was in Cuba during the crisis of 1962, was incapable of changing his mind. The Americans remained his enemies. In Paris, during the signing ceremony, Yazov muttered to himself: 'This treaty means we have lost World War III without a shot being fired.'[6]

Soviet Collapse

In January–March 1990, Gorbachev convened a special Congress that introduced political pluralism and elected him the president of the USSR – so that Party stalwarts could not remove him from power. Gorbachev's new partners, Bush, Kohl, and Mitterrand, helped him as well: they needed the Soviet leader as the signatory and the guarantor of the treaties and agreements that locked in the end of the Cold War in Europe. The Bush administration also wanted to deal with Gorbachev to secure the reduction of Soviet nuclear forces, and conducted negotiations with Moscow to this effect.

In August 1990, another international crisis propelled the US–Soviet partnership to a higher level. The Iraqi dictator Saddam Hussein invaded oil-rich Kuwait and posed a threat to the entire Gulf region. Immediately, Shevardnadze, and then Gorbachev, joined the US administration in denouncing the invasion and calling for Iraq to leave. President Bush and his entourage were hugely impressed: Iraq had been a crucial Soviet ally for years, and now the Kremlin had repudiated it. The Soviet Union and the United States were finally on the same side, sharing the same values. For Secretary of State Baker, this was the day when the Cold War ended. Bush and Scowcroft thought that in eastern Europe in 1989 and in the case of German unification the Soviet leadership had to react to unforeseen developments; now they made a choice that nobody forced them to make. Bush met with the Soviet leader in September in Helsinki and offered to build

Figure 4.6
Russians turn against the communist state, Moscow, February 1991.

a new world order together. In October, Gorbachev received the Nobel Peace Prize for 'his leading role in the peace process which today characterizes important parts of the international community'.[7] Had the Cold War finally ended?

There are two camps when it comes to describing how the Cold War ended. On the one hand, some claim that it ended in 1988–90, and then the Soviet Union collapsed for some internal reasons of its own. Many influential observers, among them the US ambassador to Moscow at this time, held this view. The great confrontation, they say, was essentially over once the Soviet leadership repudiated its communist ideology. One prominent scholar wrote: 'It was Gorbachev who ended the Cold War.'[8] On the other hand, President Bush seemed to hold a different view when he said in his State of the Union address in January 1992: 'The biggest thing that has happened in the world in my life, in our lives, is this: By the grace of God, America won the cold war.' This pronouncement, two full years after the Malta summit, suggested that for the US leadership the Cold War was not quite over as long as the Soviet Union existed. Scowcroft reflected many years later: 'Had Gorbachev possessed the authoritarian and Stalin-like political will and determination of his predecessors, we might be still facing the Soviet Union.'[9] In other words, the Soviet Union was a geopolitical base for the Cold War to come back even without communism. Those who have been affected by Vladimir Putin's Russian revanchism and aggression may nod in emphatic agreement. Both viewpoints are irrefutable, because they cannot be disproved by facts alone. It is a matter of different perspectives. This disagreement on the end of the Cold War ran deep in the United States in 1990–91, as well as inside the Soviet Union. Important political rivals of Gorbachev's project rejected his claim that the Cold War was over. Many in the Baltic republics (and their numerous supporters in North America) held the view that the Soviet Union, a continuation of the Russian empire, had to be destroyed with or without communism in power. In 1990, this camp was joined by many among the democratic-minded elites of the Russian Federation, Ukraine, and other parts of the USSR that asserted their sovereignty.

The greatest challenge to Gorbachev's international, as well as domestic, authority came from inside the Russian Federation: his political rival Boris Yeltsin. He was Gorbachev's political twin: born the same year, one month earlier, Yeltsin came from a family of peasants in the Urals and Siberia, benefited from the social mobility enabled by a

Soviet education and the Party, and was brought to Moscow from the provinces to refurbish the rusty system. In 1985–87, Yeltsin was Gorbachev's ally in the Politburo and supervised Moscow, but then had an emotional breakdown, criticized Gorbachev's reforms as insufficient, and was demoted. His political career seemed to be finished. Then he made a remarkable political comeback as a democratic or rather populist leader. In the March 1989 elections to the Congress of People's Deputies, Yeltsin won most of the votes in contested elections in Moscow. His convictions changed remarkably fast. His trip to the United States half a year later helped to transform a communist apparatchik into a self-styled liberal democrat. By early 1990, Yeltsin came to believe that the Soviet Union was an 'evil empire' that oppressed the Russians even more than non-Russians. He convinced himself that the Cold War could not be ended as long as the USSR still existed, and Gorbachev stayed in power. Yeltsin's political career proceeded with meteoric speed, buoyed by the growing crisis of Gorbachev's reforms and leadership. In March 1990, he got himself elected to the new parliament of the Russian Federation; in June he was elected its chairman. This meant a duality of power in Moscow: Yeltsin was the leader of Russia, while Gorbachev presided over the Union.

While Gorbachev made liberalization possible, he was an apparatchik and master of compromise. Yeltsin, in contrast, mingled with crowds and charmed common Russians, workers, and peasants. When 'Gorbynomics' kept failing, Yeltsin became the embodiment of populist anger: in June 1990 he enthusiastically made a claim for 'Russian sovereignty' – a path to the destruction of the Soviet Union. In July, Yeltsin walked out of the Party. In October, he declared that the Russian Federation would undertake a radical leap to a free market, like Poland and other eastern European countries. He and his Russian government refused to pay taxes to the Soviet Union's budget. Yeltsin's mission was to build a 'free democratic Russia' and help other republics, such as the Baltic states and Ukraine, to break out of the 'totalitarian empire' and build something from scratch – either a confederation or a commonwealth. In his scheme, this was the only way to transform the world: a new Russia would be able to become a genuine ally of the US.

Yeltsin gained influential friends in Washington, in Congress, in Cold War think-tanks, and among Republicans and Democrats. Many viewed him as a 'true democrat' as opposed to Gorbachev. A new transnational alliance emerged between American Cold Warriors, promoters of democratization and human rights, and the Politburo maverick who turned his back on the father of perestroika. In the White House and the State Department, however, the Russian politician was viewed as a gadfly. Yeltsin's rebellion, as well as the Baltic drive for independence, threatened to upset the Americans' careful management of Soviet decline, which was the preferred course of the Bush administration. Scowcroft in particular viewed Yeltsin as a demagogue and 'an ambitious opportunist of the first order'. He wrote to Bush that Yeltsin's 'credentials as a democrat are suspicious at best'.[10] Yet this 'opportunist' promised the Americans all the right things, including freedom for the Balts and the end of the 'evil empire'.

In January 1991, the Soviet military and the KGB used force in Lithuania, causing civilian casualties. Western media blamed Gorbachev. The uproar showed how tenuous Gorbachev's foreign policy success was. Suddenly, he was losing the respect and trust of the West by killing unarmed people (many more were killed by the Soviet military in Baku in January 1990, but it did not attract so much attention). The Russian democratic opposition ran amok, fearing a dictatorship, as if Gorbachev had not given them freedom to speak and act. Bush, however, needed Gorbachev's support in the Gulf, where the forces of the United States and their allies prepared to kick the Iraqi army out of Kuwait. After the extended air war came the ground war, called Operation Desert Storm: after just one hundred hours the Iraqi army was defeated, scattered, and sent running. This was the first war after the end of the superpowers' conflict. It demonstrated the vast preponderant military power of the United States over a Soviet-armed Third World country. As the Soviet army was in plain retreat from eastern Europe, this war also showed that the United States had become the only existing pole of the emerging world order, unrivalled and unopposed. Gorbachev tried to prevent the war, but the Americans ignored him. The co-architect of a new world order had no allies at home, and felt weak and humiliated internationally.

It began to dawn on people that the days of the Soviet Union might be numbered. In April 1991, a desperate Gorbachev offered a partnership to his main domestic enemy, Yeltsin. The Soviet president offered to build a new voluntary union, with Yeltsin's Russia as its core member. Yeltsin agreed, but it was only a tactical step. He used a truce with Gorbachev to get himself elected president of Russia, and demanded a place in the Kremlin next to Gorbachev. His goal was to destroy the central state. As the Americans had long feared, the KGB and the army leadership had to respond to this existential threat to the Soviet Union. On 19 August, the top ministers of Gorbachev's government formed a ruling junta and removed Gorbachev from power.

Just weeks earlier, President Bush visited Moscow and signed the START treaty alongside Gorbachev. Suddenly, the world seemed to be set back to restarting the Cold War. In fact, it was not what the junta members wanted to do, but the hundreds of tanks deployed in Moscow spoke louder than any words of reassurance. Yeltsin was not arrested and resisted the coup, and soon hundreds of thousands in Moscow, St Petersburg, and other cities in Russia rose to support him, and protest in favour of democracy and freedom. The junta contemplated the prospect of Western sanctions, financial

Figure 4.7
Bush arrives at the last summit with Gorbachev in Moscow, July 1991. Three weeks later the coup of hardliners ruins the Soviet Union.

bankruptcy, and possibly a civil war. Its members decided to refrain from repeating a Tiananmen Square in Moscow, and the coup folded with a whimper.

The botched coup was a fluke of history that made Yeltsin an unexpected winner, allowing him to dismantle the central Soviet state, ban the Party, cut down the KGB, and proceed with his programme of finishing off the 'evil empire'. It was like a leap into the abyss. Nobody around Yeltsin knew what to do next: there were no cadres, habits, and ideas in 'Russia' to build a functioning liberal-democratic state. And the state coffers were nearly empty, a hard fact that had doomed the junta. At the same time, the shock and the dramatic televised coverage of the events in Moscow irrevocably changed the common narrative of why and how the Cold War came to an end. It was no longer the result of Gorbachev's charm and diplomacy. Yeltsin, who suddenly eclipsed Gorbachev in international stature, emerged as a dragon slayer. His televised triumph conflated the end of the Cold War and the crumbling of the Soviet Union.

Western leaders, above all the Bush administration, were hardly ready for such a unique development. Their former Cold War foe had barely become a partner in the construction of a new order before immediately beginning to implode, and now had been dismantled from the inside. The Balts celebrated independence, with Yeltsin's agreement. The communist leaders of Ukraine, previously quite cautious, joined the nationalists and rushed to declare the independence of the second-largest Slavic republic. Many criticized Bush for timidity and reluctance to recognize a new reality. The White House, however, was concerned about what would happen to Soviet nuclear weapons. In the end, the US administration decided to delay recognition of Yeltsin's Russia and other republics until they satisfied the demands of nuclear safety and took care of Soviet debts and other commitments. Ukraine, meanwhile, held a popular referendum on 1 December. This was a unilateral move that was not accounted for by the Soviet constitution, but by that time the constitution, just like the state, had become defunct. Yeltsin recognized Ukrainian independence two days later, and in a week, he, the Ukrainian president Leonid Kravchuk, and the leaders of Belarus, decided to liquidate the Soviet Union. Gorbachev, the leader without a state, was presented with a fait accompli.

Many years after Gorbachev lost power, a Latvian theatre director staged a play in Moscow about his life. He asked 'Why Gorbachev?' and answered: he was a quirk of history, a humane person who could not be defeated by a dehumanizing political system. The play was cancelled in February 2022, after Vladimir Putin attacked Ukraine. Gorbachev, who had sought to end the Cold War so that his country could be part of an undivided international community, sacrificed his power to achieve this objective. He ended up without a country and a job. Yeltsin and those who shared his vision were triumphant. The first move of 'free Russia' after disbanding the Soviet Union was to send emissaries to Washington, Brussels, and other Western capitals with a message: the totalitarian empire was dismantled and it was – finally – time to celebrate the end of the Cold War. The United States and NATO were now faced with fifteen post-Soviet states. Yeltsin's Russia, after some delicate negotiations, became the internationally recognized legal successor to the Soviet Union. It inherited Soviet debts as well as the Soviet permanent seat on the United Nations Security Council, and became legally responsible for dozens of treaties and obligations reached between 1945 and 1991. The new Russian state, of course, was not entirely new: most of its leaders and public servants came from the Soviet apparatus, bureaucracies, and elites.

In January 1992, just days after Bush declared America's victory in the Cold War, he received a letter from Yeltsin stating that he wanted Russia and the United States to become special allies, to build a new world order based on common human values. Soon Yeltsin arrived to meet Bush at Camp David and restated his offer of an alliance. Bush politely declined. The Russian leader apparently assumed that Russia, as a legal successor to the Soviet Union, had also won the Cold War and demanded special relations and a special status. Instead, there was only one superpower in the world, and everyone else was supposed to be equal. It would take American leaders an entire decade to manage Russia's downgrade from a nuclear superpower to a regional partner. We are still living with the consequences of the failure of this endeavour.

CONCLUSION
The Time of Mercury – After the Cold War

The Cold War ended with a spectacular victory for the US and the West – fortunately, not on the battlefield. The winners did not force the Kremlin to surrender. Nor was it the case that the Soviet Union simply 'ran out of steam' as some have argued.[1] The meltdown of eastern Europe had been caused by the economic failure of the Soviet bloc, but the collapse of the Soviet Union was triggered by Gorbachev's misguided economic reforms, political liberalization, and loss of control over the Soviet state and finances. Rather than using force to regain control over runaway political movements and the countries of the Soviet bloc, the Soviet leader decided to let them go, and accepted the end of the Cold War on Western terms, banking, in return, on Western acceptance of the reformed Soviet Union into 'the civilized community'. Such acceptance was granted only to Gorbachev personally; his country was quickly consumed by internal disorder, unassisted and undefended.

The dissolution of the Soviet bloc and the Soviet Union brought to life a host of independent nation-states and an unprecedented wave of democratization around the world. Not only eastern European countries, but most post-Soviet nations, and even some Soviet satellites, such as Nicaragua, pledged allegiance to democratic principles and began to elect their leaders in competitive elections. Even the remaining autocratic regimes (excluding China, Cuba and North Korea) had to pay lip service to those procedures: democratic *appearances* seemed to have become a necessary condition for international legitimacy and recognition. The same went for human rights and the protection of minorities, as defined by the UN Charter and the Helsinki Final Act. The US government explicitly linked these criteria to its recognition of post-Soviet independent states. Indeed, these norms became synonyms for a 'civilized world', just like European bourgeois table manners and hygiene habits had once been.

The triumph of democratic conventions and freedoms normalized a highly unusual phenomenon: for the first time in history, the world became unipolar. All roads now led to Washington DC. Nobody recognized this fact better than the new leader in the Kremlin. While attending the jubilee UN General Assembly in New York, Yeltsin beseeched Bush to say publicly that the former rivalry had now been transformed into a 'deep mutual trust and alliance'. It appeared as though the bear was once again at American throats, but this time it was going in for a bear hug. For Bush and Scowcroft, with their long memories of the 1970s détente, this insistence felt like déjà vu, harking back to Brezhnev's proposal of a special partnership. Much to Yeltsin's frustration, Bush politely declined such an alliance.

For the next two decades, the United States did not have any rivals when it came to global power. The US dollar headed the snake of global convertible currencies and later towered over the euro, the new common currency of the European Union. By the end of the 1990s, the US even returned to a federal budget surplus. Yet the deficits ballooned despite periodic threats from Congress to shut the government down. Why bother about fiscal solvency if the future finally and indivisibly belonged to America? US military expenditure began to shrink after 1991, but then remained high – around $280–90 billion per year – and later grew again. This was despite the obvious truth that the country faced no threats that justified the enormous military might it possessed. The hostile regimes of North Korea, Iran, Iraq, and Cuba appeared to be desperate and doomed outliers without Soviet assistance, the last blotches on the brightening horizon. Most former enemies, including eastern European countries, the Baltic nations, Ukraine, and post-Soviet Russia, scrambled to join 'the family of civilized nations'. American political scientists insisted that the US towered over the world not because of its military power but because it held the 'soft' power of attractive democratic society, inclusivity, and mass culture.

American leaders and their Western partners could never really understand what caused their Soviet rival to disappear. Yet the Cold War victory proclaimed by Bush in January 1992 brought to life a narrative that shaped the next era. Western Cold War policies, such as 'containment of communism', began, retrospectively, to seem more far-sighted and wise than they actually had been; it was only natural to perpetuate Cold War policies into the new era. The Atlantic alliance, the resilience of NATO, and the remarkable success of European integration had been enshrined, not just as a means to prevent intra-European war, but as the unassailable foundations of the new liberal order. Many aspects of the Western Cold War, however, could not be displayed in this new pantheon. How could one defend many trillions directly spent on military containment, generally bloated military budgets, and marginally effective ideological and cultural propaganda? Or the use of missiles and nukes that seemed to have been equally marginal to the peaceful outcome of the Cold War? Could one really be certain that Gorbachev would not have become the leader of the USSR without Pershing missiles in West Germany in 1983? Furthermore, the policy balance sheets in the Third World were downright contradictory and embarrassing. Was the carpet-bombing of North Korea necessary to produce a prosperous South Korea? What about the folly of engagement in Vietnam, the lasting tolerance of colonialism in Africa and Asia, or the cynical instalment and support of dictatorships in the Middle East in the name of control over oil supplies? Such uncomfortable subjects, the food of revisionist muck-racking research by journalists and historians, were on the margins in the glorious 1990s, treated as a necessary price for freedom, as 'collateral damage' of the overall strategic triumph. This triumphalism encouraged an unlearning of the Cold War.

Francis Fukuyama, a Hegelian philosopher and a junior strategist in the Bush administration in 1990–91, became world famous by talking about 'the end of history': the death of all imaginable ideological alternatives to Western liberalism. The 'end' was also supposed to last endlessly, as if the spirit of Hegel had finally come to rest in New York or London. The main loser of the Cold War, Marxist-Leninist communism, seemed to share the fate of Count Dracula: buried with a stake through its heart. Few dared at the time to recognize that the Marxist-Leninist criticism of capitalism was at least in part valid.

The triumph of the Western liberal order bore a resemblance to the world of the 19th century, dominated by the British empire – but now this domination appeared even more final. Gone seemed to be the scourges of slavery, aggressive nationalism, the subjugation of women, colonialism, imperialism, great power wars – these were turned into objects of castigation and exorcism on Western campuses. The only real spirit that remained alive seemed to be the materialistic faith in mass consumerism and its main provider – capitalist globalization. The 1990s and 2000s were the era of Mercury, the Roman god of commerce and trade. During those two decades the volume of global trade, having already risen exponentially since the 1960s, soared into the stratosphere. The share of global trade during those decades jumped from 15 per cent of worldwide GDP to one-quarter.

In 1925, US president Calvin Coolidge said: 'After all, the chief business of the American people is business.' In 1992, a strategist of young presidential candidate Bill Clinton coined an updated version: 'It's the economy, stupid.' Clinton, inexperienced in foreign affairs, ran against the incumbent president and Cold War winner George H.W. Bush. Nevertheless, Clinton won, just as Churchill had been defeated in 1945 by Attlee. Privately, Clinton admitted he would not have won the US elections in 1992 had the Soviet Union still existed and been run by hardliners. The new Democratic administration had much to learn but believed one thing: that liberal capitalism had conquered the world for democracy. They thought they had discovered a magic formula for eternal peace: global free trade would raise millions for the middle classes; middle-class societies would veer to liberal democracy; democracies would abstain from war. Not just Hegel but also Immanuel Kant seemed to bow to Mercury, who would direct humanity to its happy-ever-after. As if to confirm this, the Russian and Chinese elites seemed to comply and competed to join the West – which they understood not as a kingdom of reason, freedom, and peace, but rather a club of the rich and successful. From St Petersburg and Moscow to Beijing and Shanghai, people adhered to the mantra that the chief business of Russia and China was business. Chequebooks trumped all other books; the early electronic revolution spread the mantra of unbridled consumption. Erstwhile communist bosses were in the vanguard of money-makers. Business centres in Russia and elsewhere had statues of Mercury in their entryways, with the youthful deity wearing a winged cap, with one foot on the globe and another in the air. It seemed a more fitting symbol of the times than statues of revolutionaries, tyrants, and liberators.

Just as all 'isms' seemed to be buried and banished, history struck back against the liberal capitalist order from an unexpected corner. Osama bin Laden's family were beneficiaries of liberal globalization; he had inherited wealth from the construction business that his father had built in Saudi Arabia and other countries. Bin Laden, however, took a different road: he cut his teeth fighting the Soviets in Afghanistan. His mission, after the Soviet collapse, was to drive the

THE TIME OF MERCURY – AFTER THE COLD WAR

Figure 5.1
Statue of Mercury in front of the World Trade Center, Moscow, 2004.

United States out of the Middle East and help to restore an Islamic caliphate there. For his followers, who formed a global network called al-Qaida, the West was 'the anti-world', to be undermined and destroyed by any means available. During the early Cold War, American and British experts on the Middle East thought that Islam was a fading phenomenon in the rapidly modernizing and secularizing region. Islamic fundamentalism and political Islamism, however, emerged, as the logical product of growing Western liberal modernity, and a furious effort to negate it. The first victory of political Islamists was the revolution in Iran in 1978–79. Having suffered the humiliation of the hostage crisis, the United States excommunicated Iran from the liberal trade system and strangled its economy by sanctions. The problem seemed to be contained and marginalized. Overall, however, the Cold War baggage of containment and sanctions could not stop the spread of Islamism. It also led to a certain complacency about the problem. The terrorist acts of 9/11 in New York and Washington DC caught the American national security state, intelligence agencies, and experts strangely off-guard. The shock was arguably even stronger than the effect of the Japanese attack on Pearl Harbor in 1941. The Second World War was fully ablaze when the US Pacific Navy was hit. The lethal strike on American soil, in the heartlands of US financial and political power, came literally out of the blue.

The Republican administration of George W. Bush included many hardline Cold War veterans, who had worked under Reagan and under Bush's father, George H.W. Bush. They believed in the immutable future of the US-led liberal order and saw this as their opportunity to protect and defend it. And they were convinced that their experience of the Cold War had perfectly equipped them to do it: after all, they had defeated communism and knew how to wield power. Their reaction to the 9/11 attacks was emotional, as they feared new terrorist strikes.[2] Yet, even more than this, it betrayed their hubris: a feeling of superiority, righteousness of power, and desire to stamp out a sudden rebellion against the 'natural' order of things. The two years after the terrorist strikes were marked by both psychological phenomena that recalled the Cold War and by post-Cold War triumphalism. 'Nuke them! Bomb them!' was the frantic call on millions of American car bumper stickers. But whom to strike exactly? For decades the enormous power of America had contained the Soviet Union in the Middle East and protected the oil states. This time, however, the worst enemies of America seemed to be not communists but a bunch of fanatical Islamists, many of them originating from Saudi Arabia, a country under US protection throughout much of the Cold War.

The previous cohorts of Cold Warriors, such as Bush, Scowcroft, Kissinger, and others, shared an awareness that American power, as awesome as it appeared, was limited. In the Middle East, Americans had cooperated with the British and listened to their hard-nosed post-colonial lessons. The exception was in Vietnam, where the Americans did not listen to the French, leading to the tragic failure of their efforts to modernize and build the state of Vietnam. The resulting 'Vietnam syndrome' curbed the American appetite to meddle and build democracy in other countries. This syndrome, however, was quickly forgotten when the US won the Cold War. The people of the young Bush administration

(2001–8) did not heed the cautionary tales of history. Even the secretary of defense, Donald Rumsfeld, schooled during the days of détente under Nixon, Ford, and Reagan, decided to wield this unprecedented American power to achieve what prudent Cold Warriors had thought to be unachievable. It took a matter of weeks to crush al-Qaida, the terrorist network created by Osama bin Laden, along with his Taliban allies in Afghanistan. Yet it did not seem like an achievement commensurate with the universalist mission to protect and secure the global liberal order. This messianic goal had a momentum of its own. Nothing less than remaking the entire Middle East seemed to be enough. The Republicans wanted to dismantle the dictatorship of Saddam Hussein in Iraq, and perhaps, in the future, the Islamist regime in Iran as well. Hubris, not fear of another terrorist attack on American soil, was the real reason behind the American invasion of Iraq in 2003. This invasion was conceived and executed without the sanction of the United Nations and against the will of Germany and France, two key American allies in Europe.

It is remarkable, in retrospect, that the last cohort of American Cold Warriors in power had walked into the same quagmire in the Middle East in 2001–3 as their predecessors had in Vietnam. The lessons of the past were overridden or unlearned. Instead of withdrawing from Afghanistan after their spectacular victory, the Bush administration unfurled the slippery and unrealizable goals of nation-building and democratization. The result of this quixotic effort was two decades of unwinnable wars in Afghanistan and Iraq that cost 3 trillion dollars while the Western-funded and trained 'civil society' of the Afghans either fled in the face of the return of the Taliban or became its victim.[3] Even more consequential was the tragic and misguided 'reform' of Iraq that reopened its sectional-religious divides, unleashed years of bloody civil strife, and produced ISIS (the Islamic State of Iraq and Syria), a new Islamist movement commanded by officers of Saddam Hussein's army, which the Americans had defeated and ousted. The US military authorities and contractors to whom the US government delegated pacification of the conquered Iraq tried every strategy but ultimately failed – albeit in a less dramatic way than in Afghanistan. The US overreach in the Middle East sapped the vast reservoir of trust in the American-led global liberal order.

Another strategic miscalculation concerned the rise of China. The US–China alliance against the Soviet Union was a major triumph of Nixon and Kissinger in Asia. That strategic success, in hindsight, could be seen as mitigating the American defeat in Vietnam. During the last years of the Cold War, under Reagan, Washington viewed the US–China partnership as calibrated and conditional. The brutal suppression of the students' revolt in Tiananmen Square led to a decisive deviation from this policy in 1989–91. The Bush administration faced a tough choice: to salvage its relationship with a resurgent communist autocracy in China or follow public opinion and sanction it. The administration decided to ignore human rights considerations. They adhered to Nixonian geopolitics and valued an alliance with Beijing as a geostrategic check on an increasingly improbable resurgence of Soviet power.

Then came the era of Mercury. The disappearance of the Soviet Union coincided with the tour of Deng Xiaoping to southern regions of China, where 'the butcher of Tiananmen' relaunched the transition to a market economy. This opened, as if by magic, the way for enormous flows of American, Japanese, and western European investments and technology into a country that had just reasserted its Party-state regime. While in 1979–91, $44 billion of direct foreign investments had gone to China, in 1992–99 the amount increased to $283 billion.[4] While Gorbachev and his successor Yeltsin struggled and failed to receive a promise of aid or investment for Russia, Deng's China received amounts that surpassed the Marshall Plan of 1948–52 many times over.

The conditions and dynamics of this Western investment into China's rise vastly differed from Cold War policies in West Germany and Japan during the 1950s. Then, the Americans had invested into the countries that were secured as part of their geostrategic zone of influence, with their troops on the ground. Those countries had experienced liberal democracies earlier, vowed to rebuild them, and fully accepted their dependence on the United States. To reward their new allies, the US government opened American markets for German and Japanese businesses and backed their integrationist drive. In the end, several decades of the Cold War and liberal integration forged a Western community, bonded not just by temporary security concerns and economic interests but also by common values. No such thing had happened between China and the West in the 1990s. The American government opened the US domestic market to cheaper 'made in China' goods with the justification that the scheme of consumerism–middle class–democratization would eventually transform China and bring the 'Middle Empire' into the liberal order under a benevolent US hegemony.

Ultimately, however, American attitudes to China were shaped by the irresistible logic of profit-making, not by strategic considerations. Mercury became the god of 'Ameri-China', as journalists between to call the symbiosis of the US and Chinese economies. Big Western corporations and investors, not strategists and statesmen, became the architects of this economic miracle. China joined the US-led capitalist globalization as the main 'Asian factory' of goods and products – many of them licensed and outsourced by Western corporations. Western investors, as well as their Asian partners of Japan, Hong Kong, Singapore, and Taiwan, used Chinese stability, ensured by the Party-state and communist discipline, to take advantage of cheap, educated labour.

In the 1950s, America had opened its markets to its former enemies so that they did not fall to communism and chaos, and it had worked remarkably, thanks to many supportive factors. In the 1990s, the West opened its markets to communist China and helped it to build a modern industrial-technological base, ignoring the ghosts of Tiananmen Square. But the expectation that economic and trade symbiosis between the two giants would eventually make China increasingly look like America was a grand delusion. The levers of economic and financial controls in China remained in the hands of 'Red families', members of the senior Chinese communist leadership, who had successfully combined Leninist politics and liberal economics. China's historical memories and its leadership's long-term intentions were bound to drive the two empires apart. In the eyes of the Chinese rulers, Mao's course of the 1940s was essentially correct: the alternative was a regime such as that of the Guomindang, a weak autocracy that depended on Washington. The Soviet collapse became Beijing's nightmare: all Chinese rulers concluded that uncontrollable democratization and liberalization could be a death knell to China's sovereignty, unity, and internal order.

Finally, a major – if not unexpected – breach in the US-constructed global liberal order was Russia becoming a rogue state. The vast federation, legal successor to the Soviet Union, had an extremely dramatic and chaotic 'democratic moment' in 1992–94. Pro-Western euphoria was strong among Russians; Yeltsin and his supporters regarded the West, particularly the United States, as a teacher and a partner. They claimed that Russia had played the decisive role in destroying communism and a totalitarian state. Scholars continue to debate what happened to make this moment fade away, replaced by a chauvinist and imperialist upsurge. Many in the West argued, retrospectively, that 'path dependency' in Russian history was too great. To put it simply, the country that had hardly ever lived under a functioning parliamentary liberal democracy was doomed to slide back to authoritarianism and thereby to its old demons of imperialist greatness. There are also many disgruntled Russian liberals who argue – also retrospectively – that the democratic moment in Russia was wasted. They find that without a complete purge of the old elites, the re-emergence of autocrats, namely Vladimir Putin, was inevitable. A few Russian liberal politicians, however, point to the unfortunate collaboration between reformist leadership and Western governments that, instead of rapid progress, led to backsliding. Indeed, Russian GDP slid down by over 40 per cent, over half of the employed population was thrown into poverty, and Soviet-era safety nets, such as free crèches, kindergartens, schools, and medicine disappeared. Life expectancy, particularly for males, dropped to record lows for any developed country in peacetime. Market forces and consumption levels only began to pick up in Moscow and other large cities around 1997, but then a default, caused by unregulated financial speculation, erased people's savings for the second time since 1991.

In the 1930s the Great Depression had caused major social upheaval in established democracies such as the United States and France. It also killed Weimar Germany and spawned the Third Reich. In Russia, the post-Soviet recession devastated the middle classes and produced widespread nostalgia for late Soviet stability, might, and glory. Liberal reformers, where they were still in power, feared such a communist-nationalist ressentiment. Unfortunately, for some of them, Chile's under Augusto Pinochet was a better model than the system of checks and balances. When the Russian parliament in 1992–93 exploded in opposition to Yeltsin's reforms and many leaders of the Russian Federation units sided with parliament, Yeltsin and his advisers prepared an anti-constitutional coup. The president ordered the dissolution of parliament. When this triggered civil strife, Yeltsin sent tanks to fire at the building where parliament sat. The Russian democratic moment went up in flames. The victorious Yeltsin changed the Russian constitution, making the parliament and federal units dependent on the super-presidency. The oligarchy of Russian billionaires, created by robber-baron privatization, entered into a concordat with the deeply unpopular Yeltsin. The new regime was democratic in name only; a few well-connected entrepreneurs snatched state property for pennies and pumped money into Yeltsin's re-election. The media were corrupted and television became the main tool of political manipulation. Russia ended up where much of Latin America and South Korea had been during the 1950s: its powerful military-industrial-scientific complex was in a shambles, without any promising modern replacement in sight.

American influence on Russian affairs was limited, but far from negligible. The Clinton administration sought to bring Russia into the Western orbit and bet on Yeltsin and a younger crop of Russian liberal technocrats. On balance, however, the US government did not do enough to steady Russia on its pro-Western track. And some US policies weakened Russian reformers and nourished anti-Americanism. Those policies, just like in the Middle East, repeated the mistakes of American Cold War practices and ignored the bitter lessons of the past.

One such lesson was the US experience in non-democratic countries in the global south. American support of pro-Western but corrupt leaders had only made the US more unpopular, produced more corruption, and ultimately led to a widespread backlash. Clinton made a similar error in Russia: he had a personal relationship with 'Tsar Boris' Yeltsin, and this made the White House support Yeltsin as the ultimate 'guarantor of Russian democracy' and approve his coup of 1993, and later his war against the breakaway republic of Chechnya in 1994–95. It would have been better for all had America instead promoted institutional checks and balances in Russia, rather than backing 'their guy' in the Kremlin. This would have better preserved their reputation as 'honest friends' among Russian pro-Western elites. Instead, the Americans and their Russian reformist partners came to be associated with Yeltsin's disastrous rule. When Yeltsin's presidency began to disintegrate, Clinton and US diplomats argued that at least they could reach some important objectives, and managed to make Russia part of the global economic order. Perhaps, the logic went, one day Russia would also become part of the liberal political order.

The flaw of this approach, however, became clear after Yeltsin bequeathed his powers to an ex-KGB colonel, Vladimir Putin. The new Russian president wanted to be a player in the Western club, but on his own terms. He gradually revealed the same inclinations as the rulers of China. In 2007, Putin had already begun to try to get off what he perceived as the American hook: he no longer wanted to be a US partner on American terms. At an international forum on European security in Munich, Putin attacked the unipolar world order and came up with a list of grievances against US hegemony. He also called NATO enlargement a violation of promises made to Gorbachev in 1990. And a year later, Putin ordered the Russian army to invade Georgia, allegedly in response to its military provocation.

One good lesson from the Cold War was that US security and commercial commitments, when they worked in harmony, helped to transform former enemies into friends. This did not happen in Russia. As we have already seen, there was no chance of Marshall-Plan-like aid for Gorbachev, or subsequently for Yeltsin's government. In 1992, the State Department began to work on a large aid package for Russia, yet this effort fell victim to the presidential elections, where Bush was defeated by Clinton. The economic dimension of US relations with Russia was, from the start, delegated to international and non-government organizations, and private businesses and entrepreneurs. The logic of Mercury in Russia, however, worked in a skewed way, the very opposite of the way it worked in China. In the stable authoritarian China with its cheap, educated labour, the US corporations made the US government subordinate American national interests to business interests. Russia, with its rapidly shrinking economy and financial free-for-all, attracted primarily American seekers of quick profit, not serious investors. From a business angle, Russia seemed like a secondary country, one that could be ignored.

Washington remained highly ambiguous regarding the future role of Russia in the US-led global order, especially in the post-Cold War security and economic structures in Europe. During German reunification, Western powers worked out an informal understanding with Gorbachev and the Soviet military that NATO would not be expanded eastwards to include Poland and other countries beyond Germany. The sudden Soviet collapse created a new situation: the West could not ignore a geostrategic vacuum in eastern Europe. To complicate this ambiguity, the Russian government signalled to NATO leaders that Russia wanted to be first among equals among the new members of the Atlantic alliance. Yeltsin warned of the flipside of his offer: an expansion of NATO without Russia could paint him and

Russian pro-Western forces into a corner and feed the surging nationalist and communist opposition.

George H.W. Bush's White House understood the strategic risks involved in choosing eastern European security over a partnership with Russia. Experts correctly assumed that the expansion of NATO would immediately create a new security dilemma in eastern Europe, undermining pro-Western liberals in Russia and eventually imposing on Washington a commitment to defend countries of which the US public rarely heard. This had been successfully done during the Cold War. There was, however, no valid cause to repeat such a feat again, given a weak and compliant Russia. Those in the US national security structures who, since the Cuban Missile Crisis, had viewed control over nuclear weapons as the most important issue, came up with the innovative idea of a 'Partnership for Peace' that would include all eastern European and post-Soviet countries, including Russia. Nothing was more important, they claimed, than keeping a nuclear Russia, however weakened, in partnership with the United States.[5]

Clinton's impromptu decision in 1993 to invite Poland, the Czech Republic, and Hungary to join NATO upended these careful calculations and ended the strategic ambiguity. The American foreign policy community, and the Clinton administration itself, became badly split over this new idea. George Kennan penned a sharp critique of NATO enlargement into eastern Europe. With uncanny clairvoyance, he predicted that the 'open door' expansion would ultimately bring NATO to the borders of Russia and trigger a war over Ukraine. This warning was dismissed by many of the same people who had lionized Kennan's wisdom and the policy of containment.[6] Clinton and his advisers claimed, then and later, that Russia received a fair deal from the West in the form of the NATO–Russia partnership, as well as the offer of a place in the G7 group of developed countries. The problem, however, was that this partnership did not anchor Russia in the NATO-based European security architecture. And this sort of relationship left Russia without a real stake in the European integration process. Russian nationalists dismissed the arrangement as a ruse. The sense of Russia being marginalized grew when the European Union, formed in 1992 at Maastricht, began also to accept countries of eastern Europe and the Baltic states; in 2013, Brussels offered an association agreement to Ukraine. In the eyes of Russian nationalists, including Putin, NATO and the EU were acting as strategic twins, both aimed at Russia's exclusion from European security and economic blocs.

It was not entirely unrealistic to expect Russia to 'join the West' and develop along a different, non-authoritarian path. Although Russia had never known democracy, it was culturally European and had a long-standing (if limited) liberal and humanitarian tradition. In the eyes of the West, however, China always seemed more attractive as a candidate for inclusion in the global order than Russia. No doubt capitalism and profitability played a decisive role. But this sense was also informed by the fact that the Soviet Union and Russia had often played the role of the Other to the concept of Europe and Euro-Atlanticism, especially during the Cold War. In the early 1990s, Yeltsin and Moscow liberals still hoped they could overcome this bias and turn their country into a member of the Euro-Atlantic 'concert'. They ended up disappointed and frustrated. US hegemony, Yeltsin began to suspect, was at the root of Washington's reluctance to accept Russia as a full member of its alliance. NATO's first secretary general, Lord Ismay, had defined its triple mission as follows: 'To keep Americans in [Europe], Germans down, and Russians out.' This formula resurfaced during the 1990s with a new component: 'bringing eastern Europeans in'. The countries that had been forced into the Soviet bloc and annexed to the Soviet Union by Stalin zealously capitalized on this anti-Russian bias; their elites demanded American protection against a probable resurgence of the 'bear'. Before long, their concerns became self-fulfilling prophecies.

The enlargement of Western security and economic blocs, and their 'open door' policy for new entrants, including Ukraine and Georgia – but still excluding Russia – became enshrined in the discourse of the liberal order. Some would later say that this approach had been always correct: they pointed to subsequent conflict between Putin's Russia and the European order as the inevitable consequence of Russia's decline and continuing collapse. It is good, they claimed later, that the West had judiciously used Russia's weakness to expand its alliance and helped post-Soviet republics, above all Ukraine, to detach themselves from Moscow. This reading of history mirrored almost exactly the dark, deterministic futurism of the chauvanistic forces in Russia. The latter always accused the United States of a plot to weaken Russia and play sheriff in Europe and in the post-Soviet space. The original liberal narrative of a joint Russian–eastern European–Western victory over communism and totalitarianism was lost between the two antagonistic discourses. By 1999, when

NATO bombed Serbia, ostensibly to protect the rights of Kosovo Albanians, anti-Americanism exploded in Russia, even among some liberals.[7]

The triumphalism of the liberal order and the mislearned or unlearned lessons from the past appear self-evident thirty years after the end of the Cold War. At the same time, it would be another folly, perhaps the ultimate one, to assume that at any time, in any country, a new generation of political leaders can avoid the mistakes of the past purely by being excellent students of history. There is no perfect knowledge or universal theory about how and why things may go wrong in international relations. New democratic elites, just like new autocratic rulers, are bound to walk into the same minefields, in semi-ignorance, driven by uncertainty, fear, arrogance, selfishness, and myopic readings of the past. As one diplomatic veteran remarked: 'Almost every government works day-to-day, by the seat of its pants, responding with inadequate information to events beyond its control driven by timetables set by others.'[8]

Those are words of deep experience. I took them to heart when finishing this book. The historian's task is to give coherent interpretation to chaotic developments; they should abstain from didactic attempts at wisdom and resist the temptation to overinterpret and impose grand schemes on messy human affairs. All the varied traditionalist, revisionist, or post-revisionist interpretations of the Cold War remain simply interpretations.

Our century has already delivered multiple shocks: the pandemic, the Russia–Ukraine war, repeated outbreaks of violence in the Middle East. More are surely in store, above all a looming confrontation between China and the United States. The media keep proclaiming 'a new Cold War'. Should this book have been called *The First Cold War*? Time will tell. For now, let it just be 'A New History' of the old global confrontation – the greatest the world has seen so far.

Further Reading

OVERVIEWS

John Lambertons Harper, *Cold War* (Oxford University Press, 2011); John Lewis Gaddis, *The Cold War* (London: Penguin, 2007); Melvyn Leffler, *For the Soul of Mankind: The United States, the Soviet Union, and the Cold War* (New York: Hill and Wang, 2007); Odd Arne Westad, *The Cold War: A World History* (London: Allen Lane, 2017); Vladislav M. Zubok, *A Failed Empire: The Soviet Union in the Cold War from Stalin to Gorbachev* (Chapel Hill: University of North Carolina Press, 2007); Lorenz M. Lüthi, *Cold Wars: Asia, the Middle East, Europe* (Cambridge University Press, 2020); Sergey Radchenko, *To Run the World: The Kremlin's Cold War Bid for Global Power* (London: Cambridge University Press, 2024).

PART ONE

On Europe's international system after the First World War and its failures see: Zara Steiner, *The Lights That Failed: European International History, 1919–1933* (Oxford: Oxford University Press, 2005); Patrick O. Cohrs, *The New Atlantic Order: The Transformation of International Politics 1860–1933* (Cambridge University Press, 2022). On postwar conditions and the Yalta agreements see: Tony Judt, *Postwar: A History of Europe Since 1945* (London: Vintage, 2010).

On Joseph Stalin see: Simon Sebag Montefiore, *Stalin: The Court of the Red Tsar* (London: Weidenfeld & Nicolson, 2010); Stephen Kotkin, *Stalin: Waiting for Hitler, 1929–1941* (London: Penguin, 2017); Oleg Khlevniuk, *Master of the House: Stalin and His Inner Circle* (London: Yale University Press, 2009).

FURTHER READING

On the cooperation between and clashes of interests of the Soviet Union and the United States see most recently: Francine Hirsch, *Soviet Judgment at Nuremberg: A New History of the International Military Tribunal after World War II* (Oxford: Oxford University Press, 2020), and on the ideological and cultural ingredients for US Cold War interventionism see: John Fousek, *To Lead the Free World: American Nationalism and the Cultural Roots of the Cold War* (Chapel Hill: University of North Carolina Press, 2000); David S. Foglesong, *The American Mission and the 'Evil Empire': The Crusade for a 'Free Russia' since 1881* (Cambridge University Press, 2007); Charles S. Maier, 'The Politics of Productivity: Foundations of American International Economic Policy after World War II', *International Organization*, vol. 31, issue 4 (1977), pp. 607–33.

On the peace arrangements following the Second World War see: S.M. Plokhy, *Yalta: The Price of Peace* (London: Penguin, 2011); Benn Steil, *The Battle of Bretton Woods: John Maynard Keynes, Harry Dexter White, and the Making of a New World Order* (Princeton University Press, 2013).

On Soviet behaviour in eastern Europe in 1944–46 see: Norman M. Naimark, *Stalin and the Fate of Europe: The Postwar Struggle for Sovereignty* (Belknap Press of Harvard University Press, 2019); in Turkey and Iran: Jamil Hasanli, *Stalin's Early Cold War Foreign Policy: Southern Neighbours in the Shadow of Moscow, 1945–1947* (Abingdon/New York: Routledge, 2022).

On the atomic arms race see: David Holloway, *Stalin and the Bomb: The Soviet Union and Atomic Energy, 1939–1956* (Yale University Press, 1996); Campbell Craig and Sergey Radchenko, *The Atomic Bomb and the Origins of the Cold War* (Yale University Press, 2008); Gregg Herken, *The Winning Weapon: The Atomic Bomb in the Cold War, 1945–1950* (Princeton University Press, 2014).

On the Marshall Plan, NATO, and Soviet reactions see: Benn Steil, *The Marshall Plan: Dawn of the Cold War* (New York: Simon & Schuster, 2018); William I. Hitchcock, 'The Marshall Plan and the Creation of the West', in Melvyn P. Leffler and Odd Arne Westad (eds), *The Cambridge History of the Cold War*, 3 vols (Cambridge/New York: Cambridge University Press, 2010), vol. I, pp. 154–74; Lawrence S. Kaplan, *NATO 1948: The Birth of the Transatlantic Alliance* (Lanham, MD/Plymouth: Rowman & Littlefield, 2007).

On the origins of the Cold War in Asia and the communists' victory in China see: Odd Arne Westad, *Cold War and Revolution: Soviet–American Rivalry and* the Origins of the Chinese Civil War, 1944–1946 (New York: Columbia University Press, 1993); Daniel Kurtz-Phelan, *The China Mission: George Marshall's Unfinished War, 1945–47* (New York: W.W. Norton, 2018); Niu Jun, *From Yan'an to the World: The Origin and Development of Chinese Communist Foreign Policy* (Norwalk, CT: Eastbridge, 2005).

On the Korean War see: Bruce Cumings, *Korea's Place in the Sun: A Modern History*, rev. edn (New York/London: W.W. Norton, 2005), chapter 5: 'Collision, 1948–1953', pp. 237–98; Chen Jian, *Mao's China and the Cold War* (Chapel Hill: University of North Carolina Press, 2001); Samuel F. Wells Jr, *Fearing the Worst: How Korea Transformed the Cold War* (New York: Columbia University Press, 2019); Steven Casey, *Selling the Korean War: Propaganda, Politics, and Public Opinion in the United States, 1950–1953* (Oxford/New York: Oxford University Press, 2008).

On the American and Soviet home fronts during the first years of the Cold War see: Laura McEnaney, 'Cold War Mobilization and Domestic Politics: The United States', in Melvyn P. Leffler and Odd Arne Westad (eds), *The Cambridge History of the Cold War*, 3 vols (Cambridge/New York: Cambridge University Press, 2010), vol. I, pp. 420–41; M.J. Heale, *McCarthy's Americans: Red Scare Politics in State and Nation, 1935–1965* (Basingstoke: Macmillan, 1998); Yoram Gorlizki and Oleg Khlevniuk, *Cold Peace: Stalin and the Soviet Ruling Circle, 1945–1953* (Oxford: Oxford University Press, 2004); Elena Zubkova, *Russia After the War: Hopes, Illusions, and Disappointments, 1945–1957* (Armonk, NY/London: M.E. Sharpe, 1998); Serhy Yekelchyk, *Stalin's Citizens: Everyday Politics in the Wake of Total War* (Oxford: Oxford University Press, 2014).

PART TWO

The Eisenhower administration's plans and strategies are explored in: Robert R. Bowie and Richard H. Immerman, *Waging Peace: How Eisenhower Shaped an Enduring Cold War Strategy* (New York: Oxford University Press, 1998); Saki Dockrill, *Eisenhower's New-Look National Security Policy, 1953–1961* (Basingstoke: Macmillan/New York: St Martin's Press, 1996).

The post-Stalin Soviet stand on East Germany is covered by: Hope M. Harrison, *Driving the Soviets Up the Wall: Soviet–East German Relations, 1953–1961*

(Princeton, NJ/Oxford: Princeton University Press, 2003); Christian F. Ostermann, *Between Containment and Rollback: The United States and the Cold War in Germany* (Stanford, CA: Stanford University Press, 2021).

On eastern Europe and the Polish and Hungarian 1956 revolutions see: Csaba Békés, 'East Central Europe, 1953–1956', in Melvyn P. Leffler and Odd Arne Westad (eds), *The Cambridge History of the Cold War*, 3 vols (Cambridge/New York: Cambridge University Press, 2010), vol. 1, pp. 334–52; Mark Kramer, 'The Soviet Union and the 1956 Crises in Hungary and Poland: Reassessments and New Findings', *Journal of Contemporary History*, vol. 33 issue 2 (1998), pp. 163–214; Paweł Machcewicz, *Rebellious Satellite: Poland 1956* (Stanford: Stanford University Press, 2009).

On Arab nationalism, the Suez crisis, and the Cold War see: Keith Kyle, *Suez* (London: I.B. Tauris, 2012); Nigel John Ashton, *Eisenhower, Macmillan, and the Problem of Nasser: Anglo-American Relations and Arab Nationalism, 1955–59* (Palgrave Macmillan, 1996); Nigel Ashton, *False Prophets: British Leaders' Fateful Fascination with the Middle East from Suez to Syria* (London: Atlantic Books, 2022).

About the Cold War roller-coaster, including the Berlin Crisis, see: Aleksandr Fursenko and Timothy Naftali, *Khrushchev's Cold War: The Inside Story of an American Adversary* (New York: W.W. Norton, 2006); for the Western side see: John P.S. Gearson, *Harold Macmillan and the Berlin Wall Crisis, 1958–62: The Limits of Interests and Force* (New York: St Martin's Press, 1998); Michael R. Beschloss, *Kennedy v. Khrushchev: The Crisis Years, 1960–1963* (London: Faber and Faber, 1991); W.R. Smyser, *Kennedy and the Berlin Wall* (Boston: Rowman and Littlefield, 2009); Jenny Thompson and Sherry Thompson, *The Kremlinologist: Llewellyn E. Thompson, American's Man in Cold War Moscow* (Baltimore: Johns Hopkins University Press, 2018).

On the struggle over the Third World in the early 1960s see: Alessandro Iandolo, *Arrested Development: The Soviet Union in Ghana, Guinea, and Mali, 1955–1968* (Ithaca: Cornell University Press, 2022); Sergey Mazov, *A Distant Front in the Cold War: The USSR in West Africa and the Congo, 1956–1964* (Stanford University Press, 2010). And on the Cuban revolution and the missile crisis see: Ada Ferrer, *Cuba: An American History* (New York: Scribner, 2021); Graham Allison and Philip Zelikow, *Essence of Decision: Explaining the Cuban Missile Crisis*, 2nd edn (New York/Harlow: Longman, 1999); Aleksandr Fursenko and Timothy Naftali, *'One Hell of a Gamble': Khrushchev, Castro, Kennedy, and* the Cuban Missile Crisis, 1958–1964 (London: John Murray, 1997); James G. Blight and Philip Brenner, *Sad and Luminous Days: Cuba's Struggle with the Superpowers After the Missile Crisis* (Oxford: Rowman & Littlefield, 2002); Michael Dobbs, *One Minute to Midnight: Kennedy, Khrushchev, and Castro on the Brink of Nuclear War* (New York: Knopf, 2008); Martin J. Sherwin, *Gambling with Armageddon: Nuclear Roulette from Hiroshima to the Cuban Missile Crisis, 1945–62* (New York: Knopf, 2020); Serhii Plokhy, *Nuclear Folly: A New History of the Cuban Missile Crisis* (London: Allen Lane, 2021).

PART THREE

On the Indochina conflict and the US war in Vietnam see: Fredrik Logevall, *Embers of War: The Fall of an Empire and the Making of America's Vietnam* (New York: Random House, 2012); David L. Anderson, *Trapped by Success: The Eisenhower Administration and Vietnam, 1953–1961* (New York: Columbia University Press, 1991); Ilya V. Gaiduk, *Confronting Vietnam: Soviet Policy toward the Indochina Conflict, 1954–1963* (Stanford University Press, 2003).

On European détente see: Jussi Hanhimäki, *The Flawed Architect: Henry Kissinger and American Foreign Policy* (New York: Oxford University Press, 2004); Michael Cotey Morgan, *The Final Act: The Helsinki Accords and the Transformation of the Cold War* (Princeton, NJ: Princeton University Press, 2018).

On Brezhnev and Soviet détente motivations and politics see: Zubok, *A Failed Empire*, chapter 6; Susanne Schattenberg, *Brezhnev: The Making of a Statesman* (London: I.B. Tauris, 2021); Günter Bischof, Stefan Karner, and Peter Ruggenthaler (eds), *The Prague Spring and the Warsaw Pact Invasion of Czechoslovakia in 1968* (Lanham: Lexington Books, 2010).

On the changes in the US and Soviet home fronts see: Vladislav Zubok, *Zhivago's Children: The Last Russian Intelligentsia* (Cambridge, MA: Harvard University Press, 2009); Benjamin Nathans, *To the Success of Our Hopeless Cause: The Many Lives of the Soviet Dissident Movement* (Princeton, NJ: Princeton University Press, 2024); Niall Ferguson et. al. (eds.), *The Shock of the Global: The 1970s in Perspective* (Cambridge, MA: Harvard University Press, 2011); Alexei Yurchak, *Everything Was Forever, Until It Was No More:*

The Last Soviet Generation (Princeton, NJ: Princeton University Press, 2011); Dina Fainberg, *Cold War Correspondents: Soviet and American Reporters on the Ideological Frontlines* (Baltimore: Johns Hopkins University Press, 2021).

On the rise and fall of US–Soviet détente see: Luke Nichter and Douglas Brinkley (eds), *The Nixon Tapes, 1971–1972* (Boston: Houghton Mifflin Harcourt, 2014); Matthew Evangelista, *Unarmed Forces: The Transnational Movement to End the Cold War* (Ithaca: Cornell University Press, 2002); Jeremi Suri, *Power and Protest: Global Revolution and the Rise of Détente* (Cambridge, MA: Harvard University Press, 2009); Anatoly Dobrynin, *In Confidence: Moscow's Ambassador to America's Six Cold War Presidents (1962–1986)* (New York: Random House, 1995); Anne Hessing Cahn, *Killing Détente: The Right Attacks the CIA* (Pennsylvania State University Press, 1998).

On the Global Cold War see: Odd Arne Westad, *The Global Cold War: Third World Interventions and the Making of Our Times* (New York: Cambridge University Press, 2005); Christopher Andrew and Vassily Mitrokhin, *The KGB and the World: The Mitrokhin Archive II* (London: Penguin, 2018); Greg Grandin, *The Empire's Workshop: Latin America, the United States, and the Rise of the New Imperialism* (New York: Picador, 2007); Tanya Harmer, *Allende's Chile and the Inter-American Cold War* (Chapel Hill: University of North Carolina Press, 2011); Piero Gleijeses, *Conflicting Missions: Havana, Washington, and Africa, 1959–1976* (Chapel Hill: University of North Carolina Press, 2001); Natalia Telepneva, *Cold War Liberation: The Soviet Union and the Collapse of the Portuguese Empire in Africa, 1961–1975* (Chapel Hill: University of North Carolina Press, 2023); Victor Israelyan, *Inside the Kremlin during the Yom Kippur War* (University of Pennsylvania Press, 1996); Roham Alvandi, *Nixon, Kissinger, and the Shah: The United States and Iran in the Cold War* (Oxford University Press, 2016); Hal Brands, *Latin America's Cold War* (Cambridge, MA: Harvard University Press, 2012).

On Afghanistan and the last Cold War years see: Artemy M. Kalinovsky, *A Long Goodbye: The Soviet Withdrawal from Afghanistan* (Cambridge, MA: Harvard University Press, 2011); Kristina Spohr, *The Global Chancellor: Helmut Schmidt and the Reshaping of International Order* (Oxford University Press, 2016)

PART FOUR

On the rise of the neoliberal West and its Cold War impact see: Fritz Bartel, *The Triumph of Broken Promises: The End of the Cold War and the Rise of Neoliberalism* (Cambridge, MA: Harvard University Press, 2022). On the Polish crisis see: Matthew J. Ouimet, *The Rise and Fall of the Brezhnev Doctrine in Soviet Foreign Policy* (Chapel Hill: University of North Carolina Press, 2001); Gregory F. Domber, *Empowering Revolution: America, Poland, and the End of the Cold War* (Chapel Hill: University of North Carolina Press, 2014).

On US Cold War thinking see: *The Reagan Diaries*, edited by Douglas Brinkley (New York: Harper Collins, 2007); Simon Miles, *Engaging the Evil Empire: Washington, Moscow, and the Beginning of the End of the Cold War* (Ithaca: Cornell University Press, 2020); Strobe Talbott and Michael Beschloss, *At the Highest Levels: The Inside Story of the End of the Cold War* (New York: Little, Brown, 1994); Don Oberdorfer, *From the Cold War to a New Era: The United States and the Soviet Union, 1983–1991* (Baltimore: Johns Hopkins University Press, 1998); Beth A. Fischer, *The Reagan Reversal: Foreign Policy and the End of the Cold War* (Columbia, MO: University of Missouri Press, 1997); Suzanne Massie, *Trust but Verify: Reagan, Russia and Me* (Blue Hill, ME: Heart Tree Press, 2013); George Bush and Brent Scowcroft, *A World Transformed* (New York: Vintage Books, 1999); Jeffrey A. Engel, *When the World Seemed New: George H.W. Bush and the End of the Cold War* (New York: Houghton Mifflin Harcourt, 2017).

On Gorbachev and his new thinking see: Robert D. English, *Russia and the Idea of the West: Gorbachev, Intellectuals, and the End of the Cold War* (New York: Columbia University Press, 2000); William Taubman, *Gorbachev: His Life and Times* (New York: Simon & Schuster, 2017); Vladislav M. Zubok, *Collapse: The Fall of the Soviet Union* (Yale University Press, 2021); Andrei Grachev, *Gorbachev's Gamble* (Cambridge: Polity Press, 2008).

On Soviet arms build-up see: David E. Hoffman, *The Dead Hand: The Untold Story of the Cold War Arms Race and Its Dangerous Legacy* (New York: Anchor Books, 2010); Aleksandr' G. Savel'yev and Nikolay N. Detinov, *The Big Five: Arms Control and Decision-Making in the Soviet Union* (Westport, CT: Praeger, 1995); Serhii Plokhy, *Chernobyl: History of a Tragedy* (London: Penguin, 2019).

On US–Soviet summitry and diplomacy see: Jack Matlock, *Reagan and Gorbachev: How the Cold War Ended* (New York: Random House, 2004);

FURTHER READING

James Graham Wilson, *Triumph of Improvisation: Gorbachev's Adaptability, Reagan's Engagement, and the End of the Cold War* (Ithaca: Cornell University Press, 2015); Sergey Radchenko, *Unwanted Visionaries: The Soviet Failure in Asia at the End of the Cold War* (London: Oxford University Press, 2014); Robert Service, *The End of the Cold War: 1985–1991* (London, Macmillan, 2015); Mary Elise Sarotte, *1989: The Struggle to Create Post-Cold War Europe* (Princeton, NJ: Princeton University Press, 2009); Mary Elise Sarotte, *The Collapse: The Accidental Opening of the Berlin Wall* (New York: Basic Books, 2014); M.E. Sarotte, *Not One Inch: America, Russia, and the Making of Post-Cold War Stalemate* (Yale University Press, 2021).

Notes

CHAPTER 1: THE FATE OF EUROPE

1. Karl Marx and Friedrich Engels, *The Communist Manifesto* (1848).
2. See more on this international system in: Zara Steiner, *The Lights That Failed: European International History, 1919–1933* (Oxford: Oxford University Press, 2005) and Patrick O. Cohrs, *The New Atlantic Order: The Transformation of International Politics 1860–1933* (Cambridge University Press, 2022).
3. *New York Times*, 22 April 1947.
4. The term comes from Timothy Snyder, *Bloodlands: Europe between Hitler and Stalin* (London: Vintage, 2011). I disagree with Snyder, however, in lumping together the results of Stalin's terror and Hitler's aggression.
5. From the diary of artillery captain Nikolai Inozemtsev, future speechwriter of Leonid Brezhnev, quoted in: Vladislav M. Zubok, *A Failed Empire: The Soviet Union in the Cold War from Stalin to Gorbachev* (Chapel Hill: University of Carolina Press, 2007), pp. 2–4.
6. Francine Hirsch, *The Soviet Judgment at Nuremberg: A New History of the International Military Tribunal after World War II* (Oxford: Oxford University Press, 2020), p. 6.
7. Melvyn P. Leffler, 'The Emergence of an American Grand Strategy, 1945–53', in Leffler and Odd Arne Westad (eds), *The Cambridge History of the Cold War* (Cambridge University Press, 2008), vol. I, p. 67.
8. Geir Lundestad, 'Empire by Invitation? The United States and Western Europe, 1945–1952', *Journal of Peace Research*, vol. 23, issue 3 (September 1986), pp. 263–77; Charles S. Maier, 'The Politics of Productivity: Foundations of American International Economic Policy after World War II', *International Organization*, vol. 31, issue 4 (1977), pp. 607–33.
9. John Fousek, *To Lead the Free World: American Nationalism and the Cultural Roots of the Cold War* (Chapel Hill: University of North Carolina

Press, 2000); David S. Foglesong. *The American Mission and the 'Evil Empire': The Crusade for a 'Free Russia' since 1881* (Cambridge University Press, 2008).

10. Michael David-Fox, preface to Patryk Babiracki and Kenyon Zimmer (eds), *Cold War Crossings: International Travel and Exchange Across the Soviet Bloc, 1940s–1960s* (Texas A & M University Press, 2014).
11. Memorandum, Ivan Maisky to Stalin and Molotov, 11 January 1944. AVPRF: fond 06, opis 6, papka 14, delo 145, list 3.
12. Quoted in Vladislav Zubok and Constantine Pleshakov, *Inside the Kremlin's Cold War: From Stalin to Khruschev* (Harvard University Press, 1996), p. 83.
13. Most recently see Stephen Kotkin, *Stalin: Waiting for Hitler, 1929–1941* (London: Penguin, 2017); Oleg Khlevniuk, *Master of the House: Stalin and His Inner Circle* (London: Yale University Press, 2009).
14. S. M. Plokhy, *Yalta: The Price of Peace* (London: Penguin, 2011).
15. Zubok and Pleshakov, op. cit., p. 25.
16. See Frank Costigliola, *Roosevelt's Lost Alliances: How Personal Politics Helped Start the Cold War* (Princeton University Press, 2012). Also his *Kennan: A Life between Worlds* (Princeton University Press, 2023).
17. Felix Chuev, *Molotov Remembers: Inside Kremlin Politics* (Chicago: Ivan R. Dee, 2007), p. 103.
18. Frank Costigliola (ed.), *The Kennan Diaries* (New York: W.W. Norton, 2014), p. 200.
19. Graham Allison, *Destined for War: Can America and China Escape Thucydides's Trap?* (Boston, MA: Houghton Mifflin Harcourt, 2017).
20. Hirsch, op. cit., p. 14.

CHAPTER 2: THE CONFLICT TAKES SHAPE

1. https://hansard.parliament.uk/Lords/1945-11-15/debates/079e4272-ea3e-47b8-9144-e2ea56d5b96b/AtomicEnergyTheWashingtonTalks
2. Bernard Brodie (ed.), *The Absolute Weapon: Atomic Power and World Order* (Yale University Press, 1946), pp. 40–41; Arnold Wolfers in ibid., p. 95.
3. Kai Bird and Martin J. Sherwin, *American Prometheus: The Triumph and Tragedy of J. Robert Oppenheimer* (New York: Knopf, 2006).
4. https://www.trumanlibrary.gov/library/research-files/outline-clifford-elsey-report

5. Campbell Craig and Sergey Radchenko, *The Atomic Bomb and the Origins of the Cold War* (Yale University Press, 2008), p. 110.
6. Eduard Mark, 'The War Scare of 1946 and its Consequences', *Diplomatic History*, vol. 21, no. 3 (Summer 1997), pp. 383–415 ; https://history.state.gov/historicaldocuments/frus1947v01/d437.
7. Norman M. Naimark, *The Russians in Germany* (Harvard University Press, 1996).
8. https://ghdi.ghi-dc.org/docpage.cfm?docpage_id=2998
9. Robert L. Beisner, *Dean Acheson: A Life in the Cold War* (New York: Oxford University Press, 2006), pp. 54, 62.
10. Matthew Connelly, *The Declassification Engine: What History Reveals About America's Top Secrets* (New York: Pantheon, 2023).
11. X, 'The Sources of Soviet Conduct', *Foreign Affairs*, July 1947; Frank Costigliola (ed.), *The Kennan Diaries* (New York: W.W. Norton, 2014), p. 199.
12. https://digitalarchive.wilsoncenter.org/document/110808.pdf?v=c46f797bf3d939c2c328ac98eb778f09
13. Benn Steil, *The Marshall Plan: Dawn of the Cold War* (New York: Simon & Schuster, 2018).
14. Acheson to Truman, 28 May 1953, Dean Acheson Papers, S. 1, box 30, f. 391, Sterling Library, Yale University.
15. Norman N. Naimark, *Stalin and the Fate of Europe: the Postwar Struggle for Sovereignty* (Belknap Press, 2019), p. 164.
16. Ibid., pp. 160, 164.
17. Ibid., p. 170.
18. Ibid., p. 171.
19. Ibid., p. 191.

CHAPTER 3: THE ASIAN FRONT

1. Mikoyan's account about this trip is at: https://nsarchive.gwu.edu/rus/text_files/MikoyanStalin/Rep-to-CPSS-1949.pdf; and https://digitalarchive.wilsoncenter.org/document/anastas-mikoyans-recollections-his-trip-china.
2. https://www.cia.gov/readingroom/docs/1950-01-12.pdf
3. Beisner, op. cit., p. 230.
4. Odd Arne Westad, *The Cold War: A World History* (London: Allen Lane, 2017), p. 159.

NOTES

5. Felix Chuev, *One Hundred Forty Conversations with Molotov*, p. 104.
6. https://digitalarchive.wilsoncenter.org/document/letter-feng-xi-stalin-kim-il-sung-shtytkov#:~:text=If%20a%20war%20is%20inevitable,Korea%20run%20by%20Syngman%20Rhee
7. Kennan, memorandum to Acheson, 13 March 1951, FRUS, 1951, vol. IV, pp. 1557–60.

CHAPTER 4: DOMESTIC FRONTLINES

1. *Pickett Journal*, 8 and 13 January 1951, the American Friends Archive, Philadelphia.
2. David C. Engerman, *Know Your Enemy: The Rise and Fall of America's Soviet Experts* (New York: Oxford University Press, 2011).
3. On this see Fousek, *To Lead the Free World*, p. 189.
4. M.J. Heale, *McCarthy's Americans: Red Scare Politics in State and Nation, 1935–1965* (Basingstoke: Macmillan, 1997); Lisle A. Rose, *The Cold War Comes to Main Street: America in 1950* (Lawrence: University Press of Kansas, 1999).
5. Elena Zubkova, *Russia After the War: Hopes, Illusions, and Disappointments, 1945–1957* (E.M. Sharp, 1998).
6. Zubok, *A Failed Empire*, pp. 54–55.
7. George Kennan, *Memoirs*, vol. 1, reprint edition (New York: Pantheon, 1983), p. 245.
8. Serhy Yekelchyk, *Stalin's Empire of Memory: Russian–Ukrainian Relations in the Soviet Historical Imagination* (University of Toronto Press, 2004).
9. Yuri Slezkine, *The Jewish Century* (Princeton University Press, 2006), chapter 3 and part of chapter 4.
10. Gennadi Kostyrchenko, *Out of the Red Shadows: Anti-semitism in Stalin's Russia* (Amherst, NY: Prometheus Books, 1995); Yoram Gorlizki and Oleg Khlevniuk, *Cold Peace: Stalin and the Soviet Ruling Circle, 1945–1953* (Oxford: Oxford University Press, 2004).
11. Dina Fainberg, *Cold War Correspondents: Soviet and American Reporters on the Ideological Frontlines* (Baltimore: Johns Hopkins University Press, 2020), p. 5.
12. Engerman, *Know Your Enemy*.
13. Fainberg, op. cit., p. 71.

14. Frances Stonor Saunders, *Who Paid the Piper? The CIA and the Cultural Cold War* (London: Granta Books, 1999).

CHAPTER 5: AFTER STALIN

1. The principal points made by John Foster Dulles to Eisenhower are courtesy of Richard Immerman, who discovered this document in archives.
2. The Solarium Project documents, courtesy of Richard Immerman: https://history.state.gov/historicaldocuments/frus1952-54v02p1/d69
3. The Solarium Project documents, courtesy of Richard Immerman: https://history.state.gov/historicaldocuments/frus1952-54v02p1/d76.
4. J. Robert Oppenheimer, 'Atomic Weapons and American Policy', *Foreign Affairs*, July 1953, p. 529.
5. Fredrik Logevall, *Embers of War: The Fall of an Empire and the Making of America's Vietnam* (New York: Random House, 2012).
6. https://www.newyorker.com/news/our-columnists/the-disbelief-and-horror-of-tuesday-night-were-captured-by-a-russian-poet-in-1933
7. The best biography of Khrushchev and his ascendancy is William Taubman's *Khrushchev: The Man and His Era* (London: Free Press/New York: W.W. Norton, 2003).
8. https://www.wilsoncenter.org/sites/default/files/media/documents/publication/CWIHP_Bulletin_10.pdf
9. http://digitalarchive.wilsoncenter.org/document/113924.pdf?v=d797c77fce03545353173d1076415e5; see also Geoffrey Roberts, 'Molotov's Proposal that the USSR Join NATO, March 1954', CWIHP E-dossier No. 27; and Geoffrey Roberts, *Molotov: Stalin's Cold Warrior* (Sterling, VA: Potomac Books, 2011).
10. Conversation between Georgy Zhukov and Dwight D. Eisenhower, 22 July 1955, in Aleksandr Yakovlev (ed.), *Georgii Zhukov: Stenogramma Oktyabr'skogo Plenuma (1957 g) TsK KPSS i Drugie Dokumenty* (Moscow: Mezhdunarodnyi Fond Demokratiya, 2001), p. 40.
11. Vladislav M. Zubok and Hope M. Harrison, The 'Nuclear Education of Nikita Khrushchev', in John Lewis Gaddis et al. (eds), *Cold War Statesmen Confront the Bomb: Nuclear Diplomacy Since 1945* (Oxford University Press, 1999), pp. 141–68.
12. David C. Engerman, *The Price of Aid: The Economic Cold War in India* (Cambridge, MA: Harvard University Press, 2018).

13. Keith Kyle, *Suez* (London: I.B. Tauris, 2012).
14. Ibid., p. 363.
15. Nigel John Ashton, *Eisenhower, Macmillan, and the Problem of Nasser: Anglo-American Relations and Arab Nationalism, 1955–59* (Palgrave Macmillan, 1996); Kyle, op. cit., pp. 364–6.
16. The notes of the Politburo sessions: https://digitalarchive.wilsoncenter.org/document/111882.pdf?v=57c764abd64d28b1f5d5216f2b0f8880; https://digitalarchive.wilsoncenter.org/document/111882.pdf?v=57c764abd64d28b1f5d5216f2b0f8880; https://digitalarchive.wilsoncenter.org/document/117064.pdf?v=634f40572566c230c25ec5951095e1d2

CHAPTER 6: THE WIND FROM THE EAST

1. Boris Chertok, *The Missiles and the People: From Aircraft to Missiles* (Moscow: Cosmoskop, 1994).
2. Quoted in Dina Fainberg, *Cold War Correspondents: Soviet and American Reporters on the Ideological Frontlines* (Baltimore: Johns Hopkins University Press, 2021), p. 124.
3. https://digitalarchive.wilsoncenter.org/document/mao-zedong-speech-meeting-representatives-sixty-four-communist-and-workers-parties-edited; Sergey Radchenko, *To Run the World: The Kremlin's Cold War Bid for Global Power* (London: Cambridge University Press, 2024), pp. 201–5.
4. Radchenko, op. cit., pp. 202–3.
5. https://history.state.gov/historicaldocuments/frus1958-60v12/d5
6. Alan S. Milward, 'The Springs of Integration', in Peter Gowan and Perry Anderson (eds), *The Question of Europe* (London: Verso, 1997), pp. 5–20; also Alan S. Milward, *The European Rescue of the Nation-State*, 2nd edition (New York: Routledge, 1992).
7. Hope M. Harrison, *Driving the Soviets Up the Wall: Soviet–East German Relations, 1953–1961* (Princeton, NJ/Oxford: Princeton University Press, 2003).
8. *Historical Archive*, Moscow, 1993, no. 4, pp. 27, 29.
9. Walter Ulbricht's letter to Khrushchev, 13 May 1958, in the documentary collection *The Presidium of the Central Committee, 1954–1964* (Moscow: ROSSPEN, 2006), vol. 2, pp. 792–829.

10. Rodric Braithwaite, *Armageddon and Paranoia: The Nuclear Confrontation* (London: Profile Books, 2017), p. 125.
11. Conversation between Nikita Khrushchev and Władisław Gomułka, 10 November 1958: https://www.wilsoncenter.org/sites/default/files/CWIHPBulletin11_p5.pdf
12. For the full text of the Mao–Yudin conversation see: https://digitalarchive.wilsoncenter.org/document/minutes-conversation-mao-zedong-and-ambassador-yudin
13. Taubman, *Khrushchev*, pp. 428–9.
14. Fursenko and Naftali, *Khrushchev's Cold War*, pp. 218–22; Taubman, *Khrushchev*, pp. 410–12.
15. Jacob Van Staaveren, *Air Operations in the Taiwan Crisis of 1958* (USAF Historical Division Liaison Office, 1962). Obtained by the National Security Archive: http://nsarchive.gwu.edu/nukevault/ebb249/doc11.pdf
16. The declassified evidence on SIOP-62, as the plan came to be called, is at: https://nsarchive2.gwu.edu/NSAEBB/NSAEBB130/index.htm
17. The reference is to Odd Arne Westad, *The Global Cold War: Third World Interventions and the Making of Our Times* (New York: Cambridge University Press, 2011).
18. See Alessandro Iandolo, *Arrested Development: The Soviet Union in Ghana, Guinea, and Mali, 1955–1968* (Ithaca: Cornell University Press, 2022).
19. https://history.state.gov/historicaldocuments/frus1964-68v23/d1
20. Sergey Mazov, *A Distant Front in the Cold War: The USSR in West Africa and the Congo, 1956–1964* (Stanford University Press, 2010).
21. https://digitalarchive.wilsoncenter.org/document/record-meeting-comrade-ns-khrushchev-comrade-w-ulbricht

---

CHAPTER 7: RUSSIAN ROULETTE

1. Ada Ferrer, *Cuba: An American History* (New York: Scribner, 2021).
2. Taubman, *Khrushchev*, pp. 526–7, 532–5.
3. *The Prezidium of CC CPSU*, vol. 1, pp. 498–9, 502–3.
4. Zubok and Pleshakov, *Inside the Kremlin's Cold War*, pp. 244–7.
5. https://digitalarchive.wilsoncenter.org/document/notes-conversation-comrade-ns-khrushchev-comrade-w-ulbricht-1-august-1961
6. Khrushchev's notes on the Germany question, 11 December 1961, published in *Istochnik*, no. 3 (2006), pp. 123–7.

7. W.R. Smyser, *Kennedy and the Berlin Wall* (Boston: Rowman and Littlefield, 2009).
8. For the public reaction see: Anne E. Gorsuch, '"Cuba, My Love": The Romance of Revolutionary Cuba in the Soviet Sixties', *The American Historical Review*, vol. 120, issue 2 (April 2015), pp. 497–526.
9. Read more in Philip Nash, *The Other Missiles of October: Eisenhower, Kennedy, and the Jupiters, 1957–1963* (University of North Carolina Press, 1997).
10. Aleksandr Fursenko and Timothy Naftali, *'One Hell of a Gamble': Khruschev, Castro, Kennedy, and the Cuban Missile Crisis, 1958–1964* (London: John Murray, 1997), pp. 152–3.
11. Martin J. Sherwin, *Gambling with Armageddon* (New York: Knopf, 2020), p. 162.
12. Ibid., pp. 205–7.
13. On this phenomenon and many details see: Sergey Radchenko and Vladislav Zubok, 'Blundering on the Brink: The Secret History and Unlearned Lessons of the Cuban Missile Crisis', *Foreign Affairs*, vol. 102, no. 3 (May/June 2023), pp. 44–52.
14. https://microsites.jfklibrary.org/cmc/oct16/doc3.html
15. https://digitalarchive.wilsoncenter.org/document/central-committee-communist-party-soviet-union-presidium-protocol-60
16. Fred Kaplan, *The Wizards of Armageddon* (New York: Simon & Schuster, 1983), p. 246.
17. Cited in Radchenko and Zubok, 'Blundering on the Brink', p. 63.

CHAPTER 8: VIETNAM AND THE ORIGINS OF DÉTENTE

1. Odd Arne Westad, *The Cold War: A World History* (New York: Basic Books, 2017), pp. 313–14.
2. Fredrik Logevall, *Embers of War: The Fall of an Empire and the Making of America's Vietnam* (New York: Random House, 2012); also David L. Anderson, *Trapped by Success: The Eisenhower Administration and Vietnam, 1953–1961* (New York: Columbia University Press, 1991).
3. Fredrik Logevall, *Choosing War: The Lost Chance for Peace and the Escalation of War in Vietnam* (University of California Press, 2001), p. xvi.
4. Ilya V. Gaiduk, *Confronting Vietnam: Soviet Policy toward the Indochina Conflict, 1954–1963* (Stanford University Press, 2003).

5. This motivation is richly elaborated on in Radchenko, *To Run the World*.
6. https://www.wilsoncenter.org/publication/the-1967-six-day-war
7. http://www.bits.de/NRANEU/nato-strategy/Harmel_Report_complete.pdf; https://www.nato.int/cps/en/natohq/official_texts_26700.htm
8. See more about Brezhnev in Zubok, *A Failed Empire*; also in Susanne Schattenberg, *Brezhnev: The Making of a Statesman* (London: I.B. Tauris, 2021).
9. Günter Bischof, Stefan Karner, and Peter Ruggenthaler (eds), *The Prague Spring and the Warsaw Pact Invasion of Czechoslovakia in 1968* (Lanham: Lexington Books, 2010).
10. More in Vladislav Zubok, *Zhivago's Children: The Last Russian Intelligentsia* (Cambridge, MA: Harvard University Press, 2009).

CHAPTER 9: BREZHNEV'S PEACE PROJECT

1. Jussi Hanhimäki, *The Flawed Architect: Henry Kissinger and American Foreign Policy* (New York: Oxford University Press, 2004), pp. xvi–xviii.
2. Nixon–Kissinger telephone conversation, 27 April 1971, in Luke Nichter and Douglas Brinkley (eds), *The Nixon Tapes, 1971–1972* (Boston: Houghton Mifflin Harcourt, 2014), p. 108, quoted in Westad, *The Cold War: A World History*.
3. Nixon–Kissinger telephone conversation, 12 March 1971, in Nichter and Brinkley, op. cit., p. 41.
4. Westad, *The Cold War: A World History*, pp. 405–9.
5. Rodric Braithwaite, *Armageddon and Paranoia: The Nuclear Confrontation* (London: Profile Books, 2017), pp. 163–6.
6. Ibid., p. 127.
7. Matthew Evangelista, *Unarmed Forces: The Transnational Movement to End the Cold War* (Cornell University Press, 2002).
8. Zubok, *A Failed Empire*, p. 222.
9. Jeremi Suri, *Power and Protest: Global Revolution and the Rise of Détente* (Cambridge, MA: Harvard University Press, 2009).
10. Morgan, op. cit.; Richard Davy, 'Helsinki Myths: Setting the Record Straight on the Final Act of the CSCE, 1975', *Cold War History*, vol. 9, no. 1 (2009), pp. 1–22.
11. Anatoly Dobrynin, *In Confidence: Moscow's Ambassador to America's Six Cold War Presidents (1962–1986)* (New York: Random House, 1995), pp. 276–81; Sukhodrev's remarks to the author.

12. https://history.state.gov/historicaldocuments/frus1969-76v15/d115. The author thanks Sergey Radchenko for bringing this document to my attention. See also: Viktor Sukhodrev, *Iazyk moi – drug moi. Ot Khrushcheva do Gorbacheva* (Moscow: Tonchu, 2008).
13. Radchenko, *To Run the World*, pp. 363–4.

CHAPTER 10: A PARTNERSHIP OF RIVALS

1. Dobrynin, *In Confidence*, p. 283.
2. Zubok, *A Failed Empire*, pp. 239–40; Radchenko, *To Run the World*, pp. 399–411.
3. Viktor Israelyan, *Inside the Kremlin during the Yom Kippur War* (University of Pennsylvania Press, 1996).
4. Ibid.
5. Samuel Moyn, *Human Rights and the Uses of History* (London/New York: Verso Books, 2017), p. 2.
6. See more on this in Zubok, *Zhivago's Children*; also Benjamin Nathans, *To the Success of Our Hopeless Cause: The Many Lives of the Soviet Dissident Movement* (Princeton, NJ: Princeton University Press, 2024).
7. On the roots of this see Samuel Moyn, *The Last Utopia: Human Rights in History* (Harvard University Press, 2010).
8. https://history.state.gov/historicaldocuments/frus1969-76v15/d115
9. Michael Cotey Morgan, *The Final Act: The Helsinki Accords and the Transformation of the Cold War* (Princeton University Press, 2018), p. 201; Dobrynin, *In Confidence*, p. 346; Dobrynin's remarks to the author.
10. Morgan, *The Final Act*, pp. 207–34.
11. Westad, *The Cold War: A World History*, p. 475.
12. Anne Hessing Cahn, *Killing Détente: The Right Attacks the CIA* (Pennsylvania State University Press, 1998).
13. There are dissenting views on this; see Christopher Andrew and Vasili Mitrokhin, *The KGB and the World: The Mitrokhin Archive II* (London: Penguin, 2018), p. 87.
14. Niall Ferguson et. al. (eds), *The Shock of the Global: The 1970s in Perspective* (Cambridge, MA: Harvard University Press, 2011).
15. Alexei Yurchak, *Everything Was Forever, Until It Was No More: The Last Soviet Generation* (Princeton, NJ: Princeton University Press, 2011).

CHAPTER 11: THE DESTRUCTION OF DÉTENTE

1. Greg Grandin, *Empire's Workshop: Latin America, the United States, and the Rise of the New Imperialism* (New York: Picador, 2007).
2. Ibid., p. 59.
3. Tanya Harmer, *Allende's Chile and the Inter-American Cold War* (Chapel Hill: University of North Carolina Press, 2014).
4. Ibid.
5. The classic study of the naval rivalry's destabilizing impact is Paul M. Kennedy, *The Rise of the Anglo-German Antagonism, 1860–1914* (Humanities Press, 1987).
6. Piero Gleijeses, *Conflicting Missions: Havana, Washington, and Africa, 1959–1976* (Chapel Hill: University of North Carolina Press, 2001); Natalia Telepneva, *Cold War Liberation: The Soviet Union and the Collapse of the Portuguese Empire in Africa, 1961–1975* (Chapel Hill: University of North Carolina Press, 2023), p. 183.
7. This reconstruction of the Soviet–Cuban relationship the author heard from Soviet veterans attending the conference 'Global Competition and the Deterioration of U.S.–Soviet Relations, 1977–1980', Fort Lauderdale, FL, 23–26 March 1995. See: https://nsarchive2.gwu.edu/carterbrezhnev/docs_global_competition/part7.PDF. Also Telepneva, op. cit., pp. 193–4.
8. 'Global Competition and the Deterioration of U.S.–Soviet Relations, 1977–1980', Fort Lauderdale, FL, 23–26 March 1995.
9. https://www.economist.com/china/2018/05/17/surging-numbers-of-chinese-people-going-abroad-should-be-welcomed
10. Roham Alvandi, *Nixon, Kissinger, and the Shah: The United States and Iran in the Cold War* (Oxford University Press, 2016).
11. See Artemy M. Kalinovsky, *A Long Goodbye: The Soviet Withdrawal from Afghanistan* (Cambridge, MA: Harvard University Press, 2011).
12. Zubok and Pleshakov, *Inside the Kremlin's Cold War*, pp. 260–61,
13. Kristina Spohr, *The Global Chancellor: Helmut Schmidt and the Reshaping of The International Order* (Oxford University Press, 2016), pp. 9, 86–8.
14. Dobrynin, *In Confidence*, pp. 425–6.
15. *Brezhnev's Diaries and Working Notes*, vol. 1 (Moscow: IstLit, 2016), pp. 975–9; Kalinovsky, *A Long Goodbye*, pp. 16–53. Kalinovsky describes the Soviet intervention as 'reluctant'.
16. Fainberg, op. cit., pp. 145–83.
17. Ibid., p. 160–63, 171–2; Yurchak, *Everything Was Forever, Until It Was No More*.

NOTES

18. Robert D. English, *Russia and the Idea of the West: Gorbachev, Intellectuals and the End of the Cold War* (Columbia University Press, 2000).
19. Fainberg, op. cit., pp. 184–6, 191–202, 207–8; Hedrick Smith, *The Russians* (Crown, 1976), pp. 678–9.
20. Smith, *The Russians*, p. 679.

CHAPTER 12: ANOTHER ROUND

1. The most systematic view of the Cold War before 1989 was by John Lewis Gaddis: *The Long Peace: Inquiries into the History of the Cold War* (Oxford University Press, 1989). The new frame of mind was expressed in Francis Fukuyama, *The End of History and the Last Man* (New York: Free Press, 1992) and John Lewis Gaddis, *We Now Know: Rethinking Cold War History* (Oxford University History, 1997).
2. Frank Costigliola (ed.), *The Kennan Diaries* (New York: W.W. Norton, 2014), p. 199.
3. The full text of the conversation is at https://nsarchive.gwu.edu/document/21040-1990-10-05-yakovlev-kennan-memcon-en
4. Keith Gessen, 'How the War in Ukraine Might End', *New Yorker*, 29 September 2022, at: https://www.newyorker.com/culture/annals-of-inquiry/how-the-war-in-ukraine-might-end
5. The most detailed explanation of the FRS policies are in: Allan H. Meltzer, *A History of the Federal Reserve*, vol. 2, book 2, 1970–1986 (University of Chicago Press, 2009).
6. Fritz Bartel, *The Triumph of Broken Promises: The End of the Cold War and the Rise of Neoliberalism* (Cambridge, MA: Harvard University Press, 2022), p. 341.
7. Melvyn Leffler, *For the Soul of Mankind: The United States, the Soviet Union, and the Cold War* (New York: Hill and Wang, 2007), p. 340.
8. David S. Foglesong, *The American Mission and the 'Evil Empire': The Crusade for a 'Free Russia' since 1881* (Cambridge University Press, 2007), pp. 177–78.
9. Matthew Evangelista, *Unarmed Forces: The Transnational Movement to End the Cold War* (Ithaca: Cornell University Press, 2002).
10. Matthew J. Ouimet, *The Rise and Fall of the Brezhnev Doctrine in Soviet Foreign Policy* (Chapel Hill: University of North Carolina Press, 2001); Gregory F. Domber, *Empowering Revolution: America, Poland, and the*

End of the Cold War (Chapel Hill: University of North Carolina Press, 2014).
11. Vladislav M. Zubok, 'Soviet Foreign Policy from Détente to Gorbachev', in Melvyn Leffler and Odd Arne Westad (eds), *Cambridge History of the Cold War*, vol. III, p. 106.
12. Mark Kramer, 'Soviet Deliberations during the Polish Crisis, 1980–81', Special Working Paper, Washington: Cold War International History Project, 1997.
13. Dobrynin, op. cit., p. 523.
14. Diary entries of 21 and then 3 December 1981, *The Reagan Diaries*, edited by Douglas Brinkley (New York: HarperCollins, 2007), pp. 57, 52; Domber, *Empowering Revolution*, pp. 29–35.
15. The author thanks Sergey Radchenko for sharing this document from Soviet archives.
16. Cited from the Andropov files in the Russian archive in Moscow, in Zubok, *Collapse*, p. 17.
17. The unpublished text is stored in the Russian archive of contemporary history (RGANI), f. 82, op. 1, d. 27, l. 24.
18. See more on this in David E. Hoffman, *The Dead Hand: The Untold Story of the Cold War Arms Race and Its Dangerous Legacy* (New York: Anchor Books, 2010).
19. Dobrynin, *In Confidence*, p. 478.
20. Simon Miles, *Engaging the Evil Empire: Washington, Moscow, and the Beginning of the End of the Cold War* (Ithaca: Cornell University Press, 2020), p. 70.
21. Ibid., p. 78.
22. On this time see: Braithwaite, *Armageddon and Paranoia*, pp. 352–5; Zubok, *A Failed Empire*, p. 275; the 1990 US intelligence reassessment of 1983 can be found at: https://nsarchive.gwu.edu/document/21038-4-pfiab-report-2012-0238-mr
23. The diary of Anatoly Adamishin, 16 September 1983, the Hoover Archive, Stanford University.
24. Don Oberdorfer, *From the Cold War to a New Era: The United States and the Soviet Union, 1983–1991* (Baltimore: Johns Hopkins University Press, 1998); Beth A. Fischer, *The Reagan Reversal: Foreign Policy and the End of the Cold War* (Columbia, MO: University of Missouri Press, 1997); Gordon S. Barras, *The Great Cold War: A Journey through the Hall of Mirrors* (Stanford Security Studies, 2009); https://nsarchive.gwu.edu/document/21038-4-pfiab-report-2012-0238-mr

25. Suzanne Massie, *Trust but Verify: Reagan, Russia and Me* (Blue Hill, ME: Heart Tree Press, 2013).

CHAPTER 13: THE ADVENT OF GORBACHEV

1. English, *Russia and the Idea of the West*, p. 166.
2. Vladislav Zubok, *The Idea of Russia: The Life and Works of Dmitry Likhachev* (London: I.B. Tauris, 2017).
3. General Sir John Hackett, *The Third World War* (London: Sidgwick and Jackson, 1978); and *The Third World War: The Untold Story* (London: Sidgwick and Jackson, 1982).
4. https://www.nytimes.com/1984/01/17/world/transcript-of-reagan-s-speech-on-soviet-american-relations.html
5. William Taubman, *Gorbachev: His Life and Times* (New York: Simon & Schuster, 2017), pp. 173–81, 198–201.
6. Aleksandr' G. Savel'yev and Nikolay N. Detinov, *The Big Five: Arms Control Decision-Making in the Soviet Union* (Westport, CT: Praeger, 1995), pp. 31–53, 83–4.
7. Chris Miller, *Chip War: The Fight for the World's Most Critical Technology* (New York: Simon & Schuster, 2022).
8. J. Matlock, *Reagan and Gorbachev: How the Cold War Ended* (New York: Random House, 1994), pp. 113–22; James Graham Wilson, *Triumph of Improvisation: Gorbachev's Adaptability, Reagan's Engagement, and the End of the Cold War* (Ithaca: Cornell University Press, 2015).
9. RGANI, the Gorbachev papers, fond 82, op. 1, d. 227, p. 101; Serhii Plokhy, *Chernobyl: History of a Tragedy* (London: Penguin, 2019); Taubman, *Gorbachev*, pp. 240–42.
10. Sergey Radchenko, *Unwanted Visionaries: The Soviet Failure in Asia at the End of the Cold War* (London: Oxford University Press, 2014), pp. 88–123.
11. *The Reagan Diaries*, pp. 406–7 (17 April 1986).
12. Fritz Bartel, *The Triumph of Broken Promises: The End of the Cold War and the Rise of Neoliberalism* (Harvard University Press, 2022), p. 170. More on this in Zubok, *Collapse*, pp. 27–33.
13. Robert Service, *The End of the Cold War: 1985–1991* (London: Macmillan, 2015), p. 281; Zubok, *Collapse*, p. 166.
14. Service, *The End of the Cold War*, pp. 245–7, 285–93.
15. Ibid., pp. 245, 267, 293.

16. Domber, *Empowering Revolution*, pp. 172–92.
17. Ibid., pp. 209–18; Bartel, *The Triumph of Broken Promises*, pp. 215–20.
18. Zubok, *Collapse*, p. 49.

CHAPTER 14: THE END OF CONFRONTATION

1. Jeffrey A. Engel, *When the World Seemed New: George H. W. Bush and the End of the Cold War* (New York: Houghton Mifflin Harcourt, 2017), pp. 48–99.
2. See Bartel, op. cit., pp. 233–45.
3. The Politburo minutes are in Anatoly Chernyaev et al., *V Politbiuro TsK KPSS: 1985–1991* (Moscow: Alpina, 2006), p. 93.
4. Ibid., p. 436.
5. The record is cited in Zubok, *A Failed Empire*, p. 323.
6. Mary Elise Sarotte, *1989: The Struggle to Create Post-Cold War Europe* (Princeton, NJ: Princeton University Press, 2009), p. 31.
7. One of many accounts is in: Mary Elise Sarotte, *The Collapse: The Accidental Opening of the Berlin Wall* (New York: Basic Books, 2014), pp. 112–18, 129–47.
8. The diary of Rodric Braithwaite, 17 November 1989.
9. Timothy Garton Ash, *The Magic Lantern: The Revolutions of '89* (London: Atlantic Books, 2019). The first edition appeared in 1990.
10. The private diary of Teimuraz Stepanov-Mamaladze in December 1989, the Hoover Archive, Stanford University.
11. Sarotte, *1989*, pp. 72–3.

CHAPTER 15: OTHER ENDINGS

1. Interview with Brent Scowcroft, 10–11 August 2000, the Bush Oral History Program, the Miller Center at the University of Virginia, at https://millercenter.org/the-presidency/presidential-oral-histories/brent-scowcroft-oral-history-part-ii
2. Chernyaev et al., *V Politbiuro TsK*, pp. 551–555.
3. https://nsarchive.gwu.edu/document/16116-document-05-memorandum-conversation-between
4. https://nsarchive.gwu.edu/document/16120-document-09-memorandum-conversation-between

5. https://www.csce.gov/international-impact/osce-celebrates-30-years-charter-paris?page=58
6. Zubok, *Collapse*, p. 163; Andrei Grachev, *Gorbachev's Gamble* (Cambridge: Polity Press, 2008), p. 274.
7. https://www.nobelprize.org/prizes/peace/1990/press-release/
8. Melvyn Leffler, *For the Soul of Humanity: The United States, the Soviet Union, and the Cold War* (New York: Hill and Wang, 2007), p. 448.
9. https://www.nytimes.com/1992/01/29/us/state-union-transcript-president-bush-s-address-state-union.html; George Bush and Brent Scowcroft, *World Transformed*, p. 563.
10. Zubok, *Collapse*, p. 182.

CONCLUSION: THE TIME OF MERCURY

1. The expression is from Lorenz M. Lüthi, *Cold Wars: Asia, the Middle East, Europe* (Cambridge University Press, 2020), p. 564.
2. On the role of fear see Melvin Leffler, *Confronting Saddam Hussein: George W. Bush and the Invasion of Iraq* (Oxford University Press, 2023).
3. See observations of these parallels in Fredrik Logevall, 'How America Lost its Way in Afghanistan', *New York Times*, 16 August 2021, https://www.nytimes.com/2021/08/16/books/review/carter-malkasian-the-american-war-in-afghanistan-craig-whitlock-the-afghanistan-papers.html
4. https://www.oecd.org/daf/inv/investment-policy/WP-2000_4.pdf
5. M.E. Sarotte, *Not One Inch: America, Russia, and the Making of Post-Cold War Stalemate* (Yale University Press, 2021).
6. George F. Kennan, 'A Fateful Error', *New York Times*, 5 February 1997, https://www.nytimes.com/1997/02/05/opinion/a-fateful-error.html, accessed 8 December 2022.
7. Eric Shiraev and Vladislav Zubok, *Anti-Americanism in Russia: From Stalin to Putin* (Basingstoke: Palgrave Macmillan, 2000).
8. Thomas W. Simons, 'Evaluating the Demise of the Soviet Union: A Forum', *Journal of Cold War Studies*, vol. 25, no. 3 (Summer 2023), p. 158.

Index

page locators given in *italics* refer to figures

A

'Able Archer 83' 377–9
ABM (anti-ballistic missile) treaty 272
Acheson, Dean 49, 54–5, 70, 73, 88–9, 90, 91, 95, 99, 203
Acheson-Lilienthal Report 55
Adenauer, Konrad 171, 177
Adzhubei, Alexei 212
Afghanistan 330–3, 336–8, 353, 354, 358, 371, 373, 409, 412, 464–5
Africa 6, 8, 193, 194–5, 196–7, 318–22 *see also* Angola; Congo; Egypt; Ethiopia; Ghana; Libya; Somalia; South Africa
Albania 141
Allende, Salvador 313–15, 316
Allison, Graham 50
al-Qaida 462, 464
Amalrik, Andrei 353–4
American Exhibition in Moscow 1959 184, *185*
Ames, Aldrich 394
Amin, Hafizullah 337, 338
Andropov, Yuri 250, 253, 259, 299, 332, 363–4, 366, 369, 371–5, 378, 388–9
Angola 317–20, *320*
anti-ballistic missile (ABM) treaty 272
Arab nationalism 154–5, 170
Arafat, Yasser 371
Arbatov, Georgy 389–90
Armenia 405, 414
arms control 222–3, 244–5, 269–74, 300–3

arms race 54, 57–8, 73–4, 192, 201, 203, 222, 244–5, 272, 354
arms reduction 146, 294, 298–9, 333–4, 393–5, 400–1
Asia 6, 8, 10, 132, 153, 238, 309 *see also* Cambodia; China; India; Indonesia; Japan; Korea; Laos; Middle East; Mongolia; Singapore; Tibet; Vietnam
Assad, Hafez 282, 283
Aswan dam 155
Athens 5, 50, 128
Atlee, Clement 53
Atomic Energy Commission (UN) 54
atomic weapons *see* nuclear weapons
Austria 26, 140 *see also* Vienna
Azerbaijan 405, 414, 449

B

Baghdad Pact 154
Bahr, Egon 256, 259, *260*
Baker, James 438–9, 444
Baltic states 37, 44, 45, 308, 405, 420, 428, 430, 446, 448, 451 *see also* Estonia; Latvia; Lithuania
Bangladesh 271
Bao Dai 234–5
Barre, Mohamed Siad 321–2
Baruch Plan 55
Batista, Fulgencio 207
Bay of Pigs 200–1
Belarus 44, 393, 452

503

Ben-Gurion, David 158
Beria, Lavrenty 58, 89, 137
Berlin 60, 76, 77–8, 81–2, 174–5, 187, 203 *see also* Berlin crisis; Berlin Wall; East Berlin; East Germany; Germany; West Berlin; West Germany
Berlin crisis 78, 175, 177–9, 181–3, 190–1, 197–8, 222, 371
Berlin Wall 203–5, 354, 406–7, 424, 438
Bevin, Ernest 73
Bikini atoll 57
bin Laden, Osama 460–2, 464
Bismarck, Otto von 436
Bohlen, Charles 66, 143–4
Botvinnik, Mikhail 382
Brandt, Willy 204, 256, 259–61, 260, 435
Brazil 315 *see also* Latin America
Bretton Woods agreements 40–1, 49
Brezhnev, Leonid
– and Afghanistan 332, 337
– and Andropov, Yuri 372
– and Angola 318
– and arms reduction 299
– and Carter, Jimmy 300, 335–6, 336
– Conference on Security and Cooperation in Europe 275–7, 294–5
– and Czechoslovakia 252–4
– death of 371
– détente 251–2, 256, 275
– and Egypt 283
– European identity 279–80
– and Ford, Gerald 294
– health 294, 299, 335
– and Kissinger, Henry 274, 277–8, 284, 299
– and Nixon, Richard 267, 271–3, 274, 281–2, 285
– *Ostpolitik* 259–60, 260
– as Party head 239–40
– and Poland 366
– in United States 277
British Commonwealth 197 *see also* United Kingdom
British Empire 39–40 *see also* United Kingdom
Brodie, Bernard 53–4, 221
Brodsky, Joseph 115
Brown, Harold 322, 323

Brussels Treaty (1948) 73
Brzezinski, Zbigniew 321, 322, 323, 324–5, 330
Bukovsky, Vladimir 300
Bulganin, Nikolai 153
Bulgaria 46, 70, 367, 409, 426
Bush, George H. W. 356
– and eastern Europe 421–2
– and Gorbachev, Mikhail 403, 411, 422, 427–31, 444–5, 450
– and Kohl, Helmut 431
– and Soviet Union, collapse of 451–2
Byelorussia *see* Belarus
Byrnes, James Francis 32, 49, 56–7, 61, 62

C

Cambodia 234, 257, 326, 413
capitalism 6, 7–8, 147, 459 *see also* liberal capitalism
The Captive Mind (Miłosz) 74
Carter, Jimmy 297, 298–300, 323, 324, 325–6, 328, 335–6, 336, 338, 358
Casey, William 363
Castro, Fidel 195, 207, 218, 219, 220, 314–15
Castro, Raúl 207, 211
Ceaușescu, Nicolae 421, 426–7, 432
Central America 370
Central Intelligence Agency (CIA) 64, 212
CFE (Treaty on Conventional Armed Forces in Europe) 441, 442, 443
Charter for a New Europe 441–2, 443
Cheney, Dick 412
Chernobyl accident 393–4
Chernyaev, Anatoly 344–5
Chiang Kai-shek 83–4, 85–6, 89
Chicago school of economics 359
Chile 312, 313–15, 361 *see also* Latin America
China
– and Africa 197
– civil war 85–6, 87
– communism 85–6, 88
– and Cuba 212
– Cultural Revolution 242–3, 257
– economic miracle 467
– economic reforms 398, 414–15
– foreign investment 415, 466

INDEX

- Great Leap Forward 169, 197
- Guomindang 85–6, 87, 89
- Hong Kong 87
- human rights 292, 325, 465
- and India 188
- and Korea 94
- and Korean War 96–8, 100, 101
- liberal capitalism 460
- liberalization 467–8
- Manchuria 31, 83–4, 91, 92
- military 353
- modernization 323–4
- nuclear programme 277–8
- nuclear war 180
- nuclear weapons 170, 257
- and Poland 161
- Sino-Soviet Treaty 1945 84, 90–2, 324
- and Soviet Union
 — assistance from 85–7, 141–2, 169–70
 — conflict 257–8, 266, 278–9
 — criticism of 179–80
 — ideological split 197
 — Manchuria 31, 83–4
 — normalization of relations 395, 412–14
 — nuclear weapons 188
 — US view of relationship 88
 — Vietnam War 242–3
- structural problems 169
- student protests 413–15
- submarines 180
- and Taiwan 160, 180–1
- Tiananmen Square 413, 414–15, 465
- and United States 4, 87–90, 181–2, 264–8, 322–6, 414, 431, 465–8, 472
- and US/Japan peace treaty 102
- and Vietnam 266, 326
- Xinjiang 92
Chou Enlai 91
Churchill, Winston 26, 27–8, 40, 42, 45
CIA (Central Intelligence Agency) 64, 212
Clay, Lucius 60, 70, 204
Clayton, William 49
Clifford, Clark 56
Clinton, Bill 459, 473–4
Cold War (CNN documentary) 3
Cold War comes to Asia (maps) 20–1
Cold War liberalism 106, 116, 253–4

Cominform (Communist Information Bureau) 71, 168
Comintern (Communist International) 28
Committee for State Security (KGB) 148, 302, 307
Committee of Information (Soviet Union) 68
Committee on the Present Danger (CPD) 301
Communist Information Bureau (Cominform) 71, 168
Communist International (Comintern) 28
Concert of Europe 24, 248
Conference on Security and Cooperation in Europe 143, 275–7, 294–5
Congo, Republic of 194, 195–6
Congress for Cultural Freedom 116
Congress of Vienna 24, 295
Conventional Armed Forces in Europe (CFE), Treaty on 441, 442, 443
Coolidge, Calvin 459
Council on Foreign Relations (USA) 64–5
CPD (Committee on the Present Danger) 301
Crete 40
Crimea *see* Yalta conference
Cuba *see also* Cuban Missile Crisis; Latin America
- and Angola 318–20
- Bay of Pigs 200–1
- blockade of 216
- and Central America 370
- and Chile 314–15
- and China 212
- and Ethiopia 322
- and Latin America 212
- revolution 207–8, 311
- and Soviet Union 206–8, 210–13, 318–20
- U-2 overflight 213
- and United States 200–1, 207, 212
Cuban Missile Crisis 205–8, 211, 213–21, 222–3, 371
Cultural Revolution 242–3, 257
Czechoslovakia
- coup 72, 72
- glasnost 406
- invasion of 288

- isolation from the West 74
- NATO membership 473
- occupation of 254–6
- oil 367
- political crisis 149
- Prague Spring 252–6
- quality of life 308
- and Soviet Union 70–1, 173, 254–6, 442
- velvet revolution 426

D

Daniloff, Nicholas 394
De Gasperi, Alcide 29
de Gaulle, Charles 162, 183, 248
Dead Hand project 374
Deng Xiaoping 161, 323, 325, 326, 372, 395, 398, 413–15
Denmark 26, 140
détente 246–52, 256, 275–6, 285, 292, 297–8, 300, 315, 323, 333, 336, 338, 345
Détente and Global Cold War in the 1970s (map) 230–1
Diem, Ngo Dinh 235, 236–7
Dobrynin, Anatoly 218, 224, 265, 285, 324–5, 336, 374
domino effect
- in Asia 10, 132, 238
- in Europe 253
- in Middle East 282
Dr Strangelove 216–17, 217
Dubček, Alexander 252, 254
Dulles, Allen 189, 196, 201
Dulles, John Foster 128, 130, 131, 132, 144, 145, 156–7, 184

E

East Berlin 174–5, 203, 424, 425 *see also* Berlin; Berlin crisis
East Germany *see also* Germany
- and Africa 197
- anti-government revolt 139
- borders, opening of 424
- creation of 78
- defectors 261
- and Deutsche mark 439
- economic crisis 198, 424
- emigration from 175, 197–8, 203–4
- glasnost 406
- and Hungary 418–19, 422–3
- nuclear war 377–8
- nuclear weapons 183
- oil 367
- *and Ostpolitik* 261–2
- peace treaty 177
- recognition of 176, 177, 262
- and reunification 438
- and Soviet Union 139, 173–4, 175–6, 197–8, 372, 409, 416, 423–5
- Stasi 262
- uprising of 1989 423
- and West Germany 175, 177, 197–8, 204, 262, 422, 431, 437–8
eastern Europe *see also* Belarus; Bulgaria; Czechoslovakia; East Germany; Hungary; Poland; Romania; Ukraine
- economic recession 361–2
- liberalization 421–2
- and NATO 247–8
- oil 406
- political instability 150–3
- radio broadcasts by USA 149
- revolutions of 1989 354–5
- show trials 79
- as Soviet bloc 81
- and Soviet Union 100, 140–1, 149–53, 406, 409, 421, 425
- Stalinist system 74
- and Western banks 306
Eden, Anthony 157, 158, 162
EEC (European Economic Community) 172–3
Egypt 155, 156, 157–8, 168, 243, 271, 281–5, 310, 322, 371 *see also* Middle East; Suez Canal
Eisenhower, Dwight 128–32, 144–6, 156, 156–8, 182–3, 186, 189–90, 192, 195
Eisenhower doctrine 163, 170
Elsey, George 56
'the end of history' 355, 458–9
Estonia 44, 405 *see also* Baltic states
Ethiopia 321–2
EU (European Union) 474
Euratom 172

Eurocommunism 255
Euromissile crisis 334–5, 364
Europe *see also* Albania; Austria; Belarus; Bulgaria; Czechoslovakia; Denmark; eastern Europe; Estonia; Finland; France; Georgia; Germany; Greece; Hungary; Italy; Latvia; Lithuania; Norway; Poland; Portugal; Romania; Russia; Serbia; Slovakia; Soviet Union; Spain; United Kingdom; Yugoslavia
- access to American markets 249
- collective security 143
- communism 51, 432
- Concert of 24, 248
- Conference on Security and Cooperation 143, 275–7, 294–5
- counterculture 254
- deadlock in 80–2
- détente 247–8, 275–6
- domino effect 253
- economies 339
- imperialism 339
- integration of 407, 420
- and 'maximum retaliation' doctrine 132
- nuclear missiles 368, 377–8
- nuclear war 364
- occupation of 26–8, 27
- and origins of Cold War 8
- revolutions 339
- security of 247, 249
- stability 338–9
- struggle for the fate of 23
- 'United States of' 172–3
- war, expectation of 29
- western civilization, survival of 128
- as world's powerhouse 23–4
European Coal and Steel Community 171
European Economic Community (EEC) 172–3
European Union (EU) 474

F

FDR *see* Roosevelt, Franklin D.
Federal Republic of Germany (FRG) *see* Germany; West Germany
Federal Reserve Bank (USA) 357, 358

Final Settlement with Respect to Germany, Treaty on 441, 442–3
Finland 37, 71, 140, 275–6
Finlandization 416
First World War 6, 24–5
Ford, Gerald 294, 297
Foreign Affairs 65
Formosa *see* Taiwan
Forrestal, James 49
France
- communist party 80, 116
- decolonization 193
- détente 333
- Eurocommunism 255
- First World War 25
- and Germany 26, 60
- imperialism 162
- and NATO 248, 249
- and peace in Europe 25
- post-war decline 29
- and Soviet Union 24, 26
- students revolts 254
- and Suez Canal 158
- and Vietnam 133, 234
- and West Germany 132
FRG (Federal Republic of Germany) *see* Germany; West Germany
Fukuyama, Francis 458

G

Gagarin, Yuri 201
Gandhi, Rajiv 395–6
Gates, Robert 412
GDR (German Democratic Republic) *see* East Germany
Geneva Summit 1955 144–7
Geneva Summit 1985 392
Georgia 405, 414, 420, 471, 475
Gerasimov, Gennady 430
German Democratic Republic (GDR) *see* East Germany
Germany *see also* Berlin; East Berlin; East Germany; West Berlin; West Germany
- Allied Control Council 75
- demilitarization 61
- division of 30, 59–60, 73–8, 175

- First World War 25
- food shortages 60, 61
- and France 26, 60
- industrial assets, removal of 60-1
- inflation 61
- National Socialism 25-6
- and NATO 437-41
- Nazi-Soviet pact 1939 45, 440
- neutrality 139, 436
- 1945 agreements 76, 177
- Paris Summit (1960) 187, 189-91
- peace treaty 176-7, 201
- and Poland 26
- post-war decline 29
- reunification 431, 435-44
- Socialist Unity Party of Germany (SED) 62
- and Soviet Union 26, 39, 45, 440-1, 442-3
- and United Kingdom 26
- and United States 26, 30, 442
- western zones, unification of 75, 76

Ghana 194
Gierek, Edward 338, 365
glasnost 398-400, 403, 405, 406, 411
Glassboro Summit 1967 244, 269
global Cold War 193
global financial crisis 360-1
global south *see* Third World
globalization 304-5, 459
gold standard 265-6, 304
Gomułka, Władysław 150-1, 161-2, 253, 365
Gorbachev, Mikhail
- arms reduction 146, 393, 394-5, 400
- and Bush, George H. W. 422, 427-31, 444-5
- and China 412-14
- defence expenditure 400, 402
- domestic reforms 402
- and East Germany 424-5
- and eastern Europe 406
- Europe, integration of 407
- foreign policy 420-1
- glasnost 398-400, 403, 406
- and India 395-6
- and Iraq 444, 449
- in Italy 428
- and Kohl, Helmut 436, 439-40, 442
- liberalization 354, 398-400, 405-6
- and Lithuania 448-9
- Moscow Summit 1991 450
- new thinking 390, 390, 393, 402, 412
- new world order 407
- Nobel Peace Prize 445
- perestroika 396-8, 411
- and Poland 421
- political reforms 403-4
- as president of the USSR 444
- and Reagan, Ronald 392-3, 394-5, 403, 411
- Soviet Union, collapse of 455
- in United States 401
- and Yeltsin, Boris 449-50

Gordievsky, Oleg 379
Great Britain *see* United Kingdom
Great Depression 25, 469
Great Leap Forward 169, 197
Great Patriotic War 30-1
Great Society 233
Grechko, Andrei 217, 272
Greece 5, 40, 50, 59, 63, 81, 339 *see also* Athens; Crete
Greene, Graham 236
Grenada 376
Gromyko, Andrei 177, 224, 250, 294, 299, 324, 332-3
Guevara, Che 207, 211, 311, 312
Gulf states 305-6 *see also* Middle East
Guomindang 85-6, 87, 89
Gouzenko, Igor 55

H

Hackett, Sir John 387
Hammarskjöld, Dag 196
Harmel report on NATO 247-8
Harriman, Averell W. 279
Hegel, Georg W.F. 347
Helsinki Final Act 143, 294-5
Helsinki Watch Committee 296, 300, 384
Hiss, Alger 105
Hitler, Adolf 25-6
Ho Chi Minh 133, 226, 234, 236
Honecker, Erich 262, 406-7, 421
Hong Kong 87

INDEX

House Un-American Activities Committee (HUAC) 105
Hoxha, Enver 141
HUAC (House Un-American Activities Committee) 105
human rights 286–96, 297, 325, 456
Hungary
– anti-communist revolution 426
– border controls 418–19
– and capitalism 417–19
– and East Germany 418–19, 422–3
– economic crisis 417
– liberalization 417, 422
– living standards 338
– NATO membership 473
– oil 367
– *Playboy* magazine 425
– political crisis 149
– quality of life 308
– revolution 152, 160, 161–2
– and Soviet Union 159–60, 161–2, 200–1, 409, 442
– suppression 162
– uprising 150, 152–3
– and West Germany 419, 423
– and Western banks 306
Hussein, Saddam 371, 444, 464
hydrogen bomb 136 *see also* nuclear weapons

I

ICBMs (intercontinental ballistic missiles) 136, 166–7, 208–9, 245, 250
IMF (International Monetary Fund) 48–9, 429
imperialism 6, 147, 163, 197, 339, 381–2
India 59, 153, 188, 310, 395–6
Indochina peace conference 160, 234
Indonesia 243
INF (Intermediary Nuclear Forces) treaty 401
Institute for International Relations (Soviet Union) 68
intercontinental ballistic missiles (ICBMs) 136, 166–7, 208–9, 245, 250
Intermediary Nuclear Forces (INF) treaty 401

International Meeting of Communist and Workers Parties (Moscow 1957) 167–8
International Monetary Fund (IMF) 48–9, 429
Iran 46–8, 134, 138, 154, 158, 327–9, 329, 358, 370–1, 457, 462 *see also* Middle East
Iran-Contra scandal 370–1
Iraq 170–1, 371, 444, 449, 457, 464–5 *see also* Middle East
'Iron Curtain' speech 42
Isaacs, Sir Jeremy 3
ISIS (Islamic State of Iraq and Syria) 465
Islam 128, 327–8, 329–30, 331–2, 462
Islamic State of Iraq and Syria (ISIS) 465
Israel 112, 158–9, 243–4, 271, 281–5, 290, 304, 371 *see also* Middle East
Italy 80, 116, 250, 255, 339, 428

J

Jackson, Henry 292, 293, 297
Janus, Time of 11–12
Japan 30, 83–4, 88, 97, 101, 102, 466
Jaruzelski, Wojciech 367, 369, 408, 419
Jews 111–12, 288–91, 289–92, 420
John Paul II (Pope) 365
Johnson, Lyndon B. 233, 234, 238, 239, 244, 256
Jupiter missiles 209–10 *see also* nuclear weapons

K

Kádár, János 253
KAL-007 (Korean Air Lines Flight) 375–6
Kekkonen, Urho 275–6
Kennan, George F.
– containment doctrine 56, 64–5, 355–6
– *Foreign Affairs* article 65, 66, 68–9
– and Marshall Plan 70
– on NATO enlargement 473–4
– and Russian people 346
– Solarium Project 129–30
– and Soviet propaganda 109
– telegram 43–4, 49–50
– and Truman, Harry S. 66
– and US-Soviet relations 99

INDEX

Kennedy, John F.
- assassination 222
- background 199
- Bay of Pigs landings 200-1
- Berlin Wall 204
- and Cuba 212-16, 218, 219
- funeral 223
- and Khrushchev, Nikita 200, 201-2, 206, 216, 233
- and nuclear war 200, 204
- and Soviet Union 192
- and West Berlin 202-3

Kennedy, Robert 204, 218
Keyserling, Leon 107
KGB (Committee for State Security) 148, 302, 307
Khomeini, Ayatollah Ruhollah 329
Khrushchev, Nikita
- African aid 194-5
- agriculture 187
- American Exhibition in Moscow 1959 184, 185
- Berlin Wall 204
- brinkmanship 181, 183, 197, 201, 205
- and capitalism, end of 163
- and China 141-2, 161, 188
- and communism 137
- conflict resolution 223
- criticism of 240-1
- and Cuba 206, 215, 217-19
- and East Germany 175-6
- economic reforms 187
- and Eisenhower, Dwight 145, 186, 189-90, 195
- and Finland 140
- foreign policy 187
- Geneva Summit 1955 146-7
- and German peace treaty 176-7
- and Hungary 159-61
- and ICBMs (intercontinental ballistic missiles) 166
- International Meeting of Communist and Workers Parties (Moscow 1957) 167-8
- and Kennedy, John F. 200, 201-2, 206, 216, 233
- and Mao Zedong 168-9, 179-81, 188, 197
- military reductions 140, 186-7
- military support 188
- and Molotov, Vyacheslav 138, 139-40
- and nuclear war 180
- nuclear weapons 177-9
- and 'open skies' 144, 148
- peaceful coexistence 147
- at Pitsunda 224
- and Poland 151
- removal from power 239
- —— attempted 165-6
- and Sputnik 167
- and Stalin, Joseph 78, 127, 137-8, 141, 150, 153, 165
- and Suez crisis 155
- and Third World 195
- U-2 spy plane 189
- and United Nations 195
- and US diplomats 145
- US state visit 184-6
- and Vietnam 236, 241
- and West Berlin 183, 201-3
- and Yugoslavia 141, 150

Kim Il-Sung 93, 94, 96
King, Martin Luther 254
Kissinger, Henry 264-8, 274, 277-9, 282, 284-5, 299, 314, 317-18, 320, 322-3
Kohl, Helmut 377, 419, 431, 436, 438-40, 442
Korea *see* Korean War; North Korea; South Korea
Korean Air Lines Flight 007 375-6
Korean War 88, 92-102, *101*, 116, 134, 138
Korolev, Sergei 166-7
Kosygin, Alexei 239, 242-3, 244-5
Kravchuk, Leonid 452
Kremlin doctors affair 112
Krenz, Egon 424
Kurds 47, 48
Kuwait 444, 449 *see also* Middle East
Kvitsinsky, Yuliy 368

L

Landau, Lev 382-3
Laos 234
Latin America 6, 8, 212, 311-16, 360-1 *see also* Brazil; Chile; Cuba; Nicaragua; Panama

INDEX

Latvia 44 *see also* Baltic states
League of Nations 25
Lebanon 371, 376–7 *see also* Middle East
Lend-Lease system 34–5
Lenin, Vladimir 134, 147, 172–3, 194, 356
liberal capitalism 7, 29, 51, 303–7, 460 *see also* capitalism
Libya 394
Lin Biao 267
Lithuania 44, 424, 428, 430, 448–9 *see also* Baltic states
Litvinov, Maxim 139
Liu Shaoqi 161
Lovett, Robert 66
Lumumba, Patrice 193, 194, *194*, 196

M

MacArthur, Douglas 95, 96, 99
McCarthy, Joseph 89, *105*, 106, 129
Macmillan, Harold 162, 183
McNamara, Robert 214, 245
MAD (mutual assured destruction) 220–1, 245–6, 271
Malenkov, Georgy 134, 137, 166
Malta Summit 1989 427–31
Manchuria 31, 83–4, 91, 92, 102
Mao Zedong
– and Cultural Revolution 242–3
– and Hungary 161
– imperialism and colonialism 197
– and Khrushchev, Nikita 168–9, 179–81, 188, 197
– and Korea 94
– and Korean War 96–8
– and Poland 161
– and Stalin, Joseph 85–7, 90–2, 97–8, 141–2
– and Third World 197
– and United States 266–7
– and Vietnam 236
maps *124–5*
– Cold War comes to Asia *20–1*
– Détente and Global Cold War in the 1970s *230–1*
– NATO and Warsaw Pact: Consolidation of The Cold War *120–1*
– Retraction of Soviet power in 1989–94 *350–1*
– transfers of land/territories in 1945 *19*
Mars, Time of 9
Marshall, George 62, 64, 85
Marshall Plan 69–71, 73, 74, 80–1, 116, 171
Masaryk, Jan 72
Mazowiecki, Tadeusz 419–20
Mengistu Haile Mariam 321
Mercury
– statue *461*
– Time of 14–15, 459–60
Middle East 154–9, 281–5 *see also* Egypt; Iran; Iraq; Israel; Kuwait; Lebanon; Palestine; Saudi Arabia; Syria; Turkey
– demilitarized 158–9
– domino effect 282
– Eisenhower doctrine 163
– oil embargo 304, 305
– and Soviet Union 155–7, 159, 163, 170–1
– and United States 163, 170–1, 371, 463–5
Mikoyan, Anastas 86, 91, 168, 174, 182, 202, 215, 219–20, 240
Miłosz, Czesław 74, 116
Minerva, Time of 12–14, 347
Minuteman missiles 208, 245, 250 *see also* nuclear weapons
Mitterrand, François 421, 431, 438, 444
Mobutu Sese Seko 196
Mollet, Guy 157
Molotov, Vyacheslav 38, 41, 48, 67, 91, 94, 136–40, 143, 165–6, 188
Mongolia 92, 395, 412
Monnet, Jean 171
Monroe Doctrine 63, 211
Moscow 308
– American Exhibition 184, *185*
– World Trade Center 461
Moscow Summit 1972 272–3
Moscow Summit 1988 402–3
Moscow Treaty 1970 259–60, 262–3
Mossadeq, Mohammad 154, 155, 158
MPLA (Popular Movement for Liberation of Angola) 317–18
Mujaheddin 371
mutual assured destruction (MAD) 220–1, 245–6, 271

INDEX

N

Nagorny Karabagh 405, 414
Nagy, Imre 152, 168
Nasser, Gamal Abdel 155–8, 156, 162
National Security Council (USA) 64
national security state 64, 106, 191, 200, 239, 297, 462
NATO *see* North Atlantic Treaty Organization (NATO)
NATO and Warsaw Pact: Consolidation of The Cold War (map) 120–1
Nazi-Soviet pact 1939 45, 440
Nehru, Jawaharlal 153
Németh, Miklós 418
neoliberalism 316, 357, 359, 397
Neto, Agostinho 317, 320
New Deal 58, 104
New Europe, Charter for 441–2, 443
New International Economic Order 315, 361
'new thinking' 390, 393, 402, 412
Nicaragua 370 *see also* Latin America
9/11 attacks 462–3
Nitze, Paul 104, 301, 368
Nixon, Richard
– American Exhibition in Moscow 1959 183–4, 185
– as anti-communist 257
– and Brezhnev, Leonid 267, 271–3, 274, 281–2, 285
– and Chile 313, 314
– and China 265–8
– and Soviet Union 265, 272, 292
– and Vietnam War 257, 263–4, 274–5
– Watergate 275
Nkrumah, Kwame 193, 194
Non-Aligned Movement 117, 160, 315
Noriega, Manuel 430
North Atlantic Treaty Organization (NATO)
– and détente 247–8
– and eastern Europe 247–8
– economic interdependence within 249
– expansion of 437–41, 472–6
– formation of 73
– and France 248, 249
– Harmel report 247–8
– maps 120–3
– Pershing missiles 337, 364, 377
– and Shevardnadze, Eduard 432
– and Soviet Union 140, 143, 247–8
– and Suez crisis 162–3
– and West Germany 140, 333–4, 436
– and Zero Option 368
North Korea 93, 457 *see also* Korea
North Vietnam 234, 235–6, 237, 238, 242–3, 244 *see also* Vietnam; Vietnam War
Norway 26, 140
Novikov telegram 67–8
nuclear war *see also* nuclear weapons
– in *Dr Strangelove* 216–17
– fear of 117, 362
– and Kennedy, John F. 200
– and Khrushchev, Nikita 180
– and Pershing Missile deployment 377–9
– planning for 178, 192, 205, 387
– and Reagan, Ronald 369, 377
– and roll-back of communism 129
– scenarios 129, 377, 387
– and United States 364
nuclear weapons *see also* arms race; nuclear war
– Acheson-Lilienthal Report 55
– anti-nuclear movement 132
– Baruch Plan 55
– and China 170, 188
– Cuban Missile Crisis 206–7, 210–11
– Dead Hand project 373–4
– Japan 30
– Korean War 100
– and Nixon, Richard 257
– shelters 205
– Smyth Report 53
– and Soviet Union 56–8, 89–90, 136, 146, 177–9, 210, 212
– Strategic Defence Initiative (SDI) 374, 395, 401
– test ban 222
– and Truman, Harry S. 55–6
– in Turkey 209–10
– and United Kingdom 56

– and United States 32, 54–6, 103–4, 131–2, 146
– and Zero Option 368
Nuremberg trials 51–2

O ─────────────────

oil 47, 154, 158–9, 170, 304, 305–6, 307, 367, 396, 397, 406
OPEC (Organization of Petroleum Exporting Countries) 304, 305
'open skies' proposal 144, 148
Operation Anadyr 211
Operation Condor 315
Operation Desert Storm 449
Oppenheimer, Robert 55, 106, 131
Organization of Petroleum Exporting Countries (OPEC) 304, 305
Osipovich, Gennady 375–6
Ostpolitik 256, 259–63, 333, 419, 435
Oswald, Lee Harvey 222

P ─────────────────

Pahlavi, Mohammad Reza 154, 327–8
Pakistan 271, 332
Palach, Jan 255
Palestine 59, 371 *see also* Middle East
Panama 430 *see also* Latin America
Paris Peace Conference 1946 70–1
Paris Summit 1960 187, 189–91
Paris Summit 1990 443
Partnership for Peace 473
Pearl Harbor 30
Penkovsky, Oleg 213
People's Republic of China (PRC) *see* China
perestroika 396–8, 402, 411, 423, 425
Perle, Richard 301
Pershing missiles 334, 337, 364, 368, 377, 378 *see also* nuclear weapons
Pieck, Wilhelm 62
Pinochet, Augusto 314
Pipes, Richard 301
Playboy magazine 425
Podgorny, Nikolai 240
Poland

– and Africa 197
– anti-communist revolution 426
– anti-Semitism 287
– borders 421
– and capitalism 418, 420
– and China 161
– division of 26, 37, 44
– economic crisis 367, 408
– economic recession 361–2
– elections 419
– isolation of 74
– liberalization 421–2
– living standards 338–9
– martial law 367, 369
– NATO membership 473
– as neutral country 416
– and nuclear war 377–8
– Paris Peace Conference 1946 70–1
– political crisis 149–51
– quality of life 308
– Solidarity (*Solidarność*) 354, 365–6, 369, 408–9, 416, 419, 422
– and Soviet Union 173, 366–8, 409, 419, 442
– and Stalin, Joseph 45
– strikes 365, 367, 416
– and United States 369–70, 408
– and Warsaw Pact 421
– and West Germany 261
– and Western banks 306, 361, 408
Popular Movement for Liberation of Angola (MPLA) 317–18
Portugal 317
Potsdam conference 59–60
Power, Thomas 216
Powers, Gary 189
Prague Spring 252–6
PRC (People's Republic of China) *see* China
Prebisch, Raúl 305
Putin, Vladimir 424–5, 446, 452, 468, 471

Q ─────────────────

al-Qaddafi, Muammar 394
Qasim, Abd al-Karim 170–1
The Quiet American (Greene) 236

INDEX

R

Radio Free Europe 114, 149
Radio Liberation 114, 149
Radio Liberty 296, 342
RAND Corporation 178
Rapallo treaty 440
Reagan, Ronald
- and communism 362–3
- and détente 297
- economics 358–60
- and Gorbachev, Mikhail 392–3, 394–5, 403, 411
- and nuclear war 369, 374–5, 377
- and oil industry 396
- and Soviet Union 353–4, 379–80, 387–8, 401–2
- in Soviet Union 402–3
- START I 402–3
- Strategic Defence Initiative (SDI) 374
Reaganomics 360
Retraction of Soviet power in 1989-94 (map) 350–1
Reuter, Ernst 77
Reykjavik Summit 1986 394–5, 396
Rhee, Syngman 93
rock music 342, 343
Rokossovsky, Konstantin 151
Romania 31, 44, 46, 70, 197, 256, 306, 361–2, 426, 426–7, 432
Roosevelt, Eleanor 99
Roosevelt, Franklin D. 27–8, 32, 40–1, 44–5, 127
Rosenberg, Julius and Ethel 105–6
ROV (Republic of Vietnam) *see* South Vietnam
Rumsfeld, Donald 464
Rusk, Dean 212, 224
Russia *see also* Moscow; Soviet Union
- Empire 24, 25, 87, 248, 331, 460
- Federation 355, 446–8, 452–3, 468–76
Rust, Mathias 400–1

S

Sadat, Anwar 281–3, 285, 322, 371
Sakharov, Andrei 110, 255, 288, 296, 299–300, 342, 383–4, 385, 398, 415
Salisbury, Harrison 113
SALT (strategic arms limitation talks) 269, 270, 272, 303, 335
Sandinistas 370
Saudi Arabia 159, 170, 304, 305–6 *see also* Middle East
SAVAK 327–8
Schmidt, Helmut 333–4
Scowcroft, Brent 422, 428, 436, 446, 448
SDI (Strategic Defence Initiative) 374, 395, 401
Second World War 26, 30–5, 39–40, 437
SED (Socialist Unity Party of Germany) 62
Serbia 476
Shakhnazarov, Georgy 409, 416
Shepilov, Dmitry 156–7
Shevardnadze, Eduard 390, 390, 401, 402, 404, 409, 420, 428, 432, 443
Shultz, George 356, 400, 401
Simonov, Konstantin 114–15
Singapore 309, 361
single integrated operational plan (SIOP) for nuclear war 192
Sino-Soviet alliance 414
Sino-Soviet border conflict 257–8
Sino-Soviet Treaty 1945 84, 90–2, 142
SIOP (single integrated operational plan) for nuclear war 192
Six Day War 243–4
Slovakia 44
Smyth Report 53
Socialist Unity Party of Germany (SED) 62
Sokolovsky, Vasily 75
Solarium Project 129–30
Solidarity (*Solidarność*) 354, 365, 369, 408–9, 416, 419, 422
Solzhenitsyn, Alexander 288, 296, 297, 342, 386
Somalia 321–2 *see also* Africa
South Africa 319, 320 *see also* Africa
South Korea 93, 235, 309, 361 *see also* Korea
South Vietnam 234, 235, 236–8 *see also* Vietnam; Vietnam War
Soviet Union *see also* Moscow; Russia
- Academy of Science 344
- and Afghanistan 331–3, 336–8, 353, 354, 358, 373, 409, 412

- and Africa 194–5, 318–22
- agriculture 306–7
- aid 85–7, 141–2, 169–70, 175–6, 194–5, 309, 310
- aircraft 136, 148–9
- American diplomats in 43–4
- and Angola 318–20
- anti-Semitism 111–12, 289, 293
- armaments 35, 176
- arms control 269–73
- arms reduction 401
- atomic program 49, 58, 110
- autarchy 173
- autocracy 36–7
- balance of trade 373
- Bolsheviks 24
- and Bulgaria 409
- censorship 252
- Chernobyl incident 393–4
- and China
—— assistance to 85–7, 141–2, 169–70
—— conflict 257–8, 266, 278–9
—— criticism by 179–80
—— ideological split 197
—— Manchuria 31, 83–4
—— normalization of relations 395, 412–14
—— nuclear weapons 188
—— US view of relationship 88
—— Vietnam War 242–3
- collapse of 353–6, 445, 445–53, 455
- collective security 143
- Committee for State Security (KGB) 148, 302, 307
- Committee of Information 68
- communism, triumph of 381–2
- and Congo 195–6
- conservatism 346–7
- consumerism 307–8
- coup 450–1
- and Cuba 206–8, 210–13, 318–20
- and Czechoslovakia 70–1, 173, 254–6, 442
- Dead Hand project 374
- defence expenditure 373, 399–400, 402
- and democracy 346–7
- de-Stalinization 142
- détente 250–2, 256, 275
- dissidents 288–9, 296, 299–300, 344, 346
- doctors 112
- and East Germany 139, 173–7, 197–8, 372, 409, 416, 423–5
- and eastern Europe 100, 140–1, 149–53, 406, 409, 421, 425
- economic crisis 424, 440
- economic nationalism 173
- economic reforms 372, 396–7
- economic weakness 34–5
- economy 173, 176, 249–50, 354, 420
- and Egypt 156, 157–8, 168, 281, 283, 322
- elections 415
- emigration 288–93, 420
- and Ethiopia 321–2
- Europe
—— integration of 407, 420
—— 'neutrality belt in' 139
—— occupation of 26–8, 27, 31
—— 'United States of' 172–3
- as European great power 31–2, 41, 224, 279–80, 317
- as evil empire 375, 376, 379–80, 402, 403
- exit from Cold War 381–8
- expansionism 32, 44–5, 302
- films 115
- and Finland 275–6
- foreign journalists 288–9
- foreign policy 48, 136–7, 420–1
- foreign travel 143
- and France 24, 26
- gas pipelines 277, 278, 306
- and Germany 26, 39, 45, 60–1, 63, 74–5, 175–7, 440–3
- glasnost 398–400, 403, 405, 411
- global status 241
- grain imports 306–7
- Great Patriotic War 30–1
- as great power 31–2, 41, 224, 279–80, 317
- human rights 286–8, 292, 294–6, 299, 325
- and Hungary 152, 159–60, 161–2, 200–1, 409, 442
- hydrogen bomb 136
- imperialism, theory of 37–8, 46–7, 163, 381–2
- and India 395–6
- industrialization 310
- instability 428

515

INDEX

- Institute for International Relations 68
- intercontinental ballistic missiles 136, 166–7, 208–9, 250
- and Iran 46–8, 134, 138, 154, 328–9
- and Iraq 444
- 'Iron Curtain' speech 42
- and Israel 112, 243–4
- and Italy 250
- and Japan 83–4, 102
- Jews 111–12, 288–91, 420
- Kennan telegram 43, 48
- KGB (Committee for State Security) 148, 302, 307
- and Korea 93–4
- Korean Air Lines Flight 007 375–6
- and Korean War 96, 100, 138
- Lend-Lease system 34–5
- liberalization 187, 191, 354, 398–400, 405–6
- and Manchuria 31, 83–4, 102
- and Marshall Plan 70–1
- and Middle East 155–7, 163, 170–1, 281–5
- military 49–50, 148, 302–3, 307, 353, 433
- military equipment, removal from Europe 443
- military-industrial complex 250, 302
- missile project 136, 208
- Moscow Treaty 1970 259–60
- mutual assured destruction (MAD) 271
- national identity 223
- national security 399
- nationalism 404–5, 411
- navy 316–17
- Nazi-Soviet pact 1939 45, 440
- and North Atlantic Treaty Organization (NATO) 140, 143, 247–8
- and North Vietnam 242–3
- nuclear anxiety 373–4
- nuclear submarines 179
- and nuclear war 178, 181, 183, 369, 377–9
- nuclear weapons 56–7, 89–90, 136, 177–9, 209, 210, 212, 222–3, 368, 399
- oil 306, 307, 367, 396, 397, 406
- Olympic Games 365
- Operation Anadyr 211
- other nationalities 110
- patriotism 148
- 'peaceful coexistence' 134, 138–53
- perestroika 396–8, 402, 411, 423
- pessimism 307–10
- and Poland 26, 45, 173, 366–8, 409, 419, 442
- political reforms 403–4
- political revolution 416
- propaganda 109–10, 114–15, 286–7
- public opinion 344
- punished nationalities 110–11
- religious freedom 403
- rock music 342, 343
- as Russia 248
- Russian nationalism 110
- Russians, superiority of 110–11
- sanctions 77, 78
- science and technology 372, 391–2
- Second World War 30–1
- —— post-war expectations 108
- —— post-war outcomes 4
- —— post-war reconstruction loans 48–9
- —— recovery from 112–13
- —— ruined cities 74
- secret police 108–9, 148
- security 399
- Sino-Soviet Treaty 1945 84, 90–2, 324
- socialist integration 173–4
- sovereignty 295
- Soviet Academy of Science 344
- Spaak, Paul-Henri 171
- spaceflight 201
- sport 223–4
- Sputnik 166–70
- spying 55, 89–90, 394
- SS-20 missiles 333–4, 368, 389, 400
- stereotypes of 345–6
- strategic arms limitation talks (SALT) 269–70
- strategic missiles 192–3
- strikes 420
- structural problems 169
- submarines 179
- superiority of 37, 110–11, 301, 303
- surveillance 108–9
- terror 80, 109, 110–11
- thermonuclear weapons 136, 209
- and Third World 153, 155, 163

- totalitarianism 287–8
- Tsar Bomba 209, 210
- and Turkey 46–8, 57–8, 134, 138
- U-2 spy plane 189
- and United Kingdom 24, 26, 39, 40
- and United Nations 95–6
- and United States
  — confrontation 223, 271, 324–5, 362–3, 394–5
  — containment policy 63–73, 103, 129–30, 145, 264–5, 301, 354
  — détente 268
  — diplomatic contact with 98–9
  — human rights 292–3
  — Malta Summit 1989 427–31
  — Moscow Summit 1972 272–3
  — perceptions 113–14, 341–3, 345–6
  — radio broadcasts by 114
  — SALT I 272
  — Zero Option 368–9
- and United States/Japan peace treaty 102
- and Vietnam War 266, 268
- vulnerability in 1946 50–1
- war veterans 37–8
- and Warsaw Pact 141, 151, 159, 253, 421, 432
- and Watergate 342
- West
  — attitudes to 115, 386
  — cultural influences 308
  — radio stations 342
  — sympathizers 287
- and West Berlin 98, 201–3
- and West Germany 98, 177–8, 256, 259–61, 277
- and world revolution 28–9
- youth culture 343
- and Yugoslavia 79, 141
- Zero Option 400
Spain 339
Sparta 50, 128
Sputnik 166–7
SS-20 missiles 333–4, 368, 389, 400
Stalin, Joseph
- anti-Semitism 111–12
- and arms race 73–4

- biography 38–9
- and China 90
- death of 112, 127–8
- denunciation of 136–7, 150, 153, 163, 391
- foreign policy 48
- and foreigners 44
- funeral 135
- 'Iron Curtain' speech 42
- and Kim Il-Sung 96
- and Korea 94
- and Korean War 99, 100
- Kremlin doctors affair 112
- as leader of global communism 28
- and Manchuria 102
- and Mao Zedong 85–7, 90–2, 97–8
- nuclear weapons 58
- Poland 45
- 70th birthday celebrations 90–1
- successors of 133–42
- terror 80, 109, 110–11, 128
- and Truman, Harry S. 98
- and United States/Japan peace treaty 102
- and US containment policy 66–7
- and West Berlin 78
- Yalta conference 27–8, 31, 41
- and Yugoslavia 79
- Zhdanov Doctrine 71
START I 402–3
Stasi 262
Steinbeck, John 115
Stimson, Henry 54
strategic arms limitation talks (SALT) 269, 270, 272, 303, 335
Strategic Defence Initiative (SDI) 374, 395, 401
Suez Canal 40, 155, 158, 162 *see also* Egypt
Suez crisis 155–9, 162
Sukarno, Ahmed 243
summits
- Geneva 1955 144–7
- Geneva 1985 392
- Glassboro 1967 244, 269
- Malta 1989 427–31
- Moscow 1972 272–3
- Moscow 1988 402–3
- Paris 1960 187, 189–91

- Paris 1990 443
- Reykjavik 1986 394–5, 396
- Vienna 1961 202–3
- Vienna 1979 335–6
- Vladivostok 1974 294
- Washington 1990 439

Syria 157, 159, 243, 282, 283, 371, 376–7 *see also* Middle East

T

Taiwan 88, 89, 92, 101, 180–1, 188, 267–8, 309, 361
Taraki, Nur-Mohammed 337
Thatcher, Margaret 357, 376, 390, 425, 438
thermonuclear weapons 103, 131, 136, 191, 209 *see also* nuclear weapons
Third World 153, 155, 163, 195, 197, 236, 309, 361
Thompson, Llewellyn (Tommy) 201, 215, 224
Thucydides 5, 50
Tiananmen Square 413, 414–15, 465
Tibet 92, 188
Time of Janus 11–12
Time of Mars 9
Time of Mercury 14–15, 459–60
Time of Minerva 12–14, 347
Time of Vulcan 9–10, 224–7
Tito, Josip Broz 79, 141, 161, 168
Titoism 79, 141, 151, 152
Tonkin Gulf incidents 237–8
transfers of land/territories in 1945 (map) 19
Treaty of Warsaw 1970 261, 262–3
Treaty on Conventional Armed Forces in Europe (CFE) 441, 442, 443
Treaty on the Final Settlement with Respect to Germany 441, 442–3
triangular diplomacy 264, 267, 268, 322
Trotsky 356
Truman, Harry S. 32, 36, 41–2, 53, 54–5, 56–7, 66, 90, 95, 98
Truman Doctrine 63
Tsar Bomba 209, 210
Turkey 46–8, 57–8, 59, 63, 134, 138, 206, 209–10, 218 *see also* Middle East

U

U-2 spy plane 189, 213
Ukraine 37, 44, 111, 308, 446, 448, 451, 452, 473, 474, 475
Ulbricht, Walter 62, 174, 175, 197–8, 253, 261–2
Union of Soviet Socialist Republics *see* Soviet Union
United Kingdom *see also* British Commonwealth; British Empire
- and Afghanistan 330–1
- anti-nuclear movement 132
- atomic partnership with US 56
- colonies 59
- decolonization 193
- economic crisis 357
- and EEC 172
- Europe, occupation of 28
- First World War 25
- and Germany 26
- as great power 50
- imperialism 162
- and India 59
- and Iran 154, 158
- Korea 95
- and 'maximum retaliation' doctrine 132
- Mediterranean trade routes 59
- nuclear fears 379
- and nuclear weapons 56, 191
- Palestine 59
- peace-keeping 25
- post-war alliance with US 39–40, 42
- Second World War 39–40
- and Soviet Union 24, 26, 39, 40
- Suez Canal 158
- trade unions 359
- and Yugoslavia 79
United Nations 36, 47, 54, 95–6, 98, 159, 193, 195, 286
United States
- and Afghanistan 331, 371, 464–5
- and Africa 322
- aircraft 148–9
- American dream 107
- and Angola 318, 319–20
- anti-communism 58, 107

INDEX

- anti-fascist intellectuals 104-5
- Arab-Israeli conflict 282-4
- arms control 269-73
- arms race 192
- arms reduction 401
- Asian alliance building 132-3
- atomic partnership with UK 56
- Bay of Pigs landings 200-1
- budget deficits 457
- and Central America 370
- Central Intelligence Agency (CIA) 64, 212
- and Chile 313-14
- and China 4, 87-90, 181-2, 264-8, 322-6, 414, 431, 465-8, 472
- CIA (Central Intelligence Agency) 64, 212
- Cold War liberalism 106, 116, 253-4
- Committee on the Present Danger (CPD) 301
- communists 104-5
- conformism 107
- Congress for Cultural Freedom 116
- consumerism 34
- containment policy 63-73, 103, 129-30, 145, 301, 354, 457
- Council on Foreign Relations 64-5
- cruise missiles 334, 337, 364
- and Cuba 200-1, 207, 212
- defence perimeter 88, 93, 170
- demilitarization of Germany 61
- democracy 33, 341, 342
- divine predestination 35
- economic crisis 357-60
- economic growth 359-60
- economic prosperity 107
- economy 326, 340
- and EEC (European Economic Community) 173
- and Egypt 155, 371
- Europe
  — access to markets 249
  — aid to 73
  — attitudes to in 116
  — and 'communist penetration.' 128
  — occupation of 26-30
  — security 143, 247, 249
- external threats 104
- Federal Reserve Bank 357, 358
- First World War 25
- foreign policy 64-5, 234, 296-7
- and Germany 26, 30, 60, 62-3, 139, 442
- and global financial crisis 360-1
- global power 456-7
- gold standard, end of 265-6
- Great Society 233
- and Greece 59, 63
- House Un-American Activities Committee (HUAC) 105
- human rights 286, 291-3, 297, 325
- immigration 234
- inflation 358, 359-60
- intercontinental ballistic missiles 208-9
- interest rates 358
- interventionism 236
- and Iran 154, 327, 329, 370-1, 462
- Iran hostage crisis 358
- and Iraq 449, 464-5
- isolationism 25
- and Israel 244, 371
- and Japan 30, 83, 84, 102, 466
- Jews 289-92
- Korean War 96, 97, 98-100, 107
- and Kuwait 449
- and Latin America 311-13
- and Lebanon 371, 376-7
- Lend-Lease system 34-5
- and Libya 394
- 'maximum retaliation' doctrine 131, 132
- and Middle East 163, 170-1, 282-3, 371, 463-5
- and military dictators 315
- military draft 73
- military expenditure 360, 457, 458
- military systems 302-3
- military-industrial-scientific complex 192
- mutual assured destruction (MAD) 271
- National Security Council 64
- national security state 64, 106, 191, 200, 239, 297, 462
- New Deal 58, 104
- new world order 51
- 9/11 attacks 462-3

519

- and non-democratic countries 470
- and North Vietnam 238, 244
- NSC-68 policy 103-4
- and nuclear war 178, 181, 183, 192, 362, 369, 377, 379
- nuclear weapons
— airborne patrols 149
— and anxiety 131-2, 182, 363-4
— arms control 222-3
— as deterrent 191-2
— escalation 103
— Euromissile crisis 334-5, 364
— Japan 30
— Korean War 100
— Pershing missiles 337, 364
— reductions 146
— shelters 205
— Strategic Defence Initiative (SDI) 374
— testing of 32, 57-8
— Zero Option 368
- oil 304, 305, 396
- Operation Desert Storm 449
- and *Ostpolitik* 261
- and Poland 369-70, 408
- racism 35
- radio broadcasts to Soviet Union 114
- RAND Corporation 178
- reforms 340
- and Russian Federation 453, 470-4
- and Saudi Arabia 170
- Second World War 30
— post-war alliance with UK 42
— post-war reconstruction loans 48-9
- social democracy 104
- social problems 340
- and South Korea 235
- and South Vietnam 235, 236-8
- and Soviet Jews 291, *291*, 293
- and Soviet Union
— confrontation 223, 271, 324-5, 362-3, 394-5
— containment policy 50, 63-73, 103, 129-30, 145, 264-5, 301, 354
— détente 268
— diplomatic contact with 98-9
— human rights 292-3
— Malta summit 1989 427-31

—— Moscow summit 1972 272-3
—— perceptions 113-14, 341-3, 345-6
—— SALT I 272
—— stereotypes of 345-6
—— Zero Option 368-9
- state secrecy 64
- strategic arms limitation talks (SALT) 269-70
- Strategic Defence Initiative (SDI) 374, 395, 401
- strategic systems 208, 245, 250
- student protests 263
- and Suez crisis 158-9, 162
- sunk cost fallacy 239
- superiority of 7-8, 47, 51, 131, 301
- as superpower 33-4
- thermonuclear weapons 103, 131
- Tonkin Gulf incidents 237-8
- trade unions 359
- triangular diplomacy 264, 267, 268, 322
- triumphalism 458
- and Turkey 59, 63, 206, 209-10
- U-2 spy plane 189, 213
- unemployment 358-9
- and Vietnam 133, 234, 236-8, 463
- and Vietnam War 238-9, 263-4, 268, 271, 274-5
- Watergate 275, 342
- and West Berlin 182-3, 202
- and West Germany 466
- and Yugoslavia 79
- Zero Option 400
Universal Declaration of Human Rights 286
USSR *see* Soviet Union
Ustinov, Dmitry 369

V

Vance, Cyrus 299, 323, 325
Vienna 82
Vienna, Congress of 24, 295
Vienna Summit 1961 202-3
Vienna Summit 1979 335-6
Vietnam 133, 226, 234-46, 257, 326, 413, 463
see also North Vietnam; South Vietnam; Vietnam War

INDEX

Vietnam War 238–9, 246, 247, 249, 263–4, 266, 268, 271, 274–5
Vladivostok Summit 1974 294
Voice of America 114, 342
Volcker, Paul 357, 358–9
Vulcan, Time of 9–10, 224–7

W

Wałęsa, Lech 422
Wallerstein, Immanuel 309–10
Warsaw, Treaty of 261, 262–3
Warsaw Pact 141, 151, 159, 253, 421, 432
Washington Summit 1990 439
Watergate 275, 342
Weinberger, Caspar 363
Weltpolitik 333
West Berlin *see also* Berlin; Berlin crisis
– access to 75–6, 78
– airlift 76–8
– blockades 76–8, 81, 182–3
– border with East Berlin 174–5, 203
– and East Berlin 425
– as enclave 78
– four-power treaty 1971 261
– and Kennedy, John F. 202–3
– and Khrushchev, Nikita 201–3
– 1949 agreements 78, 177, 205
– prosperity 204
– and Soviet Union 98, 201–3
– students revolts 254
– and United States 182–3, 202
– wall *see* Berlin Wall
West Germany *see also* Germany
– creation of 75–6, 78
– currency 78
– currency reserves 438
– détente 333
– and East Germany 175, 177, 197–8, 204, 262, 422, 431, 437–8
– economic recovery 171
– EEC membership 172
– and France 132

– and Hungary 419, 423
– Maoism 339
– Moscow Treaty 1970 259–60
– and NATO 140, 377
– neutrality 139
– nuclear missiles 364
– nuclear weapons 179
– *Ostpolitik* 259–63, 333
– and Poland 261
– sovereignty claims 177
– and Soviet Union 98, 177–8, 256, 259–60, 277
– students revolts 254
– and United States 466
– *Weltpolitik* 333
Wilson, Woodrow 25
Wojtyła, Karol (Pope John Paul II) 365
World Bank 48–9, 429
World Trade Center, Moscow 461

X

Xinjiang 92

Y

Yalta conference 27–8, 31, 40–1
Yazov, Dmitry 443–4
Yeltsin, Boris 446–8, 449–52, 456, 469–71, 472–3, 474–5
Yom Kippur War 282–5, 304
youth radicalism 246, 248–9
Yugoslavia 79, 141, 150

Z

Zero Option 368, 400
Zhao Ziyang 414
Zhdanov Doctrine 71, 79
Zhou Enlai 160, 165, 180, 267
Zhukov, Georgy 140, 146, 159, 166
Zionism 289